SIGNAL CORPS

Signal Corps

ARMY LINEAGE SERIES

SIGNAL CORPS

Compiled by
Rebecca Robbins Raines

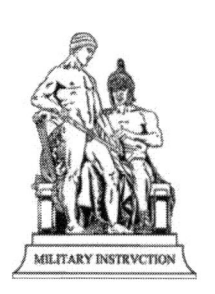

CENTER OF MILITARY HISTORY
UNITED STATES ARMY
WASHINGTON, D.C., 2005

Library of Congress Cataloging-in-Publication Data

Signal Corps / compiled by Rebecca Robbins Raines.
　　p. cm.
　Army Lineage series
　1. United States. Army. Signal Corps—History. I. Raines, Rebecca Robbins, 1952—
II. Title. III. Series.
　UG573.S486 2005
　　358'.243'0973—dc22   2005017459

CMH Pub 60–15

ARMY LINEAGE SERIES
Jeffery J. Clarke, General Editor

Advisory Committee
(As of October 2004)

Jon T. Sumida University of Maryland	Brian M. Linn Texas A&M University
Eric M. Bergerud Lincoln University	Howard P. Lowell National Archives and Records Administration
Mark Bowden *Philadelphia Inquirer*	Col. Craig Madden U.S. Army War College
Lt. Gen. Franklin L. Hagenbeck Deputy Chief of Staff for Personnel	John H. Morrow, Jr. University of Georgia
Lt. Gen. Anthony R. Jones U.S. Army Training and Doctrine Command	Reina J. Pennington Norwich University
Brig. Gen. Daniel J. Kaufman U.S. Military Academy	Ronald H. Spector George Washington University
Adrian R. Lewis University of North Texas	Brig. Gen. Volney Warner U.S. Army Command and General Staff College

U.S. Army Center of Military History
Brig. Gen. (Ret.) John S. Brown, Chief of Military History

Chief Historian	Jeffrey J. Clarke
Chief, Field Programs and Historical Services Division	Richard G. Davis
Editor in Chief	John W. Elsberg

Foreword

That the Army requires effective communications in an era known as the Information Age is axiomatic. Established in 1860 with the appointment of the first signal officer, the Signal Corps has had permanently organized units since late in the nineteenth century. Their growth in size and numbers over time highlights the increasingly specialized nature of warfare and the rise of sophisticated communications technology.

This volume, compiled by Rebecca Robbins Raines, serves as a companion to her narrative branch history, *Getting the Message Through*, published by the Center in 1996. Together these volumes provide an invaluable reference tool for anyone interested in the institutional or organizational history of the Signal Corps.

Successful military organizations depend upon the pride of their members to sustain their standards. The Army Lineage Series, of which this volume is the most recent addition, is designed to enhance the esprit de corps of United States Army units. The lineages, honors, and heraldic items included in this volume should increase the historical awareness and hence the pride of signal Soldiers. Thus it will contribute to the esprit de corps of the Signal Corps and instill within its members a greater appreciation for the history and heritage of their branch.

Washington, D.C.
3 March 2005

JOHN S. BROWN
Brigadier General, U.S. Army (Ret.)
Chief of Military History

Preface

The Signal Corps in the twenty-first century bears little resemblance to the organization founded by Maj. Albert J. Myer in 1860. Although the United States Army was the first in the world to have a separate communications branch, the legislation authorizing its establishment provided for neither permanent personnel nor units. Soldiers were detailed to signal duty from their regularly assigned units. During the Civil War small signal parties served with the various military departments, but they were disbanded at the end of the conflict. For the next thirty years, the Signal Corps remained a small organization whose members were scattered among the Army's many posts to provide communications and take weather observations. The necessity for having a separate Signal Corps continued to be debated in the halls of Congress and within the Army itself. Communications still was not widely recognized as a military specialty in and of itself.

The earliest permanent signal units were formed in the National Guard during the 1880s. New York and Illinois were among the first states to have such organizations. It took the Regular Army a little longer to follow suit. Signal companies designated A through H entered the force structure in 1898 and 1899. From this modest start, the Signal Corps continued to grow during the twentieth century as the United States and its Army assumed global responsibilities. The rise of telecommunications also meant that signaling duties became increasingly complex and an integral part of military operations. Today, the Signal Corps consists of approximately sixty-eight thousand men and women. Moreover, information dominance in the form of superior communications is considered to be *sine qua non* to modern warfare. The Signal Corps has indeed come a long way from Major Myer's original one-man branch.

The purpose of this volume is to present in compact form official organizational history information for Signal Corps units at battalion level and above that are organized under Tables of Organization and Equipment (TOE). This compilation features lineage and heraldic data for 176 signal units—7 commands, 1 center, 3 depots, 17 brigades, 8 groups, and 140 battalions. They consist of all active and inactive Regular Army and Army Reserve TOE units at battalion level and above on the rolls of the Army since 1963. The lineages are current through 30 June 2001. Also included are Army National Guard units, battalion and above, that were federally recognized and in the force structure as of 15 June 2001. Smaller units, such as separate companies and detachments, are not included because they are not authorized their own heraldic items. Units organized under Tables of Distribution and Allowances (TDA) do not appear because, in accordance with longstanding Army policy, lineage and honors are determined for TOE units only.

The lineage and honors of a unit are significant because they represent the organization's history and accomplishments. As such, they are a means to enhance troop morale and foster esprit de corps. The lineage outlines a unit's history; the honors consist of both the decorations and campaign participation credit earned by the unit. Official Lineage and Honors Certificates are prepared by the Force Structure and Unit History Branch of the U.S. Army Center of Military History (hereafter referred to as the Center). These highly stylized documents serve as a unit's birth certificate, its service record, and its deed to organizational property and historical files. The unit lineages in this volume are adapted from the official certificates. The data has been compressed to save space, but the information is similar to that on the certificates, which accounts for the technical language used. A glossary appears at the end of the volume to assist the reader in understanding these terms. The lineage begins with the official designation of the unit, followed by its special designation, if one has been approved by the Center. The recorded events in the life of a unit are restricted to a few specific actions, such as activation, inactivation, and redesignation. Campaigns and decorations for each unit are those earned by the unit itself or its lineal predecessor.

In regard to unit decorations, the general orders announcing each award are shown parenthetically along with the specific unit cited. For those awards that the Army has approved but for which it has not yet published orders, the approval announcement, usually in the form of a memorandum from the Military Awards Branch of the U.S. Army Human Resources Command, is cited. With the creation of the Army Superior Unit Award in 1985, the Army established its first peacetime unit decoration. This action, coupled with the passage by Congress in 1996 of legislation authorizing the approval of retroactive awards, has resulted in a significant increase in the honors earned by signal units. For example, in 2001 the 96th Signal Battalion received a retroactive Presidential Unit Citation (Army) for its service with the 96th Infantry Division on Okinawa during World War II. This volume includes those unit awards approved by the Military Awards Branch as of 1 July 2001. Thus participation by signal units in actions related to the Global War on Terrorism is not reflected.

Organizational history during the 1990s is anything but static. With the introduction of multiple component units, for example, the Army made a significant change in the way units are structured. They can now contain soldiers—and even entire elements—from more than one component. Headquarters and Headquarters Company, 93d Signal Brigade, a Regular Army unit stationed at Fort Gordon, Georgia, was one of the first to convert to "multi-compo" status. Since October 1999, nearly one-third of the positions within the unit have been designated as National Guard or Army Reserve. These slots are filled by full-time or drilling Guardsmen and Reservists. The conversion to multicomponent status will not ordinarily affect a unit's lineage and honors, but it will have a significant impact on how many units function. Another signal unit in the vanguard of change is the 124th Signal Battalion. As the organic signal element of the 4th Infantry Division, it has been part of the test bed for the Army's digitization initiative to transform itself into a twenty-first century fighting force using information technology to maximize combat effectiveness. Now in 2005, as this book goes to press, the upcoming implementation of the Chief of Staff's modular force redesign will mean further organizational changes for the Signal Corps and the rest of the Army.

Descriptions of the shoulder sleeve insignia, distinctive unit insignia, and other heraldic items approved for the units are included with the lineages. In some instances the text relating to the heraldic items is not as comprehensive as in the original letters of approval, amendment, or redesignation sent to the units. Minor changes in the heraldic material have been made to meet the need for brevity in this volume. Color illustrations are included for shoulder sleeve insignia, unit crests and shields, and distinctive unit insignia for those units for which these items have been approved. While the majority of distinctive unit insignia consist of the shield and motto of the unit's coat of arms, there are a number of variations. At the beginning of this section is a brief account of the evolution of these heraldic items.

The compilation of this volume has taken place in fits and starts over the course of twenty-five years, and its preparation would not have been possible without the efforts of many people. Ms Dana Purdy, a student fellow at the Center during the early 1980s, conducted the initial research that formed the basis for the unit bibliographies. These bibliographies are not intended to be comprehensive, but include both published unit histories, when available, as well as periodical articles that discuss more current unit operations and training. The *Army Communicator*, produced at the Signal Center and School at Fort Gordon, Georgia, is the primary source of the latter. After this project underwent a significant dormant period, two individuals helped bring it back to life. In 1995, Danny M. Johnson, then the historian for the Army Signal Command at Fort Huachuca, Arizona, and Dr. Carol E. Stokes, then the command historian at the Signal Center and School, lent indispensable assistance and support. Both of these individuals, now retired, are staunch champions of the Signal Corps and its history.

To my colleagues in the Force Structure and Unit History Branch (formerly the Organizational History Branch) of the Center, I owe a very great debt of gratitude. Their friendship, support, and camaraderie—in addition to their professionalism and expertise—have been invaluable through the years. Former branch chiefs Janice E. McKenney and the late John B. Wilson taught me much of what I know about organizational history. I was very fortunate to benefit from their vast knowledge and experience in this field, and their retirements during the 1990s left some big shoes to fill. Dr. Robert K. Wright, Jr., a branch alumnus who later served as Chief, Historical Resources Branch, until his retirement in 2002, has been a mentor to me and many other historians at the Center—as well as being a former Signal Corpsman. The current branch members Edward N. Bedessem, Romana M. Danysh, Stephen E. Everett, Stephen L. Y. Gammons, and Jennifer A. Nichols uphold the branch's tradition of hardworking and first-rate historians. They make my job as branch chief much easier. Dr. Richard A. Gorell, former chief of the Field Programs and Historical Services Division, generously granted me the time away from the pressing daily duties of branch chief that I needed to finish up the loose ends of the project. The current chief, Dr. Richard G. Davis, has been equally supportive in the final stages of preparation. Special kudos go to James B. Knight, the Center's librarian until his retirement in July 2004, who deserves my sincere thanks and deep appreciation for his patience and good humor in allowing me to accumulate a vast array of overdue books and periodicals. His successor, Patricia A. Ames, carries on his tradition of outstanding service.

The heraldic illustrations and descriptions provided by The Institute of Heraldry are an important part of this volume and help make the Army Lineage Series distinctive. The Force Structure and Unit History Branch is very grateful to former director, Thomas B. Proffitt, for his assistance. Since Mr. Proffitt's retirement, his successor, Fred Eichorn, has continued the Institute's outstanding support for this series. Sherry O'Connor provided the heraldic descriptions, reviewed the author's text thereof, and graciously answered my questions on heraldic terminology and usage. She taught me a great deal. After Sherry left the Institute, Bonnie Henning continued my heraldic education and saw the project through to completion. She was a tremendous help in the project's latter stages and a pleasure to work with. The credit for the striking illustrations goes to Joseph Spollen, chief of the Design and Illustration Branch, and Carl Hickey of the Institute's Technical Department who supervised their production.

Other individuals who contributed to the final product include: Lt. Col. Sherman L. Fleek and Maj. Les' Melnyk of the Historical Services Office, National Guard Bureau. Because determining the lineage and honors of National Guard units presents probably the most complex task for the organizational historian, it could not be accomplished without the Bureau's assistance. I must also thank Elizabeth Zippert of the Bureau's Force Management Division, who helped enormously by providing copies of Organizational Authorities and a computer print out of the Guard's current force structure. Denise E. Harris, Chief, Board Section, Military Awards Branch, and Pamela R. Rivera of that office verified the status of pending unit awards. This information was very helpful and much appreciated.

No book at the Center would be possible without the efforts of the editors and production staff who bring it all together. As the book's editor, Glenn R. Schwegmann brought his careful attention to detail to bear and discovered many previously undetected inconsistencies. His excellent work made this a much better volume. The author also wishes to thank John W. Elsberg, Catherine A. Heerin, Keith R. Tidman, Arthur S. Hardyman, John Birmingham, Henrietta M. Snowden, and Beth F. MacKenzie for all their hard work.

Last and far from least I thank my husband, Dr. Edgar F. Raines, Jr., for his unfailing love and support. He deserves a special award for patiently listening to long and involved discussions of lineage issues over lunches and sometimes dinners—a service above and beyond the call of duty or vows of matrimony.

I hope that this volume, along with my earlier branch history, *Getting the Message Through*, published in 1996, will serve as educational tools for both soldiers and civilians about the institutional and organizational history of the Signal Corps. I had originally intended to prepare a fairly detailed introduction to this volume, but time and resource constraints caused a change in plans. Consequently, an extensive narrative treatment of the Corps' organizational history remains to be written. Nevertheless, the lineages contained herein provide insight into the branch's organizational evolution over time and serve as a snapshot of what the Signal Corps looks like as it nears its one hundred and fiftieth anniversary.

Because the Center of Military History is responsible for the determination and publication of unit lineages and honors under Army Regulation 870-5, comments are invited and should be addressed to the Center, ATTN: DAMH-FPO, Fort McNair, DC 20319-5058.

In the end, despite the assistance of all those listed above, any mistakes, errors, or omissions are solely the responsibility of the undersigned.

Washington, D.C.
8 April 2005

Rebecca Robbins Raines

Contents

	Page
HERALDIC ITEMS	xix
LINEAGES AND HERALDIC DATA	1
Signal Corps	3
1st Signal Command	5
5th Signal Command	6
6th Signal Command	8
7th Signal Command	10
9th Signal Command	12
311th Signal Command	14
335th Signal Command	16
1st Signal Center	18
216th Signal Depot	19
801st Signal Depot	20
803d Signal Depot	22
1st Signal Brigade	23
2d Signal Brigade	26
3d Signal Brigade	29
7th Signal Brigade	31
11th Signal Brigade	33
15th Signal Brigade	37
22d Signal Brigade	39
29th Signal Brigade	41
35th Signal Brigade	43
93d Signal Brigade	46
106th Signal Brigade	49
142d Signal Brigade	51
160th Signal Brigade	53
228th Signal Brigade	55
261st Signal Brigade	58
359th Signal Brigade	61
516th Signal Brigade	63

	Page
1st Signal Group	65
4th Signal Group	67
7th Signal Group	69
12th Signal Group	70
21st Signal Group	72
199th Signal Group	74
332d Signal Group	75
505th Signal Group	76
1st Signal Battalion	77
4th Signal Battalion	79
5th Signal Battalion	81
6th Signal Battalion	83
7th Signal Battalion	86
8th Signal Battalion	87
9th Signal Battalion	89
10th Signal Battalion	92
11th Signal Battalion	94
13th Signal Battalion	96
16th Signal Battalion	101
17th Signal Battalion	103
24th Signal Battalion	105
25th Signal Battalion	108
26th Signal Battalion	110
28th Signal Battalion	112
29th Signal Battalion	115
30th Signal Battalion	117
31st Signal Battalion	119
32d Signal Battalion	121
33d Signal Battalion	123
34th Signal Battalion	125
35th Signal Battalion	127
36th Signal Battalion	129
37th Signal Battalion	131
38th Signal Battalion	133

	Page
39th Signal Battalion	135
40th Signal Battalion	138
41st Signal Battalion	141
43d Signal Battalion	144
44th Signal Battalion	147
50th Signal Battalion	150
51st Signal Battalion	153
52d Signal Battalion	156
53d Signal Battalion	158
54th Signal Battalion	160
56th Signal Battalion	163
57th Signal Battalion	165
58th Signal Battalion	167
59th Signal Battalion	169
60th Signal Battalion	171
62d Signal Battalion	173
63d Signal Battalion	175
65th Signal Battalion	178
67th Signal Battalion	179
68th Signal Battalion	181
69th Signal Battalion	183
72d Signal Battalion	186
73d Signal Battalion	188
75th Signal Battalion	190
77th Signal Battalion	191
78th Signal Battalion	193
82d Signal Battalion	195
83d Signal Battalion	198
86th Signal Battalion	200
94th Signal Battalion	203
96th Signal Battalion	204
97th Signal Battalion	206
98th Signal Battalion	208
99th Signal Battalion	210

	Page
102d Signal Battalion	213
103d Signal Battalion	215
105th Signal Battalion	217
108th Signal Battalion	219
111th Signal Battalion	221
112th Signal Battalion	223
114th Signal Battalion	226
115th Signal Battalion	227
121st Signal Battalion	229
122d Signal Battalion	234
123d Signal Battalion	238
124th Signal Battalion	241
125th Signal Battalion	245
127th Signal Battalion	249
129th Signal Battalion	252
133d Signal Battalion	254
134th Signal Battalion	257
135th Signal Battalion	260
136th Signal Battalion	263
138th Signal Battalion	265
141st Signal Battalion	267
142d Signal Battalion	270
143d Signal Battalion	273
144th Signal Battalion	275
146th Signal Battalion	277
151st Signal Battalion	279
154th Signal Battalion	281
156th Signal Battalion	283
163d Signal Battalion	287
179th Signal Battalion	289
181st Signal Battalion	291
190th Signal Battalion	293
198th Signal Battalion	296
202d Signal Battalion	302

	Page
212th Signal Battalion	304
230th Signal Battalion	306
234th Signal Battalion	308
240th Signal Battalion	311
249th Signal Battalion	314
250th Signal Battalion	316
279th Signal Battalion	319
280th Signal Battalion	322
302d Signal Battalion	325
304th Signal Battalion	327
306th Signal Battalion	329
307th Signal Battalion	331
318th Signal Battalion	333
319th Signal Battalion	335
324th Signal Battalion	337
325th Signal Battalion	339
327th Signal Battalion	341
352d Signal Battalion	345
360th Signal Battalion	346
361st Signal Battalion	348
366th Signal Battalion	350
369th Signal Battalion	352
379th Signal Battalion	355
392d Signal Battalion	357
417th Signal Battalion	359
421st Signal Battalion	362
422d Signal Battalion	363
426th Signal Battalion	366
440th Signal Battalion	368
442d Signal Battalion	371
447th Signal Battalion	373
459th Signal Battalion	375
460th Signal Battalion	377
501st Signal Battalion	379

Page

503d Signal Battalion	383
504th Signal Battalion	384
509th Signal Battalion	386
511th Signal Battalion	388
523d Signal Battalion	390
551st Signal Battalion	392
560th Signal Battalion	394
711th Signal Battalion	396
835th Signal Battalion	399
845th Signal Battalion	401
850th Signal Battalion	403
980th Signal Battalion	405
GLOSSARY OF LINEAGE TERMS	407
UNIT INDEX	411

A color illustration of the regimental insignia of the Signal Corps appears as the frontispiece. It is also included with the color illustrations of heraldic items approved for Signal Corps commands, brigades, groups, and battalions appear between pages xx and 1.

Heraldic Items

Heraldic items for Army units include coats of arms, shoulder sleeve insignia, and distinctive unit insignia. Designed on the basis of a unit's official lineage and honors, they reflect each organization's history, traditions, ideals, mission, and accomplishments. Heraldic items also serve as identifying devices and contribute to unit cohesiveness and esprit de corps.

While the custom of bearing various symbols on shields, helmets, and flags existed in antiquity, heraldry was not introduced until the Middle Ages, when the increased use of armor made it difficult to distinguish friend from foe on the battlefield. Heraldic designs included mythological beasts, emblems commemorative of heroic deeds, and other identifying marks to which specific symbolism was ascribed. These heraldic devices were placed on a surcoat worn over the armor, from which the term *coat of arms* was derived. Gradually, a formal system of heraldry evolved, complete with rules for design, use, and display.

At the present time Army regiments and separate battalions are authorized coats of arms. A complete coat of arms consists of a shield, a crest, and a motto. The shield, the most important element of the coat of arms, contains the field or ground on which the charges or symbols are placed. The crest was originally placed on top of the helmet of the chief or leader to enable his followers to recognize him during battle. Today the crest is placed upon a wreath of six skeins or twists composed of the principal metal and primary colors of the shield, alternately, in the order named. This wreath or torse represents the piece of cloth that the knight twisted around the top of his helmet and by means of which the actual crest was attached. Mottoes have been in use longer than coats of arms. Many of the older ones originated from war cries. Usually of an idealistic nature, they sometimes allude to a well-known event in the history of the unit.

The elements of the coat of arms are embroidered on the organizational flag (color), the central element of which is the American eagle. The shield of the coat of arms is the eagle's breast, a scroll bearing the motto is held in his beak, and the crest is placed above his head. A crest to the coat of arms is authorized for Regular Army units that have war service or campaign credit. Army National Guard units display the crest of the state or states in which they are located, and a special crest has been designed for all Army Reserve units.

The currently authorized embroidered shoulder sleeve insignia had their origin during World War I. They serve the same purpose as the corps symbols (badges) used during the Civil War and the War with Spain. Most corps badges were of simple design and could be cut from a single piece of cloth. These emblems, such as a four-leaf clover, a star, or a spearhead, were easily remembered and readily identified. Not only were they worn by soldiers on their headgear, they were also incorporated into the design of unit flags.

The first shoulder sleeve insignia is believed to have been worn by the men of the 81st Division during World War I. On their voyage to France they adopted as their insignia the figure of a wildcat, which they used as a distinctive marking for the division's equipment. Wear of this insignia was officially approved on 19 October 1918 by a telegram from the adjutant general, American Expeditionary Forces, to the division commander. Insignia for other units of the American Expeditionary Forces were later authorized and designs officially approved. Designs varied greatly. Many had their origin in devices already in use for organizational and equipment markings. Others were based on monograms and geometric figures alluding to a unit's numerical designation. Symbols associated with traditions, geographical locations, and unit mission were also included in some designs.

Since World War I the authorization of shoulder sleeve insignia has expanded. Under the current system, separate brigades and higher echelons are authorized shoulder sleeve insignia for wear by soldiers assigned to the units. The insignia also appear on the organizations' distinguishing flags. Over time, the designs have become more elaborate and complex owing to the increased number of authorized insignia and the availability of embroidery machinery for the production of various types of textile insignia. During the Vietnam era the policy governing the wear of subdued insignia on work uniforms was established.

Distinctive unit insignia, manufactured in metal and enamel and worn by all unit personnel, are authorized for separate battalions and higher echelons. The type of distinctive unit insignia currently in use was first authorized during the 1920s for regiments and certain other units. As in the case of shoulder sleeve insignia and coats of arms, authorization expanded as changes in the organization of the Army took place. The designs are based on symbols reflecting each unit's lineage, battle honors, traditions, and mission and usually incorporate the organization's motto. Distinctive unit insignia for most regiments and battalions include the same design elements as their coats of arms.

Today, as in the past, insignia displayed on flags and worn on uniforms are highly visible items of identification. These heraldic items serve to distinguish specific organizations and their members and are significant factors in establishing and maintaining unit esprit de corps.

Signal Corps

1st Signal Command

5th Signal Command

6th Signal Command

7th Signal Command

9th Signal Command

311th Signal Command

335th Signal Command

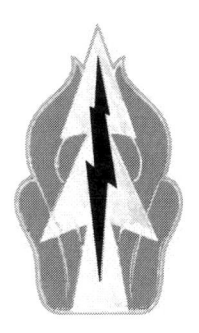

1st Signal Brigade

2d Signal Brigade

3d Signal Brigade

7th Signal Brigade

11th Signal Brigade

15th Signal Brigade

22d Signal Brigade

29th Signal Brigade

35th Signal Brigade

93d Signal Brigade

106th Signal Brigade

142d Signal Brigade

160th Signal Brigade

228th Signal Brigade

261st Signal Brigade

359th Signal Brigade

516th Signal Brigade

1st Signal Group

4th Signal Group

12th Signal Group

21st Signal Group

1st Signal Battalion

4th Signal Battalion

5th Signal Battalion

6th Signal Battalion

8th Signal Battalion

9th Signal Battalion

10th Signal Battalion

11th Signal Battalion

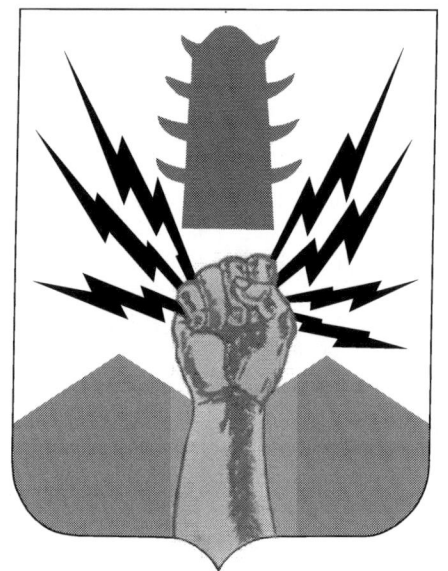

13th Signal Battalion

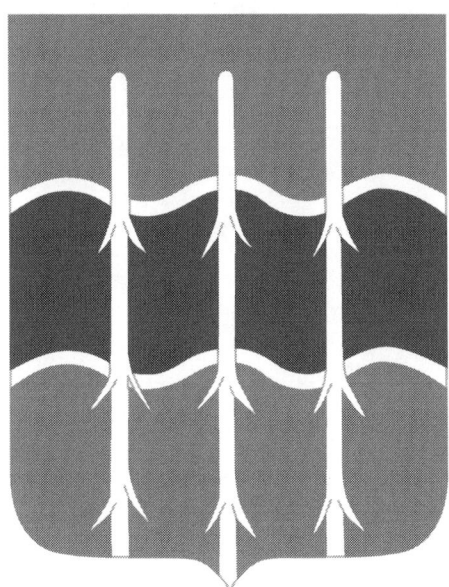

16th Signal Battalion

17th Signal Battalion

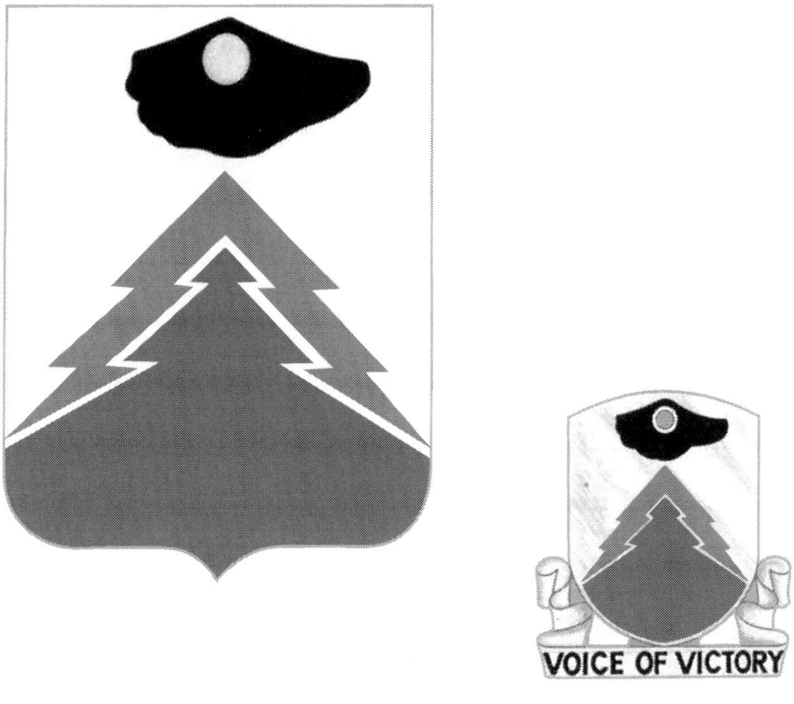

24th Signal Battalion

25th Signal Battalion

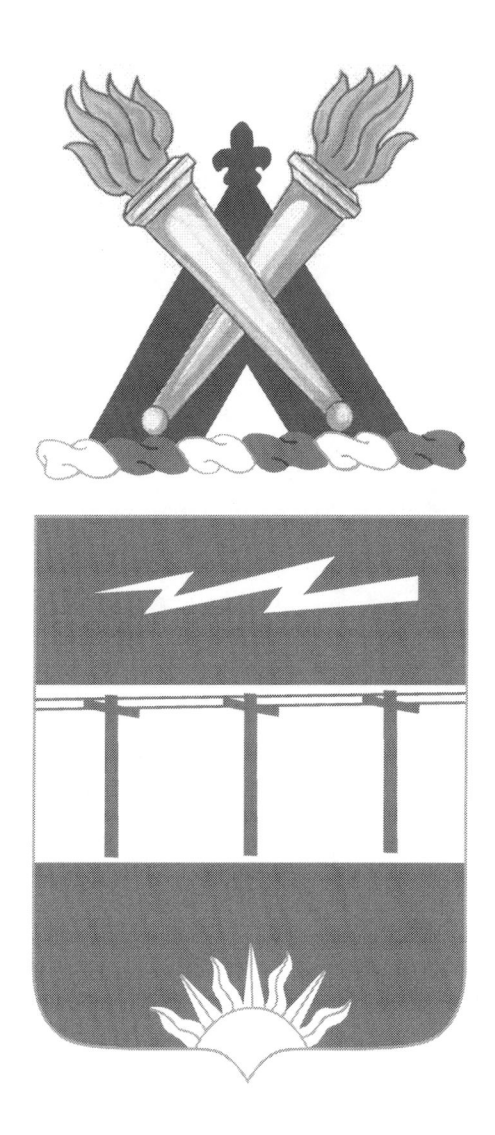

26th Signal Battalion

28th Signal Battalion

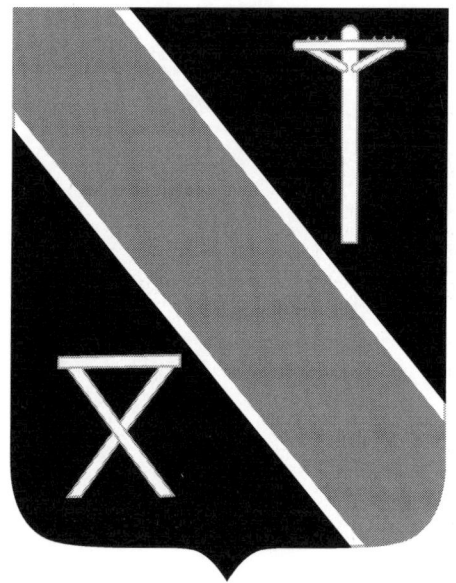

29th Signal Battalion

30th Signal Battalion

31st Signal Battalion

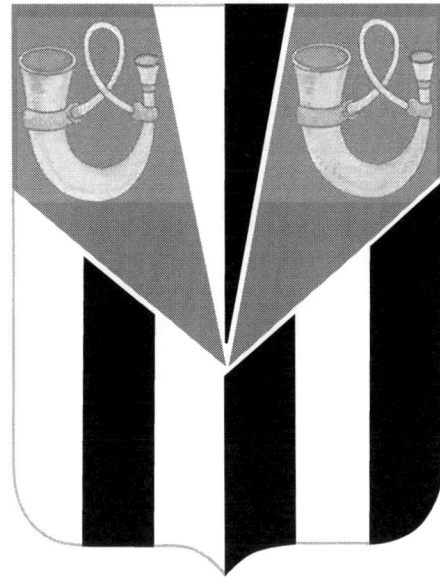

32d Signal Battalion

33d Signal Battalion

34th Signal Battalion

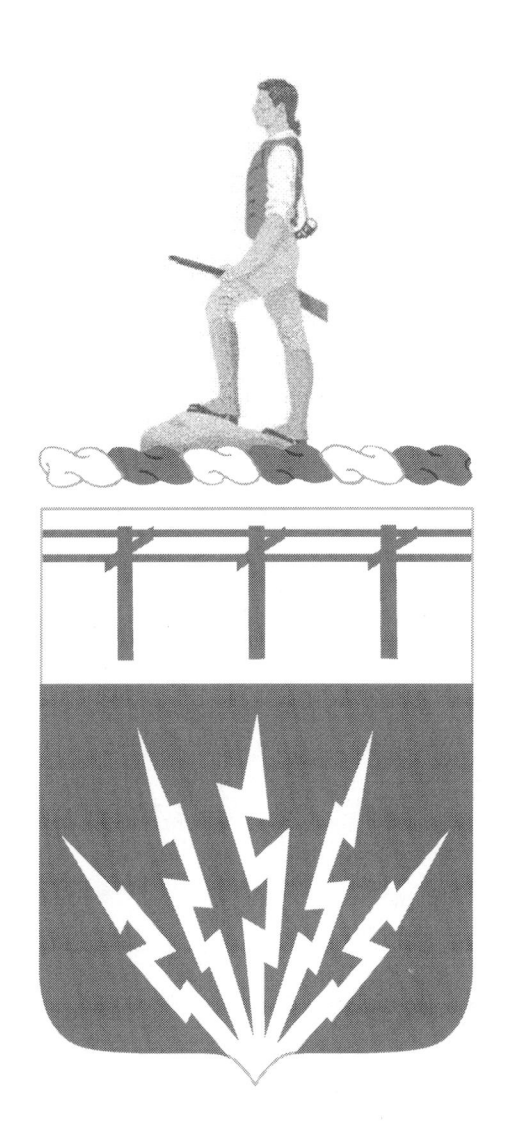

35th Signal Battalion

36th Signal Battalion

37th Signal Battalion

38th Signal Battalion

39th Signal Battalion

40th Signal Battalion

41st Signal Battalion

43d Signal Battalion

44th Signal Battalion

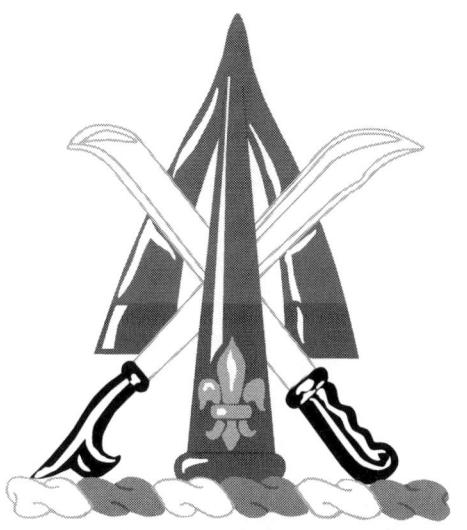

50th Signal Battalion

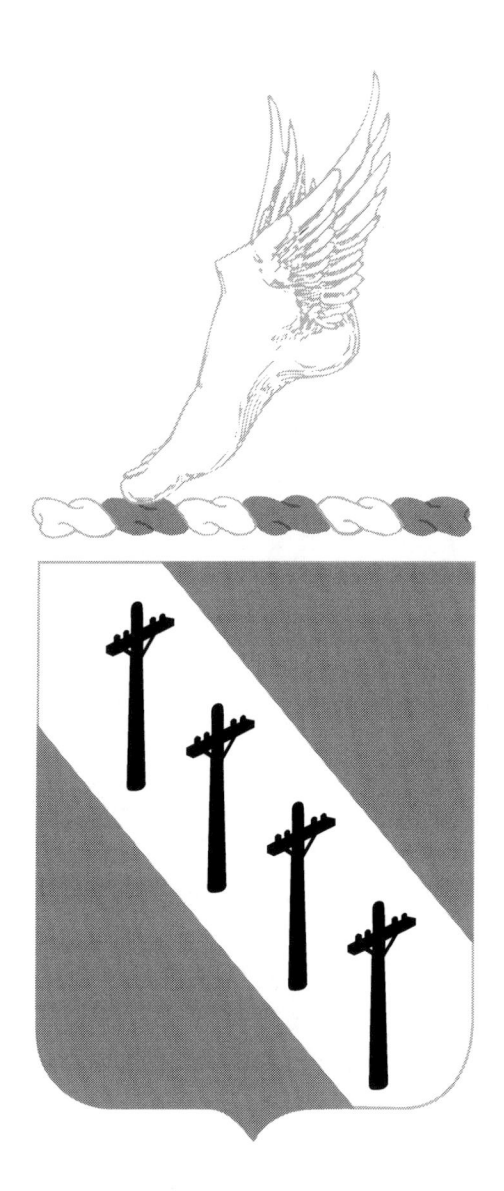

51st Signal Battalion

52d Signal Battalion

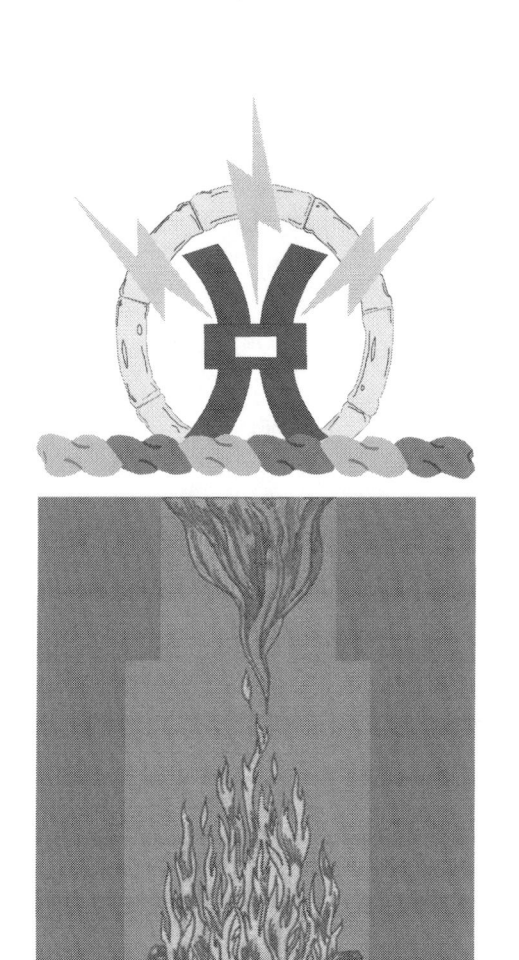

53d Signal Battalion

54th Signal Battalion

56th Signal Battalion

57th Signal Battalion

58th Signal Battalion

59th Signal Battalion

60th Signal Battalion

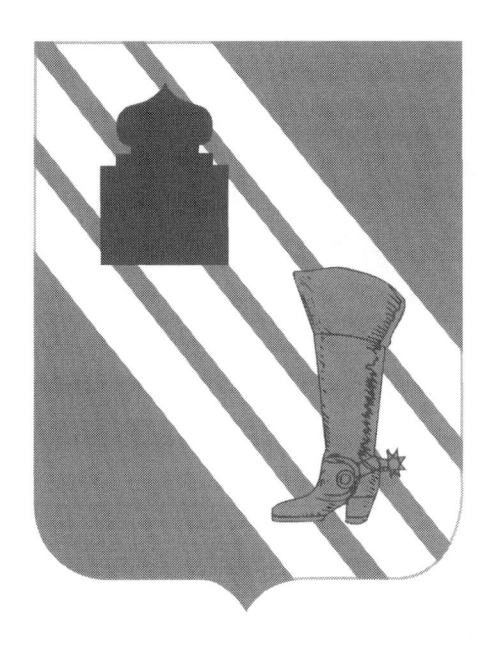

63d Signal Battalion

67th Signal Battalion

68th Signal Battalion

69th Signal Battalion

72d Signal Battalion

73d Signal Battalion

77th Signal Battalion

78th Signal Battalion

82d Signal Battalion

83d Signal Battalion

86th Signal Battalion

96th Signal Battalion

97th Signal Battalion

98th Signal Battalion

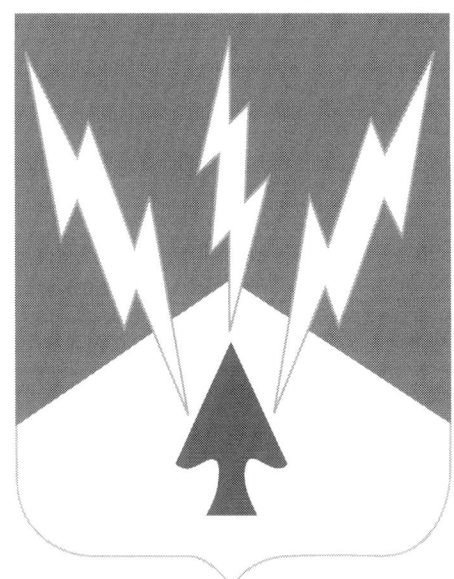

99th Signal Battalion

102d Signal Battalion

103d Signal Battalion

105th Signal Battalion

108th Signal Battalion

111th Signal Battalion

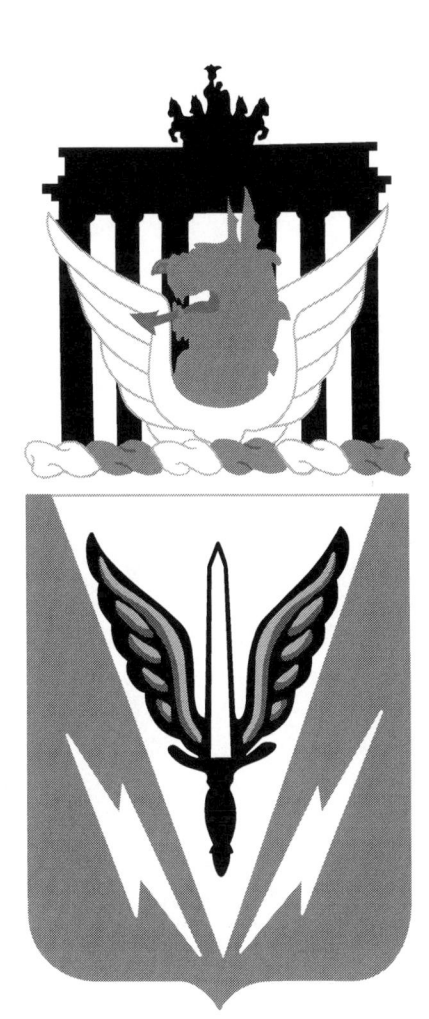

112th Signal Battalion

115th Signal Battalion

121st Signal Battalion

122d Signal Battalion

123d Signal Battalion

124th Signal Battalion

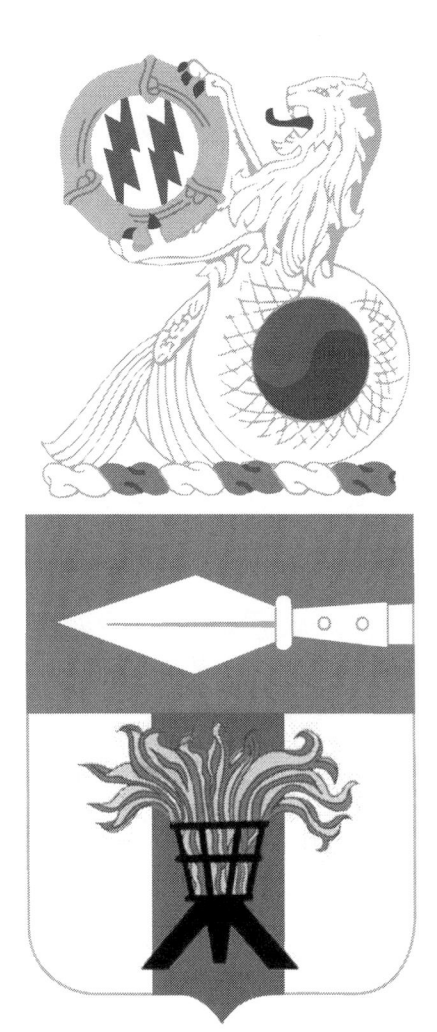

125th Signal Battalion

127th Signal Battalion

129th Signal Battalion

133d Signal Battalion

134th Signal Battalion

135th Signal Battalion

136th Signal Battalion

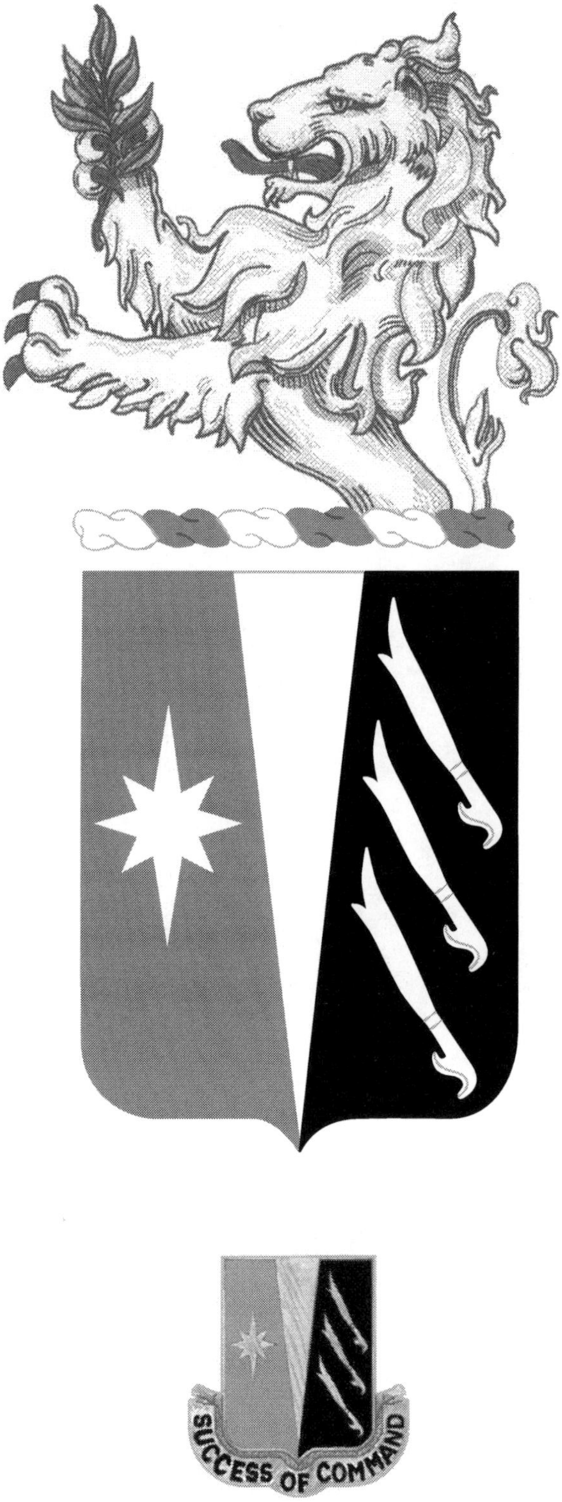

138th Signal Battalion

141st Signal Battalion

142d Signal Battalion

143d Signal Battalion

144th Signal Battalion

146th Signal Battalion

151st Signal Battalion

154th Signal Battalion

156th Signal Battalion

163d Signal Battalion

179th Signal Battalion

181st Signal Battalion

190th Signal Battalion

198th Signal Battalion

202d Signal Battalion

212th Signal Battalion

230th Signal Battalion

234th Signal Battalion

240th Signal Battalion

249th Signal Battalion

250th Signal Battalion

279th Signal Battalion

280th Signal Battalion

302d Signal Battalion

304th Signal Battalion

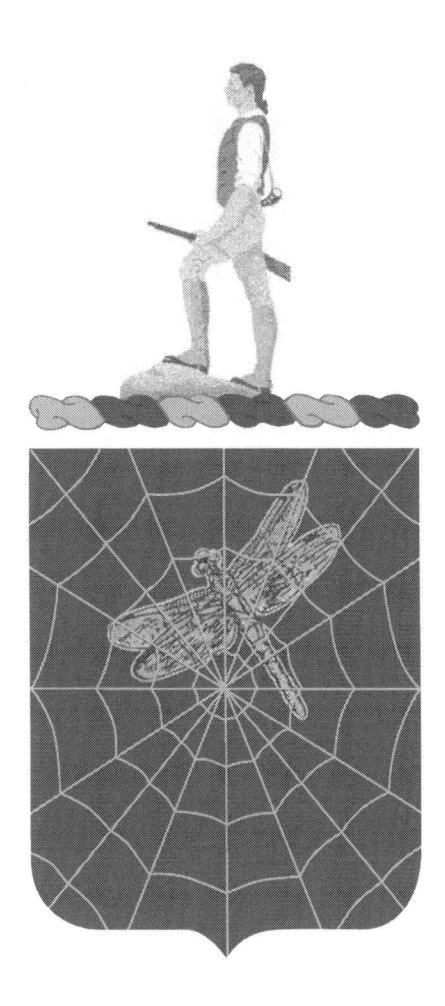

306th Signal Battalion

307th Signal Battalion

318th Signal Battalion

319th Signal Battalion

324th Signal Battalion

325th Signal Battalion

327th Signal Battalion

360th Signal Battalion

361st Signal Battalion

366th Signal Battalion

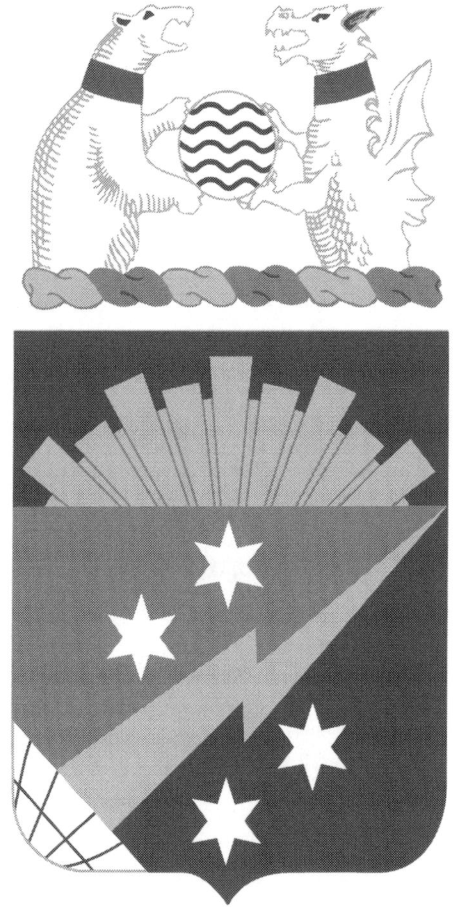

369th Signal Battalion

379th Signal Battalion

392d Signal Battalion

417th Signal Battalion

422d Signal Battalion

426th Signal Battalion

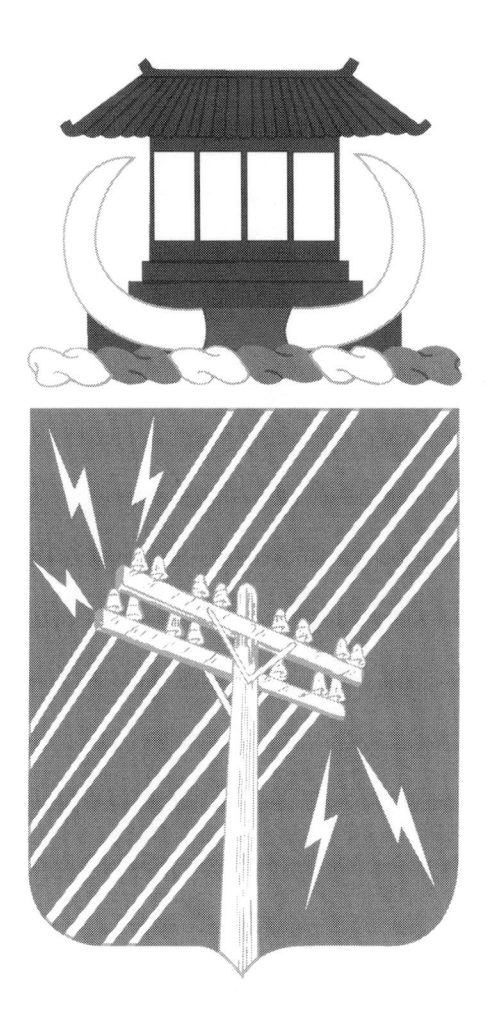

440th Signal Battalion

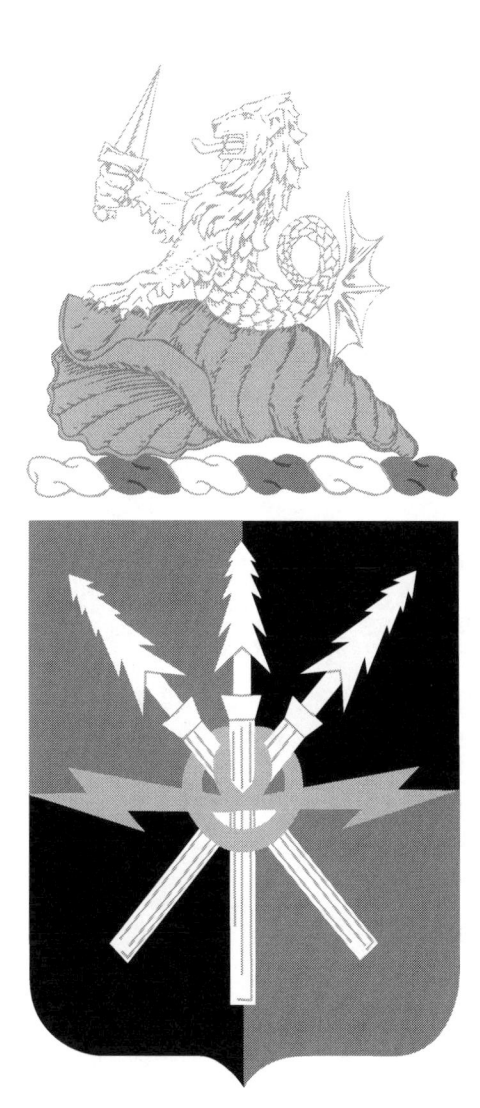

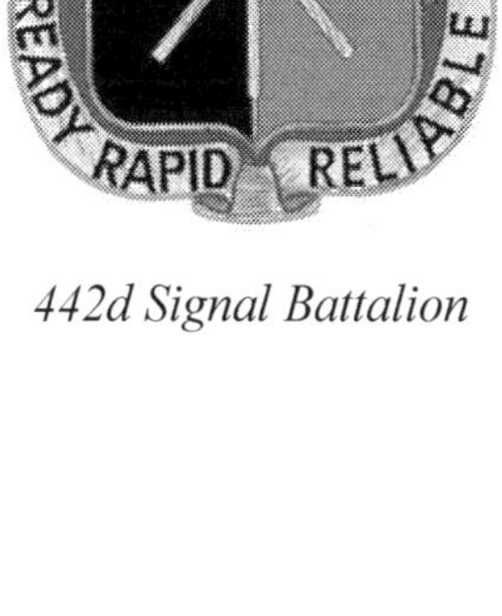

442d Signal Battalion

447th Signal Battalion

459th Signal Battalion

460th Signal Battalion

501st Signal Battalion

504th Signal Battalion

509th Signal Battalion

523d Signal Battalion

551st Signal Battalion

560th Signal Battalion

711th Signal Battalion

845th Signal Battalion

850th Signal Battalion

LINEAGES AND HERALDIC DATA

SIGNAL CORPS

HERALDIC ITEMS

COAT OF ARMS

Shield: Argent, within a bordure tenné a baton fesswise or and suspended therefrom a signal flag gules charged at center with a square of the first, in chief a mullet bronze.

Crest: On a wreath of the colors argent and tenné a dexter hand couped at the wrist, clenched, palm affronte, grasping three forked lightning flashes, all proper, flashes argent.

Motto: PRO PATRIA VIGILANS (Watchful for the Country).

Symbolism: Orange and white are the colors traditionally associated with the Signal Corps. The signal flag suspended from a baton is adopted from a badge that originated in 1865 and was called the Order of the Signal Corps. The bronze battle star represents formal recognition for participation in combat. It adorned a signal flag and was first awarded to Signal Corps soldiers in 1862.

DISTINCTIVE UNIT INSIGNIA

Description: A gold color metal and enamel device that consists of a gold eagle grasping a horizontal baton from which is suspended a red signal flag with a white center, enclosing the flag from a star at the bottom, a wreath of laurel all gold and at top left and right a white scroll inscribed PRO PATRIA at left and VIGILANS at right in gold.

Symbolism: The gold eagle holds in his talons a golden baton, from which descends a signal flag. The design originated in 1865 from a meeting of Signal Corps officers, led by Major Albert J. Myer, the chief signal officer, in Washington, D.C. The badge was a symbol of faithful service and good fellowship for those who served together in war and was called the Order of the Signal Corps. The motto PRO PATRIA VIGILANS (Watchful for the Country) was adopted from the Signal School insignia and serves to portray the cohesiveness of Signal soldiers and their affiliation with their regimental home. The laurel wreath depicts the myriad of achievements through strength made by the Corps since its inception. The battle star centered on the wreath represents formal recognition for participation in combat. It adorned a signal flag and was first awarded to Signal Corps soldiers in 1862. The battle star typifies the close operational relationship between the combined arms and the Signal Corps.

HEADQUARTERS AND HEADQUARTERS COMPANY
1st SIGNAL COMMAND

HERALDIC ITEMS

SHOULDER SLEEVE INSIGNIA

Description: On an orange disc within a white border three white rings graduating in size and having a common tangent at the base, the smallest circle surrounding a blue roundel, all surmounted by a vertical blue lightning flash issuing from lower border and extending to top border.

Symbolism: Orange and white are the colors traditionally associated with the Signal Corps. The blue lightning flash on target symbolizes the 1st Signal Command's ability to carry on all functions of its mission with speed and accuracy. The white rings refer to the emanating effect of transmitting radio waves through space. The single lightning flash further distinguishes the 1st Signal Command.

DISTINCTIVE UNIT INSIGNIA

None approved.

LINEAGE AND HONORS

RA
(inactive)

LINEAGE

Constituted 19 April 1967 in the Regular Army as Headquarters and Headquarters Company, 1st Signal Command. Activated 25 April 1967 at Fort Riley, Kansas. Inactivated March 1969 at Fort Riley, Kansas.

CAMPAIGN PARTICIPATION CREDIT

None.

DECORATIONS

None.

1st SIGNAL COMMAND BIBLIOGRAPHY

No published histories.

HEADQUARTERS AND HEADQUARTERS COMPANY 5th SIGNAL COMMAND
(Dragon Warriors)

HERALDIC ITEMS

SHOULDER SLEEVE INSIGNIA

Description: On an orange shield with a white border a stylized green demi-dragon with red eye emitting two black lightning flashes.

Symbolism: Orange and white are the colors traditionally associated with the Signal Corps. The demidragon alludes to the unit's area of operations in Germany.

DISTINCTIVE UNIT INSIGNIA

Description: A silver color metal and enamel device that consists of five lightning flashes converging at center on a silver disc with three concentric black circles, all encircled by an orange scroll inscribed PROFESSIONAL at top and COMMUNICATIONS in base in silver letters.

Symbolism: Orange and white are the colors traditionally associated with the Signal Corps. The disc with black lines alludes to the globe, and the lightning flashes form lines of longitude that symbolize the far-reaching scope of the unit's mission. The lightning also resembles a target, indicating accuracy and efficiency. The five lightning flashes refer to the unit's numerical designation.

LINEAGE AND HONORS

RA
(active)

LINEAGE

Constituted 1 July 1974 in the Regular Army as Headquarters and Headquarters Company, 5th Signal Command, and activated in Germany.

CAMPAIGN PARTICIPATION CREDIT

None.

DECORATIONS

None.

5th SIGNAL COMMAND BIBLIOGRAPHY

Baker, Jerry. "European Signal Force Drawdown." *Army Communicator* 18 (Summer 1993): 59.

Cowan, Raymond G. *Background and History of the 5th Signal Command, 1958–1977*. Worms, West Germany: Signal Corps, 5th Signal Command, 1978.

"5th Signal Command." *Army Communicator* 1 (Summer 1976): 44–45.

G6 Staff Members. "State of the Art Network Provides Faster and More Reliable Information to the Warfighter." *Army Communicator* 28 (Fall 2003): 16–19.

Gehring, Stephen P. *From the Fulda Gap to Kuwait: U.S. Army, Europe, and the Gulf War*. Washington, D.C.: Department of the Army, 1998.

Hasenauer, Heike. "Grecian Firebolt." *Soldiers* 49 (September 1994): 37–40.

Hitt, Joe. "7th Signal Brigade Joins 5th Signal Command." *Army Communicator* 7 (Winter 1982): 37.

Johnson, Danny M. "5th Signal Command Finds First Joint European Network Operations Drill to be a 'Dragon.'" *Army Communicator* 28 (Spring 2003): 58–59.

_____. *Military Communications Supporting Peacekeeping Operations in the Balkans: The Signal Corps at Its Best*. Mannheim, Germany: Headquarters, 5th Signal Command, 2000.

"McKnight Takes 5th Signal Command." *Army Communicator* 4 (Winter 1979): 59.

Rolak, Bruno J. *History of the U.S. Army Communications Command (1964–1976)*. Fort Huachuca, Ariz.: United States Army Communications Command, 1976.

Rolak, Bruno J., and George R. Thompson. *History of the United States Army Communications Command From Origin Through 1976*. Fort Huachuca, Ariz.: United States Army Communications Command, 1979.

White, Hank. "Grecian Firebolt 1994: A Real Test for Network Managers." *Army Communicator* 20 (Winter 1995): 45–51.

HEADQUARTERS AND HEADQUARTERS COMPANY
6th SIGNAL COMMAND

HERALDIC ITEMS

SHOULDER SLEEVE INSIGNIA

Description: An orange hexagon, one point up, bearing a blue falcon's head, eye white, and charged on the neck with a lightning flash point up, also white.

Symbolism: Orange and white are the colors traditionally associated with the Signal Corps. The six sides of the device reflect the designation of the command. The unit's motto, VOICE OF THE DESERT, is signified by the desert falcon, which symbolizes vigilance, speed, and clarity of communications. Blue stands for devotion to duty and loyalty. The lightning flash represents speed and electronic communication.

DISTINCTIVE UNIT INSIGNIA

Description: A silver color metal and enamel device that consists of an orange disc bearing a brown falcon's head charged on the neck with a silver lightning flash point up, issuing from and encircled by a blue motto scroll inscribed VOICE OF THE DESERT at top in silver letters and superimposed at bottom by two silver stylized scimitars crossed diagonally.

Symbolism: Orange and white are the colors traditionally associated with the Signal Corps. The falcon is associated with Saudi Arabia and the region as a respected hunting bird and desert inhabitant. With the lightning flash, it symbolizes the speed and clarity of communications required of the 6th Signal Command's mission. The crossed scimitars stand for desert service and the command's readiness for duty during its mission in Saudi Arabia. Blue denotes devotion to duty and loyalty.

LINEAGE AND HONORS

RA
(inactive)

LINEAGE

Constituted 1 July 1974 in the Regular Army as Headquarters and Headquarters Company, 6th Signal Command, and activated at Fort Shafter, Hawaii. Inactivated 30 November 1977 at Fort Shafter, Hawaii.

Activated 4 December 1990 at Fort Huachuca, Arizona. Inactivated 1 June 1992 at Fort Huachuca, Arizona.

CAMPAIGN PARTICIPATION CREDIT

Southwest Asia
    Defense of Saudi Arabia
    Liberation and Defense of Kuwait
    Cease-Fire

DECORATIONS

Meritorious Unit Commendation (Army), Streamer embroidered SOUTHWEST ASIA 1990–1991 (Headquarters, 6th Signal Command, cited; DA GO 34, 1992)

6th SIGNAL COMMAND BIBLIOGRAPHY

Brinkerhoff, John R., Ted Silva, and John A. Seitz. *The Signal Support Dilemma: The 335th Signal Command.* United States Army Reserve in Operation Desert Storm. N.p.: ANDRULIS Research Corp., 1992.

Pace, Emily Charlotte. "USAISC Before, During and After Desert Storm." *Army Communicator* 16 (Summer 1991): 13–17.

Public Affairs Officer, 6th Signal Command. *Headquarters United States Army 6th Signal Command: A Decade of Service to the Nation, 1964–1974.* San Francisco: United States Army 6th Signal Command, 1974.

Raines, Rebecca Robbins. *Getting the Message Through: A Branch History of the U.S. Army Signal Corps.* Army Historical Series. Washington, D.C.: Center of Military History, United States Army, 1996.

Rolak, Bruno J., and George R. Thompson. *History of the United States Army Communications Command From Origin Through 1976.* Fort Huachuca, Ariz.: United States Army Communications Command, 1979.

Stokes, Carol E., ed. *The U.S. Army Signal Corps in Operation Desert Shield/Desert Storm.* Fort Gordon, Ga.: Office of the Command Historian, U.S. Army Signal Center and Fort Gordon, 1994.

Stokes, Carol E., and Kathy R. Coker. "Getting the Message Through in the Persian Gulf War." *Army Communicator* 17 (Summer–Winter 1992): 17–25.

HEADQUARTERS AND HEADQUARTERS COMPANY
7th SIGNAL COMMAND

HERALDIC ITEMS

SHOULDER SLEEVE INSIGNIA

None approved.

DISTINCTIVE UNIT INSIGNIA

Description: A silver color metal and enamel device that consists of a dark blue disc bearing seven silver lightning flashes radiating from behind a silver eagle displayed between an orange motto scroll bearing in silver letters the words DIFFICILE EST SUMMISSO ESSE inclosing the base from wing tip to wing tip.

Symbolism: Orange and white are the colors traditionally associated with the Signal Corps. The blue refers to the atmosphere from the Atlantic to the Pacific Oceans and from the Caribbean to the Bering Seas through which the unit operates. The eagle suggests vigilance and dedication to duty and country. The seven lightning flashes refer to the unit's mission of communication and to its numerical designation.

LINEAGE AND HONORS

RA
(inactive)

LINEAGE

Constituted 1 July 1975 in the Regular Army as Headquarters and Headquarters Company, 7th Signal Command, and activated at Fort Ritchie, Maryland. Inactivated 1 October 1993 at Fort Ritchie, Maryland.

CAMPAIGN PARTICIPATION CREDIT

None.

DECORATIONS

None.

7th SIGNAL COMMAND BIBLIOGRAPHY

Britsch, Ellen A. "7th Signal to Upgrade Phone System." *Army Communicator* 8 (Summer 1983): 10–11.

Davenport, Vernon, Jr. "Blueprints for the Future." *Army Communicator* 15 (Spring–Summer 1990): 58.

Hinton, Albert F., and D. Jean Maire. "7th Signal Command: The Army's Voice in CONUS." *Army Communicator* 1 (Fall 1976): 51–52.

Jackson, Ruth. "Tower Power." *Army Communicator* 4 (Fall 1979): 20–22.

Rolak, Bruno J. *History of the U.S. Army Communications Command (1964–1976).* Fort Huachuca, Ariz.: United States Army Communications Command, 1976.

Rolak, Bruno J., and George R. Thompson. *History of the United States Army Communications Command From Origin Through 1976.* Fort Huachuca, Ariz.: United States Army Communications Command, 1979.

Rossiter, Charles. "Communicate to Operate." *Army Communicator* 3 (Spring 1978): 55.

———. "7th Signal Command Keeps Us on the Move." *Army Communicator* 3 (Summer 1978): 38–39.

"The 7th Signal Command ATC is Unique." *Army Communicator* 10 (Winter 1985): 38–39.

"A Towering Job." *Army Communicator* 5 (Spring 1980): 60.

HEADQUARTERS AND HEADQUARTERS COMPANY
9th SIGNAL COMMAND

HERALDIC ITEMS

SHOULDER SLEEVE INSIGNIA

Description: On a shield divided diagonally from upper left to lower right with white above and orange below, a globe with grid lines and outlines in orange above and white below and superimposed thereon from upper left to lower right a yellow lightning flash all within a yellow border.

Symbolism: Orange and white are the colors traditionally associated with the Signal Corps. The globe indicates the worldwide nature of the communications controlled by the command, and the lightning flash depicts its dynamic and strategic capabilities.

DISTINCTIVE UNIT INSIGNIA

Description: A gold color metal and enamel device that consists of three gold swords on a black background one vertical and two saltirewise between and encircled by six orange lightning flashes and surmounted by a white globe having gold grid lines, all beneath an arched gold scroll bearing the inscription VOICE OF THE ARMY in black letters.

Symbolism: Orange and white are the colors traditionally associated with the Signal Corps. The swords are indicative of the military establishment supported by the command and refer to operational readiness. The globe and lightning flashes, adopted from the shoulder sleeve insignia, symbolize the worldwide aspects of communications and the organization's dynamic and strategic capabilities.

LINEAGE AND HONORS

RA
(active)

LINEAGE

Constituted 14 February 1918 in the Regular Army as the 9th Service Company, Signal Corps. Activated 19 April 1918 in Hawaii. Redesignated in June 1922 as Service Company Number 9, Signal Corps. Redesignated 12 May 1925 as the 9th Signal Service Company. Redesignated 24 April 1943 as the 972d Signal Service Company.

Reorganized and redesignated 8 January 1944 as the 972d Signal Service Battalion. Inactivated 18 October 1948 at Fort Shafter, Hawaii. Redesignated 14 May 1958 as the 972d Signal Battalion.

LINEAGES AND HERALDIC DATA

Headquarters and Headquarters Detachment, 972d Signal Battalion, activated 23 June 1958 at Tobyhanna Signal Depot, Pennsylvania. Reorganized and redesignated 4 May 1965 as Headquarters and Headquarters Company, 972d Signal Battalion. Inactivated 20 October 1967 in Vietnam. Activated 10 May 1968 at Fort Lewis, Washington. Inactivated 29 November 1969 in Vietnam.

Redesignated 16 September 1997 as Headquarters and Headquarters Company, 9th Signal Command, and activated at Fort Huachuca, Arizona.

CAMPAIGN PARTICIPATION CREDIT

World War II
  Central Pacific

Vietnam
  Defense
  Counteroffensive
  Counteroffensive, Phase II
  Counteroffensive, Phase III
  Counteroffensive, Phase V
  Counteroffensive, Phase VI
  Tet 69/Counteroffensive
  Summer–Fall 1969
  Winter–Spring 1970

DECORATIONS

Meritorious Unit Commendation (Army), Streamer embroidered PACIFIC THEATER (972d Signal Service Battalion cited; GO 392, Central Pacific Base Command, 23 October 1945)

Meritorious Unit Commendation (Army), Streamer embroidered VIETNAM 1966–1967 (Headquarters and Headquarters Company, 972d Signal Battalion, cited; DA GO 54, 1968)

9th SIGNAL COMMAND BIBLIOGRAPHY

Bergen, John B. *Military Communications: A Test for Technology*. United States Army in Vietnam. Washington, D.C.: Center of Military History, United States Army, 1986.

Rienzi, Thomas M. *Communications-Electronics, 1962–1970*. Vietnam Studies. Washington, D.C.: Department of the Army, 1972.

Thompson, George Raynor, Dixie R. Harris, Pauline M. Oakes, and Dulany Terrett. *The Signal Corps: The Test (December 1941 to July 1943)*. United States Army in World War II. Washington, D.C.: Office of the Chief of Military History, Department of the Army, 1957.

HEADQUARTERS AND HEADQUARTERS COMPANY
311th SIGNAL COMMAND

HERALDIC ITEMS

SHOULDER SLEEVE INSIGNIA

Description: On a blue shield with a white border a yellow phoenix arising from a red flame, all above an orange demiglobe grid lined blue in base.

Symbolism: The phoenix arising from the flame represents rebirth and is indicative of a new command. The orange demiglobe symbolizes the worldwide capabilities of the organization. The blue background alludes to the sky and the transmission of voice, picture, and data via satellite.

DISTINCTIVE UNIT INSIGNIA

Description: A silver color metal and enamel device that consists of a silver broad arrow upon a blue background between two silver lightning bolts chevronwise conjoined at the top, all above an orange demiglobe with silver grid lines. Attached at base a blue scroll inscribed THE THEATER VOICE in silver.

Symbolism: Orange and white (silver) are the colors traditionally associated with the Signal Corps. The lightning bolts signify the harnessed power of communications. The arrowhead represents combat readiness and points to the sky, symbolizing the transmission of data via satellite. The globe symbolizes the worldwide capability of the organization. The motto highlights the unit's mission as the theater's communication link.

LINEAGE AND HONORS

AR
(active)

LINEAGE

Constituted 26 January 1944 in the Army of the United States as Headquarters, 3112th Signal Service Battalion. Activated 1 February 1944 at Fort Monmouth, New Jersey. Reorganized and redesignated 7 June 1945 as Headquarters and Headquarters Company, 3112th Signal Service Battalion. Inactivated 5 December 1946 in Germany.

Redesignated 27 March 1952 as Headquarters and Headquarters Company, 311th Signal Group, and allotted to the Organized Reserve Corps. Activated 10 April 1952 at Baltimore, Maryland. (Organized Reserve Corps redesignated 9 July

1952 as the Army Reserve.) Reorganized and redesignated 26 April 1954 as Headquarters and Headquarters Detachment, 311th Signal Group. Inactivated 20 February 1963 at Baltimore, Maryland.

Redesignated 16 June 1996 as Headquarters and Headquarters Company, 311th Signal Command, and activated at Fort George G. Meade, Maryland.

CAMPAIGN PARTICIPATION CREDIT

World War II
   Normandy
   Northern France
   Rhineland
   Ardennes-Alsace
   Central Europe

DECORATIONS

None.

311th SIGNAL COMMAND BIBLIOGRAPHY

"Army Signal Command Directs Worldwide Signal Exercise." *Army Communicator* 24 (Fall 1999): 6. Discusses Grecian Firebolt 1999.

Birmingham, Crista M., and Patrick A. Swan. "GF '03 Tests New Communication Capabilities for Homeland Defense, Global War on Terrorism." *Army Communicator* 28 (Fall 2003): 28–30. Grecian Firebolt 2003.

"Grecian Firebolt 2002 Tests Interoperability in Homeland Defense Communications Scenario." *Army Communicator* 27 (Fall 2002): 28.

"Practical Training for Thirty-five Units in LOGEX 61." *Army Reservist* 7 (July–August 1961): 12–13.

Siemieniec, Jack. "Grecian Firebolt Connects, Supports Multiple Exercises." *Army Communicator* 26 (Fall 2001): 2–4.

———. "Grecian Firebolt Puts Web to Use." *Army Communicator* 26 (Fall 2001): 10.

HEADQUARTERS AND HEADQUARTERS COMPANY
335th SIGNAL COMMAND

HERALDIC ITEMS

SHOULDER SLEEVE INSIGNIA

Description: A dark blue vertical rectangle arched at top and bottom with a white border having in base the polar section of an orange globe with white grid lines and issuant therefrom two white-edged orange lightning flashes with points converging at top center.

Symbolism: Orange and white are the colors traditionally associated with the Signal Corps. Dark blue signifies the atmosphere, and the lightning flashes and globe are symbolic of the unit's worldwide communication capability.

DISTINCTIVE UNIT INSIGNIA

Description: A gold color metal and enamel device that consists of two quadrates conjoined with point up, the left quadrate of white and the right of black, surmounted by two orange lightning flashes chevronwise and extending above and below the quadrates. In base a green open wreath of live oak, all above a semicircular gold scroll folded back at the base of each flash and inscribed READY LIGHTNING in black letters; areas between quadrates and flashes at top and quadrates and live oak in base pierced.

Symbolism: Orange and white are the colors traditionally associated with the Signal Corps. The white and black quadrates and the lightning flashes symbolize the organization's day and night mission to direct and coordinate the operations, training, administration, and logistics support of assigned and attached units. The live oak, the state tree of Georgia, symbolizes ever-ready strength in reserve and alludes to the organization's origin and home station in Atlanta, Georgia.

LINEAGE AND HONORS

AR
(active)

LINEAGE

Constituted 13 February 1953 in the Army Reserve as Headquarters and Headquarters Company, 335th Signal Group. Activated 28 February 1953 at Atlanta, Georgia. Reorganized and redesignated 31 December 1953 as Headquarters and Headquarters Detachment, 335th Signal Group. Reorganized and redesignated 30

June 1954 as Headquarters, 335th Signal Group. Reorganized and redesignated 31 March 1955 as Headquarters and Headquarters Detachment, 335th Signal Group. Ordered into active military service 15 October 1961 at Atlanta, Georgia; released 3 August 1962 from active military service and reverted to reserve status. Location changed 19 April 1971 to East Point, Georgia. Reorganized and redesignated 15 March 1972 as Headquarters and Headquarters Company, 335th Signal Group.

Redesignated 16 October 1984 as Headquarters and Headquarters Company, 335th Signal Brigade. Reorganized and redesignated 16 April 1986 as Headquarters and Headquarters Company, 335th Signal Command.

CAMPAIGN PARTICIPATION CREDIT

None.

DECORATIONS

None.

335th SIGNAL COMMAND BIBLIOGRAPHY

Bowman, George F. "335th Signal Command Shines at Bright Star '94." *Army Communicator* 19 (Summer 1994): 21–23.

Brinkerhoff, John R., Ted Silva, and John A. Seitz. *The Signal Support Dilemma: The 335th Signal Command*. United States Army Reserve in Operation Desert Storm. N.p.: ANDRULIS Research Corp., 1992.

Currie, James T., and Richard B. Crossland. *Twice the Citizen: A History of the United States Army Reserve, 1908–1995*. Washington, D.C.: Office of the Chief, Army Reserve, 1997.

Harrell, Rickey E. "TCMC: Charting the Course of Future Theater Communications." *Army Communicator* 20 (Winter 1995): 2–4. Discusses the command's theater communications management cell.

Majewski, Greg. "Army Reserve Signal Command Receives Networking Award." *Army Communicator* 28 (Winter 2003): 48–49

Mauldin, Curtis A. "An Important Part of the Rapid Deployment Force." *Army Communicator* 14 (Winter 1989): 33.

Reed, Anthony. "Grecian Firebolt 2000: Army Signal Command Sponsors Army's Largest Communications Exercise." *Army Communicator* 25 (Fall 2000): 16–17.

Smalls, Michael. "The 335th Signal Command in Action at Bright Star '95: 'An Olympic Performance.'" *Army Communicator* 21 (Summer 1996): 8–9.

Ward, Jim. "335th Theater Army Signal Command Spearheads Reserve Signal Global Revolution in Telecommunications, 'Shrinking Planet,' Satellites Give Commander Vision of Unit's Role," *Army Communicator* 23 (Spring 1998): 59–60.

———. "Grecian Firebolt '98 Makes Active/Reserve Signal Community One Team." *Army Communicator* 23 (Summer 1998): 39–41.

Wilson, Ronnie, et al. "Go Between Circuits V." *Army Communicator* 7 (Summer 1982): 50–53.

1st SIGNAL CENTER

HERALDIC ITEMS

None approved.

LINEAGE AND HONORS

RA
(inactive)

LINEAGE

Constituted 1 July 1968 in the Regular Army as the 1st Signal Center. Activated 22 November 1968 in Vietnam. Inactivated 24 February 1969 in Vietnam.

CAMPAIGN PARTICIPATION CREDIT

Vietnam
- Counteroffensive, Phase VI
- Tet 69/Counteroffensive

DECORATIONS

None.

1st SIGNAL CENTER BIBLIOGRAPHY

No published histories.

HEADQUARTERS AND HEADQUARTERS COMPANY
216th SIGNAL DEPOT

HERALDIC ITEMS

None approved.

LINEAGE AND HONORS

RA
(inactive)

LINEAGE

Constituted 11 May 1942 in the Army of the United States as the 216th Signal Depot Company. Activated 25 January 1943 at the Lexington Signal Depot, Avon, Kentucky. Inactivated 6 March 1946 at Camp Kilmer, New Jersey.

Redesignated 21 January 1955 as Headquarters and Headquarters Company, 216th Signal Depot, and allotted to the Regular Army. Activated 10 March 1955 at Fort Sam Houston, Texas. Inactivated 24 June 1966 at the Sacramento Army Depot, California.

CAMPAIGN PARTICIPATION CREDIT

World War II
  Normandy
  Northern France
  Rhineland
  Ardennes-Alsace
  Central Europe

DECORATIONS

Meritorious Unit Commendation (Army), Streamer embroidered EUROPEAN THEATER (216th Signal Depot Company cited: GO 148, Communications Zone, U.S. Forces, European Theater, 27 July 1945)

216th SIGNAL DEPOT BIBLIOGRAPHY

Thompson, George Raynor, and Dixie R. Harris. *The Signal Corps: The Outcome (Mid-1943 through 1945)*. United States Army in World War II. Washington, D.C.: Office of the Chief of Military History, United States Army, 1966.

HEADQUARTERS AND HEADQUARTERS COMPANY
801st SIGNAL DEPOT

HERALDIC ITEMS

None approved.

LINEAGE AND HONORS

LINEAGE

AR (inactive)

Constituted 17 December 1943 in the Army of the United States as the 583d Signal Depot Company. Activated 12 January 1944 at Camp Crowder, Missouri. Inactivated 30 June 1946 in France.

Redesignated 9 December 1947 as the 801st Signal Depot Company and allotted to the Organized Reserves. Activated 22 December 1947 at Raleigh, North Carolina. (Organized Reserves redesignated 25 March 1948 as the Organized Reserve Corps; redesignated 9 July 1952 as the Army Reserve.) Reorganized and redesignated 1 September 1950 as the 801st Signal Base Maintenance Company.

Reorganized and redesignated 30 September 1953 as Headquarters and Headquarters Company, 801st Signal Base Depot. Reorganized and redesignated 30 June 1954 as Headquarters and Headquarters Company, 801st Signal Depot. Location changed 11 October 1955 to Charlotte, North Carolina. Ordered into active military service 15 October 1961 at Charlotte, North Carolina; released from active military service 8 August 1962 and reverted to reserve status. Inactivated 31 January 1968 at Charlotte, North Carolina.

CAMPAIGN PARTICIPATION CREDIT

World War II
  Northern France
  Rhineland
  Ardennes-Alsace
  Central Europe

DECORATIONS

Meritorious Unit Commendation (Army), Streamer embroidered FRANCE AND BELGIUM (583d Signal Depot Company cited; GO 197, Theater Service Forces, European Theater, 14 August 1945)

Meritorious Unit Commendation (Army), Streamer embroidered GERMANY (583d Signal Depot Company cited; GO 53, Western Base Section, U.S. Forces, European Theater, 26 June 1946)

801st SIGNAL DEPOT BIBLIOGRAPHY

583d Signal Depot Company History. N.p., 1945.

HEADQUARTERS AND HEADQUARTERS COMPANY
803d SIGNAL DEPOT

HERALDIC ITEMS

None approved.

LINEAGE AND HONORS

AR
(inactive)

LINEAGE

Constituted 18 December 1944 in the Army of the United States as Headquarters and Headquarters Company, 3911th Signal Base Depot. Activated 25 January 1945 on New Guinea. Inactivated 31 May 1946 in the Philippine Islands.

Redesignated 26 April 1948 as Headquarters and Headquarters Company, 803d Signal Base Depot, and allotted to the Organized Reserve Corps. Activated 20 May 1948 at New York, New York. (Organized Reserve Corps redesignated 9 July 1952 as the Army Reserve.) Reorganized and redesignated 1 February 1955 as Headquarters and Headquarters Company, 803d Signal Depot. Inactivated 31 January 1968 at New York, New York.

CAMPAIGN PARTICIPATION CREDIT

World War II
   Luzon

DECORATIONS

Philippine Presidential Unit Citation, Streamer embroidered 17 OCTOBER 1944 TO 4 JULY 1945 (3911th Signal Base Depot Company cited; DA GO 47, 1950)

803d SIGNAL DEPOT BIBLIOGRAPHY

No published histories.

HEADQUARTERS AND HEADQUARTERS COMPANY
1st SIGNAL BRIGADE
(First To Communicate)

HERALDIC ITEMS

SHOULDER SLEEVE INSIGNIA

Description: On a shield divided into three vertical stripes, one blue between two orange, the blue center stripe surmounted by an unsheathed sword point to top with the hilt yellow and the blade consisting of a white three-jagged bolt of lightning, all within a yellow border.

Symbolism: The orange field of the shield and the yellow border are adopted from the authorized shoulder sleeve insignia of the former Strategic Communications Command. The lightning bolt, which also appeared on the Strategic Communications Command shoulder sleeve insignia, is depicted on the distinctive unit insignia (badge) of the 1st Signal Brigade. In this instance, the lightning bolt, a symbol of communication, has been used as a sword blade and attached to a hilt, the sword thus referring to both the tactical and support missions of the organization. The blue vertical stripe with "sword" (adopted from the authorized shoulder sleeve insignia for the United States Army, Vietnam) alludes to the unit's numerical designation.

DISTINCTIVE UNIT INSIGNIA

Description: A silver color metal and enamel device that consists of a silver barbed arrowhead, the tip conjoined with orange flames issuing at base from each side of the arrowhead, and a lightning bolt superimposed in black.

Symbolism: The one bolt of lightning (streak of electricity) alludes to communications and to the numerical designation of the organization. The barbed arrowhead with superimposed lightning bolt refers to both the tactical and strategic support missions of the organization. The flames allude to fire being the oldest source of signal communication at a distance and thus the first. The orange symbolizes "fire by night," and the black "smoke by day."

LINEAGE AND HONORS

LINEAGE

RA
(active)

Constituted 26 March 1966 in the Regular Army as Headquarters and Headquarters Company, 1st Signal Brigade. Activated 1 April 1966 in Vietnam.

CAMPAIGN PARTICIPATION CREDIT

Vietnam
  Counteroffensive
  Counteroffensive, Phase II
  Counteroffensive, Phase III
  Tet Counteroffensive
  Counteroffensive, Phase IV
  Counteroffensive, Phase V
  Counteroffensive, Phase VI
  Tet 69/Counteroffensive
  Summer–Fall 1969
  Winter–Spring 1970
  Sanctuary Counteroffensive
  Counteroffensive, Phase VII
  Consolidation I
  Consolidation II
  Cease-Fire

DECORATIONS

Meritorious Unit Commendation (Army), Streamer embroidered VIETNAM 1966–1967 (Headquarters and Headquarters Company, 1st Signal Brigade, cited; DA GO 17, 1968)

Meritorious Unit Commendation (Army), Streamer embroidered VIETNAM 1967–1969 (Headquarters and Headquarters Company, 1st Signal Brigade, cited; DA GO 48, 1971)

Meritorious Unit Commendation (Army), Streamer embroidered VIETNAM 1970–1972 (Headquarters and Headquarters Company, 1st Signal Brigade, cited; DA GO 6, 1974)

1st SIGNAL BRIGADE BIBLIOGRAPHY

Arnold, Emmett R. "Signal Communications in Vietnam." *Military Review* 47 (March 1967): 92–96.

Bergen, John D. *Military Communications: A Test for Technology*. United States Army in Vietnam. Washington, D.C.: Center of Military History, United States Army, 1986.

Betterton, Charles A. "Communications-Vietnam." *Army Digest* 22 (February 1967): 44–47.

Eckhardt, George S. *Command and Control, 1950–1969*. Vietnam Studies. Washington, D.C.: Department of the Army, 1974.
Eggenspargar, James, ed. *The First Signal Team*. Taipei, Formosa: China Color Printing Company, 1971.
1st Signal Team. Vietnam, 1969.
Grissom, Kenneth R., II, ed. *The Jagged Sword, A History of the 1st Signal Brigade*. Information Office, 1st Signal Brigade, Republic of Vietnam, c. 1970. Special issue of brigade's quarterly magazine.
Hasenauer, Heike. "Grecian Firebolt." *Soldiers* 49 (September 1994): 37–40.
Hay, John H., Jr. *Tactical and Materiel Innovations*. Vietnam Studies. Washington, D.C.: Department of the Army, 1974.
Heiser, Joseph M., Jr. *Logistic Support*. Vietnam Studies. Washington, D.C.: Department of the Army, 1974.
The History of the 1st Signal Brigade (USACC). Seoul: Public Affairs Office, Headquarters, 1st Signal Brigade, 1974.
Loudermilk, Jack. "'First' Time Deployment in Korea." *Army Communicator* 10 (Winter 1985): 24–28.
McKinney, John B. "Signal Planning Needs Innovators." *Army* 18 (March 1968): 35–42.
———. "They Communicate and Shoot." *Army* 18 (September 1968): 54–60.
Myer, Charles R. *Division-Level Communications, 1962–1973*. Vietnam Studies. Washington, D.C.: Department of the Army, 1982.
Pearson, Willard. *The War in the Northern Provinces, 1966–1968*. Vietnam Studies. Washington: Department of the Army, 1975.
Raines, Rebecca Robbins. *Getting the Message Through: A Branch History of the U.S. Army Signal Corps*. Army Historical Series. Washington, D.C.: Center of Military History, United States Army, 1996.
Rienzi, Thomas M. *Communications-Electronics, 1962–1970*. Vietnam Studies. Washington, D.C.: Department of the Army, 1972.
Rolak, Bruno J., and George R. Thompson. *History of the United States Army Communications Command From Origin Through 1976*. Fort Huachuca, Ariz.: United States Army Communications Command, 1979.
St. Clair, Jim. "The Defense of Vung Chua Mountain." *Signal* 23 (March 1969): 10–12.
Siemieniec, Jack. "Grecian Firebolt Connects, Supports Multiple Exercises." *Army Communicator* 26 (Fall 2001): 2–4.
Sokalski, Walt. "Splendid Isolation: Duty on the 'Backbone.'" *Army Communicator* 6 (Spring 1981): 30–32.
Teifel, Gordon F. *Buddies Together, Cung Than Thien, First Signal Brigade*. Saigon: Nai Suvit Phongsasvithes, 1971.

HEADQUARTERS AND HEADQUARTERS COMPANY
2d SIGNAL BRIGADE

HERALDIC ITEMS

SHOULDER SLEEVE INSIGNIA

Description: Centered upon a diamond shape two vertical orange lightning flashes on and over a white globe with blue grid lines, all on a white field enclosed by an orange border.

Symbolism: Orange and white are the colors traditionally associated with the Signal Corps. The lightning flashes are an allusion to the basic mission of the organization, and the color blue refers to the unit's capability to support the combat mission. The two flashes simulate the Roman numeral II and suggest the unit's numerical designation. The globe alludes to the worldwide scope of the unit's mission and the unit's affiliation with the former U.S. Army Communications Command.

DISTINCTIVE UNIT INSIGNIA

Description: A gold color metal and enamel device that consists of a dark green disc within an annulet divided horizontally orange and gold, the orange half inscribed EXCELLENCE in gold letters, and the lower gold half forming an open wreath of laurel. On the upper part of the disc, and extending on to the annulet, a gold Vietnamese hat that bears three horizontal orange bands, the center band cut at regular intervals. In base surmounting the wreath and extending over the lower part of the hat an orange fleur-de-lis.

Symbolism: Orange is a color traditionally associated with the Signal Corps. The fleur-de-lis, emblem of France, refers to the unit's initial activation in that country and to its World War II service in the European Theater. The distinctive Vietnamese hat stands for service in Vietnam. The three orange bands on the gold hat allude to the flag of the Republic of Vietnam. The center band is broken to represent minus signs in reference to the negative charge of electrical impulses. The three bands stand for lines of communication and refer to the unit's major mission of providing and expanding electrical communications systems and facilities. The wreath of laurel is the traditional award for high achievements and alludes to the motto EXCELLENCE. Green refers to the jungles and terrain of Vietnam.

LINEAGE AND HONORS

LINEAGE

RA
(active)

Constituted 24 October 1944 in the Army of the United States as Headquarters and Headquarters Detachment, 3348th Signal Service Group, and activated in France. Inactivated 13 March 1946 in France.

Activated 9 May 1946 at Fort Monmouth, New Jersey. Redesignated 14 March 1947 as Headquarters and Headquarters Detachment, 2d Signal Service Group. Allotted 1 March 1949 to the Regular Army. Reorganized and redesignated 16 December 1949 as Headquarters, 2d Signal Service Group. Reorganized and redesignated 25 March 1953 as Headquarters, 2d Signal Group. Inactivated 4 April 1955 at Camp Gordon, Georgia.

Redesignated 27 April 1961 as Headquarters and Headquarters Detachment, 2d Signal Group. Activated 21 June 1961 at Fort Bragg, North Carolina. Inactivated 23 October 1971 at Fort Lewis, Washington. Activated 1 June 1974 in Germany.

Redesignated 1 October 1979 as Headquarters and Headquarters Company, 2d Signal Brigade.

CAMPAIGN PARTICIPATION CREDIT

World War II
European-African-Middle Eastern Theater, Streamer without inscription

Vietnam
Defense
Counteroffensive
Counteroffensive, Phase II
Counteroffensive, Phase III
Tet Counteroffensive
Counteroffensive, Phase IV
Counteroffensive, Phase V
Counteroffensive, Phase VI
Tet 69/Counteroffensive
Summer–Fall 1969
Winter–Spring 1970
Sanctuary Counteroffensive
Counteroffensive, Phase VII
Consolidation I

DECORATIONS

Meritorious Unit Commendation (Army), Streamer embroidered VIETNAM 1965–1967 (Headquarters and Headquarters Detachment, 2d Signal Group [Army], cited; DA GO 17, 1968)

Meritorious Unit Commendation (Army), Streamer embroidered VIETNAM 1967–1968 (Headquarters and Headquarters Detachment, 2d Signal Group, cited; DA GO 54, 1968)

2d SIGNAL BRIGADE BIBLIOGRAPHY

Bergen, John D. *Military Communications: A Test for Technology*. United States Army in Vietnam. Washington, D.C.: Center of Military History, United States Army, 1986.

Carland, John M. *Combat Operations: Stemming the Tide, May 1965 to October 1966*. United States Army in Vietnam. Washington, D.C.: Center of Military History, United States Army, 2000.

Inge, Nick. "Vital Links Between Ports, U.S. Army Europe and CENTCOM." *Army Communicator* 28 (Fall 2003): 4–6. Unit's support to Operation Iraqi Freedom.

Johnson, Danny M. *Military Communications Supporting Peacekeeping Operations in the Balkans: The Signal Corps at Its Best*. Mannheim, Germany: Headquarters, 5th Signal Command, 2000.

Myer, Charles R. *Division-Level Communications 1962–1973*. Vietnam Studies. Washington, D.C.: Department of the Army, 1982.

Neindorf, David F. *2d Signal Group, 1946–1978*. Mannheim, Germany, 1978.

Raines, Rebecca Robbins. *Getting the Message Through: A Branch History of the U.S. Army Signal Corps*. Army Historical Series. Washington, D.C.: Center of Military History, United States Army, 1996.

Rienzi, Thomas M. *Communications-Electronics, 1962–1970*. Vietnam Studies. Washington, D.C.: Department of the Army, 1972.

Rolak, Bruno J. *History of the U.S. Army Communications Command (1964–1976)*. Fort Huachuca, Ariz.: United States Army Communications Command, 1976.

Rolak, Bruno J., and George R. Thompson. *History of the United States Army Communications Command From Origin Through 1976*. Fort Huachuca, Ariz.: United States Army Communications Command, 1979.

"Units Renamed." *Army Communicator* 4 (Fall 1979): 60.

HEADQUARTERS AND HEADQUARTERS COMPANY 3d SIGNAL BRIGADE

HERALDIC ITEMS

SHOULDER SLEEVE INSIGNIA

Description: On an orange shield and within a white border a blue star fimbriated white between three white lightning flashes.

Symbolism: Orange and white are the colors traditionally associated with the Signal Corps. The star, a reference to Texas, the "Lone Star State," is the place of the unit's initial activation and refers to guidance and achievement. The lightning flashes, symbolic of the speed of communications, also refer numerically to the present designation of the brigade. The color blue is indicative of support to the Infantry and other combat forces.

DISTINCTIVE UNIT INSIGNIA

Description: A gold color metal and enamel device that consists of three blue discs conjoined—two above one and centered—thereon a red triangular area with one point down bordered by three gold lightning flashes with points conjoined, and in base on a semicircular gold scroll the motto TRIPLE THREAT in blue letters.

Symbolism: The three roundels represent rounds of ammunition and, together with the colors blue, gold, and scarlet, refer to the organization's mission to support the combat arms: Infantry, Armor, and Artillery. The three lightning flashes denote the unit's triple-threat capability in the performance of its mission, adding emphasis to the motto TRIPLE THREAT.

LINEAGE AND HONORS

RA
(active)

LINEAGE

Constituted 16 September 1979 in the Regular Army as Headquarters and Headquarters Company, 3d Signal Brigade, and activated at Fort Hood, Texas.

CAMPAIGN PARTICIPATION CREDIT

Southwest Asia
   Defense of Saudi Arabia
   Liberation and Defense of Kuwait
   Cease-Fire

DECORATIONS

None.

3d SIGNAL BRIGADE BIBLIOGRAPHY

Kennedy, Randy. "3rd Signal Brigade." *Army Communicator* 12 (Summer 1987): 52–53.

Martin, Patrick, Rosielynn Banzon, and John Cox. "Hood Signaleers Test Teamwork in Road Runner '00 Exercise." *Army Communicator* 25 (Spring 2000): 39–41.

Slupik, Jean M. "3d Signal Brigade on REFORGER." *Army Communicator* 13 (Winter 1988): 26–31.

Stallings, Caroline. "3d Signal Brigade Provides 'Voice of Phantom Warriors' in 5-Month Exercise Series." *Army Communicator* 26 (Fall 2001): 16–18.

White, David E. "REFORGER '87: A Commander's Report." *Army Communicator* 12 (Fall 1987): 12–13.

Windon, Michael Leon, "3d Signal Brigade Conquers Voice, Data and Video." *Army Communicator* 28 (Summer 2003): 22–23.

HEADQUARTERS AND HEADQUARTERS COMPANY 7th SIGNAL BRIGADE

HERALDIC ITEMS

SHOULDER SLEEVE INSIGNIA

Description: A shield arched at top and base and divided chevronwise blue (ultramarine) and white, a seven-stepped orange area (one step in center and three on either side) issuing from base onto the white area, and in chief two orange diagonal lightning flashes with both ends pointed emitting from the top step of the orange stepped area, all within a white border.

Symbolism: Orange and white are the colors traditionally associated with the Signal Corps. The blue area alludes to the troposphere, the lower part of the atmosphere that extends, more or less, seven miles above the surface of the earth; the stratosphere forms the atmosphere's upper part. The seven steps of the orange area—antenna, wavelength, frequency, modulation, selectivity, volume, and control—also allude to the numerical designation of the brigade. The two lightning flashes or impulses symbolize transmitting and receiving radio and radar signals and communication. The white pointed area simulates the "bending" or breaking of electric waves (beams) in the troposphere and the scattering of a portion of them back to earth.

DISTINCTIVE UNIT INSIGNIA

Description: A silver color metal and enamel device that consists of a silver knight's helmet facing front and bearing a crest of three ostrich plumes, one orange between two white, all upon a field of four silver lightning flashes pilewise and contained on the two sides and bottom by a blue serpentine scroll inscribed with the motto VOICE OF FREEDOM in silver letters, the scroll ending at either side next to the white plumes.

Symbolism: Orange and white are the colors traditionally associated with the Signal Corps. The background of lightning flashes represents the function of signal communications. The knight's orange and white plumed helmet on the wavy blue band, simulating a winding river, is a reference to the brigade's unofficial "Order of the Orange and White Knights of the Rhine."

LINEAGE AND HONORS

LINEAGE

RA
(active)

Constituted 15 February 1970 in the Regular Army as Headquarters and Headquarters Company, 7th Signal Brigade. Activated 24 February 1970 in Germany.

CAMPAIGN PARTICIPATION CREDIT

None.

DECORATIONS

None.

7th SIGNAL BRIGADE BIBLIOGRAPHY

Curry, Michael L., and Wallace Ricks. "Data Transmissions Across the Seamless Network." *Army Communicator* 18 (Fall–Winter 1993): 14–19.

Hamilton, Brian. "Atlantic Resolve: Order Out of Chaos, Or Creating Communications Links for a Joint Multinational Exercise." *Army Communicator* 20 (Fall 1995): 40–43.

Hasenauer, Heike. "Grecian Firebolt." *Soldiers* 49 (September 1994): 37–40.

Hitt, Joe. "7th Signal Brigade Joins 5th Signal Command." *Army Communicator* 7 (Winter 1982): 37.

Hochstetler, R.R. "'Weather' Or Not." *Army Communicator* 15 (Summer–Fall 1990): 26–27. Discusses challenges posed by weather during REFORGER '90.

Johnson, Danny M. *Military Communications Supporting Peacekeeping Operations in the Balkans: The Signal Corps at Its Best*. Mannheim, Germany: Headquarters, 5th Signal Command, 2000.

Rolak, Bruno J. *History of the U.S. Army Communications Command (1964–1976)*. Fort Huachuca, Ariz.: United States Army Communications Command, 1976.

Rudd, Gordon W. *Humanitarian Intervention: Assisting the Iraqi Kurds in Operation PROVIDE COMFORT, 1991*. Washington, D.C.: Center of Military History, United States Army, 2004.

"7th Signal Brigade Helicopters Fight SNOW." *Army Aviation Digest* 23 (March 1977): 46.

Tegen, Carl M., and Roger L. Todd. "DGM Fielding in the 7th Signal Brigade." *Army Communicator* 14 (Fall 1989): 26–29.

Williamson, Stan. "It Ain't the Eiffel, but . . . ." *Army Communicator* 3 (Fall 1978): 36.

HEADQUARTERS AND HEADQUARTERS COMPANY
11th SIGNAL BRIGADE
(Desert Thunderbirds)

HERALDIC ITEMS

SHOULDER SLEEVE INSIGNIA

Description: Centered on a white oblong shield with a yellow border, arched at top and bottom, a white globe with orange grid lines surmounted by a black thunderbird with yellow lightning bolts extending over the globe from its orange eye.

Symbolism: Orange and white are the colors traditionally associated with the Signal Corps. The globe signifies the worldwide scope of the unit's mission. The thunderbird, an American Indian symbol of great power that controls the skies and sees all that occurs on the ground, refers to the unit's current southwestern location. The lightning, which issues from the thunderbird's eye as in American Indian legend, denotes the speed and abilities of electronic communications. The black thunderbird and white background symbolize the night and day capability of the unit.

DISTINCTIVE UNIT INSIGNIA

Description: Two silver beacons, the baskets conjoined at the upper edge and the ladders reversed, with orange and silver flames, the three areas within the confines of the beacons black with the center area charged with a silver fleur-de-lis, all above a silver motto scroll inscribed FLEXIBILITY–DEPENDABILITY in black letters.

Symbolism: Flaming beacons are among the oldest devices used for signaling and communications. Two have been used in reference to the sending and receiving of messages; the two poles also simulate the number "11," the organization's numerical designation. The three black areas and the fleur-de-lis refer to the organization's three campaigns in Europe during World War II.

LINEAGE AND HONORS

RA
(active)

LINEAGE

Constituted 1 September 1943 in the Army of the United States as the 3103d Signal Service Battalion. Activated 20 December 1943 at Fort Monmouth, New Jersey. Inactivated 8 October 1945 at Fort Monmouth, New Jersey.

Consolidated 4 September 1964 with Headquarters and Headquarters Detachment, 11th Signal Group (constituted 1 May 1963 in the Regular Army and activated at Fort Lewis, Washington), and consolidated unit designated as Headquarters and Headquarters Detachment, 11th Signal Group. Reorganized and redesignated 25 April 1966 as Headquarters and Headquarters Company, 11th Signal Group.

Redesignated 1 October 1979 as Headquarters and Headquarters Company, 11th Signal Brigade.

CAMPAIGN PARTICIPATION CREDIT

World War II
  Northern France
  Rhineland
  Central Europe

Southwest Asia
  Defense of Saudi Arabia
  Liberation and Defense of Kuwait
  Cease-Fire

DECORATIONS

Meritorious Unit Commendation (Army), Streamer embroidered EUROPEAN THEATER (3103d Signal Service Battalion cited; GO 12, Twelfth Army Group, 15 March 1945)

Meritorious Unit Commendation (Army), Streamer embroidered SOUTHWEST ASIA 1990–1991 (Headquarters and Headquarters Company, 11th Signal Brigade, cited; DA GO 17, 1992, as amended by DA GO 12, 1994)

11th SIGNAL BRIGADE BIBLIOGRAPHY

Ackerman, Robert K. "Tactical Signalers Learn to Pack Light, Travel Right." *Signal* 54 (April 2000): 37–39.

———. "U.S. Forces Provide Deployable Communications to East Timor." *Signal* 54 (April 2000): 44–45.

Alley, Lisa. "Thunderbird Brigade Overcomes Challenges of East Timor." *Army Communicator* 25 (Fall 2000): 13–15.

Bell, T. Anthony. "Fire Stompers of the 11th Signal Brigade." *Army Communicator* 18 (Summer 1993): 10–11.

———. "Signal on the Move." *Soldiers* 48 (October 1993): 24–25.

Bergen, John D. *Military Communications: A Test for Technology*. United States Army in Vietnam. Washington, D.C.: Center of Military History, United States Army, 1986.

"Brrrr . . . It's Jack Frost!" *Army Communicator* 4 (Spring 1979): 60. Refers to a joint readiness exercise in Alaska.

Conner, Carol. "Signal Command Provides Commercial Communications in Afghanistan." *Army* 53 (April 2003): 45–47.

Cox and Harris. "On the Level." *Army Communicator* 13 (Spring–Summer 1988): 52. Exercise "Level Road II."

Davis, Richard, Jr. "Inside USACC's 'fire brigade.'" *Army Communicator* 7 (Summer 1982): 5–11.

11th Signal Group (USACC) Ft. Huachuca, Ariz. N.p., 1973.

11th Signal Group (USACC) Ft. Huachuca, Ariz. N.p., 1974.

Gordon, Charles L. "Communications in Central America." *Army Communicator* 10 (Summer 1985): 36–41.

Gourley, Scott. "Thunderbirds Ready to Stage to Any Theatre." *Jane's Defence Weekly* 29 (21 Jan 1998): 26–29.

Grossman, Larry, and Rudi Williams. "7000+ Service Members Test Systems in Summer's Worldwide Signal Exercise." *Army Communicator* 21 (Winter 1996): 34–35. Discusses Exercise Grecian Firebolt '95.

"Gulf War Communications Quickly Fielded, Efficient." *Signal* 45 (August 1991): 44–45.

Hake, Janet. "One of a Kind." *Soldiers* 32 (January 1977): 48–49.

Hausenauer, Heike. "Grecian Firebolt." *Soldiers* 49 (September 1994): 37–40.

Hinton, Al. "The Transportable Communications Center. " *Army Communicator* 9 (Summer 1984): 11–12.

Huffman, Larry. "Signal Provides Communications Support for Bright Star Exercise." *Army Communicator* 21 (Summer 1996): 2–7.

Kennedy, Randy. "11th Signal Brigade." *Army Communicator* 13 (Winter 1988): 36–37.

Kollegger, James G. "Instant Communications to Anywhere." *Army Digest* 21 (July 1966): 32–35.

Meyer, Roger G. "Establishing Training Standards Through Initiative and Exercises." *Army Communicator* 13 (Fall 1988): 44–47.

Pace, Emily Charlotte. "USAISC Before, During and After Desert Storm." *Army Communicator* 16 (Summer 1991): 13–17. U.S. Army Information Systems Command (USAISC) successor to the U.S. Army Communications Command.

Raines, Rebecca Robbins. *Getting the Message Through: A Branch History of the U.S. Army Signal Corps*. Army Historical Series. Washington, D.C.: Center of Military History, United States Army, 1996.

Rawles, James W. "Voice in the Wilderness: Fort Huachuca's 11th Signal Brigade Provides Strategic Communications Support for Army Operations." *Defense Electronics* 20 (August 1988): 93.

Reed, Anthony. "Grecian Firebolt 2000: Army Signal Command Sponsors Army's Largest Communications Exercise." *Army Communicator* 25 (Fall 2000): 16–17.

Rienzi, Thomas M. *Communications-Electronics, 1962–1970*. Vietnam Studies. Washington, D.C.: Department of the Army, 1972.

Robinson, Clarence A., Jr. "Signal Brigade Mounts Plan for Far-Flung Contingencies." *Signal* 47 (April 1993): 27–28.

Rolak, Bruno J. *History of the U. S. Army Communications Command (1964–1976)*. Fort Huachuca, Ariz.: United States Army Communications Command, 1976.

Rolak, Bruno J., and George R. Thompson. *History of the United States Army Communications Command From Origin Through 1976*. Fort Huachuca, Ariz.: United States Army Communications Command, 1979.

Scales, Robert H., Jr. *Certain Victory*. Washington, D.C., Office of the Chief of Staff, U.S. Army, 1993.

Scelza, Matthew. "Communications Brigade Receives High-Tech Repair Equipment." *Army Communicator* 24 (Spring 1999): 38.

Schad, Dave. "Dial Eleven." *Soldiers* 42 (March 1987): 42–44.

Schubert, Frank N., and Theresa L. Kraus, eds. *The Whirlwind War*. Washington, D.C.: Center of Military History, United States Army, 1995.

Siemieniec, Jack. "Grecian Firebolt Connects, Supports Multiple Exercises." *Army Communicator* 26 (Fall 2001): 2–4.

Smith, Cornelius C., Jr. *Fort Huachuca: The Story of a Frontier Post*. Fort Huachuca, Ariz., 1978.

Stokes, Carol E., ed. *The U.S. Army Signal Corps in Operation Desert Shield/Desert Storm*. Fort Gordon, Ga.: Office of the Command Historian, U.S. Army Signal Center and Fort Gordon, 1994.

Stokes, Carol E., and Kathy R. Coker. "Getting the Message Through in the Persian Gulf War." *Army Communicator* 17 (Summer–Winter 1992): 17–25.

Thompson, George Raynor, and Dixie R. Harris. *The Signal Corps: The Outcome (Mid-1943 through 1945)*. United States Army in World War II. Washington, D.C.: Office of the Chief of Military History, United States Army, 1966.

Timberlake, Wrenne. "ISC Takes the Desert by Storm." *Army Communicator* 16 (Spring 1991): 16–18.

"Units Renamed." *Army Communicator* 4 (Fall 1979): 60.

Volkert, Tim. "Joint Exercises Benefit 11th Signal Brigade Troops." *Army Communicator* 26 (Fall 2001): 4–5.

White, Hank. "Grecian Firebolt 1994: A Real Test for Network Managers." *Army Communicator* 20 (Winter 1995): 45–51.

HEADQUARTERS AND HEADQUARTERS DETACHMENT 15th SIGNAL BRIGADE

HERALDIC ITEMS

SHOULDER SLEEVE INSIGNIA
None approved.

DISTINCTIVE UNIT INSIGNIA

Description: A gold color metal and enamel device that consists of a shield blazoned as follows: Per bend argent and tenné, in sinister chief a lamp of knowledge sable, flammant proper. Attached below the shield a gold scroll inscribed FIDELITER SERVIMUS (Faithfully We Serve) in black letters.

Symbolism: Orange and white are the colors traditionally associated with the Signal Corps. The lamp of knowledge represents the scholastic activities of the school at which the unit serves.

LINEAGE AND HONORS

TRADOC
(active)

LINEAGE

Constituted 30 November 1940 in the Army of the United States as the 15th Signal Service Battalion. Activated 1 December 1940 at Fort Monmouth, New Jersey. Redesignated 15 September 1941 as the 15th Signal Service Regiment. Redesignated 14 December 1942 as the 15th Signal Training Regiment. Disbanded 31 May 1945 at Fort Monmouth, New Jersey.

Headquarters and Headquarters Company, 15th Signal Training Regiment, reconstituted 23 September 1986 in the Regular Army as Headquarters and Headquarters Detachment, 15th Signal Brigade, transferred to the United States Army Training and Doctrine Command, and activated at Fort Gordon, Georgia.

CAMPAIGN PARTICIPATION CREDIT
None.

DECORATIONS
None.

15th SIGNAL BRIGADE BIBLIOGRAPHY

Brigade Staff. "Getting the Job Done: Training with the 15th." *Army Communicator* 13 (Fall 1988): 32–35.

Sheldon, John J., and Bozidar W. Brown. "Reorganizing Training at the Signal School." *Army Communicator* 15 (Winter–Spring 1990): 26–28.

Thompson, George Raynor, and Dixie R. Harris. *The Signal Corps: The Outcome (Mid-1943 through 1945)*. United States Army in World War II. Washington, D.C.: Office of the Chief of Military History, United States Army, 1966.

HEADQUARTERS AND HEADQUARTERS COMPANY
22d SIGNAL BRIGADE

HERALDIC ITEMS

SHOULDER SLEEVE INSIGNIA

Description: A rectangular shaped shield arched at top and bottom and consisting of a white eagle's head erased, eye and tongue blue, and beaked and crowned gold above in base two white lightning flashes crossed saltirewise, all on an orange background and within a white border.

Symbolism: Orange and white are the colors traditionally associated with the Signal Corps. The lightning flashes symbolize communications and speed; crossed, they represent strength. The eagle, a symbol of vigilance and swiftness, is adopted from the city of Frankfurt's coat of arms and refers to the unit's former location in Germany.

DISTINCTIVE UNIT INSIGNIA

Description: A silver color metal and enamel device that consists of a silver pentagram, point up, bearing five orange lightning flashes converging in center from each point of the pentagram above a horizontal orange scroll inscribed EAGER ELITES in silver letters.

Symbolism: Orange and white (silver) are the colors traditionally associated with the Signal Corps. The lightning flashes are indicative of communications and speed; converging in center they reflect accuracy and purpose. The pentagram is adopted from the V Corps' devices and reflects the brigade's support mission to the corps.

LINEAGE AND HONORS

RA
(active)

LINEAGE

Constituted 14 November 1945 in the Army of the United States as Headquarters and Headquarters Company, 22d Signal Service Group. Activated 13 December 1945 in Germany. Inactivated 20 June 1948 in Germany.

Redesignated 27 September 1951 as Headquarters and Headquarters Company, 22d Signal Group, and allotted to the Regular Army. Activated 1 November 1951 in Korea. Reorganized and redesignated 15 April 1954 as Headquarters and Headquarters Detachment, 22d Signal Group. Inactivated 13 May 1955 in Korea.

Activated 19 August 1963 in Germany. Reorganized and redesignated 15 October 1963 as Headquarters and Headquarters Company, 22d Signal Group. Reorganized and redesignated 15 September 1965 as Headquarters and Headquarters Detachment, 22d Signal Group. Inactivated 13 November 1967 in Germany.

Redesignated 16 March 1981 as Headquarters and Headquarters Company, 22d Signal Brigade, and activated in Germany.

CAMPAIGN PARTICIPATION CREDIT

Korean War
 UN Summer–Fall Offensive
 Second Korean Winter
 Korea, Summer–Fall 1952
 Third Korean Winter
 Korea, Summer 1953

DECORATIONS

Meritorious Unit Commendation (Army), Streamer embroidered KOREA 1952–1953 (Headquarters and Headquarters Company, 22d Signal Group, cited; DA GO 78, 1953)

Army Superior Unit Award, Streamer embroidered 1995–1996 (Headquarters and Headquarters Company, 22d Signal Brigade, cited; DA GO 25, 2001)

22d SIGNAL BRIGADE BIBLIOGRAPHY

Hamilton, Brian. "Atlantic Resolve: Order Out of Chaos, Or Creating Communications Links for a Joint Multinational Exercise." *Army Communicator* 20 (Fall 1995): 40–43.

G6 Staff Members. "State of the Art Network Provides Faster and More Reliable Information to the Warfighter." *Army Communicator* 28 (Fall 2003): 16–19.

Harris, Louis. "Signal Regiment Supports Task Force Hawk in Albania." *Army Communicator* 24 (Winter II 1999): 31–34.

Howard, Richard A. "22d Signal Uses TACSAT to the Fullest Extent." *Army Communicator* 18 (Fall–Winter 1993): 40–43.

Johnson, Danny M. *Military Communications Supporting Peacekeeping Operations in the Balkans: The Signal Corps at Its Best*. Mannheim, Germany: Headquarters, 5th Signal Command, 2000.

Rolak, Bruno J. *History of the U.S. Army Communications Command (1964–1976)*. Fort Huachuca, Ariz.: United States Army Communications Command, 1976.

Turner, William R., ed. *Consolidated Unit History 22d Signal Group, 29 October 1974*. N.p., 1974.

HEADQUARTERS AND HEADQUARTERS DETACHMENT
29th SIGNAL BRIGADE

HERALDIC ITEMS

SHOULDER SLEEVE INSIGNIA
None approved.

DISTINCTIVE UNIT INSIGNIA

Description: A gold color metal and enamel device that consists of a shield blazoned: Azure, an annulet emitting eight lightning flashes gyronwise or. Attached below the shield a blue scroll doubled and inscribed INSTANTANEOUS CONTACT in gold.

Symbolism: Ultramarine blue and gold are the colors representative of the parent organization, the 928th Signal Battalion, Air Support Command. The annulet in the center of the shield represents the center of signal operations, and the lightning flashes radiating in all directions are symbolic of the various phases of signal activities. The motto INSTANTANEOUS CONTACT expresses the mission of the unit.

LINEAGE AND HONORS

TRADOC
(inactive)

LINEAGE

Constituted 28 February 1942 in the Army of the United States as the 928th Signal Battalion. Activated 27 June 1942 at Mitchel Field, New York. Redesignated 17 April 1944 as the 928th Signal Battalion, Separate, Tactical Air Command. Disbanded 1 March 1945 in the Pacific area.

Reconstituted 4 August 1945 in the Army of the United States as the 928th Signal Battalion, Separate, Tactical Air Command. Headquarters, 928th Signal Battalion, Separate, Tactical Air Command, redesignated 12 September 1966 as Headquarters and Headquarters Detachment, 29th Signal Group; concurrently allotted to the Regular Army and activated in Thailand. Inactivated 30 June 1971 in Thailand.

Redesignated 23 September 1986 as Headquarters and Headquarters Detachment, 29th Signal Brigade, transferred to the United States Army Training and Doctrine Command, and activated at Fort Gordon, Georgia. Inactivated 1 August 1990 at Fort Gordon, Georgia.

CAMPAIGN PARTICIPATION CREDIT

World War II
   New Guinea
   Leyte

DECORATIONS

Philippine Presidential Unit Citation, Streamer embroidered 17 OCTOBER 1944 TO 4 JULY 1945 (928th Signal Battalion, Tactical Air Command [Separate], cited; DA GO 47, 1950)

29th SIGNAL BRIGADE BIBLIOGRAPHY

Bergen, John D. *Military Communications: A Test for Technology.* United States Army in Vietnam. Washington, D.C.: Center of Military History, United States Army, 1986.

Rienzi, Thomas M. *Communications-Electronics, 1962–1970.* Vietnam Studies. Washington, D.C.: Department of the Army, 1972.

Sheldon, John J., and Bozidar W. Brown. "Reorganizing Training at the Signal School." *Army Communicator* 15 (Winter–Spring 1990): 26–28.

Thompson, George Raynor, and Dixie R. Harris. *The Signal Corps: The Outcome (Mid-1943 through 1945).* United States Army in World War II. Washington, D.C.: Office of the Chief of Military History, United States Army, 1966.

HEADQUARTERS AND HEADQUARTERS COMPANY
35th SIGNAL BRIGADE

HERALDIC ITEMS

SHOULDER SLEEVE INSIGNIA

Description: On a rectangular shaped device arched at the top and bottom, quartered orange and white, a blue lion's head jessant of two lightning flashes saltirewise—one white and one orange—all within a blue border.

Symbolism: Orange and white are the colors traditionally associated with the Signal Corps. The lion, a symbol of courage and fierceness, is blue in allusion to the unit's Airborne designation. The lightning flashes symbolize communications, and their saltirewise position implies strength.

TAB

Description: Immediately above and touching the shoulder sleeve insignia a blue arc tab containing the inscription AIRBORNE in white letters.

DISTINCTIVE UNIT INSIGNIA

Description: A gold color metal and enamel device that consists of an orange sun of twelve rays charged with a gold bell. The sun is surmounted on either side by two white lions, respectant and sitting on an orange scroll inscribed UTMOST OF OUR ABILITY in gold letters. The space between the sun and scroll and behind the lion is black.

Symbolism: Orange and white are the colors traditionally associated with the Signal Corps. The design commemorates the unit's service in World War II for which it was awarded the Meritorious Unit Commendation. The two lions are from the coat of arms of Burma and stand for participation in the Central Burma and India-Burma campaigns. The lion is also one of India's state emblems; it forms the capital of one of the great stone pillars erected by Emperor Asoka about 350 B.C. The sun with twelve rays is from the flag of China; the bell, an ancient instrument for signaling, is of a type used in the Orient where bells were first introduced and are widely used today. The sun and bell refer to the installation and operation of telephone communications during the China Offensive in 1945.

LINEAGE AND HONORS

RA
(active)

LINEAGE

Constituted 11 January 1943 in the Army of the United States as the 931st Signal Battalion. Activated 15 January 1943 at Esler Field, Louisiana. Reorganized and redesignated 15 December 1943 as the 931st Signal Battalion, Separate, Tactical Air Force. Reorganized and redesignated 12 June 1944 as the 931st Signal Battalion. Inactivated 29 December 1945 in India.

Headquarters and Headquarters Company, 931st Signal Battalion, redesignated 28 March 1967 as Headquarters and Headquarters Detachment, 35th Signal Group, and allotted to the Regular Army. Activated 25 April 1967 at Fort Bragg, North Carolina. Reorganized and redesignated 16 December 1979 as Headquarters and Headquarters Company, 35th Signal Brigade.

CAMPAIGN PARTICIPATION CREDIT

World War II
  Central Burma
  India-Burma
  China Offensive

Southwest Asia
  Defense of Saudi Arabia
  Liberation and Defense of Kuwait

DECORATIONS

Meritorious Unit Commendation (Army), Streamer embroidered PACIFIC THEATER (931st Signal Battalion Aviation [Special] cited; GO 212, Army Air Forces, India Burma Theater, 14 September 1945)

Meritorious Unit Commendation (Army), Streamer embroidered SOUTHWEST ASIA 1990–1991 (Headquarters and Headquarters Company, 35th Signal Brigade, cited; DA GO 12, 1994)

35th SIGNAL BRIGADE BIBLIOGRAPHY

Blanton, Nancy C. "Go Between Circuits III." *Army Communicator* 5 (Summer 1980): 19–23.

Charest, Jeff. "35th Signal Reorganizes." *Army Communicator* 3 (Winter 1978): 16–17.

Crocker, Robert W. "Go Between Circuits IV." *Army Communicator* 6 (Summer 1981): 50–53.

Guidotti, John A. "The 35th Signal's New Go-to-War Concept." *Army Communicator* 16 (Fall–Winter 1991): 20–23.

Kennedy, Randy. "35th Signal Brigade." *Army Communicator* 12 (Fall 1987): 30–33.

Raines, Rebecca Robbins. *Getting the Message Through: A Branch History of the U.S. Army Signal Corps*. Army Historical Series. Washington, D.C.: Center of Military History, United States Army, 1996.

Robinson, Clarence A., Jr. "Airborne Corps' Style Shapes Vital Communications Security." *Signal* 51 (March 1997): 17–21.

Rottman, Gordon L. "The 35th Signal Brigade (Airborne)." *Trading Post* 40 (July–September 1981): 56

Scheips, Paul J. *The Role of Federal Military Forces in Domestic Disorders, 1945–1992*. Washington, D.C.: Center of Military History, United States Army, 2005

Stokes, Carol E., ed. *The U.S. Army Signal Corps in Operation Desert Shield/Desert Storm*. Fort Gordon, Ga.: Office of the Command Historian, U.S. Army Signal Center and Fort Gordon, 1994.

Stokes, Carol E., and Kathy R. Coker. "Getting the Message Through in the Persian Gulf War." *Army Communicator* 17 (Summer–Winter 1992): 17–25.

Whittaker, Chris. "Logistics and Maintenance in an Airborne Signal Brigade." *Army Communicator* 22 (Winter 1997): 23–24.

Wilson, Ronnie, et al. "Go Between Circuits V." *Army Communicator* 7 (Summer 1982): 50–53.

HEADQUARTERS AND HEADQUARTERS COMPANY
93d SIGNAL BRIGADE

HERALDIC ITEMS

SHOULDER SLEEVE INSIGNIA

Description: Centered upon a blue disc a white nine-pointed star, and centered thereon in a triangular form three orange lightning flashes.

Symbolism: The colors blue and white are a reference to the organization that is served by the unit. Orange and white are the colors traditionally associated with the Signal Corps. The lightning flashes refer to the signal communications mission of the organization. The outward points of the star connote signals transmitted, and the inward points connote signals received. The nine points and three flashes allude to the unit's numerical designation.

DISTINCTIVE UNIT INSIGNIA

Description: A gold color metal and enamel device that consists of the organization's shield and motto emblazoned: Azure over a lightning flash in bend argent, and a torch (bronze metal) proper, inflamed of the last, in sinister three mullets palewise or.

Motto: LOYALTY, HARMONY, ACCURACY.

Symbolism: The blue background denotes loyalty to country, friends, promises, and duty. The lightning flash is indicative of communications and accuracy. The stars and torch are taken from the flag of the state of Indiana. The three stars are symbolic of the unit's early affiliation with the New England Telephone and Telegraph Company, the Indiana Bell Telephone Company, and its site of activation at Camp Crowder, Missouri. The motto LOYALTY, HARMONY, ACCURACY alludes to the outstanding characteristics manifested from the first days of the unit's existence and throughout the performance of all its duties.

LINEAGE AND HONORS

RA
(active)

LINEAGE

Constituted 3 November 1941 in the Regular Army as the 93d Signal Battalion. Activated 15 May 1942 at Camp Crowder, Missouri. Inactivated 3 January 1946 at Camp Patrick Henry, Virginia. Activated 24 February 1955 at Fort Huachuca, Arizona. Inactivated (less Company D) 21 September 1972 in Germany. (Company D concurrently inactivated at Fort Hood, Texas.)

Headquarters and Headquarters Company, 93d Signal Battalion, redesignated 16 March 1981 as Headquarters and Headquarters Company, 93d Signal Brigade, and activated in Germany. Inactivated 15 December 1991 in Germany.

Activated 16 February 1998 at Fort Gordon, Georgia.

CAMPAIGN PARTICIPATION CREDIT

World War II
   Northern France
   Rhineland
   Ardennes-Alsace
   Central Europe

Southwest Asia
   Defense of Saudi Arabia
   Liberation and Defense of Kuwait
   Cease-Fire

DECORATIONS

None.

93d SIGNAL BRIGADE BIBLIOGRAPHY

Brohm, Gerald P., and Jerry W. McElwee. "Communications Agility in a Multinational, Heavy/Light Corps." *Army Communicator* 15 (Summer–Fall 1990): 46–53. Discusses the brigade's participation in REFORGER '90.

DeGroot, Vincent. "93d Signal Paves Way for Information Superhighway." *Army Communicator* 24 (Winter 1999): 36.

Dyer, George. *XII Corps, Spearhead of Patton's Army*. Baton Rouge: Army and Navy Publishing Company, 1947.

"Gerstein Made Impact on 93d Signal Brigade." *Army Communicator* 28 (Summer 2003): 53–55.

Henry, Cora. "Gallant Warriors: 93d Signal Brigade Trains Soldiers for Missions." *Army Communicator* 23 (Fall 1998): 4–6.

"93d Signal Brigade Activates at Gordon." *Army Communicator* 23 (Spring 1998): 41.

Powell, Dallas, Jr. "Active Component Signal Unit Passes First Year as Multicomponent Unit." *Army Communicator* 25 (Winter 2000): 11–13.

Raines, Rebecca Robbins. *Getting the Message Through: A Branch History of the U.S. Army Signal Corps.* Army Historical Series. Washington, D.C.: Center of Military History, United States Army, 1996.

Reed, Anthony. "Grecian Firebolt 2000: Army Signal Command Sponsors Army's Largest Communications Exercise." *Army Communicator* 25 (Fall 2000): 16–17.

Rhem, Kathleen. "93d Signal Brigade Brings Communications to Devastated Region." *Army Communicator* 24 (Spring 1999): 32–34. Describes unit's involvement after Hurricane Mitch in Central America.

Rhodes, Brad. "Lessons in Commercial-Off-The-Shelf." *Army Communicator* 25 (Spring 2000): 36–38. Discusses the brigade's participation in Grecian Firebolt '99.

Siemieniec, Jack. "Grecian Firebolt Connects, Supports Multiple Exercises." *Army Communicator* 26 (Fall 2001): 2–4.

"Signal Soldiers Diagnose Tangled Technical Issues." *Signal* 45 (August 1991): 37–39.

Stokes, Carol E., ed. *The U.S. Army Signal Corps in Operation Desert Shield/Desert Storm.* Fort Gordon, Ga.: Office of the Command Historian, U.S. Army Signal Center and Fort Gordon, 1994.

Stokes, Carol E., and Kathy R. Coker. "Getting the Message Through in the Persian Gulf War." *Army Communicator* 17 (Summer–Winter 1992): 17–25.

Ward, Jim. "Grecian Firebolt '98 Makes Active/Reserve Signal Community One Team." *Army Communicator* 23 (Summer 1998): 39–41.

HEADQUARTERS AND HEADQUARTERS COMPANY
106th SIGNAL BRIGADE

HERALDIC ITEMS

SHOULDER SLEEVE INSIGNIA

Description: On an orange rectangle arched at top and bottom with a white border, two diagonally crossed white lightning flash swords are between two blue arcs issuing from either side.

Symbolism: Orange and white are the colors traditionally associated with the Signal Corps. The two blue arcs simulate the Atlantic and Pacific Oceans and the Isthmus of Panama, and refer to the unit's location during the 1990s and its far-reaching mission and capabilities. The swords are crossed to indicate strength and support, with the blades in the form of lightning flashes to symbolize electronics and speed, underscoring the vital part of communications in military preparedness.

DISTINCTIVE UNIT INSIGNIA

Description: A silver color metal and enamel device that consists of a blue disc charged with an orange sunburst, encircled at top by an orange scroll inscribed TROPIC and at bottom by a like scroll inscribed COMMUNICATORS, all in silver letters, and overall two diagonally crossed silver lightning flash swords, the hilts passing beneath the scroll at bottom.

Symbolism: Orange and white are the colors traditionally associated with the Signal Corps. The blue disc alludes to the globe and the worldwide scope and impact of the unit's mission. The sunburst refers to the unit's location in the tropics during the 1990s; its multi-directional rays also denote the far-reaching capabilities of the unit. The swords are crossed to indicate strength and support, with the blades in the form of lightning flashes to symbolize electronics and speed, underscoring the vital part of communications in military preparedness.

LINEAGE AND HONORS

LINEAGE

RA
(inactive)

Constituted 12 February 1943 in the Army of the United States as the 932d Signal Battalion. Activated 15 February 1943 at Birmingham, Alabama. Reorganized and redesignated 20 April 1944 as the 932d Signal Battalion, Separate, Tactical Air Command. Inactivated 13 October 1945 at Camp Kilmer, New Jersey (organic elements concurrently disbanded).

Headquarters, 932d Signal Battalion, Separate, Tactical Air Command, redesignated 24 April 1963 as Headquarters and Headquarters Detachment, 106th Signal Group, and allotted to the Regular Army. Activated 12 August 1963 in France. Inactivated 13 November 1967 in Germany.

Redesignated 16 October 1991 as Headquarters and Headquarters Company, 106th Signal Brigade, and activated in Panama. Inactivated 15 October 1997 in Panama.

CAMPAIGN PARTICIPATION CREDIT

World War II
- Normandy
- Northern France
- Rhineland
- Ardennes-Alsace
- Central Europe

DECORATIONS

None.

106th SIGNAL BRIGADE BIBLIOGRAPHY

Hasenauer, Heike. "Grecian Firebolt." *Soldiers* 49 (September 1994): 37–40.

Rolak, Bruno J., and George R. Thompson. *History of the United States Army Communications Command From Origin Through 1976*. Fort Huachuca, Ariz.: United States Army Communications Command, 1979.

Vann, Irvin, Michael Welsh, and Greg Lucas. "Joint Communications in Fuertes Caminos '92." *Army Communicator* 18 (Spring 1993): 13–16. Discusses signal support for a road-building project in Honduras.

HEADQUARTERS AND HEADQUARTERS COMPANY
142d SIGNAL BRIGADE

HERALDIC ITEMS

SHOULDER SLEEVE INSIGNIA

Description: On a white square with one angle up four orange barbed lightning flashes arranged per cross and surmounted by a scarlet saltire, all within an orange border.

Symbolism: Orange and white are the colors traditionally associated with the Signal Corps. The red saltire is adopted from the Alabama state flag and refers to the unit's location. The radiating lightning flashes and arrowheads symbolize the command control, training, and logistic support provided by the unit. The lightning flashes also refer to speed and communications. The shape of the insignia alludes to an early radio antenna.

DISTINCTIVE UNIT INSIGNIA

Description: A gold color metal and enamel device that consists of a diamond-shaped figure divided vertically into black and white areas surmounted by four orange lightning flashes points inward saltirewise and extending beyond the diamond shape. Issuing from a center disc four gold arrows crosswise, all between at top a semicircular gold scroll behind the ends of the lightning flashes, folded back at each end and inscribed FOR STATE, and in base a scroll of the like inscribed AND NATION, all in black letters with pierced areas between the diamond shape and scroll.

Symbolism: Orange and white are the colors traditionally associated with the Signal Corps. The diamond shape alludes to an early radio antenna, and the colors black and white refer to the night and day efficiency of the organization. The arrows and disc symbolize the command control, training, and logistic support provided by the unit. The lightning flashes saltirewise represent the unit's speed in communications. The saltire is adopted from the Alabama state flag and alludes to Decatur, Alabama, the original home station of the unit.

LINEAGE AND HONORS

ARNG
(Alabama)

LINEAGE

Constituted 25 October 1960 in the Alabama Army National Guard as Headquarters and Headquarters Detachment, 142d Signal Group. Organized and federally recognized 1 November 1960 at Decatur. Ordered into active Federal service 11 June 1963 at Decatur; released 16 June 1963 from active Federal service and reverted to state control. Ordered into active Federal service 10 September 1963 at Decatur; released 12 September 1963 from active Federal service and reverted to state control. Reorganized and redesignated 1 April 1978 as Headquarters and Headquarters Company, 142d Signal Brigade.

Home Station: Decatur

CAMPAIGN PARTICIPATION CREDIT

None.

DECORATIONS

None.

142d SIGNAL BRIGADE BIBLIOGRAPHY

Carney, David. "Multicomponent After One Year: How's It Working?" *Army Communicator* 25 (Fall 2000): 31–32.

———. 142d Signal Brigade 'lifts bosses.'" *Army Communicator* 28 (Spring 2003): 38.

———. "142d Signal Brigade Paves Path in First Brigade Multicomponent Change of Command." *Army Communicator* 25 (Fall 2000): 30–31.

———. "Reserve Component Signaleers Provide Real-Life and Battlefield-Scenario Communications for Pacific Strike Exercise." *Army Communicator* 26 (Spring 2001): 26–28.

———. "The 20-Year Transformation of the Multi-Compo 142d Signal Brigade." *Army Communicator* 28 (Spring 2003): 39–40.

"Signal Troops Train in Germany." *The National Guardsman* 28 (January 1974): 5.

Toland, Ray B. "Training to the Army Standard." *Army Communicator* 9 (Winter 1984): 13–14.

HEADQUARTERS AND HEADQUARTERS COMPANY
160th SIGNAL BRIGADE

HERALDIC ITEMS

SHOULDER SLEEVE INSIGNIA

Description: A vertical rectangle arched at top and base and having in base the upper portion of a blue globe with white grid lines. Above the globe on an orange background two yellow lightning flashes, one issuant from either side, with their points crossed at the upper center, all within a white border.

Symbolism: Orange and white are the colors traditionally associated with the Signal Corps. The color blue refers to the unit's ability to support the combat mission. The yellow lightning flashes are an allusion to the basic mission of the organization and, along with the globe, denote the worldwide scope of the unit's mission. They also indicate the unit's affiliation with the former U.S. Army Communications Command.

DISTINCTIVE UNIT INSIGNIA

Description: A gold color metal and enamel device that consists of a gold oriental semidragon facing to the left on an orange wedge shape with point in base, all between a pair of black wings conjoined, each wing charged with a gold fleur-de-lis and flanked with a red lightning flash, all below an arched gold scroll inscribed FINEST OF THE FIRST in red letters.

Symbolism: Orange is a color traditionally associated with the Signal Corps. The wings charged with two fleurs-de-lis allude to service in the Rhineland and Central Europe. The red lightning flashes symbolize the Meritorious Unit Commendation awarded to the unit for service during World War II. The oriental semidragon symbolizes the unit's combat service in Vietnam.

LINEAGE AND HONORS

RA
(inactive)

LINEAGE

Constituted 6 March 1945 in the Army of the United States as the 3160th Signal Service Battalion and activated in France. Inactivated 20 June 1947 in Germany.

Redesignated 3 December 1954 as Headquarters and Headquarters Detachment, 160th Signal Group, and allotted to the Regular Army. Activated 28 January 1955 in Germany. Inactivated 1 October 1961 in Germany. Activated 25 March 1963 at Fort Hood, Texas. Inactivated 3 June 1972 at Oakland, California. Activated 1 July 1974 in Germany.

Redesignated 1 October 1979 as Headquarters and Headquarters Company, 160th Signal Brigade. Inactivated 22 August 1991 in Germany.

CAMPAIGN PARTICIPATION CREDIT

World War II
- Rhineland
- Central Europe

Vietnam
- Counteroffensive, Phase II
- Counteroffensive, Phase III
- Tet Counteroffensive
- Counteroffensive, Phase IV
- Counteroffensive, Phase V
- Counteroffensive, Phase VI
- Tet 69/Counteroffensive
- Summer–Fall 1969
- Winter–Spring 1970
- Sanctuary Counteroffensive
- Counteroffensive, Phase VII
- Consolidation I
- Consolidation II
- Cease-Fire

DECORATIONS

Meritorious Unit Commendation (Army), Streamer embroidered EUROPEAN THEATER (3160th Signal Service Battalion [long lines] cited; GO 32, Theater Service Forces, European Theater, 28 February 1946)

160th SIGNAL BRIGADE BIBLIOGRAPHY

Bergen, John D. *Military Communications: A Test for Technology*. United States Army in Vietnam. Washington, D.C.: Center of Military History, United States Army, 1986.

Headquarters, 160th Signal Group Unit History. Karlsruhe, Germany, 1979.

History of the 160th Signal Group. N.p., 1974.

Raines, Rebecca Robbins. *Getting the Message Through: A Branch History of the U.S. Army Signal Corps*. Army Historical Series. Washington, D.C.: Center of Military History, United States Army, 1996.

Rienzi, Thomas M. *Communications-Electronics, 1962–1970*. Vietnam Studies. Washington, D.C.: Department of the Army, 1972.

Rolak, Bruno J. *History of the U.S. Army Communications Command (1964–1976)*. Fort Huachuca, Ariz.: United States Army Communications Command, 1976.

Rolak, Bruno J., and George R. Thompson. *History of the United States Army Communications Command From Origin Through 1976*. Fort Huachuca, Ariz.: United States Army Communications Command, 1979.

"Units Renamed." *Army Communicator* 4 (Fall 1979): 60.

HEADQUARTERS AND HEADQUARTERS COMPANY
228th SIGNAL BRIGADE

HERALDIC ITEMS

SHOULDER SLEEVE INSIGNIA

Description: Centered on a blue shield arched at the top and bottom a broad orange bar arched at top and bottom. Centered overall a white bayonet surmounted above the hilt by a white crescent bearing two orange lightning flashes, all within a white border.

Symbolism: Orange and white are the colors traditionally associated with the Signal Corps. Blue and white, the colors associated with the Infantry and the South Carolina Army National Guard, refer to the unit's heritage and war experience. The bayonet suggests the unit's long military history, which began as an Infantry unit in 1907. The white crescent is taken from the flag of the unit's home state. The lightning flashes allude to the unit's mission and motto.

DISTINCTIVE UNIT INSIGNIA

Description: A silver color metal and enamel device that consists of three stylized mountain peaks divided horizontally blue and green in back of a white crescent bearing an orange lightning flash throughout and surmounted vertically by a silver bayonet, the blade between two silver fleurs-de-lis within the crescent and the guard below the crescent, all enclosed at sides and base by a wavy silver scroll passing over the hilt of the bayonet and inscribed STRENGTH IN ELECTRONICS in black letters.

Symbolism: Orange and white are the colors traditionally associated with the Signal Corps. Blue and white are the colors associated with the South Carolina Army National Guard. A bayonet is indicative of Infantry. The fleur-de-lis of France and the wavy scroll, which simulates water, refer to the heritage and service of the organization. As a unit of the 1st Regiment of Infantry in 1916, the organization served on the Mexican border. As a unit of the 118th Infantry during World War I, it participated in the Somme Offensive, Ypres-Lys, and Flanders 1918 campaigns in France, and in the Northern France and Rhineland campaigns during World War II. The white crescent from the flag of South Carolina represents the home state of the organization and, with the lightning flash, alludes to both the unit's motto and its overall mission. The stylized mountain peaks refer to the Blue Ridge Mountains and allude to Spartanburg, the unit's home station, located at the foot of the mountains.

LINEAGE AND HONORS

ARNG
(South Carolina)

LINEAGE

Organized in 1907 in the South Carolina National Guard at Spartanburg as Company I (Hampton Guards), 1st Regiment of Infantry. Redesignated 1 April 1915 as Company F, 1st Regiment of Infantry. Mustered into Federal service 1 July 1916 at Camp Moore, South Carolina; mustered out of Federal service 6 December 1916 at Camp Moore, South Carolina. Ordered into Federal service 17 April 1917; drafted into Federal service 5 August 1917. Redesignated 12 September 1917 as Company F, 118th Infantry, an element of the 30th Division. Demobilized 1 April 1919 at Camp Jackson, South Carolina.

Reorganized and federally recognized 22 August 1923 in the South Carolina National Guard at Spartanburg as Company F, 118th Infantry, an element of the 30th Division. Inducted into Federal service 16 September 1940 at Spartanburg. (118th Infantry relieved 24 August 1942 from assignment to the 30th Division.) Inactivated 15 January 1946 at Camp Kilmer, New Jersey.

Reorganized and federally recognized 3 February 1947 at Spartanburg as Headquarters Company, 218th Infantry, an element of the 51st Infantry Division. Converted and redesignated 1 April 1959 as Headquarters Company, 151st Transportation Battalion, an element of the 51st Infantry Division. Converted and redesignated 1 April 1963 as Headquarters Detachment, 51st Quartermaster Battalion, and relieved from assignment to the 51st Infantry Division.

Consolidated 1 January 1968 with Headquarters and Headquarters Detachment, 228th Signal Group (organized and federally recognized 30 April 1964 in Saluda), and consolidated unit designated as Headquarters and Headquarters Detachment, 228th Signal Group, at Spartanburg. Reorganized and redesignated 1 July 1980 as Headquarters and Headquarters Company, 228th Signal Brigade.

Home Station: Spartanburg

CAMPAIGN PARTICIPATION CREDIT

World War I
　Somme Offensive
　Ypres-Lys
　Flanders 1918

World War II
　Northern France
　Rhineland

DECORATIONS

None.

228th SIGNAL BRIGADE BIBLIOGRAPHY

American Battle Monuments Commission. *30th Division, Summary of Operations in the World War*. Washington: Government Printing Office, 1944.

Brawders, Jean Marie. "CAPSTONE Effects Training Changes." *National Guard* 40 (November 1986): 30–34.

Brinkerhoff, John R., Ted Silva, and John A. Seitz. *The Signal Support Dilemma: The 335th Signal Command*. United States Army Reserve in Operation Desert Storm. N.p.: ANDRULIS Research Corp., 1992.

Crocker, Robert W. "Go Between Circuits IV." *Army Communicator* 6 (Summer 1981): 50–53.

Davis, Nora Marshall. *History of the 118th Infantry (Palmetto Regiment)*. Columbia, S.C., 1935.

51st Infantry Division, Ready to Strike, 1956. N.p., 1956.

Hasenauer, Heike. "Grecian Firebolt." *Soldiers* 40 (September 1994): 37–40.

Historical and Pictorial Review, 30th Infantry Division, Army of the United States, Fort Jackson, South Carolina, 1941. Baton Rouge: Army and Navy Publishing Company, 1941.

Historical Annual, National Guard of the State of South Carolina, 1938. Baton Rouge: Army and Navy Publishing Company, 1938.

Murphy, Elmer A., and Robert S. Thomas. *The Thirtieth Division in the World War*. Lepato, Alaska: Old Hickory Publishing Company, 1936.

Reed, Anthony. "Grecian Firebolt 2000: Army Signal Command Sponsors Army's Largest Communications Exercise." *Army Communicator* 25 (Fall 2000): 16–17.

Royall, Sam J. *History of the 118th Infantry, American Expeditionary Force, France*. Columbia, S.C.: State Company, 1919.

Siemieniec, Jack. "Grecian Firebolt Connects, Supports Multiple Exercises." *Army Communicator* 26 (Fall 2001): 2–4.

Stevens, Larry. "Signal Support at Gallant Eagle 86." *Army Communicator* 11 (Fall 1986): 18–20.

Theodore, Peter C. "Viewpoint: 67th Signal Battalion." *Army Communicator* 2 (Spring 1977): 57–58.

"228th Signal Grows to Brigade Level." *National Guard* 34 (December 1980): 7.

Ward, Jim. "Grecian Firebolt '98 Makes Active/Reserve Signal Community One Team." *Army Communicator* 23 (Summer 1998): 39–41.

White, Hank. "Grecian Firebolt 1994: A Real Test for Network Managers." *Army Communicator* 20 (Winter 1995): 45–51.

HEADQUARTERS AND HEADQUARTERS COMPANY
261st SIGNAL BRIGADE

HERALDIC ITEMS

SHOULDER SLEEVE INSIGNIA

Description: A lozenge that consists of four lozenges conjoined, the upper of colonial blue and bearing a white five-pointed star and each of the remaining three divided into white and orange areas by a zigzag partition line, all within a buff border.

Symbolism: Orange and white are the colors traditionally associated with the Signal Corps. Colonial blue and buff are adopted from the flag of the state of Delaware. The single star alludes to Delaware as the first state to sign the Constitution and also indicates the capital city of Dover, the unit's home station. The pattern formed by the conjoined lozenges is indicative of precise planning and represents the unit's capabilities. The white and orange zigzag simulates electrical flashes and refers to the technology of a communications system and the unit's mission.

DISTINCTIVE UNIT INSIGNIA

Description: A silver color metal and enamel device that consists of four orange lightning flashes issuing vertically from a blue lozenge charged with a white star between four white vertical arching lightning bolts, all above an orange scroll inscribed FORESEE in silver letters.

Symbolism: Orange and white (silver) are the colors traditionally associated with the Signal Corps. The four white lightning bolts represent the four "Cs" of a modern military signal organization: command, control, communications, and computers. The diamond shape and blue color refer to the Delaware state flag, and the star refers to Dover, the state capital and the unit's home station. The orange lightning flashes represent the unit's mission to disseminate and direct communications efforts over a wide area.

LINEAGE AND HONORS

ARNG
(Delaware)

LINEAGE

Constituted 25 February 1943 in the Army of the United States as Headquarters and Headquarters Battery, 68th Antiaircraft Artillery Brigade. Activated 10 August 1943 on New Caledonia. Inactivated 28 February 1946 in Japan.

Redesignated 16 May 1946 as Headquarters and Headquarters Battery, 261st Antiaircraft Artillery Brigade, and allotted to the Delaware National Guard. Organized and federally recognized 5 December 1949 at Wilmington. Redesignated 1 April 1959 as Headquarters and Headquarters Battery, 261st Artillery Brigade. Location changed 31 January 1968 to Dover.

Converted and redesignated 1 January 1970 as Headquarters and Headquarters Company, 261st Signal Command. Reorganized and redesignated 1 June 1971 as Headquarters and Headquarters Company, 261st United States Army Strategic Communications Command. Reorganized and redesignated 1 July 1974 as Headquarters and Headquarters Company, 261st Signal Command.

Reorganized and redesignated 1 September 1996 as Headquarters and Headquarters Company, 261st Signal Brigade.

Home Station: Dover

CAMPAIGN PARTICIPATION CREDIT

World War II
  Northern Solomons
  Luzon

DECORATIONS

Philippine Presidential Unit Citation, Streamer embroidered 17 OCTOBER 1944 TO 4 JULY 1945 (Headquarters and Headquarters Battery, 68th Antiaircraft Artillery Brigade, cited; DA GO 47, 1950)

261st SIGNAL BRIGADE BIBLIOGRAPHY

Beveridge, Reid K. "First State Guardsmen Provide BrightStar '85 Communications." *National Guard* 39 (Nov 1985): 20–23.

Beveridge Reid K., and Charles J. Anderson. "The One-Army Reality." *Army Communicator* 10 (Fall 1985): 40–51.

Duncan, William H. "Wiring Gallant Eagle: The Force Isn't Total Until It Is Able to Talk." *Army* 37 (Nov 1987): 36–43.

"GALLANT EAGLE '84: The Army's Role in CENTCOM." *National Guard* 39 (Feb 1985): 10–14.

Grossman, Larry, and Rudi Williams. "7000+ Service Members Test Systems in Summer's Worldwide Signal Exercise." *Army Communicator* 21 (Winter 1996): 34–35. Discusses Exercise Grecian Firebolt '95.

"Guard Unit Exercise." *Army Communicator* 1 (Fall 1976): 59.

Hasenauer, Heike. "Grecian Firebolt." *Soldiers* 49 (September 1994): 37–40.

Lee, James M., and Dennis C. Hall. "WESTCOM-Spanning the Pacific." *National Guard* 34 (May 1985): 14–16.

Reilly, Belinda. "National Guard Takes on High Frequency Training in Delaware." *National Guard* 46 (May 1992): 18, 21.

Siemieniec, Jack. "Grecian Firebolt Connects, Supports Multiple Exercises." *Army Communicator* 26 (Fall 2001): 2–4.

Stevens, Larry. "Signal Support at Gallant Eagle 86." *Army Communicator* 11 (Fall 1986): 18–20.

"Team Spirit." *National Guard* 36 (March 1982): 38.

White, Hank. "Grecian Firebolt 1994: A Real Test for Network Managers." *Army Communicator* 20 (Winter 1995): 45–51.

HEADQUARTERS AND HEADQUARTERS COMPANY
359th SIGNAL BRIGADE

HERALDIC ITEMS

SHOULDER SLEEVE INSIGNIA

Description: On a rectangle arched at the top and bottom with a golden yellow border, the background quartered orange and white with a blue globe outlined and gridlined white. Overall issuing from upper left to lower right a golden yellow lightning flash.

Symbolism: Orange and white are the colors traditionally associated with the Signal Corps. The lightning flash symbolizes the unit's mission and connotes speed and accuracy. The blue globe signifies the unit's worldwide capabilities.

DISTINCTIVE UNIT INSIGNIA

Description: A gold color metal and enamel device that consists of a yellow diamond with a green border and bearing at its center a blue disc surmounted by a horizontal white lightning flash, all within and surmounting a continuous orange scroll, lined scarlet, the upper area inscribed COMMAND and the lower area COMMUNICATE in gold letters.

Symbolism: Orange and white are the colors traditionally associated with the Signal Corps. The yellow diamond with the green border and the blue disc are adopted from the national flag of Brazil and allude to the unit's service in Brazil during 1944–1945. The color scarlet refers to the award of the Meritorious Unit Commendation streamer for that service. The lightning flash symbolizes the basic mission of the organization.

LINEAGE AND HONORS

AR
(active)

LINEAGE

Constituted 10 October 1944 in the Army of the United States as Headquarters and Headquarters Detachment, 3359th Signal Service Battalion. Activated 1 November 1944 in Brazil. Inactivated 21 October 1945 in Brazil.

Redesignated 16 September 1955 as Headquarters and Headquarters Detachment, 359th Signal Group, and allotted to the Army Reserve. Activated 1 November 1955 at New York, New York. Inactivated 1 March 1963 at New York, New York.

Activated 31 January 1968 at Syracuse, New York. Reorganized and redesignated 15 March 1972 as Headquarters and Headquarters Company, 359th Signal

Group. Reorganized and redesignated 16 September 1987 as Headquarters and Headquarters Company, 359th Signal Brigade. Location changed 18 September 1995 to Fort Gordon, Georgia.

CAMPAIGN PARTICIPATION CREDIT

World War II
    American Theater, Streamer without inscription

DECORATIONS

Meritorious Unit Commendation (Army), Streamer embroidered AMERICAN THEATER (3359th Signal Service Battalion cited; GO 3, Army Service Forces, Office of the Chief Signal Officer, 26 May 1945)

359th SIGNAL BRIGADE BIBLIOGRAPHY

Blanton, Nancy C. "Go Between Circuits III." *Army Communicator* 5 (Summer 1980): 19–23.

Carroll, Bill. "Gagetown '87." *Army Communicator* 13 (Winter 1988): 48–49. Field exercise held in New Brunswick, Canada

———. "Testing Rapid Deployment." *Army Communicator* 8 (Summer 1983): 35–38.

Crocker, Robert W. "Go Between Circuits IV." *Army Communicator* 6 (Summer 1981): 50–53.

Hasenauer, Heike. "Grecian Firebolt." *Soldiers* 49 (September 1994): 37–40.

"28 Units Play Logistical CPX." *Army Reserve Magazine* 17 (November–December 1971): 24.

Ward, Jim. "Grecian Firebolt '98 Makes Active/Reserve Signal Community One Team." *Army Communicator* 23 (Summer 1998): 39–41.

Wilson, Ronnie, et al. "Go Between Circuits V." *Army Communicator* 7 (Summer 1982): 50–53.

HEADQUARTERS AND HEADQUARTERS COMPANY
516th SIGNAL BRIGADE

HERALDIC ITEMS

SHOULDER SLEEVE INSIGNIA

Description: On an orange vertical rectangle arched at top and bottom with a white border, two white diagonally crossed lightning flashes superimposed by a stylized black South Pacific spear issuing from base.

Symbolism: Orange and white are the colors traditionally associated with the Signal Corps. Black represents strength, solidity, and twenty-four-hour military preparedness. The lightning flashes, indicative of communications and electronics, are crossed to symbolize strength. The flashes form two arrowheads pointing inward, suggesting the processing of signal communications. The spear reflects the fighting aspect, suggesting the unit's aggressiveness and its heritage and home location in Hawaii.

DISTINCTIVE UNIT INSIGNIA

Description: A gold color metal and enamel device that consists of a blue disc encircled by a black scroll issuing from a gold conch shell detailed black at bottom and bearing the motto VOICE OF THE PACIFIC at the top in gold letters, and interlaced with three gold stylized South Pacific spears, one vertical and two diagonal. Issuing to top from the center point of the spears two orange lightning flashes.

Symbolism: Orange is a color traditionally associated with the Signal Corps. Black represents strength, solidity, and twenty-four-hour military preparedness. Blue is symbolic of the water of the Pacific. The disc alludes to a globe and refers to the worldwide aspect of the unit's mission. The lightning flashes are indicative of communications and electronics. The spears are adopted from the state seal of Hawaii, recalling the heritage and home location of the unit, thus emphasizing the vital role communications play in total military preparedness. The conch shell refers to the unit's location and is reminiscent of early means of communication in the Pacific.

LINEAGE AND HONORS

LINEAGE

RA
(active)

Constituted 10 October 1944 in the Army of the United States as Headquarters and Headquarters Detachment, 3367th Signal Service Battalion. Activated 25 November 1944 on New Guinea. Inactivated 27 February 1947 in the Philippine Islands.

Redesignated 19 August 1947 as the 516th Signal Service Battalion (organic elements concurrently constituted). Activated 12 September 1947 on Guam. Inactivated 27 January 1950 on Guam (organic elements concurrently disbanded).

Redesignated 14 January 1954 as Headquarters and Headquarters Detachment, 516th Signal Group, and allotted to the Regular Army. Activated 10 February 1954 in Germany. Inactivated 13 November 1967 in Germany.

Redesignated 16 October 1992 as Headquarters and Headquarters Company, 516th Signal Brigade, and activated at Fort Shafter, Hawaii.

CAMPAIGN PARTICIPATION CREDIT

World War II
　　New Guinea
　　Leyte
　　Luzon
　　Southern Philippines

DECORATIONS

Philippine Presidential Unit Citation, Streamer embroidered 17 OCTOBER 1944 TO 4 JULY 1945 (3367th Signal Service Battalion cited; DA GO 47, 1950)

516th SIGNAL BRIGADE BIBLIOGRAPHY

McMullen, Seth, and Bill McPherson. "Hawaii 'Team Signal' Supports Tribute to WWII Vets." *Army Communicator* 21 (Winter 1996): 48–49.

McPherson, Bill. "Donahue Takes Command of 516th." *Army Communicator* 28 (Fall 2003): 70–71. Colonel Brian J. Donahue becomes brigade commander.

_____. "'The East Timor Tapes': Interview with COL Randolph Strong, U.S. Forces East Timor Commander." *Army Communicator* 25 (Fall 2000): 6–12. Colonel Strong served as both commander of the 516th Signal Brigade and the U.S. Forces East Timor.

_____. "516th Signal Brigade Soldiers Support Balikatan." *Army Communicator* 25 (Summer 2000): 19–20. An exercise held in the Philippines.

_____. "Signaleers Support East Timor Operation." *Army Communicator* 25 (Fall 2000): 2–5.

Rolak, Bruno J., and George R. Thompson. *History of the United States Army Communications Command From Origin Through 1976*. Fort Huachuca, Ariz.: United States Army Communications Command, 1979.

Siemieniec, Jack. "Grecian Firebolt Connects, Supports Multiple Exercises." *Army Communicator* 26 (Fall 2001): 2–4.

HEADQUARTERS AND HEADQUARTERS DETACHMENT 1st SIGNAL GROUP

HERALDIC ITEMS

DISTINCTIVE UNIT INSIGNIA

Description: A gold color metal and enamel device that consists of a stylized green evergreen tree bordered by two white lightning flashes, all terminating at a central apex and issuant from the center of a semicircular orange scroll in base. The scroll bears the inscription EXPECTATIONS EXCEEDED in gold letters, and the ends turn upward on the sides, forming three curves around the trailing points of the flashes.

Symbolism: Orange and white are the colors traditionally associated with the Signal Corps. The lightning flashes suggest the communications function of the 1st Signal Group. The single evergreen tree at center refers to the numerical designation of the group. It further alludes to the natural beauty of Fort Lewis, one of the unit's former stations, and to the western hemlock, the official tree of the state of Washington.

LINEAGE AND HONORS

RA
(inactive)

LINEAGE

Constituted 24 January 1946 in the Army of the United States as the 1st Signal Service Group. Activated 1 February 1946 at Camp Crowder, Missouri. Redesignated 13 February 1946 as Headquarters and Headquarters Detachment, 1st Signal Group. Reorganized and redesignated 29 March 1949 as Headquarters, 1st Signal Service Group, and allotted to the Regular Army. Inactivated 20 August 1952 in Camp San Luis Obispo, California.

Redesignated 9 June 1953 as Headquarters, 1st Signal Group. Activated 1 July 1953 at Fort Monmouth, New Jersey. Reorganized and redesignated 10 June 1955 as Headquarters and Headquarters Detachment, 1st Signal Group. Inactivated 9 December 1957 at Fort Huachuca, Arizona.

Activated 1 May 1960 in France. Inactivated 15 September 1979 at Fort Hood, Texas.

CAMPAIGN PARTICIPATION CREDIT
None.

DECORATIONS
None.

1st SIGNAL GROUP BIBLIOGRAPHY
No published histories.

HEADQUARTERS AND HEADQUARTERS DETACHMENT 4th SIGNAL GROUP

HERALDIC ITEMS

DISTINCTIVE UNIT INSIGNIA

Description: A gold color metal and enamel device that consists of an orange equilateral triangle one point up. Contained between two gold stars in base a gold sea lion holding a gold sword erect in his right paw. The triangle surmounting four white lightning flashes all enclosed and supported by a gold laurel wreath, its branches bound together by a red band.

Symbolism: Orange and white are the colors traditionally associated with the Signal Corps. The four lightning flashes in base are symbolic of the basic signaling function and allude to the unit's numerical designation. The two stars represent the unit's participation in the Leyte and Luzon campaigns of World War II. The sea lion and triangle, symbols adopted from the seal of the president of the Philippines, refer to the award of the Philippine President Unit Citation. The laurel wreath tied in the scarlet color of the streamer represents the Meritorious Unit Commendation received for service in the Asiatic-Pacific Theater by an element of the group.

LINEAGE AND HONORS

RA
(inactive)

LINEAGE

Constituted 29 March 1945 in the Army of the United States as the 4025th Signal Service Group. Activated 1 June 1945 in the Philippine Islands. Redesignated 30 June 1947 as the 4th Signal Service Group. Inactivated 1 June 1949 in the Philippine Islands.

Redesignated 7 March 1951 as Headquarters, 4th Signal Service Group, and allotted to the Regular Army. Activated 20 March 1951 in Germany. Reorganized and redesignated 1 April 1953 as Headquarters, 4th Signal Group. Reorganized and redesignated 20 October 1953 as Headquarters and Headquarters Company, 4th Signal Group. Reorganized and redesignated 15 November 1954 as Headquarters and Headquarters Detachment, 4th Signal Group. Reorganized and redesignated 15 November 1956 as the 4th Signal Group. Reorganized and redesignated 19 August 1963 as Headquarters and Headquarters Detachment, 4th Signal Group. Reorganized and redesignated 15 October 1963 as Headquarters and Headquarters Company, 4th Signal Group.

Reorganized and redesignated 25 September 1965 as Headquarters and Headquarters Detachment, 4th Signal Group. Inactivated 13 November 1967 in Germany. Activated 31 July 1971 in Korea. Inactivated 15 May 1975 in Korea.

CAMPAIGN PARTICIPATION CREDIT

World War II
 Leyte
 Luzon

DECORATIONS

Philippine Presidential Unit Citation, Streamer embroidered 17 OCTOBER 1944 TO 4 JULY 1945 (4025th Signal Service Group cited; DA GO 47, 1950)

4th SIGNAL GROUP BIBLIOGRAPHY

Hughes, Howard A. *History of the 4th Signal Service Group, Philippines Command, 1947–1949.* N.p., 1949.

Rolak, Bruno J. *History of U.S. Army Communications Command (1964–1976).* Fort Huachuca, Ariz.: United States Army Communications Command, 1976.

Rolak, Bruno J., and George R. Thompson. *History of the United States Army Communications Command From Origin Through 1976.* Fort Huachuca, Ariz.: United States Army Communications Command, 1979.

Thompson, George Raynor, and Dixie R. Harris. *The Signal Corps: The Outcome (Mid-1943 through 1945).* United States Army in World War II. Washington, D.C.: Office of the Chief of Military History, United States Army, 1966.

HEADQUARTERS AND HEADQUARTERS DETACHMENT
7th SIGNAL GROUP

HERALDIC ITEMS

None approved.

LINEAGE AND HONORS

RA
(inactive)

LINEAGE

Constituted 6 August 1965 in the Regular Army as Headquarters and Headquarters Detachment, 7th Signal Group. Activated 10 September 1965 in Germany. Inactivated 2 June 1969 in Germany.

CAMPAIGN PARTICIPATION CREDIT

None.

DECORATIONS

None.

7th SIGNAL GROUP BIBLIOGRAPHY

No published histories.

HEADQUARTERS AND HEADQUARTERS DETACHMENT 12th SIGNAL GROUP

HERALDIC ITEMS

DISTINCTIVE UNIT INSIGNIA

Description: A gold color metal and enamel device that consists of a rectangular base divided diagonally from upper left to lower right, the upper area gold and the lower area orange, within at top three parallel boxed cables connected at the sides by field splices, all of scarlet. Immediately above in base a convex arched insulated portion of black, surmounted along the diagonal division line by a white lightning flash, the top bearing two gold five-pointed stars and extending over the left side and the tip terminating at the inner edge of the black insulation, which is inscribed LOUD AND CLEAR in gold letters.

Symbolism: Orange and white are the colors traditionally associated with the Signal Corps. The color red refers to the Meritorious Unit Commendation received by the organization for the North Apennines and Po Valley campaigns in Italy during World War II; the two campaigns are represented by the stars. The splices signify electrical continuity and imply a high incidence of electrical use, as well as to symbolize the direction and coordination aspects of the unit's mission. The lightning flash represents the vitality of the group, and the three red cables on the yellow (gold) area allude to Vietnam and denote the area where the organization served.

LINEAGE AND HONORS

RA
(inactive)

LINEAGE

Constituted 1 March 1945 in the Army of the United States as the 935th Signal Battalion, Separate, Tactical Air Command. Activated 1 April 1945 in Italy. Inactivated 24 December 1945 at Camp Pinedale, California (organic elements concurrently disbanded).

Headquarters and Headquarters Detachment, 935th Signal Battalion, Separate, Tactical Air Command, redesignated 1 September 1963 as Headquarters and Headquarters Detachment, 12th Signal Group, and allotted to the Regular Army. Activated 24 September 1963 in Germany. Inactivated 1 December 1966 in Germany.

Activated 1 July 1969 in Vietnam. Inactivated 27 February 1972 at Fort Lewis, Washington. Activated 1 July 1974 in Germany. Inactivated 1 July 1975 in Germany.

CAMPAIGN PARTICIPATION CREDIT

World War II
  North Apennines
  Po Valley

Vietnam
  Summer–Fall 1969
  Winter–Spring 1970
  Sanctuary Counteroffensive
  Counteroffensive, Phase VII
  Consolidation I
  Consolidation II

DECORATIONS

Meritorious Unit Commendation (Army), Streamer embroidered NORTHERN ITALY (935th Signal Battalion, Separate, Tactical Air Command, cited; GO 147, Twelfth Air Force, 3 July 1945)

12th SIGNAL GROUP BIBLIOGRAPHY

Bergen, John D. *Military Communications: A Test for Technology*. United States Army in Vietnam. Washington, D.C.: Center of Military History, United States Army, 1986.

Rienzi, Thomas M. *Communications-Electronics, 1962–1970*. Vietnam Studies. Washington, D.C.: Department of the Army, 1972.

Rolak, Bruno J. *History of the U.S. Army Communications Command (1964–1976)*. Fort Huachuca, Ariz.: United States Army Communications Command, 1976.

HEADQUARTERS AND HEADQUARTERS DETACHMENT
21st SIGNAL GROUP

HERALDIC ITEMS

DISTINCTIVE UNIT INSIGNIA

Description: A gold color metal and enamel device that consists of a sword pointed up with gold hilt and white blade between two orange lightning flashes that originate at the sword's pommel and terminate on either side of its point, all entwined by an S-shaped gold scroll extending from upper left to lower right and bearing the inscription EDGE OF THE SWORD in black letters.

Symbolism: Orange and white are the colors traditionally associated with the Signal Corps. The lightning flashes flanking the sword represent the signal function in support of the military mission. The motto is indicative of the spirit of the organization.

LINEAGE AND HONORS

RA
(inactive)

LINEAGE

Constituted 22 June 1965 in the Regular Army as Headquarters and Headquarters Detachment, 21st Signal Group. Activated 1 September 1965 at Fort Bragg, North Carolina. Inactivated 27 November 1971 at Fort Lewis, Washington.

CAMPAIGN PARTICIPATION CREDIT

Vietnam
    Counteroffensive
    Counteroffensive, Phase II
    Counteroffensive, Phase III
    Tet Counteroffensive
    Counteroffensive, Phase IV
    Counteroffensive, Phase V
    Counteroffensive, Phase VI
    Tet 69/Counteroffensive
    Summer–Fall 1969
    Winter–Spring 1970
    Sanctuary Counteroffensive
    Counteroffensive, Phase VII
    Consolidation I

DECORATIONS

Meritorious Unit Commendation (Army), Streamer embroidered VIETNAM 1966–1968 (Headquarters and Headquarters Detachment, 21st Signal Group, cited; DA GO 73, 1968)

21st SIGNAL GROUP BIBLIOGRAPHY

Bergen, John D. *Military Communications: A Test for Technology*. United States Army in Vietnam. Washington, D.C.: Center of Military History, United States Army, 1986.

Pearson, Willard. *The War in the Northern Provinces, 1966–1968*. Vietnam Studies. Washington, D.C.: Department of the Army, 1975.

Raines, Rebecca Robbins. *Getting the Message Through: A Branch History of the U.S. Army Signal Corps*. Army Historical Series. Washington, D.C.: Center of Military History, United States Army, 1996.

Rienzi, Thomas M. *Communications-Electronics, 1962–1970*. Vietnam Studies. Washington, D.C.: Department of the Army, 1972.

HEADQUARTERS AND HEADQUARTERS DETACHMENT 199th SIGNAL GROUP

HERALDIC ITEMS

None approved.

LINEAGE AND HONORS

AR (inactive)

LINEAGE

Constituted 20 June 1946 in the Army of the United States as Headquarters and Headquarters Platoon, 199th Signal Service Group, and activated at Fort Richardson, Alaska. Reorganized and redesignated 5 August 1946 as Headquarters and Headquarters Detachment, 199th Signal Service Group. Inactivated 10 January 1948 at Fort Richardson, Alaska.

Redesignated 6 August 1953 as Headquarters, 199th Signal Group, and allotted to the Army Reserve. Activated 1 September 1953 at Pasadena, California. Inactivated 10 November 1955 at Pasadena, California. Redesignated 4 May 1959 as Headquarters and Headquarters Detachment, 199th Signal Group. Activated 20 May 1959 at San Jose, California. Inactivated 29 February 1968 at San Jose, California.

CAMPAIGN PARTICIPATION CREDIT

None.

DECORATIONS

None.

199th SIGNAL GROUP BIBLIOGRAPHY

"USAR Units Named for LOGEX 65." *Army Reserve* 11 (January 1965): 8.

HEADQUARTERS AND HEADQUARTERS DETACHMENT 332d SIGNAL GROUP

HERALDIC ITEMS

None approved.

LINEAGE AND HONORS

LINEAGE

AR (inactive)

Constituted 12 May 1959 in the Army Reserve as Headquarters and Headquarters Detachment, 332d Signal Group. Activated 25 May 1959 at Fort Snelling, Minnesota. Inactivated 15 March 1963 at Fort Snelling, Minnesota.

CAMPAIGN PARTICIPATION CREDIT

None.

DECORATIONS

None.

332d SIGNAL GROUP BIBLIOGRAPHY

No published histories.

HEADQUARTERS AND HEADQUARTERS DETACHMENT 505th SIGNAL GROUP

HERALDIC ITEMS

None approved.

LINEAGE AND HONORS

RA
(inactive)

LINEAGE

Constituted 28 July 1944 in the Army of the United States as Headquarters and Headquarters Detachment, 3146th Signal Service Group. Activated 29 July 1944 in France. Inactivated 10 July 1946 in Germany.

Redesignated 30 December 1946 as Headquarters and Headquarters Detachment, 505th Signal Service Group, and activated at Fort Shafter, Hawaii. Inactivated 18 October 1948 at Fort Shafter, Hawaii.

Redesignated 4 February 1952 as Headquarters and Headquarters Company, 505th Signal Group, and allotted to the Regular Army. Activated 5 March 1952 at Camp San Luis Obispo, California. Reorganized and redesignated 23 November 1953 as Headquarters and Headquarters Detachment, 505th Signal Group. Inactivated 10 September 1965 in Germany.

CAMPAIGN PARTICIPATION CREDIT

World War II
Northern France
Rhineland
Central Europe

DECORATIONS

Meritorious Unit Commendation (Army), Streamer embroidered EUROPEAN THEATER 1944 (Headquarters Detachment, 3146th Signal Service Group, cited; GO 212, U.S. Forces, European Theater, 13 July 1946)

Meritorious Unit Commendation (Army), Streamer embroidered EUROPEAN THEATER 1944–1945 (Headquarters Detachment, 3146th Signal Service Group, cited; GO 212, U.S. Forces, European Theater, 13 July 1946)

Meritorious Unit Commendation (Army), Streamer embroidered EUROPEAN THEATER 1945 (Headquarters Detachment, 3146th Signal Service Group cited; GO 212, U.S. Forces, European Theater, 13 July 1946)

505th SIGNAL GROUP BIBLIOGRAPHY

Smith, Cornelius C., Jr. *Fort Huachuca: The History of a Frontier Post*. Fort Huachuca, Ariz., 1977.

1st SIGNAL BATTALION

HERALDIC ITEMS

COAT OF ARMS

Shield: Per bend argent and tenné.
Crest: On a wreath of the colors argent and tenné and issuing of the first a torch bearing a fleur-de-lis gules and flamed or charged with an arrowhead vert.
Motto: IN MEDIAS RES (Into the Midst of Things).
Symbolism: Orange and white are the colors traditionally associated with the Signal Corps.

The fleur-de-lis alludes to Europe where the unit fought during World War II; its color refers to the award of the Meritorious Unit Commendation streamer for service in the European Theater. The torch and arrowhead represent Operation Torch, indicating the unit's assault landing in the Algeria-French Morocco campaign during World War II.

DISTINCTIVE UNIT INSIGNIA

The distinctive unit insignia is the shield and motto of the coat of arms.

LINEAGE AND HONORS

RA
(inactive)

LINEAGE

Constituted 18 October 1927 in the Regular Army as the 59th Signal Battalion. Activated 1 February 1941 at Fort Knox, Kentucky. Reorganized and redesignated 7 August 1941 as the 1st Signal Armored Battalion. Redesignated 24 January 1942 as the 1st Armored Signal Battalion. Reorganized and redesignated 24 July 1944 as the 1st Signal Battalion. Inactivated 29 September 1945 in Germany.

Activated 1 October 1961 in Germany. Inactivated 30 June 1993 in Germany.

CAMPAIGN PARTICIPATION CREDIT

World War II
   Algeria-French Morocco (with arrowhead)
   Sicily
   Rome-Arno
   Southern France
   Rhineland
   Ardennes-Alsace
   Central Europe

Southwest Asia
   Defense of Saudi Arabia
   Liberation and Defense of Kuwait
   Cease-Fire

Company C additionally entitled to:

World War II
    Naples-Foggia

DECORATIONS

Meritorious Unit Commendation (Army), Streamer embroidered EUROPEAN THEATER (1st Signal Battalion cited: GO 389, Seventh Army, 10 August 1945)

1st SIGNAL BATTALION BIBLIOGRAPHY

Hitt, Joe. "7th Signal Brigade Joins 5th Signal Command." *Army Communicator* 7 (Winter 1982): 37.

Stokes, Carol E., ed. *The U.S. Army Signal Corps in Operation Desert Shield/Desert Storm*. Fort Gordon, Ga.: Office of the Command Historian, U.S. Army Signal Center and Fort Gordon, 1994.

Stokes, Carol E., and Kathy R. Coker. "Getting the Message Through in the Persian Gulf War." *Army Communicator* 17 (Summer–Winter 1992): 17–25.

Thompson, George Raynor, and Dixie R. Harris. *The Signal Corps: The Outcome (Mid-1943 through 1945)*. United States Army in World War II. Washington, D.C.: Office of the Chief of Military History, United States Army, 1966.

Thompson, George Raynor, Dixie R. Harris, Pauline M. Oakes, and Dulany Terrett. *The Signal Corps: The Test (December 1941 to July 1943)*. United States Army in World War II. Washington, D.C.: Office of the Chief of Military History, Department of the Army, 1957.

4th SIGNAL BATTALION

HERALDIC ITEMS

COAT OF ARMS

Shield: Argent, issuant from base four mountains tenné, and spanning each peak a lightning flash gules. In chief a bear's head erased sable.
Crest: None approved.
Motto: WE GET THE MESSAGE THROUGH.
Symbolism: Orange and white are the colors traditionally associated with the Signal Corps. The functions of the organization are implied by the four mountains representative of California, the state of the unit's original activation, and connected by the signal or lightning flashes, implying immediate contact. The bear's head, which further refers to the grizzly of California, symbolizes a policy equal to the great strength of the bear and also was employed in ancient times as an emblem of ferocity in the protection of kindred.

DISTINCTIVE UNIT INSIGNIA

The distinctive unit insignia is the shield and motto of the coat of arms.

LINEAGE AND HONORS

RA
(USMA)

LINEAGE

Constituted 27 August 1942 in the Army of the United States as the 4th Signal Battalion. Activated 5 September 1942 at Camp Young, California. Redesignated 1 December 1942 as the 4th Armored Signal Battalion. Reorganized and redesignated 20 June 1944 as the 4th Signal Battalion. Inactivated 29 September 1945 in Germany.

Activated 15 January 1946 at Fort Jackson, South Carolina. Reorganized and redesignated 27 September 1949 as the 4th Signal Battalion, Corps. Allotted 25 October 1951 to the Regular Army. Reorganized and redesignated 13 December 1954 as the 4th Signal Battalion. Inactivated 27 April 1956 in Japan. Activated 25 April 1960 in Korea. Inactivated 1 January 1966 in Korea.

Activated 1 May 1966 at West Point, New York.

CAMPAIGN PARTICIPATION CREDIT

World War II
  Rhineland
  Central Europe

Korean War
  UN Defensive
  UN Offensive
  CCF Intervention
  First UN Counteroffensive
  CCF Spring Offensive
  UN Summer–Fall Offensive
  Second Korean Winter
  Korea, Summer–Fall 1952
  Third Korean Winter
  Korea, Summer 1953

DECORATIONS

Meritorious Unit Commendation (Army), Streamer embroidered EUROPEAN THEATER (4th Signal Battalion cited; GO 38, XIII Corps, 31 May 1945)

Meritorious Unit Commendation (Army), Streamer embroidered KOREA 1950–1951 (4th Signal Battalion, Corps, cited; DA GO 38, 1952)

Meritorious Unit Commendation (Army), Streamer embroidered KOREA 1951–1952 (4th Signal Battalion, Corps, cited; DA GO 53, 1952)

Meritorious Unit Commendation (Army), Streamer embroidered KOREA 1952–1953 (4th Signal Battalion, Corps, cited; DA GO 55, 1953)

Republic of Korea Presidential Unit Citation, Streamer embroidered INCHON–HUNGNAM (4th Signal Battalion cited; DA GO 8, 1952)

Republic of Korea Presidential Unit Citation, Streamer embroidered KOREA 1951–1954 (4th Signal Battalion, Corps, cited; DA GO 82, 1954)

4th SIGNAL BATTALION BIBLIOGRAPHY

Appleman, Roy E. *South to the Naktong, North to the Yalu: June–November 1950.* United States Army in the Korean War. Washington, D.C.: Office of the Chief of Military History, Department of the Army, 1961.

Company C, 4th Signal Battalion, European Theater of Operations. Hanover, Germany: Gerbruder Janecke, 1945.

Nall, Thomas, ed. *History of the Fourth Signal Battalion.* Bad Wildungen, Germany, 1945.

"One if by Land," A Pictorial Story of the 4th Signal Battalion in Korea. Tokyo: Hosokawa Printing Company, 1952.

Rios, Carol E. "Those Crazy Signal Joes." *Army Communicator* 12 (Winter 1987): 42–43. Title refers to nickname applied to battalion members during Korean War.

Westover, John G. *Combat Support in Korea.* Washington, D.C.: Combat Forces Press, 1955.

5th SIGNAL BATTALION

HERALDIC ITEMS

COAT OF ARMS

Shield: Tenné, five fleurs-de-lis—one, two, and two—at the points of an imaginary pentagon azure, fimbriated argent.
Crest: None approved.
Motto: WE MOVE FAST.
Symbolism: Orange and white are the colors traditionally associated with the Signal Corps. The five fleurs-de-lis symbolize the numerical designation of the unit and the battle honors awarded the unit for service in France during World War I. Voided blue, they also represent five major engagements in Europe during World War II.

DISTINCTIVE UNIT INSIGNIA

Description: Superimposed on an orange pentagon edged in silver, one point up, five silver fleurs-de-lis. Across the base a silver scroll bearing the motto WE MOVE FAST in orange letters.
Symbolism: Orange and white are the colors traditionally associated with the Signal Corps. The five fleurs-de-lis on the pentagon symbolize the numerical designation of the unit and the battle honors awarded to the unit for service in Europe in World Wars I and II.

LINEAGE AND HONORS

RA

LINEAGE (5th Infantry Division) (inactive)

Constituted 1 July 1916 in the Regular Army as a Signal Corps battalion. Organized 10 July 1917 at Leon Springs, Texas, as the 9th Field Battalion, Signal Corps. Reorganized and redesignated 3 August 1917 as the 9th Field Signal Battalion. Assigned 1 December 1917 to the 5th Division (later redesignated as the 5th Infantry Division). Reorganized and redesignated 12 February 1921 as the 5th Signal Company. Inactivated 27 October 1921 at Camp Alfred Vail, New Jersey. Activated 2 October 1939 at Fort Sheridan, Illinois. Inactivated 20 September 1946 at Camp Campbell, Kentucky.

Activated 6 July 1948 at Fort Jackson, South Carolina. Inactivated 30 April 1950 at Fort Jackson, South Carolina. Activated 1 March 1951 at Indiantown Gap Military Reservation, Pennsylvania. Inactivated 1 September 1953 at Indiantown Gap Military Reservation, Pennsylvania. Activated 25 May 1954 in Germany. Inactivated 1 June 1957 at Fort Ord, California.

Redesignated 19 February 1962 as Headquarters and Headquarters Company, 5th Signal Battalion, and activated at Fort Carson, Colorado (organic elements concurrently constituted and activated). Inactivated 15 December 1970 at Fort Carson,

Colorado. Activated 21 August 1975 at Fort Polk, Louisiana. Inactivated 16 December 1992 at Fort Hood, Texas.

CAMPAIGN PARTICIPATION CREDIT

World War I
St. Mihiel
Meuse-Argonne
Alsace 1918
Lorraine 1918

World War II
Normandy
Northern France
Rhineland
Ardennes-Alsace
Central Europe

DECORATIONS

None.

5th SIGNAL BATTALION BIBLIOGRAPHY

American Battle Monuments Commission. *5th Division, Summary of Operations in the World War*. Washington, D.C.: Government Printing Office, 1944.

Barta, Edward J. *Red Diamond's First Fifty, A History of the 5th Infantry Division, 1917–1967*. Fort Carson, Colo.: Information Office, 1967.

Blumenson, Martin. *Breakout and Pursuit*. United States Army in World War II. Washington, D.C.: Office of the Chief of Military History, Department of the Army, 1961. 5th Infantry Division cited.

Cole, Hugh M. *Ardennes: The Battle of the Bulge*. United States Army in World War II. Washington, D.C.: Office of the Chief of Military History, United States Army, 1965. 5th Infantry Division cited.

———. *The Lorraine Campaign*. United States Army in World War II. Washington, D.C.: Historical Division, Department of the Army, 1950. 5th Infantry Division cited.

5th Infantry Division, Fort Ord, California. San Antonio: Newsfoto Publishing Company, 1956.

Fifth Infantry Division Historical Section. *The Fifth Infantry Division in the ETO*. Atlanta: Albert Love Enterprises, 1945. Reprint, Nashville, Tenn.: Battery Press, 1981.

Historical and Pictorial Review, 5th Infantry Division, United States Army, Fort Custer, Michigan, 1941. Baton Rouge: Army and Navy Publishing Company, 1941.

MacDonald, Charles B. *The Last Offensive*. United States Army in World War II. Washington, D.C.: Office of the Chief of Military History, Department of the Army, 1973. 5th Infantry Division cited.

Myer, Charles R. *Division-Level Communications 1962–1973*. Vietnam Studies. Washington, D.C.: Department of the Army, 1982.

Stevenson, Kenyon. *The Official History of the Fifth Division, U.S.A., During the Period of Its Organization and of Its Operations in the European World War, 1917–1919: The Red Diamond (Meuse) Division*. Washington, D.C., Society of the Fifth Division, 1919.

6th SIGNAL BATTALION

HERALDIC ITEMS

COAT OF ARMS

Shield: Per chevron wavy tenné and argent, issuant from base a demi–sea lion azure bearing in dexter paw a Luzon fighting spear and in sinister paw a New Guinea sword club of the first. On a chief of the second, three lightning flashes—two saltirewise and one fesswise—of the first enfiled with a pierced mullet of six points of the third.

Crest: None approved.

Motto: SOLDIERS–COMMUNICATORS.

Symbolism: Orange and white are the colors traditionally associated with the Signal Corps. The battalion's historic descent from the 6th Signal Company, which was organic to the 6th Infantry Division during World War II, is depicted by the six-pointed mullet. The sea lion with weapons refers to the unit's campaign service in Luzon and New Guinea during World War II. The amphibious assault landings at New Guinea and the Lingayen Gulf, Philippine Islands, are depicted by the spear and sword club. The lightning flashes allude to the battalion's command of multichannel communications facilities and its provision of a swift division-level communication system.

DISTINCTIVE UNIT INSIGNIA

Description: A silver color metal and enamel device that consists of three silver lightning flashes—one fesswise and two saltirewise—surmounted by a blue demi–sea lion in pale, charged on its mane with a silver pierced mullet of six points, and grasping in its dexter paw an orange Luzon fighting spear and in its sinister paw an orange New Guinea sword club. The device within a silver scroll inscribed SOLDIERS–COMMUNICATORS in orange letters.

Symbolism: Orange and white (silver) are the colors traditionally associated with the Signal Corps. The battalion's historic descent from the 6th Signal Company, which was organic to the 6th Infantry Division during World War II, is depicted by the six pointed mullet. The sea lion with weapons refers to the unit's campaign service in Luzon and New Guinea during World War II. The amphibious assault landings at New Guinea and the Lingayen Gulf, Philippine Islands, are depicted by the spear and sword club. The flashes allude to the battalion's command of multichannel communications facilities and provision of a swift division-level communication system.

LINEAGE AND HONORS

RA
(6th Infantry Division) (inactive)

LINEAGE

Constituted 1 July 1916 in the Regular Army as a Signal Corps battalion. Organized 25 July 1917 at the Presidio of Monterey, California, as the 8th Field Battalion, Signal Corps. Reorganized and redesignated 3 August 1917 as the 8th Field Signal Battalion. Assigned 19 November 1917 to the 4th Division. Reorganized and redesignated 17 February 1921 as the 4th Signal Company. Inactivated 21 September 1921 at Camp Lewis, Washington.

Activated 15 September 1937 at Fort Sam Houston, Texas. Relieved 16 October 1939 from assignment to the 4th Division and assigned to the 6th Division (later redesignated as the 6th Infantry Division). Redesignated 1 June 1940 as the 6th Signal Company. Inactivated 10 January 1949 in Korea. Activated 4 October 1950 at Fort Ord, California. Inactivated 3 April 1956 at Fort Ord, California. Relieved 15 May 1958 from assignment to the 6th Infantry Division, assigned to the United States Military Academy, and activated at West Point, New York. Inactivated 1 May 1966 at West Point, New York.

Redesignated 24 November 1967 as Headquarters and Headquarters Detachment, 6th Signal Battalion; concurrently assigned to the 6th Infantry Division and activated at Fort Campbell, Kentucky (organic elements concurrently constituted and activated). Inactivated 25 July 1968 at Fort Campbell, Kentucky. Activated 16 April 1986 at Fort Richardson, Alaska. Inactivated 15 July 1994 at Fort Richardson, Alaska.

CAMPAIGN PARTICIPATION CREDIT

World War I
Aisne-Marne
St. Mihiel
Meuse-Argonne
Champagne 1918
Lorraine 1918

World War II
New Guinea (with arrowhead)
Luzon (with arrowhead)

DECORATIONS

Meritorious Unit Commendation (Army), Streamer embroidered PACIFIC THEATER (6th Signal Company cited; GO 108, 6th Infantry Division, 14 June 1945)

Philippine Presidential Unit Citation, Streamer embroidered 17 OCTOBER 1944 TO 4 JULY 1945 (6th Infantry Division cited; DA GO 47, 1950)

6th SIGNAL BATTALION BIBLIOGRAPHY

American Battle Monuments Commission. *4th Division, Summary of Operations in the World War*. Washington, D.C.: Government Printing Office, 1944.

Bach, Christian A., and Henry N. Hall. *The Fourth Division, Its Services and Achievements in the World War*. Garden City, N.Y.: Country Life Press, 1920.

Pictorial Review, Sixth Infantry Division, "The Sightseeing Sixth." United States Army. Atlanta: Army and Navy Publishing Company, 1941.

6th Infantry Division, Public Relations Section. *The 6th Infantry Division in World War II, 1939–1945*. Washington, D.C.: Infantry Journal Press, 1947.

Smith, Robert Ross. *The Approach to the Philippines*. United States Army in World War II. Washington, D.C.: Office of the Chief of Military History, Department of the Army, 1953. 6th Infantry Division cited.

———. *Triumph in the Philippines*. United States Army in World War II. Washington, D.C.: Office of the Chief of Military History, Department of the Army, 1963. 6th Infantry Division cited.

7th SIGNAL BATTALION

HERALDIC ITEMS

None approved.

LINEAGE AND HONORS

RA
(inactive)

LINEAGE

Constituted 1 September 1943 in the Army of the United States as the 3101st Signal Service Battalion. Activated 20 April 1944 at Camp Crowder, Missouri. Inactivated 5 February 1946 in India.

Redesignated 10 November 1948 as Headquarters and Headquarters Detachment, 7th Signal Service Battalion. Activated 16 December 1948 on Guam. Reorganized and redesignated 13 June 1949 as Headquarters, 7th Signal Service Battalion. Inactivated 27 January 1950 on Guam.

Redesignated 12 January 1951 as the 7th Signal Service Battalion; concurrently allotted to the Regular Army and activated at Camp Kilmer, New Jersey. Reorganized and redesignated 21 May 1953 as the 7th Signal Battalion. Inactivated 1 July 1966 in France.

CAMPAIGN PARTICIPATION CREDIT

World War II
  Central Burma

DECORATIONS

None.

7th SIGNAL BATTALION BIBLIOGRAPHY

No published histories.

8th SIGNAL BATTALION

HERALDIC ITEMS

COAT OF ARMS

Shield: Bendy of four tenné and argent, a Mercury's foot azure, sandal of the second between two lightning flashes issuant respectively from dexter and sinister chiefs to fess or. In base an electronics symbol silver.
Crest: None approved.
Motto: CELERITAS–DILIGENTIA (Speed–Diligence).
Description: Orange and white are the colors traditionally associated with the Signal Corps. The four stripes represent the unit's World War II campaign honors. Blue, the color for Infantry, indicates the World War II decoration awarded for support of the 8th Infantry Division. Mercury's winged sandal symbolizes the unit's basic function, the swift delivery of messages. The electronics symbol alludes to the technical skill involved in the fulfillment of the organization's mission.

DISTINCTIVE UNIT INSIGNIA

The distinctive unit insignia is the shield and motto of the coat of arms.

LINEAGE AND HONORS

RA
(8th Infantry Division) (inactive)

LINEAGE

Constituted 1 July 1916 in the Enlisted Reserve Corps as a Signal Corps battalion. Organized 17 July 1917 at Monmouth Park, New Jersey, as the 10th Reserve Field Signal Battalion. Ordered into active military service 30 October 1917 at Camp Dodge, Iowa; concurrently redesignated as the 320th Field Signal Battalion. Assigned 19 December 1917 to the 8th Division. Demobilized 17 February 1919 at Camp Lee, Virginia.

Reconstituted 24 March 1923 in the Regular Army as the 8th Signal Company and assigned to the 8th Division (later redesignated as the 8th Infantry Division). Activated 1 July 1940 at Camp Jackson, South Carolina. Inactivated 10 November 1945 at Fort Leonard Wood, Missouri. Activated 17 August 1950 at Fort Jackson, South Carolina.

Reorganized and redesignated 1 August 1957 as the 8th Signal Battalion (organic elements constituted 16 July 1957 and activated 1 August 1957 in Germany). Inactivated 16 November 1991 in Germany.

CAMPAIGN PARTICIPATION CREDIT

World War II
   Normandy
   Northern France
   Rhineland
   Central Europe

DECORATIONS

Meritorious Unit Commendation (Army), Streamer embroidered EUROPEAN THEATER (8th Signal Company cited; GO 32, 8th Infantry Division, 14 February 1945)

Luxembourg Croix de Guerre, Streamer embroidered LUXEMBOURG (8th Infantry Division cited; DA GO 59, 1969)

8th SIGNAL BATTALION BIBLIOGRAPHY

Blumenson, Martin. *Breakout and Pursuit*. United States Army in World War II. Washington, D.C.: Office of the Chief of Military History, Department of the Army, 1961. 8th Infantry Division cited.

Eighth Infantry Division, A Combat History by Regiments and Special Units. Baton Rouge: Army and Navy Publishing Company, 1946.

Greisbach, Marc F., ed. *Combat History of the Eighth Infantry Division in World War II*. Baton Rouge: Army and Navy Publishing Company, 1954.

Historical and Pictorial Review, 8th Motorized Division, United States Army, Fort Jackson, 1942. 3 vols. Baton Rouge: Army and Navy Publishing Company 1942.

History and Roster, 320th Field Signal Battalion, United States Army. Richmond, Va., c. 1919.

Hogan, Jerry H., and Lorry R. Ruth. "Signal Communications for the Division in the Field." *Army Communicator* 2 (Spring 1977): 40–43.

Thompson, George Raynor, and Dixie R. Harris. *The Signal Corps: The Outcome (Mid-1943 through 1945)*. United States Army in World War II. Washington, D.C.: Office of the Chief of Military History, United States Army, 1966.

9th SIGNAL BATTALION

HERALDIC ITEMS

COAT OF ARMS

Shield: Per fess wavy argent and tenné, a lion rampant counterchanged, and in dexter chief a mullet interlaced vert.

Crest: On a wreath of the colors argent and tenné a plate embattled bearing a lightning bolt bendwise, overall, surmounted in saltire by a winged foot tenné.

Motto: WITH SPEED AND CERTAINTY.

Symbolism: Orange and white are the colors traditionally associated with the Signal Corps. The lion represents the unit's two Belgian Army citations, and its placement atop the wavy partition line symbolizes the unit's action at the Ludendorff Bridge on the Rhine during World War II. The green star denotes an assault landing in North Africa during World War II by elements of the 9th Signal Company.

The crest is adapted from the badge of the former 9th Signal Company. The winged foot and lightning bolt refer to swift communications service, the function of the unit. The battlements have been added to the white disc to denote the battalion's eight World War II campaigns.

DISTINCTIVE UNIT INSIGNIA

Description: A gold color metal and enamel disc. On a white background an orange lightning flash issuing from dexter surmounted by an orange winged foot.

Symbolism: Orange and white are the colors traditionally associated with the Signal Corps. The lightning and winged foot, the badge of the former 9th Signal Company, refer to swift communications service, the function of the unit.

LINEAGE AND HONORS

RA
(9th Infantry Division) (inactive)

LINEAGE

Constituted 8 July 1918 in the Regular Army as the 209th Field Signal Battalion and assigned to the 9th Division. Organized 31 July 1918 at Camp Sheridan, Alabama. Demobilized 5 February 1919 at Camp Sheridan, Alabama.

Reconstituted 24 March 1923 in the Regular Army as the 9th Signal Company and assigned to the 9th Division (later redesignated as the 9th Infantry Division).

Activated 1 August 1940 at Fort Bragg, North Carolina. Inactivated 15 January 1947 in Germany.

Activated 12 July 1948 at Fort Dix, New Jersey. Reorganized and redesignated 1 December 1957 as Headquarters and Headquarters Company, 9th Signal Battalion (organic elements constituted 13 November 1957 in the Regular Army and activated 1 December 1957 at Fort Carson, Colorado). Inactivated 31 July 1962 at Fort Carson, Colorado. Activated 1 February 1966 at Fort Riley, Kansas. Inactivated 25 September 1969 in Hawaii.

Activated 21 June 1972 at Fort Lewis, Washington. Inactivated 15 July 1991 at Fort Lewis, Washington.

CAMPAIGN PARTICIPATION CREDIT

World War II
- Algeria-French Morocco (with arrowhead)
- Tunisia
- Sicily
- Normandy
- Northern France
- Rhineland
- Ardennes-Alsace
- Central Europe

Vietnam
- Counteroffensive, Phase II
- Counteroffensive, Phase III
- Tet Counteroffensive
- Counteroffensive, Phase IV
- Counteroffensive, Phase V
- Counteroffensive, Phase VI
- Tet 69/Counteroffensive
- Summer–Fall 1969

DECORATIONS

Presidential Unit Citation (Army), Streamer embroidered REMAGEN BRIDGEHEAD (9th Signal Company cited; WD GO 68, 1945)

Meritorious Unit Commendation (Army), Streamer embroidered EUROPEAN THEATER (9th Signal Company cited; GO 53, 9th Infantry Division, 18 April 1945)

Meritorious Unit Commendation (Army), Streamer embroidered VIETNAM 1966–1967 (9th Signal Battalion cited; DA GO 48, 1968)

Meritorious Unit Commendation (Army), Streamer embroidered VIETNAM 1967–1968 (9th Signal Battalion, 9th Infantry Division, cited; DA GO 43, 1969)

Meritorious Unit Commendation (Army), Streamer embroidered VIETNAM 1968–1969 (9th Signal Battalion, 9th Infantry Division, cited; DA GO 13, 1974)

Belgian Fourragere 1940 (9th Signal Company cited; DA GO 43, 1950)

Cited in the Order of the Day of the Belgian Army for action at the Meuse River (9th Signal Company cited; DA GO 43, 1950)

Cited in the Order of the Day of the Belgian Army for action in the Ardennes (9th Signal Company cited; DA GO 43, 1950)

Republic of Vietnam Cross of Gallantry with Palm, Streamer embroidered VIETNAM 1966–1968 (9th Signal Battalion cited; DA GO 31, 1969)

Republic of Vietnam Cross of Gallantry with Palm, Streamer embroidered VIETNAM 1969 (9th Signal Battalion cited; DA GO 59, 1969)

Republic of Vietnam Civil Action Honor Medal, First Class, Streamer embroidered VIETNAM 1966–1969 (9th Signal Battalion cited; DA GO 59, 1969)

9th SIGNAL BATTALION BIBLIOGRAPHY

Bergen, John D. *Military Communications: A Test for Technology.* United States Army in Vietnam. Washington, D.C.: Center of Military History, United States Army, 1986.

Blumenson, Martin. *Breakout and Pursuit.* United States Army in World War II. Washington, D.C.: Office of the Chief of Military History, Department of the Army, 1961. 9th Infantry Division cited.

Dierking, Barbara A., Donald R. Love, and Isabelle J. Swartz, comps. *History of the 9th Infantry Division: The Old Reliables.* Fort Lewis, Washington, [1977–1979]

Fulton, William B. *Riverine Operations, 1966–1969.* Vietnam Studies. Washington, D.C.: Department of the Army, 1973.

Garland, Albert N., and Howard McGaw Smyth. *Sicily and the Surrender of Italy.* United States Army in World War II. Washington, D.C.: Office of the Chief of Military History, United States Army, 1965. 9th Infantry Division cited.

Hall, Dennis C. "'There's Nothing Here But Communications, Sir!'" *Army Communicator* 4 (Fall 1979): 37–41.

Harrison, Gordon A. *Cross-Channel Attack.* United States Army in World War II. Washington, D.C.: Office of the Chief of Military History, Department of the Army, 1951. 9th Infantry Division cited.

Historical and Pictorial Review, Ninth Division (Special Units), United States Army, Fort Bragg, North Carolina, 1941. Baton Rouge: Army and Navy Publishing Company, 1941.

Howe, George F. *Northwest Africa: Seizing the Initiative in the West.* United States Army in World War II. Washington, D.C.: Office of the Chief of Military History, Department of the Army, 1957. 9th Infantry Division cited.

Mittelman, Joseph B. *Eight Stars to Victory: A History of the Veteran Ninth U.S. Infantry Division.* Columbus, Ohio: F.J. Heer Printing Company, 1948.

Myer, Charles R. *Division-Level Communications, 1962–1973.* Vietnam Studies. Washington, D.C.: Department of the Army, 1982.

Raines, Rebecca Robbins. *Getting the Message Through: A Branch History of the U.S. Army Signal Corps.* Army Historical Series. Washington, D.C.: Center of Military History, United States Army, 1996.

Reysen, Frank, ed. *Delta Division, 1969.* N.p., 1969.

———. *9th Infantry Division, 1918–1968.* Vietnam, 1968.

Rienzi, Thomas M. *Communications-Electronics, 1962–1970.* Vietnam Studies. Washington, D.C.: Department of the Army, 1972.

Rios, Carol. "Vietnam Challenges the Signal Corps." *Army Communicator* 13 (Winter 1988): 24–25.

Thompson, George Raynor, and Dixie R. Harris. *The Signal Corps: The Outcome (Mid-1943 through 1945).* United States Army in World War II. Washington, D.C.: Office of the Chief of Military History, United States Army, 1966.

10th SIGNAL BATTALION

HERALDIC ITEMS

COAT OF ARMS

Shield: Per fess dancetty azure and tenné, overall two swords in saltire points up argent, their blades in the form of lightning bolts.

Crest: On a wreath of the colors argent and tenné a wreath of oak leaves or enclosing a mountain peak azure capped of the first, and overall two lightning flashes in saltire of the second.

Motto: VOICE OF THE MOUNTAIN.

Symbolism: Orange and white are the colors traditionally associated with the Signal Corps. The unit's service in Italy during World War II is symbolized by the dancetty partition line, which alludes to the Po Valley and mountains of Italy. The mountain symbols further refer to the unit's early designation as a mountain signal company and to its association with Colorado. The crossed swords with lightning bolt blades denote the presence of the signal battalion within the division.

The crest symbolizes the unit's World War II service in the North Apennines and Po Valley campaigns in Italy. The lightning flashes signify the Signal Corps' mission and refer to the numerical designation of the unit.

DISTINCTIVE UNIT INSIGNIA

The distinctive unit insignia is the shield and motto of the coat of arms.

LINEAGE AND HONORS

RA
(10th Mountain Division) (active)

LINEAGE

Constituted 27 August 1942 in the Army of the United States as the 110th Signal Company. Activated 9 September 1942 at Camp Carson, Colorado. Reorganized and redesignated 15 July 1943 as the 110th Signal Platoon and assigned to the 10th Light Division (later redesignated as the 10th Mountain Division). Reorganized and redesignated 6 November 1944 as the 110th Mountain Signal Company. Inactivated 15 November 1945 at Camp Carson, Colorado.

Redesignated 18 June 1948 as the 10th Signal Company. Allotted 25 June 1948 to the Regular Army. Activated 1 July 1948 at Fort Riley, Kansas.

Reorganized and redesignated 1 July 1957 as Headquarters and Headquarters Company, 10th Signal Battalion (organic elements constituted 14 June 1957 and activated 1 July 1957 in Germany). Inactivated 14 June 1958 at Fort Benning, Georgia. Activated 1 February 1986 at Fort Drum, New York.

CAMPAIGN PARTICIPATION CREDIT

World War II
    North Apennines
    Po Valley

DECORATIONS

None.

10th SIGNAL BATTALION BIBLIOGRAPHY

Casewit, Curtis W. *Mountain Troopers! The Story of the Tenth Mountain Division.* New York: Crowell, 1972.

Fisher, Ernest F., Jr. *Cassino to the Alps*. United States Army in World War II. Washington, D.C.: Center of Military History, United States Army, 1977. 10th Mountain Division cited.

Girard, Jeff. "Supporting Split-Based Operations." *Army Communicator* 25 (Winter 2000): 16–20.

Harper, Frank. *Night Climb: The Story of the Skiing Tenth.* New York: Longmans, Green and Company, 1946.

Hartley, William B., and M. R. Morton, eds. *Tenth Infantry Division*. Atlanta: Albert Love Enterprises, 1944.

Jantzen, Linda. "10th Signal in Mogadishu, Somalia." *Army Communicator* 18 (Summer 1993): 3–7.

Johnson, Danny M. *Military Communications Supporting Peacekeeping Operations in the Balkans: The Signal Corps at Its Best.* Mannheim, Germany: Headquarters, 5th Signal Command, 2000.

Newbern, Pam. "Warfighter: 10th Mountain Division's Winter Training Exercise. *Army Communicator* 28 (Summer 2003): 17–20.

Story of the 10th Infantry Division. Dallas: Taylor Publishing Company, 1957.

Templeton, Kenneth S. *10th Mountain Division, America's Ski Troops*. Chicago: 1945.

10th Infantry Division, Fort Riley, Kansas. Marceline, Mo.: Walsworth Publishing Company, 1954.

Washington, Roger, and Lori McCreary. "10th Signal Battalion Performs Its First MSE Slingload." *Army Communicator* 19 (Fall 1994): 14–15.

11th SIGNAL BATTALION

HERALDIC ITEMS

COAT OF ARMS

Shield: Tenné, between two pallets a lightning flash all argent, and a chief nebuly sable surmounting the pallets and terminating in chief two arrows, points up counterchanged.
Crest: None approved.
Motto: SURE AND READY.
Symbolism: Orange and white are the colors traditionally associated with the Signal Corps. The two vertical white bars, simulating pillars for support, the nebuly, heraldic symbol for clouds, and the lightning flash symbolize the basic mission of the battalion. The two vertical bars further allude to the numeral "11," the numerical designation of the organization. The arrows, their barbs penetrating space, symbolize Air Defense, the former function of the battalion.

DISTINCTIVE UNIT INSIGNIA

Description: A silver color metal and enamel device that consists of an orange pale between two silver pallets, nebuly at top, each pallet charged with a black vertical arrow point up. On the orange background a silver lightning flash. All are within a three-segmented silver scroll inscribed SURE on the dexter segment, AND on the middle segment, and READY on the sinister segment in black letters.
Symbolism: Orange and white (silver) are the colors traditionally associated with the Signal Corps. The two vertical bars, simulating pillars for support, the nebuly, heraldic symbol for clouds, and the lightning flash symbolize the basic mission of the battalion. The two vertical bars further allude to the numeral "11," the numerical designation of the organization. The arrows, their barbs penetrating space, symbolize Air Defense, the former function of the battalion.

LINEAGE AND HONORS

RA
(inactive)

LINEAGE

Constituted 1 July 1944 in the Army of the United States as the 3181st Signal Service Battalion. Activated 5 July 1944 at Camp Kohler, California. Reorganized and redesignated 1 December 1946 as the 3181st Signal Service Company. Reorganized and redesignated 29 April 1947 as the 11th Signal Service Battalion. Inactivated 12 April 1950 on Okinawa.

Redesignated 7 June 1954 as Headquarters, 11th Signal Battalion, and allotted to the Regular Army. Activated 15 July 1954 at Fort Huachuca, Arizona. Inactivated 9 December 1957 at Fort Huachuca, Arizona. Redesignated 31 December 1966 as Headquarters and Headquarters Company, 11th Signal Battalion, and activated in Germany (organic elements concurrently constituted and activated). Inactivated 15 June 1993 in Germany.

CAMPAIGN PARTICIPATION CREDIT

World War II
  Ryukyus

DECORATIONS

None.

11th SIGNAL BATTALION BIBLIOGRAPHY

Patrick, Harold L. "11th Air Defense Signal Battalion." *Army Communicator* 2 (Winter 1977): 49.

Smith, Cornelius C., Jr. *Fort Huachuca: The Story of a Frontier Post*. Fort Huachuca, Ariz., 1978.

Thompson, George Raynor, and Dixie R. Harris. *The Signal Corps: The Outcome (Mid–1943 through 1945)*. United States Army in World War II. Washington, D.C.: Office of the Chief of Military History, United States Army, 1966.

13th SIGNAL BATTALION

HERALDIC ITEMS

COAT OF ARMS

Shield: Per fess dancetté abased of two argent and tenné, issuant from base overall a cubit arm palewise proper grasping seven lightning flashes—three and four sable—in chief a Korean temple azure.

Crest: On a wreath of the colors argent and tenné a scimitar and an officer's sword points down saltirewise proper surmounted by a Philippine sun per fess gules and argent; overall two arrows saltirewise or surmounted by a taeguk fimbriated and charged with a bugle horn of the like garnished and stringed sable.

Motto: VOICE OF COMMAND.

Symbolism: Orange and white are the colors traditionally associated with the Signal Corps. The two mountains are symbolic of the mountainous areas of the Pacific in which the unit provided communications for the 1st Cavalry Division during World War II. They also represent the invasions of the Bismarck Archipelago and Leyte. The arm grasping the lightning flashes alludes to the mission of the unit to enable information and orders to be sent and received. The seven lightning flashes commemorate the seven decorations awarded the unit for service in World War II and Korea. The temple refers to action in Korea during the Korean War.

World War II service is represented by the sunburst, adapted from the Philippine flag and divided in scarlet and white, signifying courage and honor. The thirteen scarlet and thirteen white points of the sunburst allude to the unit's designation. The arrows recall assault landings by the unit during World War II. The taeguk symbolizes service in the Korean War and the many decorations awarded for that service, including the Republic of Korea Presidential Unit Citation. The officer's sword refers to the unit's awards in recognition of Vietnam service. The horn represents the signal mission and reflects the unit's service in Southwest Asia. Gold signifies excellence.

DISTINCTIVE UNIT INSIGNIA

The distinctive unit insignia is the shield and motto of the coat of arms.

LINEAGE AND HONORS

RA
(1st Cavalry Division) (active)

LINEAGE

Constituted 1 July 1916 in the Regular Army as a Signal Corps battalion. Organized 14 July 1917 at Fort Oglethorpe, Georgia, as the 7th Field Battalion, Signal Corps. Reorganized and redesignated 3 August 1917 as the 7th Field Signal Battalion. Assigned in December 1917 to the 15th Cavalry Division; relieved 12 May 1918 from assignment to the 15th Cavalry Division. Disbanded 16 September 1921 at Fort Bliss, Texas.

Reconstituted 19 September 1932 in the Regular Army and consolidated with the 1st Signal Troop (organized 16 September 1921 at Fort Bliss as the 13th Signal Troop and assigned to the 1st Cavalry Division; redesignated 13 December 1923 as the 1st Signal Troop); consolidated unit designated as the 1st Signal Troop, an element of the 1st Cavalry Division. Redesignated 25 March 1949 as the 13th Signal Company.

Reorganized and redesignated 15 October 1957 as Headquarters and Headquarters Company, 13th Signal Battalion, an element of the 1st Cavalry Division (organic elements constituted 22 August 1957 and activated 1 November 1957 in Korea).

CAMPAIGN PARTICIPATION CREDIT

World War II
- New Guinea
- Bismarck Archipelago (with arrowhead)
- Leyte (with arrowhead)
- Luzon

Korean War
- UN Defensive
- UN Offensive
- CCF Intervention
- First UN Counteroffensive
- CCF Spring Offensive
- UN Summer–Fall Offensive
- Second Korean Winter

Vietnam
- Defense
- Counteroffensive
- Counteroffensive, Phase II
- Counteroffensive, Phase III
- Tet Counteroffensive
- Counteroffensive, Phase IV
- Counteroffensive, Phase V
- Counteroffensive, Phase VI
- Tet 69/Counteroffensive
- Summer–Fall 1969
- Winter–Spring 1970
- Sanctuary Counteroffensive
- Counteroffensive, Phase VII

Southwest Asia
- Defense of Saudi Arabia
- Liberation and Defense of Kuwait
- Cease–Fire

DECORATIONS

Presidential Unit Citation (Army), Streamer embroidered PLEIKU PROVINCE (13th Signal Battalion cited; DA GO 40, 1967)

Valorous Unit Award, Streamer embroidered FISH HOOK (13th Signal Battalion cited: DA GO 43, 1972)

Meritorious Unit Commendation (Army), Streamer embroidered ADMIRALTY ISLANDS (1st Signal Troop cited; GO 8, 1st Cavalry Division, 1 February 1945)

Meritorious Unit Commendation (Army), Streamer embroidered PHILIPPINES 1944 (1st Signal Troop cited: GO 21, 1st Cavalry Division, 22 February 1945)

Meritorious Unit Commendation (Army), Streamer embroidered PHILIPPINES 1944–1945 (1st Signal Troop cited; GO 205, 1st Cavalry Division, 28 October 1945)

Meritorious Unit Commendation (Army), Streamer embroidered KOREA 1950–1951 (13th Signal Company cited; DA GO 53, 1952)

Meritorious Unit Commendation (Army), Streamer embroidered VIETNAM 1965–1967 (13th Signal Battalion cited; DA GO 17, 1968)

Meritorious Unit Commendation (Army), Streamer embroidered VIETNAM 1968 (13th Signal Battalion cited; DA GO 39, 1970)

Meritorious Unit Commendation (Army), Streamer embroidered VIETNAM 1968–1970 (13th Signal Battalion cited; DA GO 50, 1971)

Meritorious Unit Commendation (Army), Streamer embroidered VIETNAM 1970 (13th Signal Battalion cited; GO 1541, U.S. Army, Vietnam, 6 May 1971)

Meritorious Unit Commendation (Army), Streamer embroidered SOUTHWEST ASIA 1990–1991 (13th Signal Battalion cited; DA GO 27, 1994)

Army Superior Unit Award, Streamer embroidered 1987–1989 (13th Signal Battalion cited; DA GO 15, 1990)

Army Superior Unit Award, Streamer embroidered 1989–1990 (13th Signal Battalion cited; DA GO 6, 1992)

Philippine Presidential Unit Citation, Streamer embroidered 17 OCTOBER 1944 TO 4 JULY 1945 (1st Signal Troop cited; DA GO 47, 1950)

Republic of Korea Presidential Unit Citation, Streamer embroidered WAEGWAN–TAEGU (13th Signal Company cited; DA GO 35, 1951)

Chryssoun Aristion Andrias (Bravery Gold Medal of Greece), Streamer embroidered KOREA (13th Signal Company cited; DA GO 2, 1956)

Republic of Vietnam Cross of Gallantry with Palm, Streamer embroidered VIETNAM 1965–1969 (Headquarters and Headquarters Company and Company A, 13th Signal Battalion, cited; DA GO 59, 1969)

Republic of Vietnam Cross of Gallantry with Palm, Streamer embroidered VIETNAM 1969–1970 (13th Signal Battalion cited: DA GO 42, 1972 as amended by DA GO 11, 1973)

Republic of Vietnam Cross of Gallantry with Palm, Streamer embroidered VIETNAM 1970–1971 (13th Signal Battalion cited; DA GO 42, 1972)

Republic of Vietnam Civil Action Honor Medal, First Class, Streamer embroidered VIETNAM 1969–1970 (13th Signal Battalion cited; DA GO 42, 1972)

Company A additionally entitled to:

Presidential Unit Citation (Army), Streamer embroidered BINH THUAN PROVINCE (Company A, 13th Signal Battalion, cited; DA GO 2, 1973)

13th SIGNAL BATTALION BIBLIOGRAPHY

Appleman, Roy E. *South to the Naktong, North to the Yalu: June–November 1950*. United States Army in the Korean War. Washington, D.C.: Office of the Chief of Military History, Department of the Army, 1961. 1st Cavalry Division cited.

Bergen, John D. *Military Communications: A Test for Technology*. United States Army in Vietnam. Washington, D.C.: Center of Military History, United States Army, 1986.

Cannon, M. Hamlin. *Leyte: The Return to the Philippines*. United States Army in World War II. Washington, D.C.: Office of the Chief of Military History, Department of the Army, 1954. 1st Cavalry Division cited.

Coleman, J. D., ed. *The 1st Air Cavalry Division, Memoirs of the First Team, Vietnam, August 1965–December 1969*. Tokyo: Dai Nippon Printing Company, 1970.

1st Cavalry Division, Information Section. *1st Cavalry Division. "The First Team." Korea 1959*. Tokyo: Tosho Insatsu, 1959.

The First Team...The First Cavalry Division in Korea, 18 July 1950–18 January 1952. Atlanta: Albert Love Enterprises, 1952.

Gregory, Robyn M. "Signal Corps Names Divisional Battalion Commander." *Army Communicator* 16 (Summer 1991): 26. Lt. Col. Marilyn A. Quagliotti became the first female commander of a divisional signal battalion on 29 May 1991.

Hay, John H., Jr. *Tactical and Materiel Innovations*. Vietnam Studies. Washington, D.C.: Department of the Army, 1974.

Hermes, Walter G. *Truce Tent and Fighting Front*. United States Army in the Korean War. Washington, D.C.: Office of the Chief of Military History, United States Army, 1966. 1st Cavalry Division cited.

Hymoff, Edward. *The First Air Cavalry Division: Vietnam*. New York: M. W. Lads Publishing Company, 1967.

Johnson, Danny M. *Military Communications Supporting Peacekeeping Operations in the Balkans: The Signal Corps at Its Best*. Mannheim, Germany: Headquarters, 5th Signal Command, 2000.

Mahr, Warren C., comp. *The First Cavalry Division on Hokkaido, January 1952–June 1954*. Atlanta: Albert Love Enterprises, 1954.

Martin, Patrick, Rosielynn Banzon, and John Cox. "Hood Signaleers Test Teamwork in Road Runner '00 Exercise." *Army Communicator* 25 (Spring 2000): 39–41.

Miller, John Jr. *CARTWHEEL: The Reduction of Rabaul*. United States Army in World War II. Washington, D.C.: Office of the Chief of Military History, Department of the Army, 1959. 1st Cavalry Division cited.

Myer, Charles R. *Division-Level Communications, 1962–1973*. Vietnam Studies. Washington, D.C.: Department of the Army, 1982.

Raines, Rebecca Robbins. *Getting the Message Through: A Branch History of the U.S. Army Signal Corps*. Army Historical Series. Washington, D.C.: Center of Military History, United States Army, 1996.

Rienzi, Thomas M. *Communications-Electronics, 1962–1970*. Vietnam Studies. Washington, D.C.: Department of the Army, 1972.

Rogers, Charles A. *Occupation Diary, First Cavalry Division*. Tokyo: Toppan Printing Company, 1950.

Smith, Robert Ross. *Triumph in the Philippines*. United States Army in World War II. Washington, D.C.: Office of the Chief of Military History, Department of the Army, 1963. 1st Cavalry Division cited.

Stallings, Caroline. "3d Signal Brigade Provides 'Voice of Phantom Warriors' in 5-Month Exercise Series." *Army Communicator* 26 (Fall 2001): 16–18.

Stanton, Shelby. *The First Cav in Vietnam: Anatomy of a Division*. Novato, Calif.: Presidio Press, 1987.

Terrett, Dulany. *The Signal Corps: The Emergency*. United States Army in World War II. Washington, D.C.: Office of the Chief of Military History, Department of the Army, 1956.

Wright, Bertram C., comp. *The 1st Cavalry Division in World War II*. Tokyo: Toppan Printing Company, 1947.

16th SIGNAL BATTALION

HERALDIC ITEMS

COAT OF ARMS

Shield: Tenné, a fess wavy azure fimbriated argent, issuant from base palewise overall the heads of three Micronesian arrows with shafts barbed, each of six of the third.

Crest: On a wreath of the colors argent and tenné a palm frond palewise proper superimposed by two lightning bolts pilewise gules, and overall a sea lion or langued gules and holding in dexter fin a dagger or.

Motto: COMMUNICATIONS FIRST.

Symbolism: Orange and white are the colors traditionally associated with the Signal Corps. The arrowheads are the types used in the Pacific area in which the unit made three assault landings during World War II. The wavy blue band alludes to the overseas location of the battalion at the time of its activation, and the total number of charges corresponds to the four battle honors earned by the organization.

World War II campaigns in the Philippines and the award of the Philippine Presidential Unit Citation are represented by the sea lion. The palm frond refers to New Guinea and the Bismarck Archipelago. The lightning bolts allude to the unit's mission and signify speedy communications. Gold and scarlet denote excellence and courage, respectively.

DISTINCTIVE UNIT INSIGNIA

The distinctive unit insignia is the shield and motto of the coat of arms.

LINEAGE AND HONORS

RA
(active)

LINEAGE

Constituted 9 October 1942 in the Army of the United States as the 16th Signal Operation Battalion. Activated 31 October 1942 at Fort Sam Houston, Texas. Inactivated 20 February 1946 in Japan. Allotted 21 December 1950 to the Regular Army. Activated 10 February 1951 at Camp Gordon, Georgia. Reorganized and redesignated 2 June 1952 as the 16th Signal Battalion, Corps. Reorganized and redesignated 12 May 1954 as the 16th Signal Battalion.

CAMPAIGN PARTICIPATION CREDIT

World War II
    New Guinea (with arrowhead)
    Bismarck Archipelago (with arrowhead)
    Leyte (with arrowhead)
    Luzon

DECORATIONS

Philippine Presidential Unit Citation, Streamer embroidered 17 OCTOBER 1944 TO 4 JULY 1945 (16th Signal Operations Battalion cited; DA GO 47, 1950)

16th SIGNAL BATTALION BIBLIOGRAPHY

Headquarters, 16th Signal Battalion. *History of the 16th Signal Battalion*. N.p., 1961.

―――. *History of the 16th Signal Battalion*. APO 39: 1962.

Kennedy, Randy. "3rd Signal Brigade." *Army Communicator* 12 (Summer 1987): 52–53.

Killebrew, Ben E. "'Communications First, Sir!': The 16th Signal Battalion (Corps Area)." *Army Communicator* 3 (Winter 1978): 41.

Krueger, Walter. *From Down Under to Nippon: The Story of Sixth Army in World War II*. Washington, D.C.: Combat Forces Press, 1953.

Martin, Patrick, Rosielynn Banzon, and John Cox. "Hood Signaleers Test Teamwork in Road Runner '00 Exercise." *Army Communicator* 25 (Spring 2000): 39–41.

Stallings, Caroline. "3d Signal Brigade Provides 'Voice of Phantom Warriors' in 5-Month Exercise Series." *Army Communicator* 26 (Fall 2001): 16–18.

Thompson, George Raynor, and Dixie R. Harris. *The Signal Corps: The Outcome (Mid-1943 through 1945)*. United States Army in World War II. Washington, D.C.: Office of the Chief of Military History, United States Army, 1966.

17th SIGNAL BATTALION

HERALDIC ITEMS

COAT OF ARMS

Shield: Argent, issuant from base between two telegraph poles tenné a radio tower sable emitting in chief five lightning flashes of the second.
Crest: None approved.
Motto: FONS COMMUNICATIONES (Fountain of Communications).
Symbolism: Orange and white are the colors traditionally associated with the Signal Corps. The telegraph poles and radio tower symbolize the battalion's functions. The five lightning flashes represent the organization's World War II battle honors.

DISTINCTIVE UNIT INSIGNIA

The distinctive unit insignia is the shield and motto of the coat of arms.

LINEAGE AND HONORS

RA
(active)

LINEAGE

Constituted 1 November 1942 in the Army of the United States as the 17th Signal Operations Battalion. Activated 30 November 1942 at Camp Crowder, Missouri. Inactivated 18 February 1946 at Camp Bowie, Texas. Redesignated 5 July 1950 as the 17th Signal Operation Battalion and activated in Germany. Allotted 15 December 1950 to the Regular Army. Reorganized and redesignated 20 October 1953 as the 17th Signal Battalion. Inactivated 25 September 1965 in Germany. Activated 16 March 1981 in Germany.

CAMPAIGN PARTICIPATION CREDIT

World War II
    Normandy
    Northern France
    Rhineland
    Ardennes-Alsace
    Central Europe

Company C additionally entitled to:

Southwest Asia
    Defense of Saudi Arabia
    Liberation and Defense of Kuwait
    Cease-Fire

DECORATIONS

None.

17th SIGNAL BATTALION BIBLIOGRAPHY

Goda, Bryan S., and Robert M. Prudhomme. "Communications on a Mobile Battlefield in the 100 Hours War." *Army Communicator* 16 (Spring 1991): 42–47. Company C cited.

Headquarters, 17th Signal Battalion. *Unit History*. Karlsruhe, Germany: Otto Erich, c. 1951.

Headquarters, 17th Signal Operation Battalion. *Unit History*. N.p., 1950.

Hogan, David W., Jr. *A Command Post at War: First Army Headquarters in Europe, 1943–1945*. Washington, D.C.: Center of Military History, United States Army, 2000.

Johnson, Danny M. *Military Communications Supporting Peacekeeping Operations in the Balkans: The Signal Corps at Its Best*. Mannheim, Germany: Headquarters, 5th Signal Command, 2000.

Technical Historical Report. N.p., 1947.

Thompson, George Raynor, and Dixie R. Harris. *The Signal Corps: The Outcome (Mid-1943 through 1945)*. United States Army in World War II. Washington, D.C.: Office of the Chief of Military History, United States Army, 1966.

24th SIGNAL BATTALION

HERALDIC ITEMS

COAT OF ARMS

Shield: Per chevron argent and azure (light blue), two lightning flashes chevronwise conjoined at the center with points to base tenné fimbriated of the first, and in chief an oyster shell sable charged with a pearl proper.
Crest: None approved.
Motto: VOICE OF VICTORY.
Symbolism: Orange and white are the colors traditionally associated with the Signal Corps. The lightning flashes refer to the unit's function. The oyster shell with the pearl signifies the unit's presence in Hawaii on 7 December 1941. The light blue represents the battalion's service in Korea.

DISTINCTIVE UNIT INSIGNIA

The distinctive unit insignia is the shield and motto of the coat of arms.

LINEAGE AND HONORS

RA

LINEAGE (24th Infantry Division) (inactive)

Constituted 6 January 1905 in the Regular Army as Company L, Signal Corps, and organized at Benicia Barracks, California. Redesignated 1 December 1916 as Company B, 3d Field Battalion, Signal Corps. Redesignated 29 August 1917 as Company B, 3d Field Signal Battalion.

Consolidated 1 July 1921 with Company E, 53d Telegraph Battalion (see ANNEX) and consolidated unit reorganized and redesignated as the 11th Signal Company. Assigned 1 February 1922 to the Hawaiian Division (later designated as the 24th Infantry Division). Redesignated 1 October 1941 as the 24th Signal Company.

Reorganized and redesignated 5 June 1958 as Headquarters and Headquarters Company, 24th Signal Battalion (organic elements concurrently constituted and activated 1 July 1958 in Germany). Inactivated 15 April 1970 at Fort Riley, Kansas. Activated 21 November 1975 at Fort Stewart, Georgia. Inactivated 15 February 1996 at Fort Stewart, Georgia.

ANNEX

Constituted 9 April 1909 in the Regular Army as Company M, Signal Corps. Organized 27 April 1909 at the Presidio of San Francisco, California. Redesignated 1 November 1916 as Company E, 3d Telegraph Battalion, Signal Corps. Redesignated 29 August 1917 as Company E, 3d Telegraph Battalion. Redesignated in October 1917 as Company E, 53d Telegraph Battalion.

CAMPAIGN PARTICIPATION CREDIT

World War II
   Central Pacific
   New Guinea (with arrowhead)
   Leyte (with arrowhead)
   Luzon
   Southern Philippines (with arrowhead)

Korean War
   UN Defensive
   UN Offensive
   CCF Intervention
   First UN Counteroffensive
   CCF Spring Offensive
   UN Summer–Fall Offensive
   Second Korean Winter
   Korea, Summer 1953

Southwest Asia
   Defense of Saudi Arabia
   Liberation and Defense of Kuwait

Company C additionally entitled to:

Southwest Asia
   Cease-Fire

DECORATIONS

Presidential Unit Citation (Army), Streamer embroidered DEFENSE OF KOREA (24th Infantry Division cited; DA GO 45, 1950)

Meritorious Unit Commendation (Army), Streamer embroidered PACIFIC THEATER (GO 153, 24th Infantry Division, 1945)

Meritorious Unit Commendation (Army), Streamer embroidered KOREA 1950–1951 (24th Signal Company, 24th Infantry Division, cited; DA GO 49, 1951)

Philippine Presidential Unit Citation, Streamer embroidered 17 OCTOBER 1944 TO 4 JULY 1945 (24th Signal Company [24th Infantry Division], cited; DA GO 47, 1950)

Republic of Korea Presidential Unit Citation, Streamer embroidered PYONGTAEK (24th Signal Company cited; DA GO 35, 1951)

Republic of Korea Presidential Unit Citation, Streamer embroidered KOREA 1953 (24th Infantry Division cited; DA GO 24, 1954)

24th SIGNAL BATTALION BIBLIOGRAPHY

Appleman, Roy E. *South to the Naktong, North to the Yalu: June–November 1950.* United States Army in the Korean War. Washington, D.C.: Office of the Chief of Military History, Department of the Army, 1961. 24th Infantry Division cited.

Cannon, M. Hamlin. *Leyte: The Return to the Philippines.* United States Army in World War II. Washington, D.C.: Office of the Chief of Military History, Department of the Army, 1954. 24th Infantry Division cited.

Crawford, Gerald. "Special Training at the 24th." *Army Communicator* 9 (Winter 1984): 6–8.

Glines, C.V. "The Battle Log of Birdman Silver." *Air Force* 71(December 1988): 104–05. The 11th Signal Company became the caretaker for the pigeon, John Silver, after his heroic service during World War I.

Harvey, Lynn C. *24th Infantry Division (Mechanized),1963, ROAD Reorganization Day.* Germany, 1963.

Hermes, Walter G. *Truce Tent and Fighting Front.* United States Army in the Korean War. Washington, D.C.: Office of the Chief of Military History, United States Army, 1966. 24th Infantry Division cited.

Leyte: Historical Report of the 24th Infantry Division Landing Team, 20 October 1944–25 December 1944, Philippine Liberation Campaign. 67th Engineer Topographical Company, 1945.

Occupation History of the 24th Infantry Division in Japan. N.p., 1947.

Raines, Rebecca Robbins. *Getting the Message Through: A Branch History of the U.S. Army Signal Corps.* Army Historical Series. Washington, D.C.: Center of Military History, United States Army, 1996.

Smith, Robert Ross. *The Approach to the Philippines.* United States Army in World War II. Washington, D.C.: Office of the Chief of Military History, Department of the Army, 1953. 24th Infantry Division cited.

———. *Triumph in the Philippines.* United States Army in World War II. Washington, D.C.: Office of the Chief of Military History, Department of the Army, 1963. 24th Infantry Division cited.

Swindell, Archie C. *24th Infantry Division: Follow Me. Special Taro Leaf Historical Edition, Reactivation Day, 1960.* Germany, 1960.

24th Infantry Division. *The Twenty-fourth Infantry Division, A Brief History.* Kyoto, Japan: Benrido Company, Ltd., 1947.

24th Infantry Division, A Brief History: The Story of the 24th Division's Actions in the Korean Conflict. Tokyo: Japan News, 1954.

24th Infantry Division, Information Section. *24th Infantry Division, 16th Anniversary.* Tokyo: Tosho Printing Company, 1957.

Westover, John G. *Combat Support in Korea.* Washington, D.C.: Combat Forces Press, 1955.

25th SIGNAL BATTALION

HERALDIC ITEMS

COAT OF ARMS

Shield: Argent, semé of golpes and a weathercock standing on four lightning flashes saltirewise tenné.

Crest: On a wreath argent and tenné issuing from a palm frond fesswise proper a demi-lion rampant or holding in dexter paw a lightning flash bent sinisterwise gules fimbriated of the first.

Motto: NEVER UNPREPARED.

Symbolism: Orange and white are the colors traditionally associated with the Signal Corps. The purple roundels are symbolic of the grapes typical of the Rhineland and Central Europe, where the battalion was awarded battle honors during World War II. The weathercock, signal of the wind's direction, is used with four lightning flashes to symbolize communications in any quarter of the world.

The lion, embodiment of strength and courage, commemorates the unit's war service awards in World War II and Southwest Asia. The red lightning flash reflects the color of the Meritorious Unit Commendation awarded to the organization for service in Southwest Asia. The palm frond is expressive of victory and represents the campaign participation credits earned in Southwest Asia.

DISTINCTIVE UNIT INSIGNIA

The distinctive unit insignia is the shield and motto of the coat of arms.

LINEAGE AND HONORS

RA
(inactive)

LINEAGE

Constituted 3 February 1944 in the Army of the United States as the 25th Signal Construction Battalion. Activated 14 April 1944 at Camp Forrest, Tennessee, as the 25th Signal Light Construction Battalion. Reorganized and redesignated 26 June 1944 as the 25th Signal Heavy Construction Battalion. Inactivated 6 April 1946 in Japan.

Redesignated 20 November 1951 as the 25th Signal Construction Battalion and allotted to the Regular Army. Activated 1 December 1951 at Camp Edwards, Massachusetts. Reorganized and redesignated 20 October 1953 as the 25th Signal Battalion. Inactivated 1 October 1968 in Germany.

Activated 18 January 1971 at Fort Bragg, North Carolina. Inactivated 15 October 1993 at Fort Bragg, North Carolina.

CAMPAIGN PARTICIPATION CREDIT

World War II
   Rhineland
   Central Europe
   Asiatic-Pacific Theater, Streamer without inscription

Southwest Asia
   Defense of Saudi Arabia
   Liberation and Defense of Kuwait

DECORATIONS

Meritorious Unit Commendation (Army), Streamer embroidered SOUTHWEST ASIA 1990–1991 (25th Signal Battalion [less Company A] cited; DA GO 12, 1994)

25th SIGNAL BATTALION BIBLIOGRAPHY

Kennedy, Randy. "35th Signal Brigade." *Army Communicator* 12 (Fall 1987): 30–33.

Stokes, Carol E., ed. *The U.S. Army Signal Corps in Operation Desert Shield/Desert Storm*. Fort Gordon, Ga.: Office of the Command Historian, U.S. Army Signal Center and Fort Gordon, 1994.

Stokes, Carol E., and Kathy R. Coker. "Getting the Message Through in the Persian Gulf War." *Army Communicator* 17 (Summer–Winter 1992): 17–25.

26th SIGNAL BATTALION

HERALDIC ITEMS

COAT OF ARMS

Shield: Tenné, on a fess between in chief a lightning bolt fesswise and a demisun issuing from base argent three telegraph poles wired by two wires throughout of the first.

Crest: On a wreath of the colors argent and tenné, in front of a chevron, the point terminating in a fleur-de-lis gules, two torches crossed in saltire of the first, each emitting five tongues of flame or.

Motto: WEATHER OR NOT.

Symbolism: Orange and white are the colors traditionally associated with the Signal Corps. The three telegraph poles refer to the unit's former mission of installing, operating, and maintaining area signal centers as part of the Army area signal system. The lightning bolt alludes to all electric and electronic equipment used to accomplish the mission. The demisun, a symbol and source of energy and power, refers to both sunrise (day) and sunset (night) and indicates the unit's round-the-clock service regardless of weather and conditions.

The ten tongues of flame of the two torches represent the total of the combined campaigns credited the organization for service during World War II in Europe, represented by the fleur-de-lis, and in Korea, represented by the chevron, an allusion to the mountainous terrain of that area. The color red of the fleur-de-lis and chevron further alludes to the two Meritorious Unit Commendations awarded during these campaigns.

DISTINCTIVE UNIT INSIGNIA

The distinctive unit insignia is the shield and motto of the coat of arms.

LINEAGE AND HONORS

RA
(inactive)

LINEAGE

Constituted 13 July 1931 in the Regular Army as the 5th Construction Battalion, Signal Corps. Activated 10 February 1941 at Camp Claiborne, Louisiana, as the 5th Signal Construction Battalion. Redesignated 7 August 1941 as the 26th Signal Construction Battalion. Redesignated 14 May 1945 as the 26th Signal Light Construction Battalion. Inactivated 17 December 1945 at Camp Kilmer, New Jersey.

Redesignated 27 September 1951 as the 26th Signal Construction Battalion. Activated 2 November 1951 in Korea. Reorganized and redesignated 15 April 1954 as the 26th Signal Battalion. Inactivated 28 May 1955 in Korea. Activated 15 August 1961 in Germany. Inactivated 15 October 1991 in Germany.

CAMPAIGN PARTICIPATION CREDIT

World War II
  Normandy
  Northern France
  Rhineland
  Ardennes-Alsace
  Central Europe

Korean War
  UN Summer–Fall Offensive
  Second Korean Winter
  Korea, Summer–Fall 1952
  Third Korean Winter
  Korea, Summer 1953

Southwest Asia
  Defense of Saudi Arabia
  Liberation and Defense of Kuwait
  Cease-Fire

DECORATIONS

Meritorious Unit Commendation (Army), Streamer embroidered EUROPEAN THEATER (26th Signal Construction Battalion cited; GO 117, Communications Zone, European Theater, 28 June 1945)

Meritorious Unit Commendation (Army), Streamer embroidered KOREA 1953 (26th Signal Construction Battalion cited; DA GO 1, 1954)

Company B additionally entitled to:

Meritorious Unit Commendation (Army), Streamer embroidered KOREA 1953–1954 (Company B, 26th Signal Battalion [Construction], cited; DA GO 42, 1955)

26th SIGNAL BATTALION BIBLIOGRAPHY

Stokes, Carol E., ed. *The U.S. Army Signal Corps in Operation Desert Shield/Desert Storm*. Fort Gordon, Ga.: Office of the Command Historian, U.S. Army Signal Center and Fort Gordon, 1994.

Stokes, Carol E., and Kathy R. Coker. "Getting the Message Through in the Persian Gulf War." *Army Communicator* 17 (Summer–Winter 1992): 17–25.

Thompson, George Raynor, Dixie R. Harris, Pauline M. Oakes, and Dulany Terrett. *The Signal Corps: The Test (December 1941 to July 1943)*. United States Army in World War II. Washington, D.C.: Office of the Chief of Military History, Department of the Army, 1957.

28th SIGNAL BATTALION

HERALDIC ITEMS

COAT OF ARMS

Shield: Per bend or and gules, a bend wavy per bend azure and of the first, in base on a slip of grapevine point to base of the last, a Cross of Lorraine of the third. In chief a lion rampant of the second armed and langued of the third, sustaining a lightning flash azure.

Crest: That for the regiments and separate battalions of the Pennsylvania Army National Guard: On a wreath of the colors or and gules a lion rampant guardant proper holding in dexter paw a naked scimitar argent hilted or and in sinister an escutcheon argent on a fess sable three plates.

Motto: COMMUNICATE.

Symbolism: The unit's participation in the Champagne and Lorraine campaigns of World War I is symbolized by the grape leaf and cross on the red field. The wavy bend of blue and gold alludes to the Rhineland campaign of World War II. The upper field of gold, symbolic of special achievement, denotes the award of the Meritorious Unit Commendation for service in the European Theater. The red lion is adapted from the arms of Luxembourg and represents award of the Luxembourg Croix de Guerre. The blue lightning flash identifies the battalion's communications functions.

DISTINCTIVE UNIT INSIGNIA

The distinctive unit insignia consists of elements of the coat of arms.

LINEAGE AND HONORS

ARNG
(28th Infantry Division) (Pennsylvania)

LINEAGE

Organized 12 September 1908 in the Pennsylvania National Guard at Pittsburgh as Company A, Signal Corps. Redesignated 1 October 1912 as Field Company A, Signal Corps. Redesignated 14 February 1916 as the Wire Company, Field Battalion, Signal Troops. Mustered into Federal service 29 June 1916 at Mount Gretna; mustered out of Federal service 18 January 1917 as Company B, Field Battalion, Signal Troops. Mustered into Federal service 23 July 1917 at Pittsburgh as Company B, 1st Field Battalion, Signal Corps; drafted into Federal service 5 August 1917. Reorganized and redesignated 11 October 1917 as Company B, 103d Field Signal Battalion, an element of the 28th Division. Demobilized 20 May 1919 at Camp Dix, New Jersey.

LINEAGES AND HERALDIC DATA

Reorganized and federally recognized 16 December 1921 in the Pennsylvania National Guard at Pittsburgh as the 28th Signal Company and assigned to the 28th Division (later redesignated as the 28th Infantry Division). Inducted into Federal service 17 February 1941 at Pittsburgh. Inactivated 27 October 1945 at Camp Shelby, Mississippi.

Reorganized and federally recognized 10 October 1946 at Pittsburgh. Ordered into active Federal service 5 September 1950 at Pittsburgh. (28th Signal Company [NGUS] organized and federally recognized 18 August 1953 at Pittsburgh.) Released 15 June 1954 from active Federal service and reverted to state control; Federal recognition concurrently withdrawn from the 28th Signal Company (NGUS).

Expanded, reorganized, and redesignated 1 June 1959 as the 28th Signal Battalion with Headquarters at Pittsburgh. Location of Headquarters changed 1 August 1961 to Coraopolis.

Home Area: Southwestern Pennsylvania

CAMPAIGN PARTICIPATION CREDIT

World War I
  Champagne-Marne
  Aisne-Marne
  Oise-Aisne
  Meuse-Argonne
  Champagne 1918
  Lorraine 1918

World War II
  Normandy
  Northern France
  Rhineland
  Ardennes-Alsace
  Central Europe

Company B (Beaver Falls) additionally entitled to:

War with Spain
  Manila

Philippine Insurrection
  Manila
  Malolos

DECORATIONS

Meritorious Unit Commendation (Army), Streamer embroidered EUROPEAN THEATER (28th Signal Company cited; GO 37, 28th Infantry Division, 18 April 1945)

Luxembourg Croix de Guerre, Streamer embroidered LUXEMBOURG (28th Signal Company cited; DA GO 43, 1950)

28th SIGNAL BATTALION BIBLIOGRAPHY

American Battle Monuments Commission. *28th Division, Summary of Operations in the World War*. Washington, D.C.: Government Printing Office, 1944.

Colbaugh, Jack, ed. *The Bloody Patch: A True Story of the Daring 28th Infantry Division*. New York: Vantage Press, 1973.

Cole, Hugh M. *The Ardennes: Battle of the Bulge*. Washington, D.C.: Office of the Chief of Military History, Department of the Army, 1965. 28th Infantry Division cited.

Ent, Uzal W. *The First Century of the 28th Infantry Division*. Harrisburg, Pa.: Stackpole Books, 1979.

Gilbert, Eugene. *The 28th Division in France*. Nancy, France: Berger-Levrault, 1919.

MacDonald, Charles B. *The Last Offensive*. United States Army in World War II. Washington, D.C.: Office of the Chief of Military History, United States Army, 1973. 28th Infantry Division cited.

———. *The Siegfried Line Campaign*. United States Army in World War II. Washington, D.C.: Office of the Chief of Military History, Department of the Army, 1963. 28th Infantry Division cited.

Martin, Edward, comp. *The Twenty-Eighth Division, Pennsylvania's Guard in the World War*. 5 vols. Norwood, Mass: Plimpton Press, 1924.

Miller, Dan. "Guard's 28th Signal Battalion Key to Disaster Communications." *Army Communicator* 22 (Fall 1997): 22–23.

"National Guard Unit Bones Up on MSE." *Army Communicator* 21 (Winter 1996): 43.

Pennsylvania in the World War. An Illustrated History of the Twenty-Eighth Division. 2 vols. Pittsburgh: States Publications Society, 1921.

Proctor, Henry George. *The Iron Division, National Guard of Pennsylvania in the World War, the Authentic and Comprehensive Narrative of the Gallant Deeds and Glorious Achievements of the 28th Division in the World's Greatest War*. Philadelphia: John C. Winston Company, 1919.

"Riot Reaction Force: The Guard in the April Disorders." *National Guardsman* 22 (May 1968): 2–16.

28th Infantry Division. *Historical and Pictorial Review of the 28th Infantry Division in World War II*. Atlanta: Albert Love Enterprises, 1946. Reprint, Nashville: Battery Press, 1980.

Twenty-Eighth Infantry Division, United States Army, Camp Atterbury, Indiana, "Roll on 28th," Pictorial Review, 1950–1951. Atlanta: Albert Love Enterprises, 1951.

29th SIGNAL BATTALION

HERALDIC ITEMS

COAT OF ARMS

Shield: Sable, a bend tenné fimbriated argent between a telegraph pole and an X-frame of the third.

Crest: On a wreath of the colors argent and sable, in front of two lightning flashes in saltire tenné, a fleur-de-lis azure. Centered overall a castle tower or.

Motto: CLEAR AND OPEN.

Symbolism: Orange and white are the colors traditionally associated with the Signal Corps. The pole and X-frame symbolize the type of work done by the organization. The motto CLEAR AND OPEN is a standard telephone phrase that indicates a circuit has been satisfactorily constructed or repaired.

The unit's World War II service in five campaigns in France, Germany, and Central Europe is represented by the fleur-de-lis and the castle tower. The lightning flashes, which denote the unit's mission, and the tower allude to its original signal construction capability.

DISTINCTIVE UNIT INSIGNIA

The distinctive unit insignia is the shield and motto of the coat of arms.

LINEAGE AND HONORS

RA
(active)

LINEAGE

Constituted 20 March 1942 in the Army of the United States as the 29th Signal Construction Battalion. Activated 10 April 1942 at Camp Gordon, Georgia. Redesignated 14 May 1945 as the 29th Signal Light Construction Battalion. Reorganized and redesignated 15 August 1949 as the 29th Signal Construction Battalion. Allotted 31 October 1950 to the Regular Army. Reorganized and redesignated 20 October 1953 as the 29th Signal Battalion. Inactivated 12 August 1963 in France.

Activated 1 May 1983 at Fort Lewis, Washington.

CAMPAIGN PARTICIPATION CREDIT

World War II
    Normandy
    Northern France
    Rhineland
    Ardennes-Alsace
    Central Europe

DECORATIONS

None.

29th SIGNAL BATTALION BIBLIOGRAPHY

Barnes, Samuel A. "We, Too, Serve Proudly." *Army Communicator* 2 (Summer 1977): 41–45.

History of the 29th Signal Light Construction Battalion. N.p., c. 1947–57.

White, Hank. "Grecian Firebolt 1994. A Real Test for Network Managers." *Army Communicator* 20 (Winter 1995): 45–51.

HEADQUARTERS AND HEADQUARTERS DETACHMENT
30th SIGNAL BATTALION

HERALDIC ITEMS

COAT OF ARMS

Shield: Per bend dovetailed argent and tenné, on the last a terrestrial sphere with latitude and longitude lines, all of the first. The equator is composed of nine telegraph poles sable.

Crest: On a wreath of the colors argent and tenné four lightning flashes barbed radiate pilewise of the first, a Roman helm or garnished gules.

Motto: FORTITER ET STRENUE (Boldly and Strenuously).

Symbolism: Orange and white are the colors traditionally associated with the Signal Corps. The line of telegraph poles at the equator represents communications encircling the world and the willingness of the unit to perform its mission in any part of the world.

The lightning flashes symbolize electronic technology and rapid deployment and denote the battalion's four World War II campaigns. The Roman helm suggests Italy and Rome and represents the Meritorious Unit Commendation earned by the unit during World War II. Gold is emblematic of high achievement.

DISTINCTIVE UNIT INSIGNIA

The distinctive unit insignia is the shield and motto of the coat of arms.

LINEAGE AND HONORS

RA
(active)

LINEAGE

Constituted 11 May 1942 in the Army of the United States as the 30th Signal Construction Battalion. Activated 17 August 1942 at Camp Atterbury, Indiana. Reorganized and redesignated 14 June 1944 as the 30th Signal Heavy Construction Battalion. (Company A inactivated 1 January 1946 in Italy.) Inactivated (less Company A) 10 June 1946 in Italy.

Redesignated 16 October 1992 as the 30th Signal Battalion and allotted to the Regular Army; Headquarters and Headquarters Detachment concurrently activated at Fort Shafter, Hawaii.

CAMPAIGN PARTICIPATION CREDIT

World War II
    Naples-Foggia
    Rome-Arno
    North Apennines
    Po Valley

DECORATIONS

Meritorious Unit Commendation (Army), Streamer embroidered EUROPEAN THEATER (30th Signal Heavy Construction Battalion cited; GO 206, Peninsular Base Section, 1 August 1945)

30th SIGNAL BATTALION BIBLIOGRAPHY

Hiland, Kim. "New Detachment Stands Up at 30th Signal Battalion." *Army Communicator* 28 (Spring 2003): 59.

McMullen, Seth, and Bill McPherson. "Hawaii 'Team Signal' Supports Tribute to WWII Vets." *Army Communicator* 21 (Winter 1996): 48–49.

O'Connor, Laurie. "30th Signal Battalion Activates $12 Million Technology Program." *Army Communicator* 23 (Summer 1998): 42–43.

HEADQUARTERS AND HEADQUARTERS DETACHMENT
31st SIGNAL BATTALION

HERALDIC ITEMS

COAT OF ARMS

Shield: Tenné, three telephone wires bendwise interlaced with one of like palewise between two cornets, all argent.
Crest: None approved.
Motto: FIRMITER MANEO (I Remain Steadfast).
Symbolism: Orange and white are the colors traditionally associated with the Signal Corps. The functions of the organization are illustrated by the taut telephone wires and two cornets (medieval signal horns). The numerical designation is indicated by the group of three wires and the single strand. The motto FIRMITER MANEO (I Remain Steadfast) is suggestive of the character of the personnel in the performance of their duties.

DISTINCTIVE UNIT INSIGNIA

The distinctive unit insignia is the shield and motto of the coat of arms.

LINEAGE AND HONORS

RA
(inactive)

LINEAGE

Constituted 11 May 1942 in the Army of the United States as the 31st Signal Construction Battalion. Activated 17 August 1942 at Camp Atterbury, Indiana. Reorganized and redesignated 12 October 1944 as the 31st Signal Heavy Construction Battalion. Inactivated 22 November 1945 at Camp Kilmer, New Jersey.

Headquarters and Headquarters Detachment, 31st Signal Heavy Construction Battalion, redesignated 30 September 1966 as Headquarters and Headquarters Detachment, 31st Signal Battalion, and allotted to the Regular Army. Activated 1 December 1966 at Fort George G. Meade, Maryland. Inactivated 16 January 1967 at Fort George G. Meade, Maryland.

CAMPAIGN PARTICIPATION CREDIT

World War II
   Central Burma

DECORATIONS

Meritorious Unit Commendation (Army), Streamer embroidered INDIA, JANUARY–MARCH 1944 (31st Signal Heavy Construction Battalion cited; GO 62, United States Forces, India-Burma Theater, 19 March 1945)

Meritorious Unit Commendation (Army), Streamer embroidered INDIA, APRIL–NOVEMBER 1944 (31st Signal Heavy Construction Battalion cited; GO 62, United States Forces, India-Burma Theater, 19 March 1945)

31st SIGNAL BATTALION BIBLIOGRAPHY

Low, Theodore. *Unit History, 31st Signal Heavy Construction Battalion.* APO 431, 1945

Organizational History of the 31st Signal Construction Battalion. 17 August 1942 (Date of Activation) to 31 December 1942. Memphis, Tenn.: Headquarters, 31st Signal Construction Battalion, 1942.

Thompson, George Raynor, and Dixie R. Harris. *The Signal Corps: The Outcome (Mid-1943 through 1945).* United States Army in World War II. Washington, D.C.: Office of the Chief of Military History, United States Army, 1966.

32d SIGNAL BATTALION

HERALDIC ITEMS

COAT OF ARMS

Shield: Paly argent and sable two piles tenné, issuant from dexter and sinister chief and meeting in nombril point, each charged with a war horn of the first, those portions of the subordinaries that meet color fimbriated silver.

Crest: On a wreath of the colors argent and sable a sun in splendor bears a fleur-de-lis and environed by an annulet azure. Overall in base two daggers saltirewise points down of the first gripped gules.

Motto: QUINQUE PER QUINQUE (Five by Five).

Symbolism: Orange and white are the colors traditionally associated with the Signal Corps. The six pieces of the shield symbolize the unit's service during World War II. Ancient armies were summoned to the levies and ordered to move at the signal of the war horns. As symbols of the military function, the two piles, recalling the organization's signal duties in two theaters of operation during World War II, are each charged with a silver war horn.

The fleur-de-lis represents service in France and Central Europe during World War II. The sun highlights Asia and the Pacific and refers to the tropical nature of that area in which the unit also served. The blue annulet symbolizes unity and alludes to a globe and the worldwide scope of the Signal Corps' mission. The daggers symbolize combat readiness and represent the unit's Meritorious Unit Commendation and Army Superior Unit Award. Red, the color of courage and sacrifice, is adapted from these decorations.

DISTINCTIVE UNIT INSIGNIA

The distinctive unit insignia is the shield of the coat of arms.

LINEAGE AND HONORS

RA
(active)

LINEAGE

Constituted 11 May 1942 in the Army of the United States as the 32d Signal Construction Battalion. Activated 25 March 1943 at Camp Crowder, Missouri. Redesignated 20 May 1945 as the 32d Signal Light Construction Battalion. Inactivated 30 January 1946 on Okinawa.

Redesignated 3 December 1954 as the 32d Signal Battalion and allotted to the Regular Army. Activated 28 January 1955 in Germany.

CAMPAIGN PARTICIPATION CREDIT

World War II
   Normandy
   Northern France
   Rhineland
   Ardennes-Alsace
   Central Europe
   Asiatic-Pacific Theater, Streamer without inscription

DECORATIONS

Meritorious Unit Commendation (Army), Streamer embroidered EUROPEAN THEATER (32d Signal Heavy Construction Battalion [less Company B and Medical Detachment] cited; GO 69, First Army, 5 May 1945)

Army Superior Unit Award, Streamer embroidered 1990–1991 (32d Signal Battalion cited; DA GO 34, 1992)

Company B additionally entitled to:

Meritorious Unit Commendation (Army), Streamer embroidered EUROPEAN THEATER (Company B, 32d Signal Heavy Construction Battalion, cited; GO 36, First Army, 1 March 1945)

32d SIGNAL BATTALION BIBLIOGRAPHY

Hall, Wray. "New Tropo System." *Army Communicator* 8 (Winter 1983): 59.

Hamilton, Brian. "Atlantic Resolve: Order Out of Chaos, Or Creating Communications Links for a Joint Multinational Exercise." *Army Communicator* 20 (Fall 1995): 40–43.

Harris, Louis. "Signal Regiment Supports Task Force Hawk in Albania." *Army Communicator* 24 (Winter II 1999): 31–34.

Hogan, David W., Jr. *A Command Post at War: First Army Headquarters in Europe, 1943–1945*. Washington, D.C.: Center of Military History, United States Army, 2000.

Johnson, Danny M. *Military Communications Supporting Peacekeeping Operations in the Balkans: The Signal Corps at Its Best*. Mannheim, Germany: Headquarters, 5th Signal Command, 2000.

Thompson, George Raynor, and Dixie R. Harris. *The Signal Corps: The Outcome (Mid-1943 through 1945)*. United States Army in World War II. Washington, D.C.: Office of the Chief of Military History, United States Army, 1966.

HEADQUARTERS AND HEADQUARTERS DETACHMENT 33d SIGNAL BATTALION

HERALDIC ITEMS

COAT OF ARMS

Shield: Argent, three piles tenné, each charged with a bugle horn of the first, stringed azure, a chief vairé gules and of the first.

Crest: On a wreath of the colors argent and azure, issuing from the battlements of a tower of the first masoned sable, a beacon of the last fired proper.

Motto: IN ARDUIS FORTIS (Brave in Difficulties).

Symbolism: Orange and white are the colors traditionally associated with the Signal Corps. The three piles are representative of the entering wedge into enemy territory and of the piles used as foundations in construction work. The bugle horns, which illustrate the martial aspect of the organization, denote strength and fortitude. The divisions of the upper third of the shield represent the difficulties overcome by the personnel in the performance of their functions and, being above all else, signify dominion and authority. In ancient times this shield design was often granted as a special reward for protection and wisdom, as well as for successful command in war. The numerical designation is indicated by the three piles and the three bugle horns. The motto IN ARDUIS FORTIS (Brave in Difficulties) is expressive of the manner in which the personnel conduct their allotted duties.

The battlements of the tower stand for the fortifications of Europe during World War II and refer to the battalion's service in that theater for which it received the Meritorious Unit Commendation. The lighted beacon, which transmitted military information in medieval days, stands for the signal function. The two ladders, or footholds, indicate that the battalion served in both the European and the Asiatic-Pacific Theaters. The flames refer to the unit's participation in World War II.

DISTINCTIVE UNIT INSIGNIA

The distinctive unit insignia is the shield and motto of the coat of arms.

LINEAGE AND HONORS

LINEAGE

RA
(inactive)

Constituted 11 May 1942 in the Army of the United States as the 33d Signal Construction Battalion. Activated 14 December 1942 at Camp McCain, Mississippi. Reorganized and redesignated 1 June 1945 as the 33d Signal Light Construction Battalion. Inactivated 15 December 1945 in the Philippine Islands.

Redesignated 29 May 1963 as the 33d Signal Battalion and allotted to the Regular Army. Activated 16 September 1963 at Fort Richardson, Alaska. Headquarters and Headquarters Company, 33d Signal Battalion, reorganized and redesignated 16 February 1973 as Headquarters and Headquarters Detachment, 33d Signal Battalion (organic elements concurrently inactivated). Inactivated 15 April 1986 at Fort Richardson, Alaska.

CAMPAIGN PARTICIPATION CREDIT

World War II
  Normandy
  Northern France
  Rhineland
  Ardennes-Alsace
  Central Europe
  Asiatic-Pacific Theater, Streamer without inscription

DECORATIONS

Meritorious Unit Commendation (Army), Streamer embroidered EUROPEAN THEATER (33d Signal Construction Battalion cited; GO 148, Third Army, 22 June 1945)

33d SIGNAL BATTALION BIBLIOGRAPHY

Kies, Donna. "Remembrance of Things Cold." *Army Communicator* 11 (Summer 1986): 48.
"Military Successfully Links Up With Alascom." *Alascom Spectrum* 3 (1982): 19.
Raines, Rebecca Robbins. *Getting the Message Through: A Branch History of the U.S. Army Signal Corps*. Army Historical Series. Washington, D.C.: Center of Military History, United States Army, 1996.
Rolak, Bruno J. *History of the U.S. Army Communications Command (1964–1976)*. Fort Huachuca, Ariz.: United States Army Communications Command, 1976.
Thrower, Allen, and Jon M. Chelgren. "USACC-Alaska Communicates in Spite of Awesome Obstacles." *Army Communicator* 8 (Winter 1983): 48–51.

34th SIGNAL BATTALION

HERALDIC ITEMS

COAT OF ARMS

Shield: Per fess argent and tenné, on a pale between in chief two fleurs-de-lis a coconut palm tree fructed in base, all counterchanged; overall on a fess of the first fimbriated of the second a lightning flash throughout of the last.
Crest: None approved.
Motto: SKILL, ENDURANCE, SPIRIT.
Symbolism: Orange and white are the colors traditionally associated with the Signal Corps. The six checkered divisions of the shield, together with the fleur-de-lis and coconut palm tree, represent the campaign honors awarded the organization for service in the European and Asiatic-Pacific Theaters during World War II. The unit's Meritorious Unit Commendation for service in the European Theater is depicted by the second fleur-de-lis. The battalion's historic construction mission is indicated by the white band across the shield to signify the cleared rights-of-way in pole line construction. The lightning flash represents the speed with which the organization facilitated lines of communication.

DISTINCTIVE UNIT INSIGNIA

The distinctive unit insignia is the shield and motto of the coat of arms.

LINEAGE AND HONORS

RA
LINEAGE (inactive)

Constituted 11 May 1942 in the Army of the United States as the 34th Signal Construction Battalion. Activated 18 March 1943 at Camp Crowder, Missouri. Reorganized and redesignated 1 June 1945 as the 34th Signal Light Construction Battalion. Inactivated 25 January 1946 in Japan.

Redesignated 3 December 1954 as the 34th Signal Battalion and allotted to the Regular Army. Activated 28 January 1955 in Germany. Inactivated 15 November 1991 in Germany.

CAMPAIGN PARTICIPATION CREDIT

World War II
- Normandy
- Northern France
- Rhineland
- Ardennes-Alsace
- Central Europe
- Asiatic-Pacific Theater, Streamer without inscription

Southwest Asia
- Defense of Saudi Arabia
- Liberation and Defense of Kuwait
- Cease-Fire

DECORATIONS

Meritorious Unit Commendation (Army), Streamer embroidered EUROPEAN THEATER (34th Signal Construction Battalion cited; GO 139, Third Army, 14 June 1945)

34th SIGNAL BATTALION BIBLIOGRAPHY

History of the 34th Signal Battalion, Corps. Möhrigen, Germany, c. 1955.

Stokes, Carol E., ed. *The U.S. Army Signal Corps in Operation Desert Shield/Desert Storm*. Fort Gordon, Ga.: Office of the Command Historian, U.S. Army Signal Center and Fort Gordon, 1994.

Stokes, Carol E., and Kathy R. Coker. "Getting the Message Through in the Persian Gulf War." *Army Communicator* 17 (Summer–Winter 1992): 17–25.

35th SIGNAL BATTALION

HERALDIC ITEMS

COAT OF ARMS

Shield: Tenné, five lightning flashes radiate from the base point argent. On a chief of the last three telephone poles palewise connected by two wires throughout of the first.

Crest: That for the regiments and separate battalions of the Army Reserve: On a wreath of the colors argent and tenné the Lexington Minuteman proper. The statue of the Minuteman Capt. John Parker (H. H. Kitson, sculptor) stands on the Common in Lexington, Massachusetts.

Motto: WE CARRY THE WORD.

Symbolism: Orange and white are the colors traditionally associated with the Signal Corps. The telephone poles are symbolic of the construction activities of the organization. The five lightning flashes are symbolic of the unit's five battle honors for World War II. The lightning flashes also are symbolic of messages carried over the wires. The three poles and five lightning flashes are suggestive of the numerical designation of the organization.

DISTINCTIVE UNIT INSIGNIA

The distinctive unit insignia is the shield and motto of the coat of arms.

LINEAGE AND HONORS

AR
(active)

LINEAGE

Constituted 11 May 1942 in the Army of the United States as the 35th Signal Construction Battalion. Activated 23 February 1943 at Camp Crowder, Missouri. Reorganized and redesignated 20 May 1945 as the 35th Signal Light Construction Battalion. Inactivated 5 October 1945 at Camp Polk, Louisiana.

Allotted 12 January 1948 to the Organized Reserves. Activated 16 January 1948 with Headquarters at Newark, New Jersey. (Organized Reserves redesignated 25 March 1948 as the Organized Reserve Corps; redesignated 9 July 1952 as the Army Reserve.) Reorganized and redesignated 1 November 1950 as the 35th Signal Aviation Construction Battalion. Reorganized and redesignated 25 April 1952 as the 35th Signal Construction Battalion. Reorganized and redesignated 15 July 1953 as the 35th Signal Battalion. Location of Headquarters changed 7 February 1958 to Jersey City, New Jersey. Inactivated 24 July 1959 at Jersey City, New Jersey.

Activated 16 November 1980 at Fort Allen, Puerto Rico.

CAMPAIGN PARTICIPATION CREDIT

World War II
  Normandy (with arrowhead)
  Northern France
  Rhineland
  Ardennes-Alsace
  Central Europe

DECORATIONS

Meritorious Unit Commendation (Army), Streamer embroidered EUROPEAN THEATER (35th Signal Construction Battalion cited; GO 44, First Army, 16 March 1945)

35th SIGNAL BATTALION BIBLIOGRAPHY

Hogan, David W., Jr. *A Command Post at War: First Army Headquarters in Europe, 1943–1945*. Washington, D.C.: Center of Military History, United States Army, 2000.

Johnson, Danny M. *Military Communications Supporting Peacekeeping Operations in the Balkans: The Signal Corps at Its Best*. Mannheim, Germany: Headquarters, 5th Signal Command, 2000.

Matson, Ryan, and Marimer Navarette. "35th Signal Deploys off Puerto Rico for First Time in Years." *Army Communicator* 28 (Fall 2003): 36–37.

Thompson, George Raynor, and Dixie R. Harris. *The Signal Corps: The Outcome (Mid-1943 through 1945)*. United States Army in World War II. Washington, D.C.: Office of the Chief of Military History, United States Army, 1966.

Toland, Ray B. "Training to the Army Standard." *Army Communicator* 9 (Winter 1984): 13–14.

HEADQUARTERS AND HEADQUARTERS DETACHMENT
36th SIGNAL BATTALION

HERALDIC ITEMS

COAT OF ARMS

Shield: Per fess tenné and vair, in chief a lion passant guardant argent armed and langued azure.
Crest: On a wreath of the colors argent and tenné an oriental dragon passant gules in front of a torch enflamed or between two lightning flashes issuing from center base pilewise or.
Motto: FOR THE COMMANDER.
Symbolism: Orange and white are the colors traditionally associated with the Signal Corps. The lion is from the arms of Normandy, location of the first campaign in which the battalion participated during World War II. The heraldic fur known as vair, which resembles blue and white bells, refers to signaling.

The dragon is representative of Vietnam where the battalion participated in twelve campaigns during that conflict. The torch and lightning flashes are symbolically associated with the Signal Corps. Red stands for courage and sacrifice, and gold is emblematic of excellence.

DISTINCTIVE UNIT INSIGNIA

The distinctive unit insignia is an adaptation of the shield of the coat of arms and incorporates the motto.

LINEAGE AND HONORS

RA
(active)

LINEAGE

Constituted 11 May 1942 in the Army of the United States as the 36th Signal Construction Battalion. Activated 25 May 1943 at Camp Crowder, Missouri. Reorganized and redesignated 1 March 1944 as the 36th Signal Heavy Construction Battalion. Inactivated 15 June 1946 in Germany.

Redesignated 1 March 1963 as the 36th Signal Battalion and allotted to the Regular Army. Activated 26 March 1963 at Fort Bragg, North Carolina. Headquarters and Headquarters Company, 36th Signal Battalion, reorganized and redesignated 1 March 1970 as Headquarters and Headquarters Detachment, 36th Signal Battalion (organic elements concurrently inactivated in Vietnam). Headquarters and Headquarters Detachment, 36th Signal Battalion, inactivated 26 August 1971 at Fort Lewis, Washington.

Headquarters and Headquarters Detachment, 36th Signal Battalion, activated 1 July 1974 in Korea.

CAMPAIGN PARTICIPATION CREDIT

World War II
- Normandy
- Northern France
- Rhineland
- Ardennes-Alsace
- Central Europe

Vietnam
- Counteroffensive, Phase II
- Counteroffensive, Phase III
- Tet Counteroffensive
- Counteroffensive, Phase IV
- Counteroffensive, Phase V
- Counteroffensive, Phase VI
- Tet 69/Counteroffensive
- Summer–Fall 1969
- Winter–Spring 1970
- Sanctuary Counteroffensive
- Counteroffensive, Phase VII
- Consolidation I

DECORATIONS

Meritorious Unit Commendation (Army), Streamer embroidered VIETNAM 1966–1968 (Headquarters and Headquarters Company, 36th Signal Battalion, cited; DA GO 42, 1969)

Meritorious Unit Commendation (Army), Streamer embroidered VIETNAM 1968–1969 (Headquarters and Headquarters Company, 36th Signal Battalion, cited; DA GO 48, 1971)

36th SIGNAL BATTALION BIBLIOGRAPHY

Bergen, John D. *Military Communications: A Test for Technology*. United States Army in Vietnam. Washington, D.C.: Center of Military History, United States Army, 1986.

Myer, Charles R. *Division-Level Communications, 1962–1973*. Vietnam Studies. Washington, D.C.: Department of the Army, 1982.

Rienzi, Thomas M. *Communications-Electronics, 1962–1970*. Vietnam Studies. Washington, D.C.: Department of the Army, 1972.

Thompson, George Raynor, and Dixie R. Harris. *The Signal Corps: The Outcome (Mid-1943 through 1945)*. United States Army in World War II. Washington, D.C.: Office of the Chief of Military History, United States Army, 1966

HEADQUARTERS AND HEADQUARTERS DETACHMENT
37th SIGNAL BATTALION

HERALDIC ITEMS

COAT OF ARMS

Shield: Tenné, a pale argent billetty sable endorsed of the second, and on a chief wavy of the last a gunstone emitting two lightning flashes that terminates in arrowheads fesswise azure.

Crest: On a wreath of the colors argent and tenné, in front of a slip of grapevine leaved and fructed proper, a stag's head erased sable attired or.

Motto: PERFECTION IS OUR GOAL.

Symbolism: Orange and white are the colors traditionally associated with the Signal Corps. The organization's signal electronic warfare operations are symbolized by the black gunstone and simulated blue radar beams. The communication wire and cable lines are depicted by the white vertical stripes. The wavy partition line refers to the unit's ability to provide submarine cable terminals as well as land installations. The white lines also indicate the effective performance in the clearing of rights-of-way for pole line circuits and aerial installations. The series of rectangles denote the battalion's mission to provide pictorial services and aid in the dissemination of messages.

The grapevine and stag commemorate the organization's campaign award for service in the Rhineland during World War II and in the occupation of Austria.

DISTINCTIVE UNIT INSIGNIA

Description: A gold color metal and enamel device that consists of a black stag's head erased and gold antlers that have a black gunstone emitting two blue lightning flashes. The device is within an orange scroll inscribed PERFECTION IS OUR GOAL in gold letters.

Symbolism: The stag's head commemorates the organization's service in the Rhineland during World War II and in the occupation of Austria. The gunstone with lightning flashes alludes to the unit's signal electronic warfare operations.

LINEAGE AND HONORS

RA
(inactive)

LINEAGE

Constituted 11 May 1942 in the Army of the United States as the 37th Signal Construction Battalion. Activated 14 April 1944 at Camp Forrest, Tennessee, as the 37th Signal Light Construction Battalion. Reorganized and redesignated 26 June 1944 as the 37th Signal Heavy Construction Battalion. Inactivated 15 March 1947 in Germany.

Redesignated 1 August 1966 as the 37th Signal Battalion; concurrently allotted to the Regular Army and activated in Vietnam. (Companies A, B, and C inactivated 1 March 1970 in Vietnam.) Headquarters and Headquarters Detachment, 37th Signal Battalion, inactivated 29 June 1972 at Fort Lewis, Washington.

CAMPAIGN PARTICIPATION CREDIT

World War II
    Rhineland

Vietnam
    Counteroffensive, Phase II
    Counteroffensive, Phase III
    Tet Counteroffensive
    Counteroffensive, Phase IV
    Counteroffensive, Phase V
    Counteroffensive, Phase VI
    Tet 69/Counteroffensive
    Summer–Fall 1969
    Winter–Spring 1970
    Sanctuary Counteroffensive
    Counteroffensive, Phase VII
    Consolidation I
    Consolidation II
    Cease-Fire

DECORATIONS

Meritorious Unit Commendation (Army), Streamer embroidered VIETNAM 1966–1967 (37th Signal Battalion cited; DA GO 66, 1968)

Meritorious Unit Commendation (Army), Streamer embroidered VIETNAM 1967–1968 (37th Signal Battalion [Support] cited; DA GO 42, 1969)

37th SIGNAL BATTALION BIBLIOGRAPHY

Bergen, John D. *Military Communications: A Test for Technology*. United States Army in Vietnam. Washington, D.C.: Center of Military History, United States Army, 1986.

McKinney, John B. "They Communicate and Shoot." *Army* 18 (September 1968): 54–60.

Raines, Rebecca Robbins. *Getting the Message Through: A Branch History of the U.S. Army Signal Corps*. Army Historical Series. Washington, D.C.: Center of Military History, United States Army, 1996.

Rienzi, Thomas M. *Communications-Electronics, 1962–1970*. Vietnam Studies. Washington, D.C.: Department of the Army, 1972.

38th SIGNAL BATTALION

HERALDIC ITEMS

COAT OF ARMS

Shield: Tenné, three lightning flashes—two per saltire and one per pale argent—centered overall a sinister gauntlet sable.
Crest: On a wreath of the colors argent and tenné a demiglobe of the like gridlined argent surmounted by a mullet, points fleury or.
Motto: SIGNAL READY.
Symbolism: Orange and white are the colors traditionally associated with the Signal Corps. The three lightning flashes symbolize command, control, and communication. The gauntlet represents strength and unity.

The orange demiglobe represents the unit's involvement in worldwide communications. The gold five-pointed star denotes the five campaign participation credits awarded the unit for service in France and Central Europe, as represented by the fleurs-de-lis.

DISTINCTIVE UNIT INSIGNIA

The distinctive unit insignia is the shield and motto of the coat of arms.

LINEAGE AND HONORS

RA
(inactive)

LINEAGE

Constituted 11 May 1942 in the Army of the United States as the 38th Signal Construction Battalion. Activated 1 July 1943 at Camp Toccoa, Georgia. Reorganized and redesignated 20 May 1945 as the 38th Signal Light Construction Battalion. Inactivated 30 January 1946 on Okinawa.

Redesignated 17 January 1986 as the 38th Signal Battalion, allotted to the Regular Army, and activated in Germany. Inactivated 15 June 1991 in Germany.

CAMPAIGN PARTICIPATION CREDIT

World War II
    Normandy
    Northern France
    Rhineland
    Ardennes-Alsace
    Central Europe
    Asiatic-Pacific Theater, Streamer without inscription

DECORATIONS

Army Superior Unit Award, Streamer embroidered 1986 (38th Signal Battalion cited; DA GO 30, 1987)

38th SIGNAL BATTALION BIBLIOGRAPHY

Company A, 38th Signal Construction Battalion. Okinawa, 1945.

HEADQUARTERS AND HEADQUARTERS DETACHMENT 39th SIGNAL BATTALION

HERALDIC ITEMS

COAT OF ARMS

Shield: Tenné, a sword palewise argent (silver gray) debruised by a saltire argent charged with four rays issuant saltirewise sable. Overall a quatrefoil gules fimbriated of the third.

Crest: On a wreath of the colors argent and tenné a tower of the first issuing five lightning flashes pilewise gules fimbriated or superimposed in base by an oriental dragon's head of the third.

Motto: THE WILL TO SUCCEED.

Symbolism: Orange and white are the colors traditionally associated with the Signal Corps. The sword symbolizes service in Vietnam, for which the unit was awarded several Meritorious Unit Commendations. The intersecting quatrefoil, rays, and saltire represent a radio beam and reflect aspects of the unit's mission. Red, black, and silver, the former colors of Germany's national flag, allude to service in the Rhineland during World War II. Red and white are also the colors for the signal flags in the branch insignia.

The tower, a symbol of defense and strength, represents the unit's World War II service in Rhineland and Central Europe and suggests that region of Europe. Vietnam service is commemorated by the red oriental dragon, which denotes valor and sacrifice. The five lightning flashes, symbolizing quick response and electronic warfare, reflect the unit's Meritorious Unit Commendations for service in Vietnam. Red is the color of the decoration, and gold is emblematic of honor and high achievement.

DISTINCTIVE UNIT INSIGNIA

Description: A silver color metal and enamel device that consists of a silver sword point up, the blade surmounted in cross by four intersecting red discs, the intersections silver, and overall four black rays saltirewise in point; all in front of a silver encircling scroll inscribed THE WILL TO SUCCEED in black.

Symbolism: Orange and white (silver) are the colors traditionally associated with the Signal Corps. The sword symbolizes service in Vietnam, for which the unit was awarded several Meritorious Unit Commendations. The intersecting quatrefoil, rays, and saltire represent a radio beam and reflect aspects of the unit's mission. Red, black, and silver, the former colors of Germany's national flag, allude to service in the Rhineland during World War II. Red and white are also the colors for the signal flags in the branch insignia.

LINEAGE AND HONORS

RA
(active)

LINEAGE

Constituted 11 December 1944 in the Army of the United States as Headquarters and Headquarters Detachment, 3907th Signal Service Battalion. Activated 17 January 1945 in France. Inactivated 25 November 1945 in Germany.

Redesignated 19 July 1951 as Headquarters and Headquarters Company, 39th Signal Support Battalion, and allotted to the Regular Army. Activated 6 August 1951 at Camp Gordon, Georgia. Reorganized and redesignated 15 June 1954 as Headquarters and Headquarters Detachment, 39th Signal Battalion. Reorganized and redesignated 15 June 1969 as Headquarters and Headquarters Company, 39th Signal Battalion. Reorganized and redesignated 28 March 1973 as Headquarters and Headquarters Detachment, 39th Signal Battalion.

CAMPAIGN PARTICIPATION CREDIT

World War II
    Rhineland
    Central Europe

Vietnam
    Advisory
    Defense
    Counteroffensive
    Counteroffensive, Phase II
    Counteroffensive, Phase III
    Tet Counteroffensive
    Counteroffensive, Phase IV
    Counteroffensive, Phase V
    Counteroffensive, Phase VI
    Tet 69/Counteroffensive
    Summer–Fall 1969
    Winter–Spring 1970
    Sanctuary Counteroffensive
    Counteroffensive, Phase VII
    Consolidation I
    Consolidation II
    Cease-Fire

LINEAGES AND HERALDIC DATA

DECORATIONS

Meritorious Unit Commendation (Army), Streamer embroidered VIETNAM 1962–1965 (39th Signal Battalion [Support] cited; DA GO 3, 1966)

Meritorious Unit Commendation (Army), Streamer embroidered VIETNAM 1965–1966 (39th Signal Battalion [Support] cited; DA GO 17, 1968)

Meritorious Unit Commendation (Army), Streamer embroidered VIETNAM 1966–1967 (39th Signal Battalion [Support] cited; DA GO 54, 1968)

Meritorious Unit Commendation (Army), Streamer embroidered VIETNAM 1967–1969 (39th Signal Battalion cited; DA GO 48, 1971)

Meritorious Unit Commendation (Army), Streamer embroidered VIETNAM 1969–1972 (39th Signal Battalion cited; DA GO 32, 1973)

39th SIGNAL BATTALION BIBLIOGRAPHY

Bergen, John D. *Military Communications: A Test for Technology*. United States Army in Vietnam. Washington, D.C.: Center of Military History, United States Army, 1986.

Myer, Charles R. *Division-Level Communications, 1962–1973*. Vietnam Studies. Washington, D.C.: Department of the Army, 1982.

Raines, Rebecca Robbins. *Getting the Message Through: A Branch History of the U.S. Army Signal Corps*. Army Historical Series. Washington, D.C.: Center of Military History, United States Army, 1996.

Rienzi, Thomas M. *Communications-Electronics, 1962–1970*. Vietnam Studies. Washington, D.C.: Department of the Army, 1972.

Rolak, Bruno J. *History of the U.S. Army Communications Command (1964–1976)*. Fort Huachuca, Ariz.: United States Army Communications Command, 1976.

Rolak, Bruno J., and George R. Thompson. *History of the United States Army Communications Command From Origin Through 1976*. Fort Huachuca, Ariz.: United States Army Communications Command, 1979.

Smolinski, Lynn, and Theodore Kantor. "The Warfighter and the Deployable Communications Package—Strategic." *Army Communicator* 28 (Fall 2003): 2–3.

Ward, Roger L. *39th Signal Battalion, 1944–1974*. Bremerhaven, West Germany, 1974.

40th SIGNAL BATTALION

HERALDIC ITEMS

COAT OF ARMS

Shield: Sable on a bend tenné, fimbriated argent between in chief a peach leaved and in base a horse's head couped two telephone poles of single arm, each palewise of the third.

Crest: On a wreath of the colors argent and sable a mural crown of the first masoned sable and charged with a lion passant azure, armed and langued gules and enfiled by an oriental polearm of the last.

Motto: BENE FACTUM (Well Done).

Symbolism: The background of the shield is black. The bend is orange bordered in silver for the Signal Corps. The silver peach is symbolic of the state of Georgia, the origin of the unit's cadre and original officers from the 29th Signal Construction Battalion. The horse's head represents Kentucky, the state of the unit's original activation. The telephone poles are symbolic of telephone construction, the type of work done by this unit; the two poles represent the second unit from one origin, the 29th Signal Construction Battalion.

The lion adapted from the arms of Normandy commemorates the unit's initial combat service. The mural crown with its five embattlements represents the total number of campaigns credited the organization for service in Europe during World War II. The pole arm is indicative of service in Vietnam, and its two outer scarlet blades allude to the Meritorious Unit Commendations awarded to the unit during that period.

DISTINCTIVE UNIT INSIGNIA

The distinctive unit insignia is the shield and motto of the coat of arms.

LINEAGE AND HONORS

RA
(active)

LINEAGE

Constituted 31 July 1942 in the Army of the United States as the 40th Signal Construction Battalion. Activated 21 September 1942 at Camp Campbell, Kentucky. Reorganized and redesignated 25 May 1945 as the 40th Signal Light Construction Battalion. Inactivated 25 January 1946 at Camp Gruber, Oklahoma.

Redesignated 31 August 1950 as the 40th Signal Construction Battalion. Activated 19 September 1950 at Camp Gordon, Georgia. Allotted 31 October 1950 to the Regular Army.

LINEAGES AND HERALDIC DATA 139

Reorganized and redesignated 1 October 1953 as the 40th Signal Battalion. Headquarters and Headquarters Company, 40th Signal Battalion, reorganized and redesignated 1 October 1981 as Headquarters and Headquarters Detachment, 40th Signal Battalion (organic elements inactivated 30 September 1981 at Fort Huachuca, Arizona).

Reorganized and redesignated 16 January 1998 as Headquarters and Headquarters Company, 40th Signal Battalion (organic elements concurrently activated at Fort Huachuca, Arizona).

CAMPAIGN PARTICIPATION CREDIT

World War II
  Normandy
  Northern France
  Rhineland
  Ardennes-Alsace
  Central Europe

Vietnam
  Counteroffensive, Phase II
  Counteroffensive, Phase III
  Tet Counteroffensive
  Counteroffensive, Phase IV
  Counteroffensive, Phase V
  Counteroffensive, Phase VI
  Tet 69/Counteroffensive
  Summer–Fall 1969
  Winter–Spring 1970
  Sanctuary Counteroffensive
  Counteroffensive, Phase VII
  Consolidation I
  Consolidation II
  Cease-Fire

Southwest Asia
  Defense of Saudi Arabia
  Liberation and Defense of Kuwait
  Cease-Fire

DECORATIONS

Meritorious Unit Commendation (Army), Streamer embroidered VIETNAM 1966–1967 (40th Signal Battalion [Construction] cited; DA GO 73, 1968)

Meritorious Unit Commendation (Army), Streamer embroidered VIETNAM 1967–1968 (Headquarters and Headquarters Detachment, 40th Signal Battalion, cited; DA GO 36, 1970)

Meritorious Unit Commendation (Army), Streamer embroidered SOUTHWEST ASIA 1990–1991 (40th Signal Battalion cited; DA GO 17, 1992)

40th SIGNAL BATTALION BIBLIOGRAPHY

Ackerman, Robert K. "Tactical Signalers Learn to Pack Light, Travel Right." *Signal* 54 (April 2000): 37–39.

Barnes, Samuel A. "We, Too, Serve Proudly." *Army Communicator* 2 (Summer 1977): 41–45.

Bergen, John D. *Military Communications: A Test for Technology.* United States Army in Vietnam. Washington, D.C.: Center of Military History, United States Army, 1986.

Davis, Richard, Jr. "Inside USACC's 'fire brigade.'" *Army Communicator* 7 (Summer 1982): 5–11.

Fitzgerald, Paula M. "Can You Hear Me Now?: 40th Signal Battalion Keeps CJTK-HOA Communications Up and Running." *Army Communicator* 28 (Summer 2003): 21–22. Discusses Company A's operations in the Horn of Africa.

"40th Battalion Members Are Off Again." *Army Communicator* 4 (Winter 1979): 60. Company B cited.

Hasenauer, Heike. "Grecian Firebolt." *Soldiers* 49 (September 1994): 37–40.

Huffman, Larry. "Signal Provides Communications Support for Bright Star Exercise." *Army Communicator* 21 (Fall 1996): 2–7.

Kennedy, Randy. "35th Signal Brigade." *Army Communicator* 13 (Winter 1988): 36–37.

Petersen, M. William. "Troops Phone Home Courtesy of 40th Signal Team." *Army Communicator* 28 (Summer 2003): 45–46. Team serving in Kuwait comprised members of Company B.

Raines, Rebecca Robbins. *Getting the Message Through: A Branch History of the U.S. Army Signal Corps.* Army Historical Series. Washington, D.C.: Center of Military History, United States Army, 1996.

Rienzi, Thomas M. *Communications-Electronics, 1962–1970.* Vietnam Studies. Washington, D.C.: Department of the Army, 1972.

Rippee, Tom. "Signal Infantry Soldiers." *Army Communicator* 6 (Summer 1981): 12–14. Company B cited. Describes combined arms training at Fort Huachuca.

Rolak, Bruno J. *History of the U.S. Army Communications Command (1964–1976).* Fort Huachuca, Ariz.: United States Army Communications Command, 1976.

Smith, Cornelius C., Jr. *Fort Huachuca: The Story of a Frontier Post.* Fort Huachuca, Ariz., 1978.

Stokes, Carol E., ed. *The U.S. Army Signal Corps in Operation Desert Shield/Desert Storm.* Fort Gordon, Ga.: Office of the Command Historian, U.S. Army Signal Center and Fort Gordon, 1994.

Stokes, Carol E., and Kathy R. Coker. "Getting the Message Through in the Persian Gulf War." *Army Communicator* 17 (Summer–Winter 1992): 17–25.

Thompson, George Raynor, and Dixie R. Harris. *The Signal Corps: The Outcome (Mid-1943 through 1945).* United States Army in World War II. Washington, D.C.: Office of the Chief of Military History, United States Army, 1966.

Volkert, Tim. "40th Signal Battalion Gets Hot at Hood." *Army Communicator* 26 (Fall 2001): 5–6.

―――. "Networking Soldiers." *Army Communicator* 26 (Fall 2001): 6–7. Features tactical satellite team of Company A.

HEADQUARTERS AND HEADQUARTERS DETACHMENT 41st SIGNAL BATTALION

HERALDIC ITEMS

COAT OF ARMS

Shield: Argent on a fess tenné an ogress throughout fimbriated of the first surmounted by two lightning flashes of the like, that issuing from dexter side point to base and on the sinister reversed, and in chief a fleur-de-lis of the second.

Crest: On a wreath of the colors argent and tenné an eagle head or gorged with a collar gules charged with a lightning flash of the first superimposed in base by a palm frond fesswise proper.

Motto: PAX NOSTRA FINIS (Peace Is Our Goal).

Symbolism: Orange and white are the colors traditionally associated with the Signal Corps. The fess crossing the field represents a wire or cable, and the black circle represents the soft iron diaphragm in telephonic equipment. The lightning flashes allude to the currents that cause the diaphragm to vibrate and, thus, transmit sound. The black circle symbolizes a sounding board for all types of signal apparatus and its construction and maintenance. The fleur-de-lis signifies combat service in Europe during World War II.

The eagle embodies strength and vigilance. It represents the organization's service in Europe during World War II and in Vietnam. Gold is emblematic of honor and high achievement. The red reflects valor and is the color of the Meritorious Unit Commendation; two were awarded to the unit for service in Vietnam. The lightning flash highlights electronic capabilities and quick response, and the palm refers to the tropical nature of Vietnam.

DISTINCTIVE UNIT INSIGNIA

The distinctive unit insignia is the shield of the coat of arms.

LINEAGE AND HONORS

RA
(active)

LINEAGE

Constituted 8 January 1943 in the Army of the United States as the 41st Signal Construction Battalion. Activated 25 January 1943 at Camp Forrest, Tennessee. Reorganized and redesignated 14 May 1945 as the 41st Signal Light Construction Battalion. Inactivated 7 December 1945 in Germany.

Redesignated 20 October 1950 as the 41st Signal Construction Battalion and allotted to the Regular Army. Activated 13 November 1950 at Camp Rucker, Alabama. Reorganized and redesignated 29 October 1953 as the 41st Signal Battalion. (Companies A, B, C, and D inactivated 1 March 1970 in Vietnam.) Headquarters and Headquarters Company, 41st Signal Battalion, inactivated 27 February 1972 at Fort Lewis, Washington.

Headquarters and Headquarters Company, 41st Signal Battalion, redesignated 1 July 1974 as Headquarters and Headquarters Detachment, 41st Signal Battalion, and activated in Korea.

CAMPAIGN PARTICIPATION CREDIT

World War II
- Normandy
- Northern France
- Rhineland
- Ardennes-Alsace
- Central Europe

Vietnam
- Defense
- Counteroffensive
- Counteroffensive, Phase II
- Counteroffensive, Phase III
- Tet Counteroffensive
- Counteroffensive, Phase IV
- Counteroffensive, Phase V
- Counteroffensive, Phase VI
- Tet 69/Counteroffensive
- Summer–Fall 1969
- Winter–Spring 1970
- Sanctuary Counteroffensive
- Counteroffensive, Phase VII
- Consolidation I
- Consolidation II

DECORATIONS

Meritorious Unit Commendation (Army), Streamer embroidered VIETNAM 1965–1966 (41st Signal Battalion [CA] cited; DA GO 20, 1967 as amended by DA GO 53, 1967)

Meritorious Unit Commendation (Army), Streamer embroidered VIETNAM 1967–1968 (Headquarters and Headquarters Company, 41st Signal Battalion, cited; DA GO 42, 1969)

41st SIGNAL BATTALION BIBLIOGRAPHY

Barnes, Samuel A. "We, Too, Serve Proudly." *Army Communicator* 2 (Summer 1977): 41–45.

Bergen, John D. *Military Communications: A Test for Technology.* United States Army in Vietnam. Washington, D.C.: Center of Military History, United States Army, 1986.

Castorina, Susan. "The Deung San Challenge: 'To Climb a Mountain With Pack'." *Army Communicator* 26 (Spring 2001): 30–31.

Coxwell, Richard L. "Quality Assurance: A Key to Success." *Army Communicator* 17 (Spring 1992): 38–40.

Fields, Robert. "Tower Climbing in 41st Signal Battalion." *Army Communicator* 27 (Spring 2002): 57–58.

41st Signal Construction Battalion. Baton Rouge: Army and Navy Publishing Company, 1952.

HHC, 41st Signal Battalion, 1971. Quinhon, South Vietnam, c. 1971.

History of the 41st Signal Battalion (Combat Area). Fort Ord, Calif., 1960.

Myer, Charles R. *Division-Level Communications, 1962–1973.* Vietnam Studies. Washington, D.C.: Department of the Army, 1982.

Raines, Rebecca Robbins. *Getting the Message Through: A Branch History of the U.S. Army Signal Corps.* Army Historical Series. Washington, D.C.: Center of Military History, United States Army, 1996.

Rienzi, Thomas M. *Communications-Electronics, 1962–1970.* Vietnam Studies. Washington, D.C.: Department of the Army, 1972.

Rolak, Bruno J. *History of the U.S. Army Communications Command (1964–1976).* Fort Huachuca, Ariz.: United States Army Communications Command, 1976.

Rolak, Bruno J., and George R. Thompson. *History of the United States Army Communications Command From Origin Through 1976.* Fort Huachuca, Ariz.: United States Army Communications Command, 1979.

St. Clair, Jim. "The Defense of Vung Chua Mountain." *Signal* 23 (March 1969): 10–12. Company B cited.

HEADQUARTERS AND HEADQUARTERS DETACHMENT
43d SIGNAL BATTALION
(Always Professional)

HERALDIC ITEMS

COAT OF ARMS

Shield: Per chevron sable and tenné, on a chevron argent between in chief two unicorn heads erased of the third and in base a Vietnamese building of the first, charged with a fountain, two lightning flashes azure, chevronwise.

Crest: On a wreath of the colors argent and sable, in front of two towers gules, two scimitars hilts to base saltirewise or. Between the points an annulet of bamboo proper charged with a fleur-de-lis azure.

Motto: TEAMWORK STRENGTH SPEED.

Symbolism: The unicorn, the heraldic animal with the body and head of a horse and the legs and feet of a deer, is strong as a horse and as swift as a deer. The two unicorns symbolize the teamwork, strength, and speed of the 43d Signal Battalion and its heavy construction duties. Because the unit was activated at Camp Crowder, Missouri, the horses further allude to the early history of the area when the starting points of the Santa Fe Trail and the Pony Express were in Missouri. The white chevron represents the lights and beacons of the Signal Corps. The Far Eastern structure and the fountain, a conventional heraldic representation of water, refer to the unit's overseas service, the buildings and rice paddies of Vietnam. The lightning flashes are symbolic of communications, and the four jagged points of the flashes represent the four battle honors of Ardennes-Alsace, Central Europe, Northern France, and the Rhineland. The colors black and white refer to the day and night vigilance of the unit, and orange is a color traditionally associated with the Signal Corps.

The towers, recalling medieval signal towers, symbolize World War II service in the Rhineland and Central Europe, and the fleur-de-lis recalls participation in campaigns in Northern France and Ardennes-Alsace. The many campaigns the unit saw during the Vietnam conflict are represented by the annulet of bamboo. The two scimitars represent the unit's more recent service in the defense of Saudi Arabia and Kuwait. Blue denotes integrity and worldwide service. Scarlet and gold signify courage and excellence, respectively.

DISTINCTIVE UNIT INSIGNIA

The distinctive unit insignia is the shield and motto of the coat of arms.

LINEAGE AND HONORS

LINEAGE

RA
(active)

Constituted 8 February 1944 in the Army of the United States as the 43d Signal Construction Battalion and activated at Camp Crowder, Missouri. Reorganized and redesignated 1 March 1944 as the 43d Signal Heavy Construction Battalion. Inactivated 28 May 1946 in Germany.

Redesignated 1 August 1966 as the 43d Signal Battalion; concurrently allotted to the Regular Army and activated in Vietnam. (Companies A, B, C, D, and E inactivated 1 March 1970 in Vietnam.) Headquarters and Headquarters Detachment, 43d Signal Battalion, inactivated 30 May 1971 in Vietnam.

Headquarters and Headquarters Detachment, 43d Signal Battalion, activated 1 July 1974 in Germany.

CAMPAIGN PARTICIPATION CREDIT

World War II
- Northern France
- Rhineland
- Ardennes-Alsace
- Central Europe

Vietnam
- Counteroffensive, Phase II
- Counteroffensive, Phase III
- Tet Counteroffensive
- Counteroffensive, Phase IV
- Counteroffensive, Phase V
- Counteroffensive, Phase VI
- Tet 69/Counteroffensive
- Summer–Fall 1969
- Winter–Spring 1970
- Sanctuary Counteroffensive
- Counteroffensive, Phase VII

Southwest Asia
- Defense of Saudi Arabia
- Liberation and Defense of Kuwait
- Cease-Fire

DECORATIONS

Meritorious Unit Commendation (Army), Streamer embroidered VIETNAM 1967–1968 (Headquarters and Headquarters Detachment, 43d Signal Battalion [Support], cited; DA GO 73, 1968)

Meritorious Unit Commendation (Army), Streamer embroidered VIETNAM 1968–1970 (Headquarters and Headquarters Detachment, 43d Signal Battalion, cited; DA GO 24, 1972)

43d SIGNAL BATTALION BIBLIOGRAPHY

Bergen, John D. *Military Communications: A Test for Technology.* United States Army in Vietnam. Washington, D.C.: Center of Military History, United States Army, 1986.

43d Signal Battalion History. N.p., 1974.

Hougham, Paul R. *43rd Signal Battalion. Unit History 1944–1974.* Heidelberg, Germany, 1978.

Johnson, Danny M. *Military Communications Supporting Peacekeeping Operations in the Balkans: The Signal Corps at Its Best.* Mannheim, Germany: Headquarters, 5th Signal Command, 2000.

Jones, Frederick I., and Walter W. Martin, eds. *History of the 43rd Signal Heavy Construction Battalion from Activation to V-J Day (7 February 1944 to 2 September 1945).* Frankfurt am Main, Germany: Schwanheim, Franz Jos. Henrich Druckerei und Verlag, 1945.

McKinney, John B. "They Communicate and Shoot." *Army* 18 (September 1968): 54–60.

Rienzi, Thomas M. *Communications-Electronics, 1962–1970.* Vietnam Studies. Washington, D.C.: Department of the Army, 1972.

44th SIGNAL BATTALION

HERALDIC ITEMS

COAT OF ARMS

Shield: Tenné, on a pale cottised between four lightning flashes in saltire argent a sword azure, the blade consisting of three jagged bolts of lightning.

Crest: On a wreath of the colors argent and tenné a tower proper superimposed by two scimitars saltirewise, hilts to base interlaced with a cross voided or.

Motto: OUTSTANDING.

Symbolism: Orange and white are the colors traditionally associated with the Signal Corps. The lightning bolts symbolize communications. The white broad area between two narrow bands refers to the 44th Signal Battalion's former mission as a signal construction battalion. The sword refers to both the tactical and support missions of the battalion and alludes to man's determination to defend freedom against oppression.

The tower represents World War II service in the Rhineland and Central Europe. The gold cross symbolizes the Republic of Vietnam Cross of Gallantry with Palm and four Meritorious Unit Commendations awarded to the unit for service in Vietnam and Southwest Asia. The scimitars refer to service in the defense of Saudi Arabia and Kuwait. Gold signifies excellence.

DISTINCTIVE UNIT INSIGNIA

The distinctive unit insignia is the shield and motto of the coat of arms.

LINEAGE AND HONORS

RA
(active)

LINEAGE

Constituted 3 February 1944 in the Army of the United States as the 44th Signal Construction Battalion. Redesignated 14 April 1944 as the 44th Signal Light Construction Battalion and activated at Camp Forrest, Tennessee. Reorganized and redesignated 26 June 1944 as the 44th Signal Heavy Construction Battalion. Inactivated 6 April 1946 in Japan.

Redesignated 1 August 1966 as the 44th Signal Battalion, allotted to the Regular Army, and activated in Vietnam. Inactivated 1 March 1970 in Vietnam. Activated 17 March 1972 in Vietnam. Inactivated 3 June 1972 at Oakland, California. Activated 16 March 1981 in Germany.

CAMPAIGN PARTICIPATION CREDIT

World War II
    Rhineland
    Central Europe
    Asiatic-Pacific Theater, Streamer without inscription

Vietnam
    Counteroffensive, Phase II
    Counteroffensive, Phase III
    Tet Counteroffensive
    Counteroffensive, Phase IV
    Counteroffensive, Phase V
    Counteroffensive, Phase VI
    Tet 69/Counteroffensive
    Summer–Fall 1969
    Winter–Spring 1970
    Consolidation II
    Cease-Fire

Southwest Asia
    Defense of Saudi Arabia
    Liberation and Defense of Kuwait
    Cease-Fire

DECORATIONS

Meritorious Unit Commendation (Army), Streamer embroidered VIETNAM 1967–1968 (44th Signal Battalion cited; DA GO 37, 1970)

Meritorious Unit Commendation (Army), Streamer embroidered VIETNAM 1968–1969 (44th Signal Battalion cited; DA GO 43, 1970)

Meritorious Unit Commendation (Army), Streamer embroidered SOUTHWEST ASIA 1990–1991 (44th Signal Battalion cited; DA GO 17, 1992)

Company C additionally entitled to:

Meritorious Unit Commendation (Army), Streamer embroidered VIETNAM 1966–1967 (Company C/44th, 39th Signal Battalion, cited; DA GO 54, 1968)

44th SIGNAL BATTALION BIBLIOGRAPHY

Bergen, John D. *Military Communications: A Test for Technology.* United States Army in Vietnam. Washington, D.C.: Center of Military History, United States Army, 1986.

Hitt, Joe. "7th Signal Brigade Joins 5th Signal Command." *Army Communicator* 7 (Winter 1982): 37.

Johnson, Danny M. *Military Communications Supporting Peacekeeping Operations in the Balkans: The Signal Corps at Its Best.* Mannheim, Germany: Headquarters, 5th Signal Command, 2000.

Rienzi, Thomas M. *Communications-Electronics, 1962–1970.* Vietnam Studies. Washington, D.C.: Department of the Army, 1972.

Rudd, Gordon W. *Humanitarian Intervention: Assisting the Iraqi Kurds in Operation Provide Comfort, 1991.* Washington, D.C.: Center of Military History, United States Army, 2004.

Stokes, Carol E., ed. *The U.S. Army Signal Corps in Operation Desert Shield/Desert Storm.* Fort Gordon, Ga.: Office of the Command Historian, U.S. Army Signal Center and Fort Gordon, 1994.

Stokes, Carol E., and Kathy R. Coker. "Getting the Message Through in the Persian Gulf War." *Army Communicator* 17 (Summer–Winter 1992): 17–25.

Thompson, James. "Bravo Sets Up Able Sentry." *Army Communicator* 24 (Winter II 1999): 24–25. Company B's service in Macedonia.

———. "Data Teams Provide Services." *Army Communicator* 24 (Winter II 1999): 27–28. Company A's service in Kosovo.

———. "44th Signal Battalion Supports Mission in Greece." *Army Communicator* 24 (Winter II 1999): 22–24.

———. "Switch 11 Soldiers Keep Connections in Macedonia." *Army Communicator* 24 (Winter II 1999): 29–30.

———. "Tactical-Satellite Team Provides Long-Distance Communications." *Army Communicator* 24 (Winter 1999): 30–31.

———. "Working Like Dawgs." *Army Communicator* 24 (Winter II 1999): 25–26. "Cable dogs" of the 44th Signal Battalion in Macedonia.

50th SIGNAL BATTALION

HERALDIC ITEMS

COAT OF ARMS

Shield: Tenné, on a bend double cottised potenté counterpotenté argent, a key sable.

Crest: On a wreath of the colors argent and tenné a broad arrow with point up divided fesswise gules and azure and charged in base with a fleur-de-lis or interlaced saltirewise by a machete and a bolo knife blades up of the first grips and pommels sable.

Motto: KEY TO COMMAND.

Symbolism: Orange and white are the colors traditionally associated with the Signal Corps. The white design is taken from the arms of Champagne where the battalion saw action during World War I and was awarded battle honors. The key from the coat of arms of the city of Lisieux is symbolic of Normandy, the key to the fortress of Europe, and represents battle honors earned during World War II.

The color blue and the gold fleur-de-lis refer to France, where the unit served during World Wars I and II. The arrow represents the assault landing in the Normandy campaign of World War II, and scarlet is the color of the Meritorious Unit Commendation awarded the organization for that action. The machete was suggested by the sugar cane crop of the Dominican Republic, and the color scarlet refers to the award of the Meritorious Unit Commendation streamer inscribed DOMINICAN REPUBLIC. The bolo knife, long associated with the Philippines, denotes service during the Philippine Insurrection.

DISTINCTIVE UNIT INSIGNIA

The distinctive unit insignia is the shield and motto of the coat of arms.

LINEAGE AND HONORS

RA
(active)

LINEAGE

Constituted 16 December 1899 in the Regular Army as Company H, Signal Corps, and organized in the Philippine Islands. Reorganized and redesignated 15 November 1913 as Telegraph Company H, Signal Corps. Consolidated 19 September 1916 with the 1st Provisional Company, Signal Corps (organized 21 May 1916 at Fort Sam Houston, Texas), and consolidated unit reorganized and redesignated as the 1st Telegraph Battalion. Redesignated 1 October 1917 as the 51st Telegraph

LINEAGES AND HERALDIC DATA 151

Battalion. Consolidated 8 March 1921 with the 52d Telegraph Battalion (organized 19 October 1916 at Columbus, New Mexico), and consolidated unit reorganized and redesignated as the 50th Signal Battalion. Inactivated 24 September 1921 at Fort Sam Houston, Texas.

Activated 1 July 1940 at Fort Sheridan, Illinois. Inactivated (less Company B) 15 December 1945 in Germany (Company B inactivated 23 April 1946 in Germany). Redesignated 27 September 1951 as the 50th Signal Battalion, Corps. Activated 24 October 1951 in Japan. Reorganized and redesignated 20 December 1954 as the 50th Signal Battalion. Reorganized and redesignated 15 May 1957 as the 50th Airborne Signal Battalion. Reorganized and redesignated 15 December 1958 as the 50th Signal Battalion.

CAMPAIGN PARTICIPATION CREDIT

Philippine Insurrection
   Streamer without inscription

World War I
   Oise-Aisne
   Meuse-Argonne
   Champagne 1918

World War II
   Normandy (with arrowhead)
   Northern France
   Rhineland
   Ardennes-Alsace
   Central Europe

Armed Forces Expeditions
   Dominican Republic

Southwest Asia
   Defense of Saudi Arabia
   Liberation and Defense of Kuwait

DECORATIONS

Meritorious Unit Commendation (Army), Streamer embroidered EUROPEAN THEATER (50th Signal Battalion cited; GO 18, VII Corps, 2 April 1945)

Meritorious Unit Commendation (Army), Streamer embroidered DOMINICAN REPUBLIC (50th Signal Battalion [Airborne Corps] cited; DA GO 20, 1967)

Meritorious Unit Commendation (Army), Streamer embroidered SOUTHWEST ASIA 1990–1991 (50th Signal Battalion cited; DA GO 12, 1994)

50th SIGNAL BATTALION BIBLIOGRAPHY

Branley, Bill. "Caber Communications." *Army Communicator* 3 (Winter 1978): 9. Field exercise Caber Dragon II.

Brawley, John. *Anyway, We Won*. Marcelline, Mo.: Walsworth Publishing Company, 1988.

Guidotti, John A. "The 35th Signal's New Go-to-War Concept." *Army Communicator* 16 (Fall–Winter 1991): 20–23.

Kennedy, Randy. "35th Signal Brigade." *Army Communicator* 12 (Fall 1987): 30–33.

Raines, Rebecca Robbins. *Getting the Message Through: A Branch History of the U.S. Army Signal Corps*. Army Historical Series. Washington, D.C.: Center of Military History, United States Army, 1996.

Scheips, Paul J. *The Role of Federal Military Forces in Domestic Disorders, 1945–1992*. Washington, D.C.: Center of Military History, United States Army, 2005.

Stokes, Carol E., ed. *The U.S. Army Signal Corps in Operation Desert Shield/Desert Storm*. Fort Gordon, Ga.: Office of the Command Historian, U.S. Army Signal Center and Fort Gordon, 1994.

Stokes, Carol E., and Kathy R. Coker. "Getting the Message Through in the Persian Gulf War." *Army Communicator* 17 (Summer–Winter 1992): 17–25.

The Story of the 50th Signal Battalion from Iceland to Germany. Paris: P. Dupont, 1945.

Terrett, Dulany. *The Signal Corps: The Emergency*. United States Army in World War II. Washington, D.C.: Office of the Chief of Military History, Department of the Army, 1956.

Thompson, George Raynor, and Dixie R. Harris. *The Signal Corps: The Outcome (Mid-1943 through 1945)*. United States Army in World War II. Washington, D.C.: Office of the Chief of Military History, United States Army, 1966.

Thompson, George Raynor, Dixie R. Harris, Pauline M. Oakes, and Dulany Terrett. *The Signal Corps: The Test (December 1941 to July 1943)*. United States Army in World War II. Washington, D.C.: Office of the Chief of Military History, Department of the Army, 1957.

51st SIGNAL BATTALION

HERALDIC ITEMS

COAT OF ARMS

Shield: Tenné, on a bend argent four telegraph poles in pale cross arm normal to bend sable.
Crest: On a wreath of the colors argent and tenné the right winged foot of Mercury argent.
Motto: SEMPER CONSTANS (Always Constant).
Symbolism: Orange and white are the colors traditionally associated with the Signal Corps. The bend is taken from the arms of Lorraine and St. Mihiel and represents two of the campaigns in which the unit participated during World War I. The four telegraph poles represent the engagements of the battalion during World War I.

The winged foot of Mercury represents rapidity in delivering messages.

DISTINCTIVE UNIT INSIGNIA

The distinctive unit insignia is the shield and motto of the coat of arms.

LINEAGE AND HONORS

RA
(active)

LINEAGE

Constituted 1 July 1916 in the Regular Army as the 5th Telegraph Battalion, Signal Corps. Activated 12 July 1917 at Monmouth Park, New Jersey. Redesignated 1 October 1917 as the 55th Telegraph Battalion.

Reorganized and redesignated 18 March 1921 as the 51st Signal Battalion. Reorganized and redesignated 1 March 1945 as the 51st Signal Operation Battalion. Reorganized and redesignated 8 September 1950 as the 51st Signal Battalion, Corps. Reorganized and redesignated 13 February 1955 as the 51st Signal Battalion.

CAMPAIGN PARTICIPATION CREDIT

World War I
    Lorraine 1918
    St. Mihiel
    Meuse-Argonne

World War II
    Sicily (with arrowhead)
    Naples-Foggia
    Rome-Arno
    North Apennines
    Po Valley

Korean War
    UN Defensive
    UN Offensive
    CCF Intervention
    First UN Counteroffensive
    CCF Spring Offensive
    UN Summer–Fall Offensive
    Second Korean Winter
    Korea, Summer–Fall 1952
    Third Korean Winter
    Korea, Summer 1953

Southwest Asia
    Defense of Saudi Arabia
    Liberation and Defense of Kuwait
    Cease-Fire

DECORATIONS

Meritorious Unit Commendation (Army), Streamer embroidered EUROPEAN THEATER (51st Signal Battalion cited; GO 129, Fifth Army, 23 December 1944)

Meritorious Unit Commendation (Army), Streamer embroidered KOREA 1950–1951 (51st Signal Battalion, Corps, cited; DA GO 35, 1952)

Meritorious Unit Commendation (Army), Streamer embroidered KOREA 1953–1954 (51st Signal Battalion cited; DA GO 14, 1955)

Republic of Korea Presidential Unit Citation, Streamer embroidered KOREA 1950–1953 (51st Signal Battalion cited; DA GO 74, 1953)

Company B additionally entitled to:

Meritorious Unit Commendation (Army), Streamer embroidered KOREA 1952 (Company B, 51st Signal Battalion [Corps], cited; DA GO 28, 1953)

51st SIGNAL BATTALION BIBLIOGRAPHY

Adcock, Thomas G., and Edward R. Baldwin, Jr. "Combined Signal Operations, Eighth U.S. Army CPX." *Signal* 27 (May 1973): 13–15.

"Field Training of the Fifty-First Signal Battalion." *Signal Corps Bulletin* 81 (November–December 1934): 71.

51st Signal Battalion. *History of the Fifty-First Signal Battalion, 1917–1978.* 51st Signal Battalion, 1978.

―――. *History of the Fifty-First Signal Battalion, Signal Corps, United States Army.* N.p., 1936.

―――. *History of the Fifty-First Signal Battalion, Signal Corps, United States Army.* Fort Monmouth, N.J., 1949.

―――. *History of the Fifty-First Signal Battalion, Signal Corps, United States Army, January 1, 1937.* Fort Monmouth, N.J., 1937.

———. *History of the Fifty-First Signal Battalion, Signal Corps, United States Army, January 1, 1938*. Fort Monmouth, N.J., 1938.

———. *History of the Fifty-First Signal Battalion, Signal Corps, United States Army, January 1, 1939*. Fort Monmouth, N.J., 1939.

———. *History of the Fifty-First Signal Battalion, Signal Corps, United States Army, January 1, 1940*. Fort Monmouth, N.J., 1940.

———. *History of the Fifty-First Signal Battalion, World War I-World War II-Korean Conflict, Signal Corps, United States Army*. Camp Red Cloud, Korea, 1959.

Haynes, Anthony. "Always Constant." *Signal* 19 (June 1965): 38–39.

Ingles, H. C. "The Fifty-First Signal Battalion." *Signal Corps Bulletin* 84 (May–June 1935): 2–10.

Olmstead, Dawson. "Organization Day of the Fifty-First Signal Battalion." *Signal Corps Bulletin* 105 (July–September 1939): 108–10.

Sherrill, S. H. "The Fifty-First Signal Battalion and the Tests of the Proposed Infantry Division." *Signal Corps Bulletin* 101 (July–September 1938): 1–13.

Stokes, Carol E., ed. *The U.S. Army Signal Corps in Operation Desert Shield/Desert Storm*. Fort Gordon, Ga.: Office of the Command Historian, U.S. Army Signal Center and Fort Gordon, 1994.

Stokes, Carol E., and Kathy R. Coker. "Getting the Message Through in the Persian Gulf War." *Army Communicator* 17 (Summer–Winter 1992): 17–25.

Storms, Harry E. "The Participation of the 51st Signal Battalion in the First Army Maneuvers, 1939." *Signal Corps Bulletin* 107 (January–March 1940): 5–17.

Terrett, Dulany. *The Signal Corps: The Emergency*. United States Army in World War II. Washington, D.C.: Office of the Chief of Military History, Department of the Army, 1956.

Thompson, George Raynor, and Dixie R. Harris. *The Signal Corps: The Outcome (Mid-1943 through 1945)*. United States Army in World War II. Washington, D.C.: Office of the Chief of Military History, United States Army, 1966.

HEADQUARTERS AND HEADQUARTERS DETACHMENT 52d SIGNAL BATTALION

HERALDIC ITEMS

COAT OF ARMS

Shield: Tenné, on a pale argent issuing from base a radio tower of the field emitting four lightning flashes counterchanged.

Crest: On a wreath of the colors argent and tenné a triangle azure within a bamboo border proper, three bars wavy argent, all in front of a flaming torch sable flamant of the second.

Motto: WE TRANSMIT.

Symbolism: Orange and white are the colors traditionally associated with the Signal Corps. The radio tower and lightning flashes represent the construction function and operation of the message center, the early mission of the battalion.

The crest commemorates the battalion's mission of support in the Mekong Delta of Vietnam, as represented by the triangle with bamboo border. The wavy blue and white bars refer to the water of the area. The torch alludes to guidance and the four tongues of flame to the four battle honors earned by the battalion during World War II.

DISTINCTIVE UNIT INSIGNIA

The distinctive unit insignia is the shield and motto of the coat of arms.

LINEAGE AND HONORS

RA
(active)

LINEAGE

Constituted 18 October 1927 in the Regular Army as the 52d Signal Battalion. Activated 10 February 1941 at Fort Sam Houston, Texas. Inactivated 25 January 1949 in Korea. Activated 1 August 1966 in Vietnam. Inactivated 13 October 1971 at Fort Lewis, Washington.

Headquarters and Headquarters Detachment, 52d Signal Battalion, activated 1 July 1974 in Germany.

CAMPAIGN PARTICIPATION CREDIT

World War II
    New Guinea
    Leyte
    Luzon
    Southern Philippines

Vietnam
    Counteroffensive, Phase II
    Counteroffensive, Phase III
    Tet Counteroffensive
    Counteroffensive, Phase IV
    Counteroffensive, Phase V
    Counteroffensive, Phase VI
    Tet 69/Counteroffensive
    Summer–Fall 1969
    Winter–Spring 1970
    Sanctuary Counteroffensive
    Counteroffensive, Phase VII
    Consolidation I

DECORATIONS

Philippine Presidential Unit Citation, Streamer embroidered 17 OCTOBER 1944 TO 4 JULY 1945 (52d Signal Battalion [Separate] cited; DA GO 47, 1950)

52d SIGNAL BATTALION BIBLIOGRAPHY

Bergen, John D. *Military Communications: A Test for Technology*. United States Army in Vietnam. Washington, D.C.: Center of Military History, United States Army, 1986.

Derr, Steve E. *52nd Signal Battalion, 1927–1977: A Unit History*. Vaihingen, West Germany, 1978.

Rienzi, Thomas M. *Communications-Electronics, 1962–1970*. Vietnam Studies. Washington, D.C.: Department of the Army, 1972.

Rolak, Bruno J. *History of the U.S. Army Communications Command (1964–1976)*. Fort Huachuca, Ariz.: United States Army Communications Command, 1976.

Rolak, Bruno J., and George R. Thompson. *History of the United States Army Communications Command From Origin Through 1976*. Fort Huachuca, Ariz.: United States Army Communications Command, 1979.

Terrett, Dulany. *The Signal Corps: The Emergency*. United States Army in World War II. Washington, D.C.: Office of the Chief of Military History, Department of the Army, 1956.

Thompson, George Raynor, and Dixie R. Harris. *The Signal Corps: The Outcome (Mid-1943 through 1945)*. United States Army in World War II. Washington, D.C.: Office of the Chief of Military History, United States Army, 1966.

Thompson, George Raynor, Dixie R. Harris, Pauline M. Oakes, and Dulany Terrett. *The Signal Corps: The Test (December 1941 to July 1943)*. United States Army in World War II. Washington, D.C.: Office of the Chief of Military History, Department of the Army, 1957.

"*We Transmit*": *A History of the 52d Signal Battalion, 1927–1974*. N.p., 1974.

53d SIGNAL BATTALION

HERALDIC ITEMS

COAT OF ARMS

Shield: Tenné, in base a signal fire and smoke proper.
Crest: On a wreath of the colors or and tenné issuing from a millrind gules, three lightning flashes of the first, all surmounting an annulet of bamboo proper.
Motto: FIRST, LAST AND ALWAYS.
Symbolism: Orange and white are the colors traditionally associated with the Signal Corps. The bonfire and curling smoke symbolize one of the primitive forms of signaling.

The millrind, a symbol of strength, represents the invaluable support and skill in communications that the battalion contributed to the Allied assaults, first in Algeria and later in other actions in North Africa and Italy during World War II. The flashes denote skill in modern communications and speedy response to mission requirements. Participation in campaigns in Vietnam is recalled by the annulet of bamboo, signifying also unity and cooperative action. Scarlet and gold denote courage and excellence, respectively.

DISTINCTIVE UNIT INSIGNIA

The distinctive unit insignia is the shield and a variation of the motto of the coat of arms.

LINEAGE AND HONORS

RA
(inactive)

LINEAGE

Constituted 18 October 1927 in the Regular Army as the 53d Signal Battalion. Activated 1 June 1941 at Camp Bowie, Texas. Inactivated 30 September 1945 in Italy. Activated 21 September 1954 at Fort Hood, Texas. Inactivated 23 June 1971 at Fort Lewis, Washington.

CAMPAIGN PARTICIPATION CREDIT

World War II
    Algeria–French Morocco (with arrowhead)
    Tunisia
    Sicily (with arrowhead)
    Naples-Foggia
    Rome-Arno
    North Apennines
    Po Valley

Vietnam
    Counteroffensive
    Counteroffensive, Phase II
    Counteroffensive, Phase III
    Tet Counteroffensive
    Counteroffensive, Phase IV
    Counteroffensive, Phase V
    Counteroffensive, Phase VI
    Tet 69/Counteroffensive
    Summer–Fall 1969
    Winter–Spring 1970
    Sanctuary Counteroffensive
    Counteroffensive, Phase VII

DECORATIONS

Meritorious Unit Commendation (Army), Streamer embroidered EUROPEAN THEATER (53d Signal Battalion cited; GO 14, II Corps, 11 May 1945)

Meritorious Unit Commendation (Army), Streamer embroidered VIETNAM 1966–1967 (53d Signal Battalion [Corps] cited; DA GO 17, 1968, as amended by DA GO 1, 1969)

Meritorious Unit Commendation (Army), Streamer embroidered VIETNAM 1967–1968 (53d Signal Battalion [Corps] cited; DA GO 56, 1969)

Meritorious Unit Commendation (Army), Streamer embroidered VIETNAM 1968–1969 (53d Signal Battalion cited; DA GO 48, 1971)

53d SIGNAL BATTALION BIBLIOGRAPHY

Bergen, John D. *Military Communications: A Test for Technology*. United States Army in Vietnam. Washington, D.C.: Center of Military History, United States Army, 1986.

53d Signal Battalion (Corps): Italy via North Africa; Texas to Tunisia; Sicily and Italy; Reactivation. Fort Hood, Tex., 1956.

Rienzi, Thomas M. *Communications-Electronics, 1962–1970*. Vietnam Studies. Washington, D.C.: Department of the Army, 1972.

Scheips, Paul J. *The Role of Federal Military Forces in Domestic Disorders, 1945–1992*. Washington, D.C.: Center of Military History, United States Army, 2005.

Thompson, George Raynor, and Dixie R. Harris. *The Signal Corps: The Outcome (Mid-1943 through 1945)*. United States Army in World War II. Washington, D.C.: Office of the Chief of Military History, United States Army, 1966.

Thompson, George Raynor, Dixie R. Harris, Pauline M. Oakes, and Dulany Terrett. *The Signal Corps: The Test (December 1941 to July 1943)*. United States Army in World War II. Washington, D.C.: Office of the Chief of Military History, Department of the Army, 1957.

HEADQUARTERS AND HEADQUARTERS DETACHMENT
54th SIGNAL BATTALION

HERALDIC ITEMS

COAT OF ARMS

Shield: Per bend tenné and azure, a bend wavy double cottised potenté counterpotenté argent.

Crest: On a wreath of the colors argent and tenné a sword bendwise sinister proper, hilted or surmounting in bend a lightning flash of the second, all in front of a section of bamboo palewise buff leaved of thirteen vert.

Motto: COMMAND CONTROL.

Symbolism: Orange and white are the colors traditionally associated with the Signal Corps. The wavy diagonal band, representing the Rhine River, refers to the battalion's combat participation in the Central European area during World War II. Blue and the patterned bands flanking the central band are taken from the arms of Ardennes. The potenté pattern also represents telegraph poles and refers to the unit's signal function.

During the Vietnam conflict the organization provided signal support, represented by the lightning flash, to the I Field Force, Vietnam. The sword is from the shoulder sleeve insignia of the supported organization and is indicative of combat support and the award of the Republic of Vietnam Cross of Gallantry to the battalion. The bamboo also refers to South Vietnam and is divided into three segments to represent the three Meritorious Unit Commendations awarded to the unit. The leaves represent the thirteen campaigns in that country in which the battalion participated.

DISTINCTIVE UNIT INSIGNIA

The distinctive unit insignia is the shield and motto of the coat of arms.

LINEAGE AND HONORS

RA
(active)

LINEAGE

Constituted 18 October 1927 in the Regular Army as the 54th Signal Battalion. Activated 10 February 1941 at Fort Ord, California. Inactivated 29 December 1945 at Camp Kilmer, New Jersey.

Activated 1 August 1962 at Fort Hood, Texas. Inactivated 17 February 1971 at Fort Lewis, Washington. Activated 16 June 1980 at Fort Hood, Texas. Inactivated 15 April 1989 at Fort Hood, Texas.

Headquarters and Headquarters Company, 54th Signal Battalion, reorganized and redesignated 1 March 1991 as Headquarters and Headquarters Detachment, 54th Signal Battalion, and activated in Saudi Arabia.

CAMPAIGN PARTICIPATION CREDIT

World War II
    Ardennes-Alsace
    Central Europe

Vietnam
    Defense
    Counteroffensive
    Counteroffensive, Phase II
    Counteroffensive, Phase III
    Tet Counteroffensive
    Counteroffensive, Phase IV
    Counteroffensive, Phase V
    Counteroffensive, Phase VI
    Tet 69/Counteroffensive
    Summer–Fall 1969
    Winter–Spring 1970
    Sanctuary Counteroffensive
    Counteroffensive, Phase VII

Southwest Asia
    Liberation and Defense of Kuwait
    Cease-Fire

DECORATIONS

Meritorious Unit Commendation (Army), Streamer embroidered VIETNAM 1965–1966 (54th Signal Battalion [Corps] cited; DA GO 17, 1968)

Meritorious Unit Commendation (Army), Streamer embroidered VIETNAM 1966–1967 (54th Signal Battalion [Corps] cited; DA GO 17, 1968)

Meritorious Unit Commendation (Army), Streamer embroidered VIETNAM 1967–1968 (54th Signal Battalion cited; DA GO 54, 1968)

Army Superior Unit Award, Streamer embroidered 1996 (Headquarters and Headquarters Detachment, 54th Signal Battalion, cited; DA GO 25, 2001)

Republic of Vietnam Cross of Gallantry with Palm, Streamer embroidered VIETNAM 1965–1971 (54th Signal Battalion cited; DA GO 54, 1974)

54th SIGNAL BATTALION BIBLIOGRAPHY

Ackerman, Robert K. "Tactical Signalers Learn to Pack Light, Travel Right." *Signal* 54 (April 2000): 37–39.

Bergen, John D. *Military Communications: A Test for Technology.* United States Army in Vietnam. Washington, D.C.: Center of Military History, United States Army, 1986.

54th Signal Battalion Association. *54th Signal Battalion Alumni Directory.* Three Lakes, Wisc.: 54th Signal Battalion Association, 1991.

⎯⎯⎯. *54th Signal Battalion Alumni Directory.* 2d ed. Three Lakes, Wisc.: 54th Signal Battalion Association, 1994.

Gunnels, William F., Jr., comp. "Carrier System Platoon, B Company, 54th Signal Battalion, 1944–1945." MS, June 1997, copy available at the U.S. Army Military History Institute, Carlisle, Pa.

Hall, David. "Getting the Word from Corps Commander to Field Units." *Army Digest* 24 (March 1969): 64–65.

Kennedy, Randy. "3rd Signal Brigade." *Army Communicator* 12 (Summer 1987): 52–53.

"Mission Accomplished." A Summary of Military Operations of the XVIII Corps (Airborne) in the European Theater of Operations, 1944–1945. Schwerin, Germany, 1945.

Pace, Emily Charlotte. "USAISC, Before, During and After Desert Storm." *Army Communicator* 16 (Summer 1991): 13–17.

Raduege, Harry, Jr., Roland LeSieur, and Michael Gasaspo. "Shifting Communications in Saudi Sands: How U.S. Central Command Communicators Quickly Relocated and Reestablished Communications Systems in Face of Terrorist Threats." *Army Communicator* 22 (Fall 1997): 13–15.

Raines, Rebecca Robbins. *Getting the Message Through: A Branch History of the U.S. Army Signal Corps.* Army Historical Series. Washington, D.C.: Center of Military History, United States Army, 1996.

Rienzi, Thomas M. *Communications-Electronics, 1962–1970.* Vietnam Studies. Washington, D.C.: Department of the Army, 1972.

Stokes, Carol E., ed. *The U.S. Army Signal Corps in Operation Desert Shield/Desert Storm.* Fort Gordon, Ga.: Office of the Command Historian, U.S. Army Signal Center and Fort Gordon, 1994.

Thompson, George Raynor, and Dixie R. Harris. *The Signal Corps: The Outcome (Mid-1943 through 1945).* United States Army in World War II. Washington, D.C.: Office of the Chief of Military History, United States Army, 1966.

Thompson, George Raynor, Dixie R. Harris, Pauline M. Oakes, and Dulany Terrett. *The Signal Corps: The Test (December 1941 to July 1943).* United States Army in World War II. Washington, D.C.: Office of the Chief of Military History, Department of the Army, 1957.

Ward, Jim. "Desert Signal Unit Underpins Southwest Asia Security." *Army Communicator* 23 (Winter 1998): 56–57.

HEADQUARTERS AND HEADQUARTERS DETACHMENT 56th SIGNAL BATTALION

HERALDIC ITEMS

COAT OF ARMS

Shield: Tenné, on a bend argent three pellets and a billet sable.
Crest: On a wreath of the colors argent and tenné the head of Mercury couped proper.
Motto: DEBIT VERBUM TRANSIRE (The Message Must Go Through).
Symbolism: Orange and white are the colors traditionally associated with the Signal Corps. Black denotes dependability and stability and, in conjunction with white, denotes day and night capabilities. The three pellets and billet suggest the letter "V" in Morse code and refer to the "V" symbolizing victory for the democracies.

Mercury was the messenger of the gods in Greek and Roman mythology and personifies the unit's mission.

DISTINCTIVE UNIT INSIGNIA

The distinctive unit insignia is the shield, crest, and motto of the coat of arms.

LINEAGE AND HONORS

RA
(active)

LINEAGE

Constituted 18 October 1927 in the Regular Army as the 56th Signal Battalion. Activated 1 February 1941 at Fort Jackson, South Carolina. Inactivated 8 March 1946 at Camp Kilmer, New Jersey.

Headquarters and Headquarters Detachment activated 16 October 1991 in Panama.

CAMPAIGN PARTICIPATION CREDIT

World War II
    Normandy (with arrowhead)
    Northern France
    Rhineland
    Ardennes-Alsace
    Central Europe

DECORATIONS

Meritorious Unit Commendation (Army), Streamer embroidered EUROPEAN THEATER (56th Signal Battalion cited; GO 52, V Corps, 11 May 1945)

56th SIGNAL BATTALION BIBLIOGRAPHY

Editors of Army Times. *A History of the U.S. Army Signal Corps*. New York: G. P. Putnam's Sons, 1961.

4th Anniversary, 56th Signal Battalion. c. 1945.

Henry, Cora. "Gallant Warriors: 93d Signal Brigade Trains Soldiers for Missions." *Army Communicator* 23 (Fall 1998): 4–6.

Thien, Carl. *56th Signal Battalion: Before the Thunder*. Spring Hill, Fla.: Sir Speedy Printers, 1992.

Thompson, George Raynor, and Dixie R. Harris. *The Signal Corps: The Outcome (Mid-1943 through 1945)*. United States Army in World War II. Washington, D.C.: Office of the Chief of Military History, United States Army, 1966.

57th SIGNAL BATTALION

HERALDIC ITEMS

COAT OF ARMS

Shield: Per fess argent and tenné, an antenna of four wires in the shape of a mascle counterchanged.

Crest: On a wreath of the colors argent and tenné a fleur-de-lis of the first, the tops of the three petals terminating in arrowheads and the lower ends conjoined and convoluted, and two lightning bolts azure issuing from the binding ring and extending upward and between the petals and conjoined with two lower points of the center arrowhead and the inner lower points of the outer two arrowheads.

Motto: VINCIMUS SPATIUM (We Conquer Space).

Symbolism: Orange and white are the colors traditionally associated with the Signal Corps. The four wires forming the antenna symbolize the nature of the activities of the organization.

The fleur-de-lis with the three petals terminating in arrowheads refers to the three assault landings in which the unit participated during World War II. The center arrowhead alludes to the landing in Southern France and the two outer petals with the two lightning bolts (which simulate the seed pods of the Florentine fleur-de-lis) to the Naples-Foggia and Rome-Arno campaigns in Italy. The lightning bolts also are symbolic of communication.

DISTINCTIVE UNIT INSIGNIA

The distinctive unit insignia is the shield and motto of the coat of arms.

LINEAGE AND HONORS

RA
(active)

LINEAGE

Constituted 18 October 1927 in the Regular Army as the 57th Signal Battalion. Activated 10 February 1941 at Camp Edwards, Massachusetts. Inactivated 29 September 1945 in Germany. Activated 16 May 1966 at Fort Hood, Texas.

CAMPAIGN PARTICIPATION CREDIT

World War II
   Naples-Foggia (with arrowhead)
   Anzio (with arrowhead)
   Rome-Arno
   Southern France (with arrowhead)
   Rhineland
   Ardennes-Alsace
   Central Europe

Southwest Asia
   Defense of Saudi Arabia
   Liberation and Defense of Kuwait
   Cease-Fire

DECORATIONS

Meritorious Unit Commendation (Army), Streamer embroidered SOUTHWEST ASIA 1990–1991 (57th Signal Battalion cited; DA GO 12, 1994)

57th SIGNAL BATTALION BIBLIOGRAPHY

Burrow, Byron L. "MSE Support of Corps Combat Operations." *Army Communicator* 16 (Fall–Winter 1991): 28–29.

Harley, William B., and Hale Mason, eds. *History of the 57th Signal Battalion, World War II, February 10, 1941 to September 29, 1945: North Africa-Italy-Europe, Salerno-Anzio-Southern France.* N.p.: W. B. Harley, 1984.

Hicks-Callaway, Vanessa. "Signal Unit Provides Eyes and Ears in 'Triple Strike.'" *Army Communicator* 23 (Spring 1998): 44. Company A cited.

Kennedy, Randy. "3rd Signal Brigade." *Army Communicator* 12 (Summer 1987): 52–53.

Martin, Patrick, Rosielynn Banzon, and John Cox. "Hood Signaleers Test Teamwork in Road Runner '00 Exercise." *Army Communicator* 25 (Spring 2000): 39–41.

Scheips, Paul J. *The Role of Federal Military Forces in Domestic Disorders, 1945–1992.* Washington, D.C.: Center of Military History, United States Army, 2005.

Stallings, Caroline. "3d Signal Brigade Provides 'Voice of Phantom Warriors' in 5-Month Exercise Series." *Army Communicator* 26 (Fall 2001): 16–18.

Stokes, Carol E., ed. *The U.S. Army Signal Corps in Operation Desert Shield/Desert Storm.* Fort Gordon, Ga.: Office of the Command Historian, U.S. Army Signal Center and Fort Gordon, 1994.

Stokes, Carol E., and Kathy R. Coker. "Getting the Message Through in the Persian Gulf War." *Army Communicator* 17 (Summer–Winter 1992): 17–25.

Thompson, George Raynor, and Dixie R. Harris. *The Signal Corps: The Outcome (Mid-1943 through 1945).* United States Army in World War II. Washington, D.C.: Office of the Chief of Military History, United States Army, 1966.

Windon, Michael Leon. "3d Signal Brigade Conquers Voice, Data and Video." *Army Communicator* 28 (Summer 2003): 22–23.

HEADQUARTERS AND HEADQUARTERS DETACHMENT 58th SIGNAL BATTALION

HERALDIC ITEMS

COAT OF ARMS

Shield: Per chevron reversed tenné and sable, issuant in base between two fountains a splice of three wires spread at fess point per chevron reversed and per pale throughout. In chief issuant from fess point two lightning flashes point to chief argent.

Crest: On a wreath of the colors argent and tenné a roundel per pale azure and gules charged with a mullet of the first between the handles of two barongs saltirewise proper, all surmounting a panache of three varieties of bird of paradise distinguishing feathers or and azure.

Motto: SPIRIT, SPEED, STRENGTH.

Symbolism: Orange and white are the colors traditionally associated with the Signal Corps. The two fountains (white and blue wavy discs) in base denote the unit's participation in two campaigns in the Pacific theater during World War II. The spliced wires suggest the battalion's particular function of cable construction, and crossing the black into the bright orange signifies the light of information brought by communications. The two lightning flashes represent signals.

The barong, a long knife of the Moros, a native people of the Philippines, and the feathers of the bird of paradise, a species indigenous to New Guinea, represent the unit's World War II campaign participation on Luzon and New Guinea. The star and the red and blue areas of the roundel refer to the Meritorious Unit Commendation and the Philippine Presidential Unit Citation, the unit's two decorations.

DISTINCTIVE UNIT INSIGNIA

The distinctive unit insignia is the shield and motto of the coat of arms.

LINEAGE AND HONORS

RA
(active)

LINEAGE

Constituted 18 October 1927 in the Regular Army as the 58th Signal Battalion. Activated 10 February 1941 at Camp Peay, Tennessee. Reorganized and redesignated 25 September 1949 as the 58th Signal Battalion, Corps. Inactivated 26 June 1950 in Japan.

Redesignated 2 March 1967 as the 58th Signal Battalion. Activated 26 May 1967 at Fort Lewis, Washington. Inactivated (less Company B) 1 February 1980 at Fort Lewis, Washington (Company B concurrently inactivated at Fort Gordon, Georgia).

Headquarters and Headquarters Company, 58th Signal Battalion, reorganized and redesignated 16 October 1992 as Headquarters and Headquarters Detachment, 58th Signal Battalion, and activated in Japan.

CAMPAIGN PARTICIPATION CREDIT

World War II
  New Guinea
  Luzon

DECORATIONS

Meritorious Unit Commendation (Army), Streamer embroidered LUZON (58th Signal Battalion [less Companies A and C] cited; GO 160, I Corps, 27 July 1945)

Philippine Presidential Unit Citation, Streamer embroidered 17 OCTOBER 1944 TO 4 JULY 1945 (58th Signal Battalion [Special] cited; DA GO 47, 1950)

58th SIGNAL BATTALION BIBLIOGRAPHY

Alessi, Anthony. "58th Signal Battalion Soldiers Learn Jungle Skills with Marines." *Army Communicator* 25 (Fall 2000): 33–34.

Fuentez, Barry. "Rollin' Rollin' Rollin' on the River...." *Army Communicator* 5 (Winter 1980): 56–57. Company B cited. Adventure training exercise.

Kille, Dale. "58th Signal Battalion Keeps Okinawa Warfighters Connected." *Army Communicator* 23 (Summer 1998): 43.

McMillan, Brett. "Signal Soldiers Challenge Northern Training Area Field-Skills Course." *Army Communicator* 24 (Winter 1999): 25–26.

———. "Team 58 Connects Okinawa." *Army Communicator* 24 (Winter 1999): 45.

Smith, Robert Ross. *Triumph in the Philippines*. United States Army in World War II. Washington, D.C.: Office of the Chief of Military History, Department of the Army, 1963.

Thompson, George Raynor, and Dixie R. Harris. *The Signal Corps: The Outcome (Mid-1943 through 1945)*. United States Army in World War II. Washington, D.C.: Office of the Chief of Military History, United States Army, 1966.

Thompson, Keith. "58th Signal Battalion Trains to Defend Fort Buckner." *Army Communicator* 24 (Spring 1999): 46–47.

———. "Signal Soldiers Take Plunge in Marine Course." *Army Communicator* 24 (Winter 1999): 29–30.

HEADQUARTERS AND HEADQUARTERS DETACHMENT
59th SIGNAL BATTALION

HERALDIC ITEMS

COAT OF ARMS

Shield: Argent, issuant from base a demisphere azure gridlined of the first, debruised by a pile twice bevilled tenné, overall a polestar of the first superimposed by a fleur-de-lis of the second.

Crest: On a wreath of the colors argent and azure five lightning flashes in point azure, overall a lion's face or.

Motto: VOICE OF THE ARCTIC.

Symbolism: Orange and white are the colors traditionally associated with the Signal Corps. The pile simulating a lightning bolt is indicative of communications and electronics while representing speed and suggesting the point of origin in the "North." The polestar is symbolic of the North Star and underscores the unit's Arctic location. The fleur-de-lis commemorates the battalion's first battle honor and baptism of fire in France.

The colors blue and gold are adapted from the state flag of Alaska. The five lightning flashes honor the battalion's World War II campaigns. The lion, a symbol of strength and courage, reflects the European Theater of Operations and the unit's World War II location and heritage.

DISTINCTIVE UNIT INSIGNIA

The distinctive unit insignia is the shield and motto of the coat of arms.

LINEAGE AND HONORS

RA
(active)

LINEAGE

Constituted 11 May 1942 in the Army of the United States as the 59th Signal Battalion. Activated 28 October 1942 at Camp Crowder, Missouri. Inactivated 24 November 1945 at Camp Kilmer, New Jersey.

Headquarters and Headquarters Detachment, 59th Signal Battalion, allotted 16 October 1992 to the Regular Army and activated at Fort Richardson, Alaska.

CAMPAIGN PARTICIPATION CREDIT

World War II
   Normandy
   Northern France
   Rhineland
   Ardennes-Alsace
   Central Europe

DECORATIONS

None.

59th SIGNAL BATTALION BIBLIOGRAPHY

Owen, Brian. "59th Signal Battalion Extends Local-Area Network More Then 1,500 Miles to Shemya." *Army Communicator* 28 (Spring 2003): 59.

Thompson, George Raynor, and Dixie R. Harris. *The Signal Corps: The Outcome (Mid-1943 through 1945)*. United States Army in World War II. Washington, D.C.: Office of the Chief of Military History, United States Army, 1966.

HEADQUARTERS AND HEADQUARTERS DETACHMENT 60th SIGNAL BATTALION

HERALDIC ITEMS

COAT OF ARMS

Shield: Per bend twice bevilled argent and tenné, overall a telegraph pole sable.
Crest: None approved.
Motto: WITH A WILL.
Symbolism: Orange and white are the colors traditionally associated with the Signal Corps. The partition line gives the appearance of a streak of lightning, and the telegraph pole symbolizes communication.

DISTINCTIVE UNIT INSIGNIA

The distinctive unit insignia is the shield and motto of the coat of arms.

LINEAGE AND HONORS

RA
(inactive)

LINEAGE

Constituted 1 October 1933 in the Regular Army as the 60th Signal Battalion. Activated 1 June 1940 at Fort Lewis, Washington. Inactivated 10 April 1946 in the Philippine Islands. Headquarters and Headquarters Company, 60th Signal Battalion, redesignated 17 March 1972 as Headquarters and Headquarters Detachment, 60th Signal Battalion, and activated in Vietnam. Inactivated 29 June 1972 at Oakland, California.

CAMPAIGN PARTICIPATION CREDIT

World War II
  New Guinea
  Luzon

Vietnam
  Consolidation II
  Cease-Fire

DECORATIONS

Philippine Presidential Unit Citation, Streamer embroidered 17 OCTOBER 1944 TO 4 JULY 1945 (60th Signal Battalion [Special] cited; DA GO 47, 1950)

60th SIGNAL BATTALION BIBLIOGRAPHY

Signal Corps, Fort Lewis, Washington, Christmas, 1941. Tacoma, Wash.: Pioneer, Inc., c. 1941.

Thompson, George Raynor, and Dixie R. Harris. *The Signal Corps: The Outcome (Mid-1943 through 1945).* United States Army in World War II. Washington, D.C.: Office of the Chief of Military History, United States Army, 1966.

Thompson, George Raynor, Dixie R. Harris, Pauline M. Oakes, and Dulany Terrett. *The Signal Corps: The Test (December 1941 to July 1943).* United States Army in World War II. Washington, D.C.: Office of the Chief of Military History, Department of the Army, 1957.

62d SIGNAL BATTALION

HERALDIC ITEMS

None approved.

LINEAGE AND HONORS

RA
(inactive)

LINEAGE

Constituted 1 October 1933 in the Regular Army as the 62d Signal Battalion. Activated 13 October 1939 at Fort Sam Houston, Texas. Redesignated 25 September 1949 as the 62d Signal Battalion, Corps. Inactivated 26 June 1950 in Japan. Redesignated 1 March 1963 as the 62d Signal Battalion. Activated 26 March 1963 at Fort Bragg, North Carolina.

Headquarters and Headquarters Detachment, 62d Signal Battalion, converted and redesignated 25 April 1966 as Headquarters and Main Support Company, 62d Maintenance Battalion. Inactivated 4 October 1972 at Oakland Army Base, California.

Converted and redesignated 1 January 1998 as the 62d Signal Battalion.

CAMPAIGN PARTICIPATION CREDIT

World War II
- Tunisia
- Rome-Arno
- North Apennines
- Po Valley

Vietnam
- Counteroffensive, Phase II
- Counteroffensive, Phase III
- Tet Counteroffensive
- Counteroffensive, Phase IV
- Counteroffensive, Phase V
- Counteroffensive, Phase VI
- Tet 69/Counteroffensive
- Summer–Fall 1969
- Winter–Spring 1970
- Sanctuary Counteroffensive
- Counteroffensive, Phase VII
- Consolidation I
- Consolidation II
- Cease-Fire

DECORATIONS

Meritorious Unit Commendation (Army), Streamer embroidered EUROPEAN THEATER (62d Signal Battalion cited; GO 16, IV Corps, 18 March 1945)

Meritorious Unit Commendation (Army), Streamer embroidered VIETNAM 1969–1970 (Headquarters and Main Support Company, 62d Maintenance Battalion, cited; DA GO 2, 1971)

62d SIGNAL BATTALION BIBLIOGRAPHY

Terrett, Dulany. *The Signal Corps: The Emergency*. United States Army in World War II. Washington, D.C.: Office of the Chief of Military History, Department of the Army, 1956.

Thompson, George Raynor, Dixie R. Harris, Pauline M. Oakes, and Dulany Terrett. *The Signal Corps: The Test (December 1941 to July 1943)*. United States Army in World War II. Washington, D.C.: Office of the Chief of Military History, Department of the Army, 1957.

63d SIGNAL BATTALION

HERALDIC ITEMS

COAT OF ARMS

Shield: Tenné, surmounting four bendlets argent in bend the silhouette of a mosque azure and a boot vert.
Crest: None approved.
Motto: AB INITIO (From the Beginning).
Symbolism: Orange and white are the colors traditionally associated with the Signal Corps. The four bendlets represent the four battle honors awarded the organization for service during World War II. The silhouette of the mosque (adopted from the Fifth Army shoulder sleeve insignia) is for service in North Africa. The green boot, representing Italy, is for service in that country.

DISTINCTIVE UNIT INSIGNIA

The distinctive unit insignia is the shield and motto of the coat of arms.

LINEAGE AND HONORS

RA
(active)

LINEAGE

Constituted 1 July 1940 in the Regular Army as the 63d Signal Battalion. Activated 1 June 1941 at Camp Claiborne, Louisiana. Reorganized and redesignated 1 March 1945 as the 63d Signal Operation Battalion. Inactivated 20 June 1948 in Austria. Activated 1 April 1950 in Austria. Reorganized and redesignated 1 October 1952 as the 63d Signal Battalion. Inactivated 10 September 1955 in Austria.

Headquarters and Headquarters Company, 63d Signal Battalion, activated 24 July 1967 at Fort Riley, Kansas. Inactivated 15 February 1972 at Fort Lewis, Washington. Redesignated 1 July 1975 as Headquarters and Headquarters Detachment, 63d Signal Battalion, and activated in Germany. Inactivated 1 October 1977 in Germany.

Reorganized and redesignated 1 October 1984 as Headquarters and Headquarters Company, 63d Signal Battalion, and activated in Germany (organic elements concurrently activated).

CAMPAIGN PARTICIPATION CREDIT

World War II
    Naples-Foggia
    Rome-Arno
    North Apennines
    Po Valley

Vietnam
    Tet Counteroffensive
    Counteroffensive, Phase IV
    Counteroffensive, Phase V
    Counteroffensive, Phase VI
    Tet 69/Counteroffensive
    Summer–Fall 1969
    Winter–Spring 1970
    Sanctuary Counteroffensive
    Counteroffensive, Phase VII
    Consolidation I
    Consolidation II

Southwest Asia
    Defense of Saudi Arabia
    Liberation and Defense of Kuwait
    Cease-Fire

Company B additionally entitled to:

World War II–EAME
    Tunisia

DECORATIONS

Meritorious Unit Commendation (Army), Streamer embroidered ITALY (63d Signal Battalion cited; GO 189, Fifth Army, 23 December 1944)

Meritorious Unit Commendation (Army), Streamer embroidered VIETNAM 1968 (Headquarters and Headquarters Company, 63d Signal Battalion, cited; DA GO 42, 1969)

Meritorious Unit Commendation (Army), Streamer embroidered VIETNAM 1968–1970 (Headquarters and Headquarters Company, 63d Signal Battalion, cited; DA GO 18, 1979)

Meritorious Unit Commendation (Army), Streamer embroidered SOUTHWEST ASIA 1990–1991 (63d Signal Battalion cited; DA GO 17, 1992)

63d SIGNAL BATTALION BIBLIOGRAPHY

Bergen, John D. *Military Communications: A Test for Technology.* United States Army in Vietnam. Washington, D.C.: Center of Military History, United States Army, 1986.

Grombacher, Gerd S. "Corps Signal Communications in Vietnam." *Signal* 23 (April 1969): 24–29.

Henry, Cora. "Gallant Warriors: 93d Signal Brigade Trains Soldiers for Missions." *Army Communicator* 23 (Fall 1998): 4–6.

In Command Communications, September 1970. Headquarters, U.S. Army, Vietnam, 1970.

Leech, John W. *The 63rd Signal Battalion Genesis and Exodus Through World War II*. The 63rd Signal Battalion World War II Association, December 1985.

Lindsay, Jock C. "Welcome 63d Signal." *Army Communicator* 9 (Fall 1984): 44.

Pearson, Willard. *The War in the Northern Provinces, 1966–1968*. Vietnam Studies. Washington, D.C.: Department of the Army, 1975.

Rienzi, Thomas M. *Communications-Electronics, 1962–1970*. Vietnam Studies. Washington, D.C.: Department of the Army, 1972.

Rutt, John A., and Jeremiah J. Jette. "From Tactical to Installational: 63d Signal Battalion in Operation IRAQI FREEDOM." *Army Communicator* 28 (Fall 2003): 11–14.

Stokes, Carol E., ed. *The U.S. Army Signal Corps in Operation Desert Shield/Desert Storm*. Fort Gordon, Ga.: Office of the Command Historian, U.S. Army Signal Center and Fort Gordon, 1994.

Stokes, Carol E., and Kathy R. Coker. "Getting the Message Through in the Persian Gulf War." *Army Communicator* 17 (Summer–Winter 1992): 17–25.

Thompson, George Raynor, and Dixie R. Harris. *The Signal Corps: The Outcome (Mid-1943 through 1945)*. United States Army in World War II. Washington, D.C.: Office of the Chief of Military History, United States Army, 1966.

Thompson, George Raynor, Dixie R. Harris, Pauline M. Oakes, and Dulany Terrett. *The Signal Corps: The Test (December 1941 to July 1943)*. United States Army in World War II. Washington, D.C.: Office of the Chief of Military History, Department of the Army, 1957.

65th SIGNAL BATTALION

HERALDIC ITEMS

None approved.

LINEAGE AND HONORS

AR
(inactive)

LINEAGE

Constituted 11 May 1942 in the Army of the United States as the 65th Signal Battalion. Activated 1 April 1943 at Fort Lewis, Washington. Inactivated 10 November 1946 in Germany.

Allotted 6 May 1959 to the Army Reserve. Activated 1 June 1959 with Headquarters at Caven Point, New Jersey. Inactivated 1 March 1963 at Caven Point, New Jersey.

CAMPAIGN PARTICIPATION CREDIT

World War II
  Rhineland
  Ardennes-Alsace
  Central Europe

DECORATIONS

Meritorious Unit Commendation (Army), Streamer embroidered EUROPEAN THEATER (65th Signal Battalion cited; GO 243, XXI Corps, 10 August 1945)

65th SIGNAL BATTALION BIBLIOGRAPHY

Thompson, George Raynor, and Dixie R. Harris. *The Signal Corps: The Outcome (Mid-1943 through 1945)*. United States Army in World War II. Washington, D.C.: Office of the Chief of Military History, United States Army, 1966.

67th SIGNAL BATTALION

HERALDIC ITEMS

COAT OF ARMS

Shield: Or, on a pale sable between two fleurs-de-lis tenné a fire arrow of the first flamant proper.
Crest: None approved.
Motto: RAPID FLEXIBLE RELIABLE.
Symbolism: Orange is a color traditionally associated with the Signal Corps. The two fleurs-de-lis allude to the two battle honors the organization earned in Central Europe and the Rhineland during World War II. The fire arrow simulates a flare and symbolizes the signal mission of the battalion.

DISTINCTIVE UNIT INSIGNIA

The distinctive unit insignia is the shield and motto of the coat of arms.

LINEAGE AND HONORS

RA
(active)

LINEAGE

Constituted 11 May 1942 in the Army of the United States as the 67th Signal Battalion. Activated 1 May 1943 at Camp Van Dorn, Mississippi. Inactivated 5 April 1946 in the Philippine Islands.

Allotted 2 March 1967 to the Regular Army. Activated 25 April 1967 at Fort Riley, Kansas.

CAMPAIGN PARTICIPATION CREDIT

World War II
    Rhineland
    Central Europe
    Asiatic-Pacific Theater, Streamer without inscription

Southwest Asia
    Defense of Saudi Arabia
    Liberation and Defense of Kuwait
    Cease-Fire

DECORATIONS

Meritorious Unit Commendation (Army), Streamer embroidered SOUTHWEST ASIA 1990–1991 (67th Signal Battalion cited; DA GO 17, 1992)

67th SIGNAL BATTALION BIBLIOGRAPHY

Blanton, Nancy C. "Go Between Circuits III." *Army Communicator* 5 (Summer 1980): 19–23.

Carroll, Bill. "Testing Rapid Deployment." *Army Communicator* 8 (Summer 1983): 35–38.

Couch, Aro. "67th Signal Battalion Provides Ears for Dominica." *Army Communicator* 5 (Winter 1980): 20–21.

Crocker, Robert W. "Go Between Circuits IV." *Army Communicator* 6 (Summer 1981): 50–53.

Dolde, Ruth. "A Combined Exercise." *Army Communicator* 11 (Winter 1986): 54. Training exercise at Fort Gordon with 82d Signal Battalion.

"Exercise Golden Pistol." *Army Communicator* 3 (Fall 1978): 61. Company D cited.

Hasenauer, Heike. "Grecian Firebolt." *Soldiers* 49 (September 1994): 37–40.

Henry, Cora. "Gallant Warriors: 93d Signal Brigade Trains Soldiers for Missions." *Army Communicator* 23 (Fall 1998): 4–6.

Hitt, Joe. "7th Signal Brigade Joins 5th Signal Command." *Army Communicator* 7 (Winter 1982): 37. Company E cited.

Kirk, William M. "2d Signal Training Brigade: Training the C-E Maintainers!" *Army Communicator* 6 (Winter 1981): 48–51.

McCargo, Kelly. "67th Signal Departs for Desert Rotation." *Army Communicator* 28 (Winter 2003): 50–51.

Rhodes, Brad. "Lessons in Commercial-Off-The-Shelf." *Army Communicator* 25 (Spring 2000): 36–38. Discusses the battalion's participation in Grecian Firebolt '99.

Stokes, Carol E., ed. *The U.S. Army Signal Corps in Operation Desert Shield/Desert Storm*. Fort Gordon, Ga.: Office of the Command Historian, U.S. Army Signal Center and Fort Gordon, 1994.

Stokes, Carol E., and Kathy R. Coker. "Getting the Message Through in the Persian Gulf War." *Army Communicator* 17 (Summer–Winter 1992): 17–29.

Theodore, Peter C. "Viewpoint: 67th Signal Battalion." *Army Communicator* 2 (Spring 1977): 57–58.

Wiggins, Richard. "Bold Eagle '84." *Army Communicator* 9 (Winter 1984): 20–23.

Wilson, Ronnie, et al. "Go Between Circuits V." *Army Communicator* 7 (Summer 1982): 50–53.

68th SIGNAL BATTALION

HERALDIC ITEMS

COAT OF ARMS

Shield: Per bend tenné and argent, a bend lozengy between two lighthouse beacons, all counterchanged.

Crest: On a wreath of the colors argent and tenné a sea lion sejant of the first charged with a return boomerang palewise sable armed and langued azure grasping a triton shell of the like.

Motto: I BURN WELL, I SEE.

Symbolism: Orange and white are the colors traditionally associated with the Signal Corps. The signal functions of the battalion are attractively and allegorically symbolized by the lighthouse beacons, reminiscent of New England and referring to the unit's former affiliation with the New England Telegraph and Telephone Company. Such types of beacons were in use along the New England coast in colonial days. The lozengy divisions of the shield are added for design. Square figures heraldically represent honesty and constancy and are probably the root of the phrase "square dealings." The motto is expressive of the alertness of the unit's personnel at all times.

The sea lion is from the flag of the president of the Philippines. It refers to the unit's service in the Philippines during the last year of World War II for which the battalion was awarded the Philippine Presidential Unit Citation. The return boomerang alludes to the fulfillment of the promise that American troops would return to the Philippines, which was made earlier in the war after the fall of Corregidor. The triton shell was used on the Pacific Islands as a war trumpet; it stands for the battalion's signal function.

DISTINCTIVE UNIT INSIGNIA

Description: A silver color metal and enamel device that consists of the Philippine sun in silver surmounted by an orange isosceles triangle. Overall a silver sea lion charged with a black return boomerang palewise grasping a silver triton shell.

Symbolism: The sea lion, triangle, and sun are from the flag of the president of the Philippines. They refer to the organization's service in the Philippines during the last year of World War II for which the battalion was awarded the Philippine Presidential Unit Citation. The return boomerang alludes to the fulfillment of the promise that American troops would return to the Philippines, which was made earlier in the war after the fall of Corregidor. The triton shell was used on the Pacific Islands as a war trumpet; it stands for the battalion's signal function.

LINEAGE AND HONORS

RA
(inactive)

LINEAGE

Constituted 13 August 1942 in the Army of the United States as the 68th Signal Battalion. Activated 15 December 1942 at Camp McCain, Mississippi. Inactivated 26 January 1946 at Camp Anza, California.

Allotted 20 September 1963 to the Regular Army. Activated 15 October 1963 in Germany. Inactivated 13 November 1967 in Germany.

CAMPAIGN PARTICIPATION CREDIT

World War II
　Luzon

DECORATIONS

Philippine Presidential Unit Citation, Streamer embroidered 17 OCTOBER 1944 TO 4 JULY 1945 (68th Signal Battalion cited; DA GO 47, 1950)

68th SIGNAL BATTALION BIBLIOGRAPHY

No published histories.

HEADQUARTERS AND HEADQUARTERS DETACHMENT 69th SIGNAL BATTALION

HERALDIC ITEMS

COAT OF ARMS

Shield: Per pale tenné and argent, in bend a cornet of the second garnished with five bands and fimbriated of the first, and in sinister chief a fleur-de-lis of the last.

Crest: On a wreath of the colors argent and tenné five embattlements of the first issuing an oriental demidragon or armed, langued, and garnished Gules, tufted vert holding five arrows of the fourth.

Motto: VOIX DE COMMANDE (Voice of Command).

Symbolism: Orange and white are the colors traditionally associated with the Signal Corps. The cornet, an ancient signal horn, denotes the communications mission of the organization. The five bands symbolize the battalion's campaign honors for World War II, and the fleur-de-lis represents the Meritorious Unit Commendation received for service in the European Theater.

The oriental demidragon commemorates the battalion's service in Vietnam. The battlements represent the unit's five campaigns in the European Theater during World War II. The cluster of red arrows honors the battalion's five Meritorious Unit Commendations and underscores valor and sacrifice.

DISTINCTIVE UNIT INSIGNIA

The distinctive unit insignia is the shield and motto of the coat of arms.

LINEAGE AND HONORS

RA
(active)

LINEAGE

Constituted 13 August 1942 in the Army of the United States as the 69th Signal Battalion. Activated 15 December 1942 at Camp McCain, Mississippi. Inactivated 20 April 1945 in Austria.

Allotted 11 March 1955 to the Regular Army and activated at Fort George G. Meade, Maryland. Inactivated 1 March 1970 in Vietnam. Headquarters and Headquarters Detachment, 69th Signal Battalion, activated 17 March 1972 in Vietnam. Inactivated 13 November 1972 at Oakland, California. Activated 1 June 1974 in Germany.

CAMPAIGN PARTICIPATION CREDIT

World War II
　Normandy
　Northern France
　Rhineland
　Ardennes-Alsace
　Central Europe

Vietnam
　Defense
　Counteroffensive
　Counteroffensive, Phase II
　Counteroffensive, Phase III
　Tet Counteroffensive
　Counteroffensive, Phase IV
　Counteroffensive, Phase V
　Counteroffensive, Phase VI
　Tet 69/Counteroffensive
　Summer–Fall 1969
　Winter–Spring 1970
　Consolidation II
　Cease-Fire

DECORATIONS

Meritorious Unit Commendation (Army), Streamer embroidered EUROPEAN THEATER (69th Signal Battalion cited; Citation, XX Corps, undated)

Meritorious Unit Commendation (Army), Streamer embroidered VIETNAM 1965–1966 (69th Signal Battalion cited; DA GO 17, 1968)

Meritorious Unit Commendation (Army), Streamer embroidered VIETNAM 1966–1967 (Headquarters and Headquarters Company, 69th Signal Battalion, cited; DA GO 46, 1969)

Meritorious Unit Commendation (Army), Streamer embroidered VIETNAM 1968–1969 (Headquarters and Headquarters Company, 69th Signal Battalion, cited; DA GO 37, 1970)

Meritorious Unit Commendation (Army), Streamer embroidered VIETNAM 1969–1970 (Headquarters and Headquarters Company, 69th Signal Battalion, cited; DA GO 51, 1971)

69th SIGNAL BATTALION BIBLIOGRAPHY

Bergen, John D. *Military Communications: A Test for Technology*. United States Army in Vietnam. Washington, D.C.: Center of Military History, United States Army, 1986.

Curbow, Linda. "Gas!" *Army Communicator* 9 (Fall 1984): 40–43. Battalion underwent nuclear, biological, chemical training.

Fitz-Enz, David G. *Why A Soldier?: A Signal Corpsman's Tour from Vietnam to the Moscow Hot Line.* New York: Ballantine Books, 2000. Fitz-Enz served with the 69th Signal Battalion in Vietnam.

McKinney, John B. "They Communicate and Shoot." *Army* 18 (September 1968): 54–60.

Myer, Charles R. *Division-Level Communications, 1962–1973.* Vietnam Studies. Washington, D.C.: Department of the Army, 1982.

O'Donnell, Diann E. *Unit History 69th Signal Battalion, 1942–1978.* Augsburg, Germany, 1978.

Raines, Rebecca Robbins. *Getting the Message Through: A Branch History of the U.S. Army Signal Corps.* Army Historical Series. Washington, D.C.: Center of Military History, United States Army, 1996.

Rienzi, Thomas M. *Communications-Electronics, 1962–1970.* Vietnam Studies. Washington, D.C.: Department of the Army, 1972.

Rolak, Bruno J. *History of the U.S. Army Communications Command (1964–1976).* Fort Huachuca, Ariz.: United States Army Communications Command, 1976.

Rolak, Bruno J., and George R. Thompson. *History of the United States Army Communications Command From Origin Through 1976.* Fort Huachuca, Ariz.: United States Army Communications Command, 1979.

69th Signal Battalion Unit History. N.p., 1974.

HEADQUARTERS AND HEADQUARTERS DETACHMENT 72d SIGNAL BATTALION

HERALDIC ITEMS

COAT OF ARMS

Shield: Per pale sable and gules, a fleur-de-lis throughout or between in chief two fusils pilewise and in fess two mullets argent.

Crest: On a wreath of the colors or and sable a staff raguly couped at each end of the like surmounted by two lightning bolts saltirewise of the first.

Motto: ALWAYS FIT TO FIGHT.

Symbolism: The fleur-de-lis represents action in France during World War II. Black, red, and gold allude to the national colors of Germany and, with white, to the three German states with which the battalion's service is associated. The stars allude to the two campaign participation credits earned by the unit in Europe during World War II. The two fusils are symbolic of radio waves and impulses, a reference to the unit's mission. Gold denotes excellence, and red signifies courage.

The ragged staff represents lookout and signal positions as well as World War II battlefields and their locations in the battle-scarred forests of the European Theater. The lightning bolts represent the Signal Corps and the battalion's World War II campaigns. Gold symbolizes excellence, and black denotes strength and solidarity.

DISTINCTIVE UNIT INSIGNIA

Description: A gold color metal and enamel device that consists of a gold fleur-de-lis placed on a trilobate shape divided vertically into black and red areas with a white star between each branch arm and the tail arms of the fleur-de-lis. A white fusil radiates outward between the top of each of the branch arms and the main stem of the fleur-de-lis.

Symbolism: The gold fleur-de-lis represents the unit's activities in France. The combination of black, red, and gold alludes to the national colors of Germany and also represents Belgium. Black and gold allude to the German state of Baden-Württemberg; red and white to the state of Hessen; and black, gold, and red to the state of Rhineland-Pfalz. The two white stars are symbolic of the two campaign participation credits earned by the battalion—Rhineland and Central Europe—as well as the battalion's activities in Europe and the Far East. The two white fusils are symbolic of radio waves (impulses).

LINEAGE AND HONORS

LINEAGE

RA
(active)

Constituted 8 May 1944 in the Army of the United States as the 3186th Signal Service Battalion. Activated 15 May 1944 at Fort Monmouth, New Jersey. Redesignated 30 June 1947 as the 72d Signal Service Battalion. Inactivated 25 January 1950 in Japan.

Redesignated 7 June 1954 as Headquarters, 72d Signal Battalion, and allotted to the Regular Army. Activated 15 July 1954 at Fort Huachuca, Arizona. Reorganized and redesignated 9 December 1957 as Headquarters and Headquarters Detachment, 72d Signal Battalion. Inactivated 1 October 1964 at Fort Huachuca, Arizona.

Activated 25 September 1965 in Germany. Inactivated 13 November 1967 in Germany. Activated 1 January 1972 in Germany.

CAMPAIGN PARTICIPATION CREDIT

World War II
Rhineland
Central Europe
Asiatic-Pacific Theater, Streamer without inscription

DECORATIONS

None.

72d SIGNAL BATTALION BIBLIOGRAPHY

Gallivan, Catherine. "Signal Team Keeps Task Force in Touch and Talking." *Army Communicator* 23 (Fall 1998): 21. Support provided to Task Force Rijeka in Croatia.

Hitt, Joe. "7th Signal Brigade Joins 5th Signal Command." *Army Communicator* 7 (Winter 1982): 37.

Hypes, G. D. *72d Signal Battalion, 1947–1978*. Karlsruhe, West Germany, 1978.

Johnson, Danny M. *Military Communications Supporting Peacekeeping Operations in the Balkans: The Signal Corps at Its Best*. Mannheim, Germany: Headquarters, 5th Signal Command, 2000.

Rolak, Bruno J. *History of the U.S. Army Communications Command (1964–1976)*. Fort Huachuca, Ariz.: United States Army Communications Command, 1976.

Rudd, Gordon W. *Humanitarian Intervention: Assisting the Iraqi Kurds in Operation Provide Comfort, 1991*. Washington, D.C.: Center of Military History, United States Army, 2004.

Shackford, Charles, ed. *Line Up, 3186th Signal Service Battalion*. N.p, 1945.

HEADQUARTERS AND HEADQUARTERS DETACHMENT 73d SIGNAL BATTALION

HERALDIC ITEMS

COAT OF ARMS

Shield: Per pile azure and tenné, between four lightning flashes argent pilewise a sea lion grasping a sword argent.
Crest: None approved.
Motto: None approved.
Symbolism: Orange and white are the colors traditionally associated with the Signal Corps. The sea lion commemorates the Philippine Presidential Unit Citation; blue alludes to the Pacific Ocean. The four lightning flashes represent the four capabilities of a signal unit.

DISTINCTIVE UNIT INSIGNIA

Description: A silver color metal and enamel device that consists of a blue diamond charged with a silver sea lion holding a sword, flanked on the bottom side by two orange triangles, each with one convex side and bearing two silver lightning flashes radiating from base.
Symbolism: Orange and white (silver) are the colors traditionally associated with the Signal Corps. The sea lion commemorates the Philippine Presidential Unit Citation; blue alludes to the Pacific Ocean. The four lightning flashes represent the four capabilities of a signal unit.

LINEAGE AND HONORS

RA
(inactive)

LINEAGE

Constituted 29 March 1945 in the Army of the United States as the 4026th Signal Photographic Battalion. Activated 20 May 1945 in the Philippine Islands. Inactivated 15 April 1946 in Japan.

Redesignated 8 September 1954 as Headquarters, 73d Signal Battalion, and allotted to the Regular Army. Activated 15 December 1954 at Fort Huachuca, Arizona. Inactivated 1 May 1957 at Fort Huachuca, Arizona. Redesignated 1 March 1963 as Headquarters and Headquarters Detachment, 73d Signal Battalion. Activated 26 March 1963 at Fort Bragg, North Carolina. Inactivated 29 June 1972 at Oakland, California.

Activated 1 July 1974 in Germany. Inactivated 15 September 1994 in Germany.

LINEAGES AND HERALDIC DATA 189

CAMPAIGN PARTICIPATION CREDIT

World War II
   Luzon

Vietnam
   Counteroffensive, Phase II
   Counteroffensive, Phase III
   Tet Counteroffensive
   Counteroffensive, Phase IV
   Counteroffensive, Phase V
   Counteroffensive, Phase VI
   Tet 69/Counteroffensive
   Summer–Fall 1969
   Winter–Spring 1970
   Sanctuary Counteroffensive
   Counteroffensive, Phase VII
   Consolidation I
   Consolidation II
   Cease-Fire

DECORATIONS

Meritorious Unit Commendation (Army), Streamer embroidered VIETNAM 1966–1968 (Headquarters and Headquarters Detachment, 73d Signal Battalion [Support], cited; DA GO 42, 1969)

Philippine Presidential Unit Citation, Streamer embroidered 17 OCTOBER 1944 TO 4 JULY 1945 (4026th Signal Photographic, Battalion Headquarters, cited; DA GO 47, 1950)

73d SIGNAL BATTALION BIBLIOGRAPHY

Bergen, John D. *Military Communications: A Test for Technology*. United States Army in Vietnam. Washington, D.C.: Center of Military History, United States Army, 1986.

The History of the 73rd Signal Battalion. N.p., c. 1978.

Rienzi, Thomas M. *Communications-Electronics, 1962–1970*. Vietnam Studies. Washington, D.C.: Department of the Army, 1972.

Royal, Lee. "Amitie." *Army Communicator* 9 (Fall 1984): 44. Report of ceremony with a French counterpart unit.

Unit History, 73rd Signal Battalion. N.p., 1974.

HEADQUARTERS AND HEADQUARTERS DETACHMENT 75th SIGNAL BATTALION

HERALDIC ITEMS

None approved.

LINEAGE AND HONORS

AR
(inactive)

LINEAGE

Constituted 20 April 1944 in the Army of the United States as the 3114th Signal Service Battalion. Activated 10 May 1944 at Corozal, Canal Zone. Redesignated 7 May 1947 as the 75th Signal Service Battalion. Inactivated 16 July 1948 at Fort Clayton, Canal Zone.

Redesignated 18 August 1959 as Headquarters and Headquarters Detachment, 75th Signal Battalion, and allotted to the Army Reserve. Activated 10 October 1959 at Chicago Heights, Illinois. Inactivated 11 January 1963 at Chicago Heights, Illinois.

CAMPAIGN PARTICIPATION CREDIT

World War II
American Theater, Streamer without inscription

DECORATIONS

None.

75th SIGNAL BATTALION BIBLIOGRAPHY

No published histories.

77th SIGNAL BATTALION

HERALDIC ITEMS

COAT OF ARMS

Shield: Argent, a torch sable enflamed surmounting in base three waves tenné and flanked in chief by two slips of grapevine of the second.

Crest: That for the regiments and separate battalions of the Army Reserve: On a wreath of the colors argent and tenné the Lexington Minuteman proper. The statue of the Minuteman Capt. John Parker (H. H. Kitson, sculptor) stands on the Common in Lexington, Massachusetts.

Motto: None approved.

Symbolism: Orange and white are the colors traditionally associated with the Signal Corps. The flaming torch, one of the oldest means of communication, alludes to the unit's function. The unit's service in World War I is represented by the two slips of grapevine with four leaves for battle honors won in France. The three waves refer to the unit's World War II service in the Pacific theater.

DISTINCTIVE UNIT INSIGNIA

The distinctive unit insignia is the shield of the coat of arms.

LINEAGE AND HONORS

AR
(77th Infantry Division) (inactive)

LINEAGE

Constituted 1 July 1916 in the Enlisted Reserve Corps as a Signal Corps battalion. Organized March–October 1917 in New York as the 1st Reserve Field Signal Battalion. Ordered into active military service 5 October 1917 at Camp Upton, New York; concurrently redesignated as the 302d Field Signal Battalion and assigned to the 77th Division. Demobilized 9 May 1919 at Camp Upton, New York.

Reconstituted 24 June 1921 in the Organized Reserves as the 77th Signal Company, an element of the 77th Division (later redesignated as the 77th Infantry Division). Organized in May 1922 at New York, New York. Ordered into active military service 24 March 1942 at Fort Jackson, South Carolina. Inactivated 15 March 1946 in Japan. Activated 19 February 1947 at New York, New York. (Organized Reserves redesignated 25 March 1948 as the Organized Reserve Corps; redesignated 9 July 1952 as the Army Reserve.)

Reorganized and redesignated 1 May 1959 as Headquarters and Headquarters Company, 77th Signal Battalion. (Companies A and B constituted 7 April 1959 and activated 1 May 1959 at Garden City, Long Island, New York, and New York, New

York, respectively; Company C constituted 25 March 1963 and activated 26 March 1963 at New York, New York.) Redesignated 21 October 1963 as Headquarters and Headquarters Detachment, 77th Signal Battalion. Inactivated 30 December 1965 at New York, New York (organic elements concurrently inactivated).

CAMPAIGN PARTICIPATION CREDIT

World War I
   Oise-Aisne
   Meuse-Argonne
   Lorraine 1918
   Champagne 1918

World War II
   Western Pacific
   Leyte
   Ryukyus

DECORATIONS

Meritorious Unit Commendation (Army), Streamer embroidered PACIFIC THEATER (77th Signal Company cited; GO 178, 77th Infantry Division, 30 May 1945)

Philippine Presidential Unit Citation, Streamer embroidered 17 OCTOBER 1944 TO 4 JULY 1945 (77th Signal Company cited; DA GO 47, 1950)

77th SIGNAL BATTALION BIBLIOGRAPHY

Adler, Julius O., ed. *History of the Seventy-Seventh Division, August 25, 1917–November 11, 1918.* New York: Wynkoop Hallenbeck Crawford Company, 1919.

American Battle Monuments Commission. *77th Division, Summary of Operations in the World War.* Washington, D.C.: Government Printing Office, 1944.

Appleman, Roy E., James M. Burns, Russell A. Gugeler, and John Stevens. *Okinawa: The Last Battle.* United States Army in World War II. Washington, D.C.: Historical Division, Department of the Army, 1948. 77th Infantry Division cited.

Cannon, M. Hamlin. *Leyte: The Return to the Philippines.* United States Army in World War II. Washington, D.C.: Office of the Chief of Military History, Department of the Army, 1954. 77th Infantry Division cited.

Crowl, Philip A. *Campaign in the Marianas.* United States Army in World War II. Washington, D.C.: Office of the Chief of Military History, Department of the Army, 1960. 77th Infantry Division cited.

McKeogh, Arthur. *The Victorious 77th Division (New York's Own) in the Argonne Fight.* New York: John H. Eggers Company, 1919.

Myers, Max, ed. *Ours to Hold It High: The History of the 77th Infantry Division in World War II by Men Who Were There.* Washington, D.C.: Infantry Journal Press, 1947.

"ONEIDA BEAR." *Army Reserve Magazine* 10 (July–August 1964): 9. Training exercise in which the 77th Signal Battalion participated.

Operation Report, Iceberg Phase I, 77th Infantry Division. N.p., 1945.

Smith, Robert Ross. *Triumph in the Philippines.* United States Army in World War II. Washington, D.C.: Office of the Chief of Military History, Department of the Army, 1963. 77th Infantry Division cited.

HEADQUARTERS AND HEADQUARTERS DETACHMENT 78th SIGNAL BATTALION

HERALDIC ITEMS

COAT OF ARMS

Shield: Per cross tenné and argent, a fret containing and interlaced with an annulet, the saltire bands terminating in lightning flashes throughout, all counterchanged.

Crest: On a wreath of the colors argent and tenné a sea lion naiant or, langued azure, supporting an equilateral triangle point up azure, charged with a sun rayonnant with eight groups of rays of the third.

Motto: NEVER BETTERED.

Symbolism: Orange and white are the colors traditionally associated with the Signal Corps. The four divisions of the shield denote the unit's heritage of installing, operating, and maintaining four area signal centers as part of an Army area signal system. The fret with lightning flashes depicts the radio relay and field cable trunk circuits between the area signal centers. The interlaced ring alludes to the message center and signal information provided by the organization. The counterchanged colors refer to the unit's signal displacement capability and also its circuit patching and switching responsibilities.

The gold sea lion and eight-rayed Philippine sun with blue background, taken from the seal of the president of the Philippines, refer to the Philippine Presidential Unit Citation earned by the unit. The triangle is associated with the presidential seal and the national flag of the Philippines. The sea lion, also represented on the coat of arms of Manila, additionally refers to campaign participation on Luzon.

DISTINCTIVE UNIT INSIGNIA

Description: A silver color metal and enamel device that consists of a stylized silver Philippine sun superimposed by silver and orange lightning flashes crossed diagonally. Overall a lozenge divided crosswise silver and orange bearing another lozenge divided crosswise orange and silver. At top an arched silver scroll inscribed NEVER, and on the bottom an arched silver scroll inscribed BETTERED, all in black letters and overall at center a gold sea lion.

Symbolism: Orange and white (silver) are the colors traditionally associated with the Signal Corps. The lightning flashes and lozenges in alternating colors refer to versatility, multiple capabilities, and the unit's heritage of circuit patching and switching. The gold sea lion and Philippine sun, adapted from the seal of the president of the Philippines, commemorate the Philippine Presidential Unit Citation awarded to the battalion for service during World War II. The sea lion also alludes to Manila and refers to the unit's campaign participation on Luzon.

LINEAGE AND HONORS

LINEAGE

RA
(active)

Constituted 26 August 1942 in the Army of the United States as the 318th Coast Artillery Barrage Balloon Battalion. Activated 10 December 1942 at Camp Tyson, Tennessee. Reorganized and redesignated 1 August 1943 as the 318th Antiaircraft Balloon Battalion, Low Altitude. Reorganized and redesignated 25 September 1943 as the 318th Antiaircraft Balloon Battalion, Very Low Altitude.

Converted, reorganized, and redesignated 17 April 1944 as the 78th Signal Light Construction Battalion. Reorganized and redesignated 1 September 1944 as the 78th Signal Heavy Construction Battalion. Inactivated 31 August 1946 in Japan.

Redesignated 20 July 1966 as the 78th Signal Battalion, allotted to the Regular Army, and activated at Fort Huachuca, Arizona. Inactivated 31 January 1971 at Fort Lewis, Washington.

Headquarters and Headquarters Company, 78th Signal Battalion, redesignated 16 October 1992 as Headquarters and Headquarters Detachment, 78th Signal Battalion, and activated in Japan.

CAMPAIGN PARTICIPATION CREDIT

World War II
    Luzon

DECORATIONS

Philippine Presidential Unit Citation, Streamer embroidered 17 OCTOBER 1944 TO 4 JULY 1945 (78th Signal [Heavy] Construction Battalion cited; DA GO 47, 1950)

78th SIGNAL BATTALION BIBLIOGRAPHY

Evers, Michelle. "Japan Defense Message System Center First in Pacific." *Army Communicator* 24 (Winter 1999): 38.

Nquyen, Luan. "78th Supports Japan's Disaster Day Exercise." *Army Communicator* 28 (Winter 2003): 49–50.

Rolak, Bruno J. *History of the U.S. Army Communications Command (1964–1976).* Fort Huachuca, Ariz.: United States Army Communications Command, 1976.

Whitehead, Tony. "78th Signal Battalion Begins Major Upgrade in Japan." *Army Communicator* 23 (Summer 1998): 46.

82d SIGNAL BATTALION

HERALDIC ITEMS

COAT OF ARMS

Shield: Per pale wavy tenné and argent, a fleur-de-lis, the outer petals each charged with a lozenge, all counterchanged. Overall on a winged chevronel abased sable fimbriated of the second, four plates accosted by six billets, three and three of the last.

Crest: None approved.

Motto: THE COMMANDER'S VOICE.

Symbolism: Orange and white are the colors traditionally associated with the Signal Corps. The wavy central partition line represents the Rhine River that flows in a northerly direction and is an essential waterway in the Rhineland where the organization served during World War II. The fleur-de-lis symbolizes France where the battalion served during World Wars I and II, a fact alluded to by the division and counterchanging of said charge. The two diamonds allude to the two leading nations in the diamond cutting industry, Belgium and the Netherlands, where the battalion served during World War II. The winged chevron indicates the unit's historic airborne mission, and the color black is taken from the field of the Belgian coat of arms. The chevron markings are the international Morse code symbols for "82," the numerical designation of the battalion.

DISTINCTIVE UNIT INSIGNIA

The distinctive unit insignia is the shield and motto of the coat of arms.

LINEAGE AND HONORS

RA

LINEAGE (82d Airborne Division) (active)

Constituted 1 July 1916 in the Enlisted Reserve Corps as a Signal Corps battalion. Organized 19 September 1917 at Camp Gordon, Georgia, as the 13th Reserve Field Signal Battalion. Ordered into active military service 5 October 1917; concurrently redesignated as the 307th Field Signal Battalion and assigned to the 82d Division. Demobilized 22 May 1919 at Camp Morrison, Virginia.

Reconstituted 24 June 1921 in the Organized Reserves as the 82d Signal Company and assigned to the 82d Division (later redesignated as the 82d Airborne Division). Organized in February 1922 at Macon, Georgia. Ordered into active military service 25 March 1942 and reorganized at Camp Claiborne, Louisiana. Reorganized and redesignated 15 August 1942 as the 82d Airborne Signal Company. (Organized Reserves redesignated 25 March 1948 as the Organized Reserve Corps.)

Withdrawn 15 November 1948 from the Organized Reserve Corps and allotted to the Regular Army. Reorganized and redesignated 1 September 1957 as Headquarters and Headquarters Detachment, 82d Signal Battalion (organic elements constituted 19 July 1957 and activated 1 September 1957 at Fort Bragg, North Carolina).

CAMPAIGN PARTICIPATION CREDIT

World War I
St. Mihiel
Meuse-Argonne
Lorraine 1918

World War II
Sicily (with arrowhead)
Naples-Foggia
Normandy (with arrowhead)
Rhineland (with arrowhead)
Ardennes-Alsace
Central Europe

Armed Forces Expeditions
Dominican Republic
Grenada
Panama

Southwest Asia
Defense of Saudi Arabia
Liberation and Defense of Kuwait

DECORATIONS

Presidential Unit Citation (Army), Streamer embroidered STE. MERE EGLISE (82d Airborne Signal Company cited; WD GO 83, 1944)

Meritorious Unit Commendation (Army), Streamer embroidered SOUTHWEST ASIA 1990–1991 (82d Signal Battalion cited; DA GO 27, 1994)

French Croix de Guerre with Palm, World War II, Streamer embroidered STE. MERE EGLISE (82d Airborne Signal Company cited; DA GO 43, 1950)

French Croix de Guerre with Palm, World War II, Streamer embroidered COTENTIN (82d Airborne Signal Company cited; DA GO 43, 1950)

French Croix de Guerre, World War II, Fourragere (82d Airborne Signal Company cited; DA GO 43, 1950)

Belgian Fourragere 1940 (82d Airborne Signal Company cited; DA GO 43, 1950)

Cited in the Order of the Day of the Belgian Army for action in the Ardennes (82d Airborne Signal Company cited; DA GO 43, 1950)

Cited in the Order of the Day of the Belgian Army for action in Belgium and Germany (82d Airborne Signal Company cited; DA GO 43, 1950)

Military Order of William (Degree of the Knight of the Fourth Class), Streamer embroidered NIJMEGEN 1944 (82d Airborne Signal Company cited; DA GO 43, 1950)

Netherlands Orange Lanyard (82d Airborne Signal Company cited; DA GO 43, 1950)

82d SIGNAL BATTALION BIBLIOGRAPHY

American Battle Monuments Commission. *82d Division, Summary of Operations in the World War*. Washington, D.C.: Government Printing Office, 1944.

Barry, Robert F., ed. *Power Pack: The 82d Airborne Division [in the Dominican Republic]*. Portsmouth, Va.: Messenger Printing Company, 1965.

Blumenson, Martin. *Breakout and Pursuit*. United States Army in World War II. Washington, D.C.: Office of the Chief of Military History, Department of the Army, 1961. 82d Airborne Division cited.

―――. *Salerno to Cassino*. United States Army in World War II. Washington: Government Publishing Office, 1969. 82d Airborne Division cited.

Burdette, Thomas W., ed. *The Jump Log. History of the 82d Airborne Division, America's "Guard of Honor."* Norfolk: C&M Offset Printing Company, 1961.

Cantelou, Campbell. "Jumping Into a 'Just Cause.'" *Army Communicator* 15 (Winter–Spring 1990): 6–11.

Combat: D-Day in Grenada (82d Airborne Division). Alexandria, Va.: Photo Press International, 1984.

Dawson, W. Forrest, comp. and ed. *Saga of the All American*. Atlanta: Albert Love Enterprises, 1946. Reprint. Nashville: Battery Press, 1978.

Dolde, Ruth. "A Combined Exercise." *Army Communicator* 11 (Winter 1986): 54. Training exercise at Fort Gordon with 67th Signal Battalion.

82d Airborne Division, Action in Central Europe, April–May 1945, Based on Official After-Action Reports. N.p., 1945.

82d Airborne Signal Company. Berlin: Druckhaus Tempelhof, 1946.

82d Signal Battalion (ABN DIV) History. N.p., c. 1964.

Ferrell, Robert S. "Operation UPHOLD DEMOCRACY: Contingency Communications and Forced Entry Operations for Haiti." *Army Communicator* 20 (Winter 1995): 7–14.

Garland, Albert N., and Howard McGaw Smyth. *Sicily and the Surrender of Italy*. United States Army in World War II. Washington, D.C: Office of the Chief of Military History, Department of the Army, 1965. 82d Airborne Division cited.

Harrison, Gordon A. *Cross-Channel Attack*. United States Army in World War II. Washington, D.C.: Office of the Chief of Military History, United States Army, 1951. 82d Airborne Division cited.

Hood, Dellman O. "History of the 307th Field Signal Battalion," in *Official History of the 82nd Division, A.E.F., "All American" Division*. Indianapolis: Bobbs-Merrill Company, 1919.

MacDonald, Charles B. *The Siegfried Line Campaign*. United States Army in World War II. Washington, D.C.: Office of the Chief of Military History, Department of the Army, 1963. 82d Airborne Division cited.

Raines, Rebecca Robbins. *Getting the Message Through: A Branch History of the U.S. Army Signal Corps*. Army Historical Series. Washington, D.C.: Center of Military History, United States Army, 1996.

Robinson, Clarence A., Jr. "Parachute Forced Entry Drives Signal Battalion's Rapid Support." *Signal* 51 (March 1997): 21–22.

Smith, Craig. "82d Signal Battalion Deploys to Former Soviet Union." *Army Communicator* 22 (Fall 1997): 2–6.

Thompson, George Raynor, and Dixie R. Harris. *The Signal Corps: The Outcome (Mid-1943 through 1945)*. United States Army in World War II. Washington, D.C.: Office of the Chief of Military History, United States Army, 1966.

83d SIGNAL BATTALION

HERALDIC ITEMS

COAT OF ARMS

Shield: Tenné, a network of nine wires fretty, five and four argent, and overall in pale a field telephone sable fimbriated of the second.

Crest: That for the regiments and separate battalions of the Army Reserve: On a wreath of the colors argent and tenné the Lexington Minuteman proper. The statue of the Minuteman Capt. John Parker (H. H. Kitson, sculptor) stands on the Common in Lexington, Massachusetts.

Motto: SIGNUM SEMPER DANS (Always Giving a Signal).

Symbolism: Orange and white are the colors traditionally associated with the Signal Corps. The network of wire represents the teamwork required for successful signal communications. The wire and telephone together allude to the mission of a signal battalion. The nine wires commemorate the nine battle honors awarded the unit, four for service in World War I and five for service in World War II.

DISTINCTIVE UNIT INSIGNIA

The distinctive unit insignia is the shield and motto of the coat of arms.

LINEAGE AND HONORS

AR
(83d Infantry Division) (inactive)

LINEAGE

Constituted 1 July 1916 in the Enlisted Reserve Corps as a Signal Corps battalion. Organized March–October 1917 in Ohio as the 20th Reserve Field Signal Battalion. Ordered into active military service 5 October 1917 at Camp Sherman, Ohio; concurrently redesignated as the 308th Field Signal Battalion and assigned to the 83d Division. Demobilized 6 August 1919 at Camp Sherman, Ohio.

Reconstituted 24 June 1921 in the Organized Reserves as the 83d Signal Company, an element of the 83d Division (later redesignated as the 83d Infantry Division). Organized in December 1921 at Columbus, Ohio. Ordered into active military service 15 August 1942 at Camp Atterbury, Indiana. Inactivated 27 March 1946 at Camp Kilmer, New Jersey. Activated 14 November 1946 at Cleveland, Ohio. (Organized Reserves redesignated 25 March 1948 as the Organized Reserve Corps; redesignated 9 July 1952 as the Army Reserve.)

Reorganized and redesignated 19 March 1959 as Headquarters and Headquarters Company, 83d Signal Battalion (Companies A and B concurrently constituted and activated, at Toledo and Marion, Ohio, respectively; Company C constituted 27

March 1963 and activated 15 April 1963 at Painesville, Ohio). Location of Headquarters changed 1 May 1959 to Youngstown, Ohio. Redesignated 1 November 1963 as Headquarters and Headquarters Detachment, 83d Signal Battalion. Inactivated 31 December 1965 at Youngstown, Ohio (organic elements concurrently inactivated).

CAMPAIGN PARTICIPATION CREDIT

World War I
Aisne-Marne
Oise-Aisne
Meuse-Argonne
Champagne 1918

World War II
Normandy
Northern France
Rhineland
Ardennes-Alsace
Central Europe

DECORATIONS

None.

83d SIGNAL BATTALION BIBLIOGRAPHY

Blumenson, Martin. *Breakout and Pursuit*. United States Army in World War II. Washington, D.C.: Office of the Chief of Military History, Department of the Army, 1961. 83d Infantry Division cited.

Cole, Hugh M. *The Ardennes: Battle of the Bulge*. United States Army in World War II. Washington, D.C.: Office of the Chief of Military History, Department of the Army, 1965. 83d Infantry Division cited.

———. *The Lorraine Campaign*. United States Army in World War II. Washington, D.C.: Historical Division, Department of the Army, 1950. 83d Infantry Division cited.

83d Infantry Division History 1917–1962. 1962 ANACDUTRA Camp A. P. Hill, Virginia. Camp A.P. Hill, Va., 1962.

Hayhow, Ernie. *The Thunderbolt Across Europe: A History of the 83d Infantry Division 1942–1945*. Munich: F. Bruckmann KG, 1946.

MacDonald, Charles B. *The Last Offensive*. United States Army in World War II. Office of the Chief of Military History, United States Army, 1973. 83d Infantry Division cited.

———. *The Siegfried Line Campaign*. United States Army in World War II. Washington, D.C.: Office of the Chief of Military History, Department of the Army, 1963. 83d Infantry Division cited.

Thunderbolt Division: The Story of the Eighty-third Infantry Division, 1945. N.p., 1945.

86th SIGNAL BATTALION
(First Voice Heard)

HERALDIC ITEMS

COAT OF ARMS

Shield: Per fess argent, radiant of six from fesspoint two gules between four sable and argent a tiger face proper grasping a lightning bolt fesswise tenné within a crescent of the first triple fimbriated vert, gules, and sable.

Crest: On a wreath of the colors argent and sable an octagon sable fimbriated argent surmounted by an irregular mullet of six in dexter chief issuing six contrails arching to sinister base of the second.

Motto: FIRST VOICE HEARD.

Symbolism: Orange and white (silver) are the colors traditionally associated with the Signal Corps. The rays in chief, suggested by the state flag of Arizona, allude to Fort Huachuca, the battalion's home station. The rays refer to campaign credits earned during two wars. The two red sectors refer to the battalion's Meritorious Unit Commendations, and the black and white rays refer to the knowledge required for night and day signal operations. The tiger symbolizes Vietnam, site of the unit's first wartime service. The lightning bolt connotes electronic communications and speed of response. The crescent, outlined in the colors of the Kuwait flag, represents the Persian Gulf region, site of the unit's second wartime service.

The meteor streaking across the octagon symbolizes swiftness. Its brilliance and speed refer to early methods of conveying information by means of signal lights and stand for the battalion's mission of providing military communications. The eight sides of the insignia, representing the eight directions of the compass, indicate that the unit can transmit information in all directions. The eight sides, combined with the six points of the meteor, also allude to the battalion's numerical designation.

DISTINCTIVE UNIT INSIGNIA

The distinctive unit insignia is the shield and motto of the coat of arms.

LINEAGE AND HONORS

LINEAGE

RA
(active)

Constituted 23 March 1966 in the Regular Army as Headquarters and Headquarters Detachment, 86th Signal Battalion. Activated 1 June 1966 at Fort Bragg, North Carolina. Inactivated 30 April 1971 in Vietnam.

Activated 1 July 1977 at Fort Huachuca, Arizona. Reorganized and redesignated 16 January 1998 as Headquarters and Headquarters Company, 86th Signal Battalion (organic elements concurrently constituted and activated at Fort Huachuca, Arizona).

CAMPAIGN PARTICIPATION CREDIT

Vietnam
- Counteroffensive, Phase II
- Counteroffensive, Phase III
- Tet Counteroffensive
- Counteroffensive, Phase IV
- Counteroffensive, Phase V
- Counteroffensive, Phase VI
- Tet 69/Counteroffensive
- Summer–Fall 1969
- Winter–Spring 1970
- Sanctuary Counteroffensive
- Counteroffensive, Phase VII

Southwest Asia
- Defense of Saudi Arabia
- Liberation and Defense of Kuwait
- Cease-Fire

DECORATIONS

Meritorious Unit Commendation (Army), Streamer embroidered VIETNAM 1966–1967 (Headquarters and Headquarters Detachment, 86th Signal Battalion [Support], cited; DA GO 42, 1969)

Meritorious Unit Commendation (Army), Streamer embroidered SOUTHWEST ASIA 1990–1991 (86th Signal Battalion cited; DA GO 17, 1992)

Republic of Vietnam Cross of Gallantry with Palm, Streamer embroidered VIETNAM 1967–1968 (Headquarters and Headquarters Detachment, 86th Signal Battalion, cited; DA GO 48, 1971)

Republic of Vietnam Civil Action Honor Medal, First Class, Streamer embroidered VIETNAM 1967–1970 (Headquarters and Headquarters Detachment, 86th Signal Battalion, cited; DA GO 51, 1971)

86th SIGNAL BATTALION BIBLIOGRAPHY

Ackerman, Robert K. "Tactical Signalers Learn to Pack Light, Travel Right." *Signal* 54 (April 2000): 37–39.

Alley, Lisa. "Thunderbird Brigade Overcomes Challenges of East Timor." *Army Communicator* 25 (Fall 2000): 13–15.

Bergen, John D. *Military Communications: A Test for Technology*. United States Army in Vietnam. Washington, D.C.: Center of Military History, United States Army, 1986.

Davis, Richard, Jr. "Inside USACC's 'Fire Brigade.'" *Army Communicator* 7 (Summer 1982): 5–11.

Hasenauer, Heike. "Grecian Firebolt." *Soldiers* 49 (September 1994): 37–40.

Kennedy, Randy. "35th Signal Brigade." *Army Communicator* 13 (Winter 1988): 36–37.

McPherson, Bill. "Signaleers Support East Timor Operation." *Army Communicator* 25 (Fall 2000): 2–5.

Raines, Rebecca Robbins. *Getting the Message Through: A Branch History of the U.S. Army Signal Corps*. Army Historical Series. Washington, D.C.: Center of Military History, United States Army, 1996.

Rienzi, Thomas M. *Communications-Electronics, 1962–1970*. Vietnam Studies. Washington, D.C.: Department of the Army, 1972.

Rolak, Bruno J. *History of the U.S. Army Communications Command (1964–1976)*. Fort Huachuca, Ariz.: United States Army Communications Command, 1976.

Stokes, Carol E., ed. *The U.S. Army Signal Corps in Operation Desert Shield/Desert Storm*. Fort Gordon, Ga.: Office of the Command Historian, U.S. Army Signal Center and Fort Gordon, 1994.

Stokes, Carol E., and Kathy R. Coker. "Getting the Message Through in the Persian Gulf War." *Army Communicator* 17 (Summer–Winter 1992): 17–25.

Williams, Ardine. "Road Test." *Army Communicator* 13 (Winter 1988): 53. Exercise "Level Road."

94th SIGNAL BATTALION

HERALDIC ITEMS

None approved.

LINEAGE AND HONORS

AR
(inactive)

LINEAGE

Constituted 24 June 1921 in the Organized Reserves as the 94th Signal Company and assigned to the 94th Division (later redesignated as the 94th Infantry Division). Organized in November 1921 at Boston, Massachusetts. Ordered into active military service 15 September 1942 at Fort Custer, Michigan. Inactivated 6 February 1946 at Camp Kilmer, New Jersey. Activated 13 February 1947 at Boston, Massachusetts. (Organized Reserves redesignated 25 March 1948 as the Organized Reserve Corps; redesignated 9 July 1952 as the Army Reserve.)

Reorganized and redesignated 1 May 1959 as Headquarters and Headquarters Company, 94th Signal Battalion (Companies A and B constituted 6 April 1959 in the Army Reserve and activated 1 May 1959 at Boston and Roslindale, Massachusetts, respectively.) Inactivated 1 March 1963 at Boston, Massachusetts, and relieved from assignment to the 94th Infantry Division (organic elements concurrently inactivated).

CAMPAIGN PARTICIPATION CREDIT

World War II
  Northern France
  Rhineland
  Central Europe

DECORATIONS

None.

94th SIGNAL BATTALION BIBLIOGRAPHY

Blumenson, Martin. *Breakout and Pursuit.* United States Army in World War II. Washington, D.C.: Office of the Chief of Military History, Department of the Army, 1961. 94th Infantry Division cited.

Byrnes, Laurence G., ed. *History of the 94th Infantry Division in World War II.* Washington, D.C.: Infantry Journal Press, 1948.

MacDonald, Charles B. *The Siegfried Line Campaign.* United States Army in World War II. Washington, D.C.: Office of the Chief of Military History, Department of the Army, 1963. 94th Infantry Division cited.

96th SIGNAL BATTALION

HERALDIC ITEMS

COAT OF ARMS

Shield: Tenné, a pile argent issuant from a foot of two waves sable fimbriated of the second, and a sea lion grasping a raised sword of the third.

Crest: That for the regiments and separate battalions of the Army Reserve: On a wreath of the colors argent and tenné the Lexington Minuteman proper. The statue of the Minuteman Capt. John Parker (H. H. Kitson, sculptor) stands on the Common in Lexington, Massachusetts.

Motto: SIGNAL, CLEF DU SUCCES (Signal, Key to Success).

Symbolism: Orange and white are the colors traditionally associated with the Signal Corps. The white pile, or wedge shape, represents the beam of a searchlight and alludes to the unit's function. The two waves at the bottom of the shield represent the unit's participation in World War II campaigns in the Pacific theater, and the sea lion is for the Philippine Presidential Unit Citation awarded the unit for service in the Philippines.

DISTINCTIVE UNIT INSIGNIA

The distinctive unit insignia is the shield and motto of the coat of arms.

LINEAGE AND HONORS

AR
(inactive)

LINEAGE

Constituted 25 July 1918 in the National Army as the 621st Field Signal Battalion and assigned to the 96th Division (later redesignated as the 96th Infantry Division). Organized in October 1918 at Camp Wadsworth, South Carolina. Demobilized 7 January 1919 at Camp Wadsworth, South Carolina.

Reconstituted 24 June 1921 in the Organized Reserves as the 96th Signal Company and assigned to the 96th Division. Organized in March 1922 at Seattle, Washington. Ordered into active military service 15 August 1942 at Camp Adair, Oregon. Inactivated 3 February 1946 at Camp Anza, California. Activated 22 October 1947 at Helena, Montana. (Organized Reserves redesignated 25 March 1948 as the Organized Reserve Corps; redesignated 9 July 1952 as the Army Reserve.) Location changed 1 June 1949 to Butte, Montana; changed 1 July 1950 to Salt Lake City, Utah.

Reorganized and redesignated 1 June 1959 as Headquarters and Headquarters Company, 96th Signal Battalion (organic elements constituted 29 April 1959 in the

Army Reserve; activated 1 June 1959 at Salt Lake City, Utah). Inactivated 15 February 1963 at Salt Lake City, Utah, and relieved from assignment to the 96th Infantry Division (organic elements concurrently inactivated).

CAMPAIGN PARTICIPATION CREDIT

World War II
    Leyte (with arrowhead)
    Ryukyus

DECORATIONS

Presidential Unit Citation (Army), Streamer embroidered OKINAWA (96th Signal Company cited; DA GO 29, 2001)

Meritorious Unit Commendation (Army), Streamer embroidered PACIFIC THEATER OCT 1944–FEB 1945 (96th Signal Company cited; GO 64, 96th Infantry Division, 2 March 1945)

Meritorious Unit Commendation (Army), Streamer embroidered PACIFIC THEATER MAR 1945–SEP 1945 (96th Signal Company cited; GO 781, 96th Infantry Division, 21 September 1945)

Philippine Presidential Unit Citation, Streamer embroidered 17 OCTOBER 1944 TO 4 JULY 1945 (96th Signal Company cited; DA GO 47, 1950)

96th SIGNAL BATTALION BIBLIOGRAPHY

Kern, Irving, ed. *Signal Communique*. Washington, D.C.: Infantry Journal Press, 1946.
96th Infantry Division, 1942–1944. San Francisco: Shannon and Firth, 1945.
96th Infantry Division, Ryukyu Campaign Action Report. N.p., 1945.

97th SIGNAL BATTALION

HERALDIC ITEMS

COAT OF ARMS

Shield: Sable, between a lightning flash bendwise in bend point to chief argent a fleur-de-lis and a bunch of grapes or.
Crest: None approved.
Motto: TRIED AND TRUE.
Symbolism: The colors of the Constabulary—black and golden orange—are used. The battle honors are symbolized by the fleur-de-lis for France and the bunch of grapes for Central Europe and the Rhineland. The lightning flash is used to represent Signal Corps service.

DISTINCTIVE UNIT INSIGNIA

The distinctive unit insignia is the shield and motto of the coat of arms.

LINEAGE AND HONORS

RA
(inactive)

LINEAGE

Constituted 3 November 1941 in the Army of the United States as the 97th Signal Battalion. Activated 10 April 1942 at Fort Sam Houston, Texas. Reorganized and redesignated 1 May 1946 as the 97th Constabulary Signal Squadron. Reorganized and redesignated 5 July 1950 as the 97th Signal Operation Battalion.

Allotted 16 February 1951 to the Regular Army. Reorganized and redesignated 15 February 1953 as the 97th Signal Battalion. Inactivated 15 September 1993 in Germany.

CAMPAIGN PARTICIPATION CREDIT

World War II
   Rhineland
   Ardennes-Alsace
   Central Europe

DECORATIONS

None.

97th SIGNAL BATTALION BIBLIOGRAPHY

Historical Section, 97th Signal Operation Battalion. *Unit History of the 97th Signal Battalion from 10 April 1942 to 10 April 1952.* Böblingen, Germany: Mobile Press of the 5th Loudspeaker and Leaflet Company, 1952.

Jones, Sylvia B., and Edwin P. Stouffer. "Fielding the SWITCH!" *Army Communicator* 9 (Fall 1984): 50–54.

"Spirit of the 97th Signal Battalion." *Signal* 5 (July–August 1951): 9–11, 74, 80.

Thompson, George Raynor, and Dixie R. Harris. *The Signal Corps: The Outcome (Mid-1943 through 1945).* United States Army in World War II. Washington, D.C.: Office of the Chief of Military History, United States Army, 1966.

HEADQUARTERS AND HEADQUARTERS DETACHMENT 98th SIGNAL BATTALION

HERALDIC ITEMS

COAT OF ARMS

None approved.

DISTINCTIVE UNIT INSIGNIA

Description: A gold color metal and enamel device that consists of a blue disc bearing a sea lion grasping in his right paw a flaming torch, all gold and all within an orange annulet inscribed in gold letters KNOWLEDGE, UNITY, SPEED, each word separated by a gold lightning flash. Issuing from the annulet eight white rays.

Symbolism: Orange and white are the colors traditionally associated with the Signal Corps. The sea lion and the eight rays of the sun are associated with the seal of the president of the Philippines. They commemorate the action for which the battalion received the Philippine Presidential Unit Citation and also refer to the unit's participation in four campaigns during World War II. The torch grasped by the sea lion stands for knowledge, the annulet symbolizes unity, and the lightning flashes represent speed. The blue disc represents Lake Ontario, which is near the battalion's former home area in New York.

LINEAGE AND HONORS

AR
(inactive)

LINEAGE

Constituted 3 November 1941 in the Regular Army as the 98th Signal Battalion. Activated 15 June 1942 at Camp Crowder, Missouri. Inactivated 31 May 1946 in Japan.

Redesignated 12 January 1948 as the 98th Signal Operations Battalion; concurrently withdrawn from the Regular Army and allotted to the Organized Reserves. (Organized Reserves redesignated 25 March 1948 as the Organized Reserve Corps; redesignated 9 July 1952 as the Army Reserve.) Redesignated 23 March 1956 as the 98th Signal Battalion. Headquarters and Headquarters Company, 98th Signal Battalion, activated 24 May 1956 at East Orange, New Jersey. Location changed 19 February 1957 to Montclair, New Jersey. Inactivated 1 June 1959 at Montclair, New Jersey.

Headquarters and Headquarters Company, 98th Signal Battalion, redesignated 31 January 1968 as Headquarters and Headquarters Detachment, 98th Signal Battalion, and activated at Rochester, New York. Location changed 1 July 1968 to Webster, New York. Inactivated 17 June 1990 at Webster, New York.

CAMPAIGN PARTICIPATION CREDIT

World War II
  New Guinea
  Leyte
  Luzon
  Southern Philippines

DECORATIONS

Meritorious Unit Commendation (Army), Streamer embroidered PACIFIC THEATER (98th Signal Battalion [less Company A] cited; GO 73, XI Corps, 14 September 1945)

Philippine Presidential Unit Citation, Streamer embroidered 17 OCTOBER 1944 TO 4 JULY 1945 (98th Signal Battalion [Separate] cited; DA GO 47, 1950)

98th SIGNAL BATTALION BIBLIOGRAPHY

Blanton, Nancy C. "Go Between Circuits III." *Army Communicator* 5 (Summer 1980): 19–23.

Cannon, M. Hamlin. *Leyte: The Return to the Philippines*. United States Army in World War II. Washington, D.C.: Office of the Chief of Military History, Department of the Army, 1961.

Carroll, Bill. "Gagetown '87." *Army Communicator* 13 (Winter 1988): 48–49. Field exercise held in New Brunswick, Canada.

Crocker, Robert W. "Go Between Circuits IV." *Army Communicator* 6 (Summer 1981): 50–53.

History of X Corps on Mindanao, 17 April 1945–30 June 1945. N.p., 1945.

A History of the X Corps in the Leyte-Samar Operation. N.p., 1945.

"28 Units Play Logistical CPX." *Army Reserve* 17 (November–December 1971): 24. Command post exercise at Camp Pickett, Virginia.

99th SIGNAL BATTALION

HERALDIC ITEMS

COAT OF ARMS

Shield: Per chevron tenné and argent, three lightning flashes, each of three zigzags—one in pale between two in bend—all counterchanged and all issuing from base above an arrowhead gules.

Crest: That for the regiments and separate battalions of the Army Reserve: On a wreath of the colors argent and tenné the Lexington Minuteman proper. The statue of the Minuteman Capt. John Parker (H. H. Kitson, sculptor) stands on the Common in Lexington, Massachusetts.

Motto: THE GOLDEN FLASH

Symbolism: Orange and white are the colors traditionally associated with the Signal Corps. The color scarlet denotes the Meritorious Unit Commendation (Army) awarded the unit for service in the Asiatic-Pacific theater during World War II. The three lightning flashes represent the unit's participation in the following campaigns: the assault landing in New Guinea, indicated by the arrowhead, and Leyte and the Southern Philippines, for which the unit was awarded the Philippine Presidential Unit Citation. The design alludes to the former heraldic devices, symbolism, and numerical designation used by the unit. The per chevron simulates a mountain, and the lightning flashes have a total of nine zigzags.

DISTINCTIVE UNIT INSIGNIA

Description: A gold color metal and enamel device that consists of a gold Philippine sun on a blue background between two orange lightning flashes issuing from opposite sides in base chevronwise. All above a black scroll bears the inscription THE GOLDEN FLASH in gold letters.

Symbolism: The orange lightning flashes symbolize the basic mission of the battalion. The sun (adopted from the national flag of the Philippines) alludes to the organization's distinguished service in the Philippines. The arrowhead, formed by the joining of the two lightning flashes, refers to the unit's assault landing in New Guinea during World War II.

LINEAGE AND HONORS

LINEAGE

AR
(inactive)

Constituted 3 November 1941 in the Regular Army as the 99th Signal Battalion. Activated 10 March 1942 at Fort Ord, California. Inactivated 31 January 1946 in Japan.

Allotted 19 January 1954 to the Army Reserve. Activated 1 March 1954 with Headquarters at Plattsburgh, New York. (Company B concurrently activated.) (Company A activated 15 February 1955 at Plattsburgh, New York; Company B concurrently inactivated.) Location of Headquarters changed 1 February 1956 to New York, New York. Headquarters and Headquarters Company, 99th Signal Battalion, inactivated 15 August 1959 at New York, New York.

Redesignated 15 September 1959 as Headquarters and Headquarters Detachment, 99th Signal Battalion. Ordered into active military service 15 October 1961 at New York, New York. Released from active military service 8 August 1962 and reverted to reserve status. Location of Headquarters changed 31 January 1966 to Fort Tilden, New York; changed 1 October 1977 to Brooklyn, New York. (Organic elements activated 31 January 1968.) Ordered into active military service (less Company A) 24 March 1970 at Fort Hamilton, New York; released from active military service 26 March 1970 and reverted to reserve status. Inactivated 15 September 1996 at Brooklyn, New York.

CAMPAIGN PARTICIPATION CREDIT

World War II
- New Guinea (with arrowhead)
- Leyte
- Southern Philippines
- Bismarck Archipelago

Company C additionally entitled to:

World War II–AP
- Luzon

DECORATIONS

Meritorious Unit Commendation (Army), Streamer embroidered PACIFIC THEATER (99th Signal Battalion [less Company C] cited; GO 84, X Corps, 14 July 1945)

Philippine Presidential Unit Citation, Streamer embroidered 17 OCTOBER 1944 TO 4 JULY 1945 (99th Signal Battalion cited; DA GO 47, 1950)

Company A additionally entitled to:

Meritorious Unit Commendation (Army), Streamer embroidered LEYTE (Company A, 99th Signal Battalion, cited; GO 68, Sixth Army, 11 April 1945)

99th SIGNAL BATTALION BIBLIOGRAPHY

The Admiralties: Operations of the 1st Cavalry Division (29 February–18 May 1944). American Forces in Action. Washington, D.C.: Historical Division, War Department, 1945.

Cannon, M. Hamlin. *Leyte: The Return to the Philippines*. United States Army in World War II. Washington, D.C.: Office of the Chief of Military History, Department of the Army, 1961.

History of X Corps on Mindanao, 17 April 1945–30 June 1945. N.p., 1945.

A History of the X Corps in the Leyte-Samar Operation. N.p., 1945.

Krueger, Walter. *From Down Under to Nippon: The Story of Sixth Army in World War II*. Washington, D.C.: Combat Forces Press, 1953.

X Corps Occupation of Japan. N.p., 1945.

Thompson, George Raynor, and Dixie R. Harris. *The Signal Corps: The Outcome (Mid-1943 through 1945)*. United States Army in World War II. Washington, D.C.: Office of the Chief of Military History, United States Army, 1966.

Thompson, George Raynor, Dixie R. Harris, Pauline M. Oakes, and Dulany Terrett. *The Signal Corps: The Test (December 1941 to July 1943)*. United States Army in World War II. Washington, D.C.: Office of the Chief of Military History, Department of the Army, 1957.

"USAR Sig Bn Goes to ONEIDA BEAR II." *Army Reserve* 11 (July–August 1965): 6.

HEADQUARTERS AND HEADQUARTERS DETACHMENT 102d SIGNAL BATTALION

HERALDIC ITEMS

COAT OF ARMS

Shield: Argent, two bars wavy azure, and overall a quill palewise tenné fimbriated on the second of the first.

Crest: On a wreath of the colors argent and azure a chevron vert superimposed by a cubit arm in armor gauntleted embowed of the first and holding a lightning flash barbed at either end bendwise or.

Motto: HONOR HERITAGE HISTORY

Symbolism: Orange and white are the colors traditionally associated with the Signal Corps. The battalion's microwave signaling functions are symbolized by the two slightly wavy bars, which also represent the Tiber and Po Rivers, thus alluding to the unit's campaigns in Italy during World War II. The quill pen is a play on the Celtic word "pen" for mountaintop, from which the name Apennine is believed to derive. It also symbolizes communications.

The arm in armor underscores combat readiness and the unit's service during World War II. The two barbs on the lightning flash commemorate the unit's campaigns in the North Apennines and Po Valley; the lightning flash itself highlights speed and electronic capabilities. The chevron suggests the rugged and forested Apennines; green alludes to the fertility of the Po Valley.

DISTINCTIVE UNIT INSIGNIA

The distinctive unit insignia is the shield and motto of the coat of arms.

LINEAGE AND HONORS

RA
(active)

LINEAGE

Constituted 11 December 1944 in the Army of the United States as the 102d Signal Heavy Construction Battalion. Activated 1 March 1945 in Italy as the 102d Signal Light Construction Battalion. Inactivated 2 October 1945 at Camp Myles Standish, Massachusetts.

Redesignated 1 February 1955 as the 102d Signal Battalion and allotted to the Regular Army. Activated 18 March 1955 in Germany. Inactivated 13 November 1967 in Germany. Headquarters and Headquarters Detachment, 102d Signal Battalion, activated 1 July 1974 in Germany.

CAMPAIGN PARTICIPATION CREDIT

World War II
    North Apennines
    Po Valley

DECORATIONS

None.

102d SIGNAL BATTALION BIBLIOGRAPHY

102d Signal Battalion, Frankfurt, Germany. N.p., c. 1974.
102d Signal Battalion, Frankfurt, Germany. N.p., c. 1976.
102d Signal Battalion, Frankfurt, Germany. N.p., c. 1978.

103d SIGNAL BATTALION

HERALDIC ITEMS

COAT OF ARMS

Shield: Argent, in base two bars embattled counterembattled tenné above a foot of the like. In bend a lightning flash throughout sable fimbriated of the first.

Crest: That for the regiments and separate battalions of the Army Reserve: On a wreath of the colors argent and tenné the Lexington Minuteman proper. The statue of the Minuteman Capt. John Parker (H. H. Kitson, sculptor) stands on the Common in Lexington, Massachusetts.

Motto: SANS FAUTE, SANS RETARD (Without Fault, Without Delay).

Symbolism: Orange and white are the colors traditionally associated with the Signal Corps. The three embattled walls refer to the battle streamers earned by the unit in Europe during World War II. The black lightning flash suggests the function of the Signal Corps.

DISTINCTIVE UNIT INSIGNIA

The distinctive unit insignia is the shield and motto of the coat of arms.

LINEAGE AND HONORS

AR
(inactive)

LINEAGE

Constituted 24 June 1921 in the Organized Reserves as the 103d Signal Company and assigned to the 103d Division (later redesignated as the 103d Infantry Division). Organized 9 September 1921 at Denver, Colorado. Ordered into active military service 15 November 1942 at Camp Claiborne, Louisiana. Inactivated 20 September 1945 at Camp Kilmer, New Jersey.

Activated 15 September 1947 at Des Moines, Iowa. (Organized Reserves redesignated 25 March 1948 as the Organized Reserve Corps; redesignated 9 July 1952 as the Army Reserve.)

Reorganized and redesignated 18 May 1959 as Headquarters and Headquarters Company, 103d Signal Battalion (organic elements constituted 20 April 1959 and activated 18 May 1959 as follows: Company A at Des Moines, Iowa; Company B [less 4th and 5th Area Support Platoons] at Watertown, Minnesota; and 4th and 5th Area Support Platoons at Shakopee, Minnesota). Inactivated 15 March 1963 at Des Moines, Iowa, and relieved from assignment to the 103d Infantry Division (organic elements concurrently inactivated).

CAMPAIGN PARTICIPATION CREDIT

World War II
　　Rhineland
　　Ardennes-Alsace
　　Central Europe

DECORATIONS

None.

103d SIGNAL BATTALION BIBLIOGRAPHY

Cactus Caravan. Atlanta: Albert Love Enterprises, 1944. A pictorial history of the 103d Infantry Division.

Mueller, Ralph, and Jerry Turk. *Report After Action, The Story of the 103d Division*. Innsbruck, Austria: Wagner'sche Universitäts-Buchdruckerei, 1945. Reprint, Nashville, Tenn.: Battery Press, 1977.

HEADQUARTERS AND HEADQUARTERS DETACHMENT
105th SIGNAL BATTALION

HERALDIC ITEMS

COAT OF ARMS

Shield: Tenné, a torch argent enflamed proper surmounted by a pair of palmetto branches saltirewise vert fimbriated of the second. Overall a crescent or environed by an annulet of lightning flashes white.

Crest: That for the regiments and separate battalions of the South Carolina Army National Guard: On a wreath of the colors argent and tenné upon a mount vert a palmetto tree proper charged with a crescent argent.

Motto: UBIQUITOUS.

Symbolism: Orange and white are the colors traditionally associated with the Signal Corps. The torch and palmetto leaves simulate the Corps insignia. The torch and annulet of lightning flashes symbolize leadership and the unit's mission and capabilities. The crescent and palmetto leaves refer to the emblems of South Carolina, the unit's home state.

DISTINCTIVE UNIT INSIGNIA

Description: A silver color metal and enamel device that consists of a vertical silver torch with a yellow flame crossed saltirewise by two green palmetto leaves. The stems surmounted by a yellow crescent with horns up conjoining the lower edge of the leaves, all on a dark blue area enclosed on either side by an arched lightning flash divided lengthwise into silver and orange from the flame to the outer edge of an orange scroll passing over the torch in base and inscribed UBIQUITOUS in silver.

Symbolism: Orange and white are the colors traditionally associated with the Signal Corps. The torch and palmetto leaves simulate the Corps insignia. The torch and annulet of lightning flashes symbolize leadership and the unit's mission and capabilities. The crescent and palmetto leaves refer to the emblems of South Carolina, the unit's home state. The arched lightning flashes, flame, and scroll parody the unit's motto.

LINEAGE AND HONORS

ARNG
(South Carolina)

LINEAGE

Constituted 15 March 1979 in the South Carolina Army National Guard as Headquarters and Headquarters Detachment, 105th Signal Battalion. Organized and federally recognized 1 May 1979 at North Charleston. Consolidated 1 October 1996 with the 113th Transportation Detachment (organized and federally recognized 23 September 1992 at North Charleston as the 118th Transportation Detachment; redesignated 1 October 1995 as the 113th Transportation Detachment) and consolidated unit designated as Headquarters and Headquarters Detachment, 105th Signal Battalion.

Home Station: North Charleston

CAMPAIGN PARTICIPATION CREDIT

None.

DECORATIONS

None.

105th SIGNAL BATTALION BIBLIOGRAPHY

Brawders, Jean Marie. "CAPSTONE Effects Training Changes." *National Guard* 40 (November 1986): 30–34.

Crocker, Robert W. "Go Between Circuits IV." *Army Communicator* 6 (Summer 1981): 50–53.

HEADQUARTERS AND HEADQUARTERS DETACHMENT 108th SIGNAL BATTALION

HERALDIC ITEMS

COAT OF ARMS

Shield: Argent, a palmetto branch stem to base vert charged with a mullet white voided green between two lightning bolts arched chevronwise reversed tenné.

Crest: That for the regiments and separate battalions of the South Carolina Army National Guard: On a wreath of the colors argent and vert upon a mount vert a palmetto tree proper charged with a crescent argent.

Motto: PRIDE IN EXCELLENCE.

Symbolism: Orange and white (silver) are the colors traditionally associated with the Signal Corps. The palmetto branch refers to South Carolina, "The Palmetto State," the unit's home area. The star implies command and guidance and represents the unit's overall mission. The lightning bolts symbolize speed and efficiency.

DISTINCTIVE UNIT INSIGNIA

Description: A silver color metal and enamel device that consists of a green palmetto branch stem to base passing under and over a voided silver five-pointed star between two orange lightning bolts arched convexly left and right, all below a blue scroll bearing the inscription PRIDE IN EXCELLENCE in silver letters.

Symbolism: Orange and white (silver) are the colors traditionally associated with the Signal Corps. The palmetto branch refers to South Carolina, "The Palmetto State," the unit's home area. The star implies command and guidance and represents the unit's overall mission. The lightning bolts symbolize speed and efficiency.

LINEAGE AND HONORS

ARNG
(South Carolina)

LINEAGE

Organized and federally recognized 1 October 1980 in the South Carolina Army National Guard at Columbia as Headquarters and Headquarters Detachment, 108th Signal Battalion. Location changed 19 December 1983 to Camden.

Home Station: Camden

CAMPAIGN PARTICIPATION CREDIT
None.

DECORATIONS
None.

108th SIGNAL BATTALION BIBLIOGRAPHY

Brawders, Jean Marie. "CAPSTONE Effects Training Changes." *National Guard* 40 (November 1986): 30–34.

111th SIGNAL BATTALION

HERALDIC ITEMS

COAT OF ARMS

Shield: Tenné, three staffs raguly palewise couped and erased argent. On a chief of the like two lightning flashes saltirewise of the first.

Crest: That for the regiments and separate battalions of the South Carolina Army National Guard: On a wreath of the colors argent and tenné upon a mount vert a palmetto tree proper charged with a crescent argent.

Motto: SIGNALING PRIDE.

Symbolism: Orange and white are the colors traditionally associated with the Signal Corps. The staff raguly is a heraldic symbol for a tree trunk or pole. The pole supports communication lines. The tree trunk refers to the palmetto tree on the state flag of South Carolina, the unit's home area. The staffs symbolize support for the mission of the Army and, in turn, for the defense of the state. The three staffs likewise suggest the unit's numerical designation. The lightning flashes refer to the multidirectional speed of electronic communications.

DISTINCTIVE UNIT INSIGNIA

The distinctive unit insignia is the shield and motto of the coat of arms.

LINEAGE AND HONORS

ARNG
(South Carolina)

LINEAGE

Constituted 20 March 1979 in the Army National Guard as the 111th Signal Battalion and allotted to Georgia, Alabama, South Carolina, and the Virgin Islands. Organized 1 April–1 June 1979 from existing units with Headquarters at Winder, Georgia. Reorganized 1 October 1980 and allotted to South Carolina, Alabama, and the Virgin Islands (location of Headquarters concurrently changed to Greenwood, South Carolina). Reorganized 1 June 1981 and allotted to South Carolina and Alabama. Reorganized 1 September 1981 and allotted to South Carolina and Florida. Reorganized 1 August 1991 and allotted to South Carolina.

Home Area: Western South Carolina

CAMPAIGN PARTICIPATION CREDIT

Company A (Abbeville) entitled to:

World War II-EAME
 Tunisia
 Sicily
 Rome-Arno
 Naples-Foggia
 North Apennines
 Po Valley

DECORATIONS

Company A (Abbeville) entitled to:

French Croix de Guerre with Silver-Gilt Star, World War II, Streamer embroidered CASSINO (Headquarters Battery, 178th Field Artillery Group, cited; DA GO 43, 1950)

111th SIGNAL BATTALION BIBLIOGRAPHY

Brawders, Jean Marie. "CAPSTONE Effects Training Changes." *National Guard* 40 (November 1986): 30–34.

Crocker, Robert W. "Go Between Circuits IV." *Army Communicator* 6 (Summer 1981): 50–53.

Morris, Al, Bill Hawkesworth, and Phyllis Prucino. "The 53d on REFORGER." *Army Communicator* 11 (Spring 1986): 26–29.

112th SIGNAL BATTALION

HERALDIC ITEMS

COAT OF ARMS

Shield: Tenné, on a pile between two lightning flashes in point a dagger argent hilted and winged sable, blade fimbriated of the last.

Crest: On a wreath of the colors argent and tenné in front of the Brandenburg Gate of Berlin sable and issuing from the center of a vol of the first a dragon's head of the second.

Motto: PENETRA LE TENEBRE (Penetrate the Shadows).

Symbolism: Orange and white (silver) are the colors traditionally associated with the Signal Corps. The pile represents the airborne route of attack, alluding to the unit's service during World War II. The dagger, an established symbol of special operations organizations, is black and white in reference to the battalion's covert and overt missions and winged to emphasize present day capabilities of rapid deployment by air. The motto is in Italian in reference to the unit's first area of combat operations. The lightning flashes symbolize electronic technology. The black color of the wings refers to the motto that is translated "Penetrate the Shadows" (special operations), and bespeaks the unit's ability to communicate continuously with deployed operational teams and command elements.

The vol (or wings) and dragon's head are suggested by the shoulder sleeve insignia of the First Airborne Army and the XVIII Airborne Corps, under which the unit served in World War II. Their colors are changed to those of the Signal Corps. The Brandenburg Gate symbolizes occupation duty in Berlin in 1945.

DISTINCTIVE UNIT INSIGNIA

Description: A silver color metal and enamel device that consists of an orange field and centered thereon between two silver lightning flashes both points down, a silver dagger with black hilt and wings enclosed on sides and in base by a black scroll folded and reversed silver at the top and inscribed PENETRA LE TENEBRE in silver.

Symbolism: Orange and white (silver) are the colors traditionally associated with the Signal Corps. The dagger, an established symbol of special operations organizations is black and white (silver) in reference to the battalion's covert and overt missions. It is winged to emphasize present day capabilities for speed of deployment by air. The black color enhances the motto that is translated "Penetrate the Shadows." The lightning flashes reflect electronic technology. The motto is in Italian in reference to the unit's first area of combat operations.

LINEAGE AND HONORS

RA
(active)

LINEAGE

Constituted 14 July 1944 in the Army of the United States as the 512th Airborne Signal Company and activated in North Africa. Disbanded 10 February 1945 in France.

Reconstituted 5 April 1945 in the Army of the United States; concurrently consolidated with the 112th Airborne Army Signal Battalion (constituted 15 January 1945 in the Army of the United States and activated 10 February 1945 in France) and consolidated unit designated as the 112th Airborne Army Signal Battalion. Inactivated 12 December 1945 at Camp Patrick Henry, Virginia.

Redesignated 17 September 1986 as the 112th Signal Battalion, allotted to the Regular Army, and activated at Fort Bragg, North Carolina.

CAMPAIGN PARTICIPATION CREDIT

World War II
  Rome-Arno
  Southern France (with arrowhead)
  Rhineland
  Ardennes-Alsace
  Central Europe

Southwest Asia
  Liberation and Defense of Kuwait

DECORATIONS

Meritorious Unit Commendation (Army), Streamer embroidered SOUTHWEST ASIA 1991 (112th Signal Battalion [Special Operations] [Airborne] cited; DA GO 17, 1992)

Army Superior Unit Award, Streamer embroidered 1994–1995 (112th Signal Battalion cited; DA GO 1, 1996)

Army Superior Unit Award, Streamer embroidered 1995–1996 (112th Signal Battalion cited; DA GO 15, 1997)

112th SIGNAL BATTALION BIBLIOGRAPHY

Flood, Patrick. "Special Ops Signal Battalion Provides Special Support for Operation IRAQI FREEDOM." *Army Communicator* 28 (Fall 2003): 19–23.

Kropp, Donald. "Joint Task Force Communications: The Special Operations Paradigm." *Army Communicator* 18 (Summer 1993): 26–28.

Mills, Brad. "112th Signal Batallion Soldiers Get Valor Awards." *Army Communicator* 28 (Spring 2003): 50.

"112th Signal Battalion Provides Commo for Purple Dragon '98." *Army Communicator* 23 (Spring 1998): 43.

Rackley, Jeffrey A. "A Special Signal Battalion." *Army Communicator* 12 (Spring 1987): 48.

Rudd, Gordon W. *Humanitarian Intervention: Assisting the Iraqi Kurds in Operation PROVIDE COMFORT, 1991*. Washington, D.C.: Center of Military History, United States Army, 2004.

Thompson, George Raynor, and Dixie R. Harris. *The Signal Corps: The Outcome (Mid-1943 through 1945)*. United States Army in World War II. Washington, D.C.: Office of the Chief of Military History, United States Army, 1966.

HEADQUARTERS AND HEADQUARTERS COMPANY
114th SIGNAL BATTALION

HERALDIC ITEMS

None approved.

LINEAGE AND HONORS

AR
(inactive)

LINEAGE

Constituted 10 October 1944 in the Army of the United States as Headquarters and Headquarters Detachment, 3364th Signal Service Battalion. Activated 28 October 1944 at Miami, Florida. Inactivated 22 April 1946 at Miami, Florida.

Redesignated 20 October 1959 as Headquarters and Headquarters Detachment, 114th Signal Battalion, and allotted to the Army Reserve. Activated 26 October 1959 at Greensboro, North Carolina. Reorganized and redesignated 5 January 1966 as Headquarters and Headquarters Company, 114th Signal Battalion. Inactivated 31 January 1968 at Greensboro, North Carolina.

CAMPAIGN PARTICIPATION CREDIT

None.

DECORATIONS

Meritorious Unit Commendation (Army), Streamer embroidered AMERICAN THEATER (3364th Signal Service Battalion cited; GO 3, Army Service Forces, 26 May 1946)

114th SIGNAL BATTALION BIBLIOGRAPHY

No published histories.

115th SIGNAL BATTALION

HERALDIC ITEMS

COAT OF ARMS

Shield: Gules, on a pile throughout between two 40-mm. shells or and overall the insignia of the Signal Corps.

Crest: That for the regiments and separate battalions of the Alabama Army National Guard: On a wreath of the colors or and gules a slip of cotton plant with full bursting boll proper.

Motto: FIRST IN DUTY.

Symbolism: Red and yellow are the colors for Artillery. The pile represents a searchlight beam to indicate the Coast Artillery origin of the unit. The shells denote the organization's former function as an Antiaircraft Artillery Automatic Weapons unit. The insignia hightlights the battalion's affiliation with the Signal Corps. The fountain, a heraldic symbol for water, depicts the battalion's campaign service during World War II in the Asiatic-Pacific Theater.

DISTINCTIVE UNIT INSIGNIA

The distinctive unit insignia is the shield and motto of the coat of arms.

LINEAGE AND HONORS

ARNG
(Alabama)

LINEAGE

Organized and federally recognized 21 December 1940 in the Alabama National Guard as the 2d Battalion, 151st Engineers, with Headquarters at Florence. Inducted into Federal service 27 January 1941 at home stations. Redesignated 12 September 1942 as the 2d Battalion, 151st Engineer Combat Regiment. Reorganized and redesignated 11 July 1944 as the 1343d Engineer Combat Battalion. (Company C, 1343d Engineer Combat Battalion, inactivated 16 January 1946 at Camp Kilmer, New Jersey.) 1343d Engineer Combat Battalion (less Company C) inactivated 26 January 1946 at Camp Kilmer, New Jersey.

Converted, redesignated, and federally recognized 15 January 1947 as the 104th Antiaircraft Artillery Automatic Weapons Battalion, with Headquarters at Florence. Ordered into active Federal service 16 January 1951 at Florence. Redesignated 11 May 1953 as the 104th Antiaircraft Artillery Battalion. Released 15 June 1954 from active Federal service and reverted to state control; concurrently, consolidated with the 278th Antiaircraft Artillery Battalion (organized and federally recognized 23 March 1953 with Headquarters at Florence), and consolidated unit designated as the 278th Antiaircraft Artillery Battalion. Reorganized and redesignated 2 May 1959 as the 1st Automatic Weapons Battalion, 278th Artillery.

Converted and redesignated 16 December 1959 as the 115th Signal Battalion. Ordered into active Federal service 11 June 1963 at home stations; released 16 June 1963 from active Federal service and reverted to state control. Ordered into active Federal service 10 September 1963 at home stations; released 12 September 1963 from active Federal service and reverted to state control.

Home Area: Northwestern Alabama

CAMPAIGN PARTICIPATION CREDIT

World War II
   Aleutian Islands
   Rhineland

DECORATIONS

None.

115th SIGNAL BATTALION BIBLIOGRAPHY

Dod, Karl C. *The Corps of Engineers: The War Against Japan.* United States Army in World War II. Washington, D.C.: Office of the Chief of Military History, United States Army, 1966. 2d Battalion, 151st Engineer Combat Regiment, cited.

121st SIGNAL BATTALION

HERALDIC ITEMS

COAT OF ARMS

Shield: Per bend enhanced argent and tenné, on the first palewise in bend six Lorraine Crosses and on the second palewise in bend three fire arrows all counterchanged.

Crest: On a wreath of the colors argent and tenné a Spanish castle argent charged with a fleur-de-lis tenné.

Motto: TO ΠPARON EY POIEIN (Do Well the Duty That Lies Before You).

Symbolism: Orange and white are the colors traditionally associated with the Signal Corps. The six Lorraine Crosses represent the unit's six World War I campaigns and are arranged to suggest a telegraph line. The three fire arrows symbolize the unit's three assault landings in World War II and also suggest the signal functions such weapons once served.

Orange and white are the colors traditionally associated with the Signal Corps. The Spanish castle taken from the Spanish campaign medal symbolizes the unit's service in Puerto Rico during the War with Spain. The fleur-de-lis represents the unit's service in France during World War I.

DISTINCTIVE UNIT INSIGNIA

The distinctive unit insignia consists of elements of the crest and the motto of the coat of arms.

LINEAGE AND HONORS

RA
(1st Infantry Division) (active)

LINEAGE

Constituted 1 July 1916 in the Regular Army as a Signal Corps battalion. Organized 16 September 1916 at Fort Sam Houston, Texas, as the 2d Field Battalion, Signal Corps, to consist of the following companies:

Company A organized 27 July 1898 as Company A, Signal Corps; redesignated 5 April 1910 as Field Company A, Signal Corps; redesignated 19 October 1915 as Radio Company A, Signal Corps; redesignated 11 November 1916 as Company A, 2d Field Battalion, Signal Corps.

Company B organized 27 July 1898 as Company D, Signal Corps; redesignated 5 April 1910 as Field Company D, Signal Corps; redesignated 11 November 1916 as Company B, 2d Field Battalion, Signal Corps.

Company C organized 11 May 1917 at Fort Sam Houston, Texas.

Battalion assigned 24 May 1917 to the 1st Expeditionary Division (redesignated 6 July 1917 as the 1st Division; redesignated 1 August 1942 as the 1st Infantry Division). Reorganized and redesignated 3 August 1917 as the 2d Field Signal Battalion. Reorganized and redesignated 9 February 1921 as the 1st Signal Company.

Reorganized and redesignated 15 February 1957 as Headquarters and Headquarters Company, 121st Signal Battalion (organic elements constituted 8 February 1957 and activated 15 February 1957 at Fort Riley, Kansas). Inactivated 15 December 1995 at Fort Riley, Kansas. Activated 16 February 1996 in Germany.

CAMPAIGN PARTICIPATION CREDIT

War with Spain
  Puerto Rico

World War I
  Montdidier-Noyon
  Aisne-Marne
  St. Mihiel
  Meuse-Argonne
  Lorraine 1918
  Picardy 1918

World War II
  Algeria-French Morocco (with arrowhead)
  Tunisia
  Sicily (with arrowhead)
  Normandy (with arrowhead)
  Northern France
  Rhineland
  Ardennes-Alsace
  Central Europe

Vietnam
  Defense
  Counteroffensive
  Counteroffensive, Phase II
  Counteroffensive, Phase III
  Tet Counteroffensive
  Counteroffensive, Phase IV
  Counteroffensive, Phase V
  Counteroffensive, Phase VI
  Tet 69/Counteroffensive
  Summer-Fall 1969
  Winter-Spring 1970

Southwest Asia
  Defense of Saudi Arabia
  Liberation and Defense of Kuwait
  Cease-Fire

DECORATIONS

Presidential Unit Citation (Army), Streamer embroidered EUROPE 1944–1945 (1st Signal Company cited; DA GO 42, 1953)

Meritorious Unit Commendation (Army), Streamer embroidered EUROPEAN THEATER (1st Signal Company cited; GO 164, 1st Infantry Division, 4 September 1953)

Meritorious Unit Commendation (Army), Streamer embroidered VIETNAM 1966–1967 (121st Signal Battalion cited; DA GO 17, 1968)

Meritorious Unit Commendation (Army), Streamer embroidered VIETNAM 1967–1968 (121st Signal Battalion cited; DA GO 1, 1969)

Meritorious Unit Commendation (Army), Streamer embroidered VIETNAM 1968–1969 (121st Signal Battalion cited; DA GO 39, 1970)

Army Superior Unit Award, Streamer embroidered 1996–1997 (Headquarters and Headquarters Company and Company B, 121st Signal Battalion, cited; DA GO 25, 2001)

Army Superior Unit Award, Streamer embroidered 1997 (Headquarters and Headquarters Company, Companies A and C, 121st Signal Battalion, cited; DA GO 25, 2001)

French Croix de Guerre with Palm, World War I, Streamer embroidered LORRAINE-PICARDY (2d Field Signal Battalion cited; WD GO 11, 1924)

French Croix de Guerre with Palm, World War I, Streamer embroidered AISNE-MARNE and MEUSE-ARGONNE (2d Field Signal Battalion cited; WD GO 11, 1924)

French Croix de Guerre with Gilt Star, World War I, Streamer embroidered FRANCE (2d Field Signal Battalion cited; WD GO 11, 1924)

French Croix de Guerre with Palm, World War II, Streamer embroidered TUNISIA (1st Signal Company cited; DA GO 43, 1950)

French Croix de Guerre with Palm, World War II, Streamer embroidered NORMANDY (1st Signal Company cited; DA GO 43, 1950)

French Medaille Militaire, Fourragere (1st Signal Company cited; DA GO 43, 1950)

Belgian Fourragere 1940 (1st Signal Company cited; DA GO 43, 1950)

Cited in the Order of the Day of the Belgian Army for action at Mons (1st Signal Company cited; DA GO 43, 1950)

Cited in the Order of the Day of the Belgian Army for action at Eupen-Malmedy (1st Signal Company cited; DA GO 43, 1950)

Republic of Vietnam Cross of Gallantry with Palm, Streamer embroidered VIETNAM 1965–1968 (121st Signal Battalion cited; DA GO 21, 1969)

Republic of Vietnam Civil Action Honor Medal, First Class, Streamer embroidered VIETNAM 1965–1970 (121st Signal Battalion cited; DA GO 53, 1970)

121st SIGNAL BATTALION BIBLIOGRAPHY

American Battle Monuments Commission. *1st Division, Summary of Operations in the World War*. Washington, D.C.: Government Printing Office, 1944.

Bergen, John D. *Military Communications: A Test for Technology*. United States Army in Vietnam. Washington, D.C.: Center of Military History, United States Army, 1986.

Blumenson, Martin. *Breakout and Pursuit*. United States Army in World War II. Washington, D.C.: Office of the Chief of Military History, Department of the Army, 1961. 1st Infantry Division cited.

———. *Salerno to Cassino*. United States Army in World War II. Washington, D.C.: Office of the Chief of Military History, United States Army, 1969. 1st Infantry Division cited.

Bowman, Patrick A. "C^3 That Is Really C^3." *Army Communicator* 7 (Spring 1982): 4–11.

Cole, Hugh M. *The Ardennes: Battle of the Bulge*. United States Army in World War II. Washington, D.C.: Office of the Chief of Military History, Department of the Army, 1965. 1st Infantry Division cited.

Garland, Albert N., and Howard McGaw Smyth. *Sicily and the Surrender of Italy*. United States Army in World War II. Washington, D.C.: Office of the Chief of Military History, Department of the Army, 1965. 1st Infantry Division cited.

Goda, Bryan, and Douglas Babb. "Providing Communications to Task Force Eagle in Bosnia: Doing More with Less." *Army Communicator* 22 (Fall 1997): 7–12.

Greenstreet, Medford, ed. *1st Infantry Division, Fort Riley, Kansas, 1956*. N.p.: Miller Publishing Company, 1956.

Harrison, Gordon A. *Cross-Channel Attack*. United States Army in World War II. Washington, D.C.: Office of the Chief of Military History, United States Army, 1951. 1st Infantry Division cited.

Horn, Tyree R. "The First Signal Company in Georgia." *Signal Corps Bulletin* 108 (April–June 1940): 31–44.

Howe, George F. *Northwest Africa: Seizing the Initiatve in the West*. United States Army in World War II. Washington, D.C.: Office of the Chief of Military History, Department of the Army, 1957. 1st Infantry Division cited.

Johnson, Danny M. *Military Communications Supporting Peacekeeping Operations in the Balkans: The Signal Corps at Its Best*. Mannheim, Germany: Headquarters, 5th Signal Command, 2000.

Knickerbocker, H. R., et al. *Danger Forward: The Story of the First Division in World War II*. Atlanta: Albert Love Enterprises, 1947. Reprint, Nashville: Battery Press, 1980.

MacDonald, Charles B. *The Siegfried Line Campaign*. United States Army in World War II. Washington, D.C.: Office of the Chief of Military History, Department of the Army, 1963. 1st Infantry Division cited.

Myer, Charles R. *Division-Level Communications, 1962–1973*. Vietnam Studies. Washington, D.C.: Department of the Army, 1982.

Noble, Thomas F., ed. *1st Infantry Division, 35th Annniversary*. Darmstadt, Germany: L. C. Wittich, 1952.

Raines, Rebecca Robbins. *Getting the Message Through: A Branch History of the U.S. Army Signal Corps*. Army Historical Series. Washington, D.C.: Center of Military History, United States Army, 1996.

A Record of the Activities of the Second Field Signal Battalion, First Division. Cologne: J. P. Bachem, 1919.

Rienzi, Thomas M. *Communications-Electronics, 1962–1970*. Vietnam Studies. Washington, D.C.: Department of the Army, 1972.

Society of the First Division. *History of the First Division During the World War, 1917–1919*. Philadelphia: John C. Winston Company, 1922.

Tasks Performed by the 121st Signal Battalion During the Period 1 June 1966 Through 31 May 1967. N.p., 1967.

Terrett, Dulany. *The Signal Corps: The Emergency*. United States Army in World War II. Washington, D.C.: Office of the Chief of Military History, Department of the Army, 1956.

Thompson, George Raynor, and Dixie R. Harris. *The Signal Corps: The Outcome (Mid-1943 through 1945)*. United States Army in World War II. Washington, D.C.: Office of the Chief of Military History, United States Army, 1966.

Vietnam, April 1967–April 1968: A Pictorial History of the 121st Signal Battalion, 1st Infantry Division. N.p., 1968.

Vietnam, October 1965–April 1967: A Pictorial History of the 121st Signal Battalion, 1st Infantry Division. N.p., 1967.

Wilson, Jimmie, ed. *1st Infantry Division in Vietnam, 1969*. Tokyo: Dai Nippon Printing Company, c. 1969.

———. *1st Infantry Division in Vietnam, July 1965–April 1967.* Tokyo: Dai Nippon Printing Company, 1967.

———. *1st Infantry Division in Vietnam, 1 May 1967–31 December 1968.* Tokyo: Dai Nippon Printing Company, c. 1969.

122d SIGNAL BATTALION

HERALDIC ITEMS

COAT OF ARMS

Shield: Per fess enhanced dancetté argent, two pallets tenné and paley of five per pale gules and azure, in base a Korean bell of the first.

Crest: On a wreath of the colors argent and tenné a carabao's head argent within an annulet tenné fimbriated of the first charged with six fleurs-de-lis of the like.

Motto: FIAT LUX (Let There Be Light).

Symbolism: The five divisions at the top of the shield, in the orange and white colors of the Signal Corps, stand for the battalion's five World War II battle honors. The ten divisions in base in the red and blue of the Korean taeguk refer to the battalion's decorations (two Republic of Korea Presidential Unit Citations) awarded for service during the Korean War.

The crest is the badge of the old 2d Signal Company. The carabao head is for service during the Philippine Insurrection, and the six fleurs-de-lis commemorate the unit's campaigns in France during World War I.

DISTINCTIVE UNIT INSIGNIA

The distinctive unit insignia is the shield and crest of the coat of arms.

LINEAGE AND HONORS

RA
(2d Infantry Division) (active)

LINEAGE

Constituted 1 July 1916 in the Regular Army as a Signal Corps battalion. Organized 10 October 1916 at Fort Bliss, Texas, as the 1st Field Battalion, Signal Corps, to consist of the following companies:

Company A organized 28 May 1899 in the Philippine Islands as Company E, Signal Corps. Redesignated 5 April 1910 as Field Company E, Signal Corps. Redesignated 11 November 1916 as Company A, 1st Field Battalion, Signal Corps.

Company B organized 1 July 1904 at Benecia Barracks, California, as Company I, Signal Corps. Redesignated 5 April 1910 as Field Company I, Signal Corps. Redesignated 11 November 1916 as Company B, 1st Field Battalion, Signal Corps.

Company C organized in May 1917 at Fort Bliss, Texas.

LINEAGES AND HERALDIC DATA 235

Reorganized and redesignated 3 August 1917 as the 1st Field Signal Battalion. Assigned 21 September 1917 to the 2d Division (later redesignated as the 2d Infantry Division). Reorganized and redesignated 23 April 1921 as the 2d Signal Company.

Reorganized and redesignated 20 June 1957 as Headquarters and Headquarters Company, 122d Signal Battalion (organic elements constituted 24 May 1957 and activated 20 June 1957 in Alaska).

CAMPAIGN PARTICIPATION CREDIT

Philippine Insurrection
  San Isidro

World War I
  Aisne
  Aisne-Marne
  St. Mihiel
  Meuse-Argonne
  Lorraine 1918
  Ile de France 1918

World War II
  Normandy
  Northern France
  Rhineland
  Ardennes-Alsace
  Central Europe

Korean War
  UN Defensive
  UN Offensive
  CCF Intervention
  First UN Counteroffensive
  CCF Spring Offensive
  UN Summer–Fall Offensive
  Second Korean Winter
  Korea, Summer–Fall 1952
  Third Korean Winter
  Korea, Summer 1953

DECORATIONS

Presidential Unit Citation (Army), Streamer embroidered WIRTZFELD, BELGIUM (2d Signal Company, 2d Infantry Division, cited; WD GO 26, 1945)

Presidential Unit Citation (Army), Streamer embroidered HONGCHON (2d Infantry Division cited; DA GO 72, 1951)

Meritorious Unit Commendation (Army), Streamer embroidered EUROPEAN THEATER (2d Signal Company cited; GO 41, 2d Infantry Division, 14 April 1945)

Meritorious Unit Commendation (Army), Streamer embroidered KOREA 1950–1951 (2d Signal Company, 2d Infantry Division, cited; DA GO 49, 1951)

French Croix de Guerre with Palm, World War I, Streamer embroidered AISNE-MARNE (1st Field Signal Battalion cited; WD GO 11, 1924)

French Croix de Guerre with Palm, World War I, Streamer embroidered MEUSE-ARGONNE (1st Field Signal Battalion cited; WD GO 11, 1924)

French Croix de Guerre, World War I, Fourragere (1st Field Signal Battalion cited; WD GO 11, 1924)

Belgian Fourragere 1940 (2d Signal Company cited; DA GO 43, 1950)

Cited in the Order of the Day of the Belgian Army for action in the Ardennes (2d Signal Company cited; DA GO 43, 1950)

Cited in the Order of the Day of the Belgian Army for action on Elsenborn Crest (2d Signal Company cited; DA GO 43, 1950)

Republic of Korea Presidential Unit Citation, Streamer embroidered NAKTONG RIVER LINE (2d Signal Company cited; DA GO 35, 1951)

Republic of Korea Presidential Unit Citation, Streamer embroidered KOREA 1950–1953 (2d Signal Company cited; DA GO 10, 1954)

122d SIGNAL BATTALION BIBLIOGRAPHY

American Battle Monuments Commission. *2d Division, Summary of Operations in the World War*. Washington, D.C.: Government Printing Office, 1944.

Appleman, Roy E. *South to the Naktong, North to the Yalu: June–November 1950*. United States Army in the Korean War. Washington, D.C.: Office of the Chief of Military History, Department of the Army, 1961. 2d Infantry Division cited.

Blumenson, Martin. *Breakout and Pursuit*. United States Army in World War II. Washington, D.C.: Office of the Chief of Military History, Department of the Army, 1961. 2d Infantry Division cited.

Carver, Curtis, et al. "2d Infantry Division's Tactical Worldwide Web: An Effective Battlefield Information System." *Army Communicator* 23 (Spring 1998): 24–28.

Cole, Hugh M. *The Ardennes: Battle of the Bulge*. United States Army in World War II. Washington, D.C.: Office of the Chief of Military History, Department of the Army, 1965. 2d Infantry Division cited.

Combat History of the Second Infantry Division, World War II. Baton Rouge: Army and Navy Publishing Company, 1946. Reprint. Nashville: Battery Press, 1979.

Harrison, Gordon A. *Cross-Channel Attack*. United States Army in World War II. Washington, D.C.: Office of the Chief of Military History, United States Army, 1951. 2d Infantry Division cited.

Hermes, Walter G. *Truce Tent and Fighting Front*. United States Army in the Korean War. Washington, D.C.: Office of the Chief of Military History, United States Army, 1966. 2d Infantry Division cited.

MacDonald, Charles B. *The Last Offensive*. United States Army in World War II. Washington, D.C.: Office of the Chief of Military History, United States Army, 1973. 2d Infantry Division cited.

———. *The Siegfried Line Campaign*. United States Army in World War II. Washington, D.C.: Office of the Chief of Military History, Department of the Army, 1963. 2d Infantry Division cited.

Munroe, Clark C. *The Second United States Infantry Division in Korea, 1950–1951*. Tokyo: Toppan Printing Company, 1952.

Murdock, Karen. "Typhoon Janis in Korea Challenges Signal Unit." *Army Communicator* 21 (Winter 1996): 43–44. 1st Platoon, Company A, cited.

122d Signal Battalion. Baton Rouge: Army and Navy Publishing Company, 1959.

"Second to None." The Second United States Infantry Division in Korea, 1 January 1953–31 December 1953. Tokyo: Toppan Printing Company, 1954.

Tatom, Louis J. "Notes on the Motorization of the Second Signal Company." *Signal Corps Bulletin* 91 (July–August 1936): 7–13.

Thompson, George Raynor, and Dixie R. Harris. *The Signal Corps: The Outcome (Mid-1943 through 1945).* United States Army in World War II. Washington, D.C.: Office of the Chief of Military History, United States Army, 1966.

Thompson, George Raynor, Dixie R. Harris, Pauline M. Oakes, and Dulany Terrett. *The Signal Corps: The Test (December 1941 to July 1943).* United States Army in World War II. Washington, D.C.: Office of the Chief of Military History, Department of the Army, 1957.

123d SIGNAL BATTALION

HERALDIC ITEMS

COAT OF ARMS

Shield: Tenné, a crowing cock, beaked, wattled, jelloped, and legged azure, perched on a triangle above a mace fesswise, all argent.
Crest: None approved.
Motto: PRIMA VOX AUDIAT (The First Voice Heard).
Symbolism: Orange and white are the colors traditionally associated with the Signal Corps. The crowing cock from the arms of one of the Marne provinces represents signal service in that area during World War I. The triangle represents the Iron Triangle in Korea, which the unit helped to hold. The mace from the arms of Colmar alludes to the unit's World War II service in the Colmar pocket.

DISTINCTIVE UNIT INSIGNIA

The distinctive unit insignia is the shield and motto of the coat of arms.

LINEAGE AND HONORS

RA
LINEAGE (3d Infantry Division) (active)

Constituted 1 July 1916 in the Regular Army as a Signal Corps battalion. Organized 26 June 1917 at Fort Leavenworth, Kansas, as the 5th Field Battalion, Signal Corps. Reorganized and redesignated 3 August 1917 as the 5th Field Signal Battalion. Assigned 12 November 1917 to the 3d Division (later redesignated as the 3d Infantry Division).

Reorganized and redesignated 14 February 1921 as the 3d Signal Company. Inactivated 1 February 1925 at Camp Lewis, Washington. Activated 1 July 1935 at Fort Lewis, Washington.

Reorganized and redesignated 1 July 1957 as Headquarters and Headquarters Company, 123d Signal Battalion (organic elements constituted 23 April 1957 and activated 1 July 1957 at Fort Benning, Georgia).

CAMPAIGN PARTICIPATION CREDIT

World War I
- Aisne
- Champagne-Marne
- Aisne-Marne
- St. Mihiel
- Meuse-Argonne
- Champagne 1918

World War II
- Algeria-French Morocco (with arrowhead)
- Tunisia
- Sicily (with arrowhead)
- Naples-Foggia
- Anzio (with arrowhead)
- Rome-Arno
- Southern France (with arrowhead)
- Rhineland
- Ardennes-Alsace
- Central Europe

Korean War
- CCF Intervention
- First UN Counteroffensive
- CCF Spring Offensive
- UN Summer–Fall Offensive
- Second Korean Winter
- Korea, Summer–Fall 1952
- Third Korean Winter
- Korea, Summer 1953

DECORATIONS

Presidential Unit Citation (Army), Streamer embroidered COLMAR (3d Infantry Division cited; WD GO 44, 1945)

Meritorious Unit Commendation (Army), Streamer embroidered EUROPEAN THEATER (3d Signal Company cited; GO 87, 3d Infantry Division, 7 March 1945)

Meritorious Unit Commendation (Army), Streamer embroidered KOREA 1950–1951 (3d Signal Company, 3d Infantry Division, cited; DA GO 62, 1952)

Meritorious Unit Commendation (Army), Streamer embroidered KOREA 1953 (3d Signal Company, 3d Infantry Division, cited; DA GO 11, 1954)

French Croix de Guerre with Silver Star, World War I, Streamer embroidered MARNE (5th Field Signal Battalion cited; WD GO 11, 1924)

French Croix de Guerre with Palm, World War II, Streamer embroidered COLMAR (3d Signal Company cited; DA GO 43, 1950)

French Croix de Guerre, World War II, Fourragere (3d Signal Company cited; DA GO 43, 1950)

Republic of Korea Presidential Unit Citation, Streamer embroidered UIJONGBU CORRIDOR (3d Signal Company cited; DA GO 20, 1953)

Republic of Korea Presidential Unit Citation, Streamer embroidered IRON TRIANGLE (3d Signal Company cited; DA GO 29, 1954)

Chryssoun Aristion Andrias (Bravery Gold Medal of Greece), Streamer embroidered KOREA (3d Signal Company cited; DA GO 2, 1956)

123d SIGNAL BATTALION BIBLIOGRAPHY

American Battle Monuments Commission. *3d Division, Summary of Operations in the World War*. Washington, D.C.: Government Printing Office, 1944.

Appleman, Roy E. *South to the Naktong, North to the Yalu: June–November 1950*. United States Army in the Korean War. Washington, D.C.: Office of the Chief of Military History, Department of the Army, 1961. 3d Infantry Division cited.

Bancroft, Delbert. "123d Signal Battalion Supports Operation Torch Overwatch." *Army Communicator* 22 (Winter 1997): 29–30.

Blumenson, Martin. *Salerno to Cassino*. United States Army in World War II. Washington, D.C.: Office of the Chief of Military History, United States Army, 1969. 3d Infantry Division cited.

Dolcater, Max W., ed. *3d Infantry Division in Korea*. Tokyo: Toppan Printing Company, 1953.

Editors of *Army Times*. *A History of the U.S. Army Signal Corps*. New York: G. P. Putnam's Sons, 1961.

Fisher, Ernest F., Jr. *Cassino to the Alps*. United States Army in World War II. Washington, D.C.: Center of Military History, United States Army, 1977. 3d Infantry Division cited.

Garland, Albert N., and Howard McGaw Smyth. *Sicily and the Surrender of Italy*. United States Army in World War II. Washington. D.C.: Office of the Chief of Military History, Department of the Army, 1965. 3d Infantry Division cited.

Hamilton, Brian. "Atlantic Resolve: Order Out of Chaos, Or Creating Communications Links for a Joint Multinational Exercise." *Army Communicator* 20 (Fall 1995): 40–43.

Hemenway, Frederic V., ed. and comp. *History of the Third Division, United States Army, in the World War, for the Period December 1, 1917 to January 1, 1919*. Cologne, Germany: M. DuMont Schauberg, 1919.

Hermes, Walter G. *Truce Tent and Fighting Front*. United States Army in the Korean War. Washington, D.C.: Office of the Chief of Military History, United States Army, 1966. 3d Infantry Division cited.

Howe, George F. *Northwest Africa: Seizing the Initiatve in the West*. United States Army in World War II. Washington, D.C.: Office of the Chief of Military History, Department of the Army, 1957. 3d Infantry Division cited.

MacDonald, Charles B. *The Last Offensive*. United States Army in World War II. Washington, D.C.: Office of the Chief of Military History, United States Army, 1973. 3d Infantry Division cited.

Taggart, Donald G., ed. *History of the Third Infantry Division in World War II*. Washington, D.C.: Infantry Journal Press, 1947.

Thompson, George Raynor, and Dixie R. Harris. *The Signal Corps: The Outcome (Mid-1943 through 1945)*. United States Army in World War II. Washington, D.C.: Office of the Chief of Military History, United States Army, 1966.

124th SIGNAL BATTALION

HERALDIC ITEMS

COAT OF ARMS

Shield: Per fess tenné and argent, in chief a dexter hand encased in a gauntlet grasping three lightning flashes—one in pale and two saltirewise—of the second, and in base a wheel arraswise sable winged of the first.

Crest: On a wreath of the colors argent and tenné a lion passant gardant grasping in dexter forepaw a pheon argent.

Motto: THE VOICE OF THE SAINTS.

Symbolism: Orange and white are the colors traditionally associated with the Signal Corps. The design, adopted from the badge of the former 4th Signal Company, symbolizes the battalion's functions.

The lion in the crest is adopted from the arms of Normandy. The heraldic representation of the spearhead held aloft is a reference to the battalion's participation in the invasion of Normandy during World War II.

DISTINCTIVE UNIT INSIGNIA

Description: A silver color metal and enamel device that consists of a square with chamfered corners, one corner up, divided horizontally. The upper half of orange charged with a right hand wearing a silver gauntlet and grasping three silver lightning flashes, one vertically between two in saltire. The lower half of silver charged with an orange winged black wheel in perspective.

Symbolism: Orange and white (silver) are the colors traditionally associated with the Signal Corps. The functions of the organization are symbolized by the strong right hand of the person grasping the lightning flashes, indicating speed. The unit's original numerical designation is indicated by the four sides of the square.

LINEAGE AND HONORS

RA
(4th Infantry Division) (active)

LINEAGE

Constituted 1 June 1940 in the Regular Army as the 4th Signal Company, assigned to the 4th Division (later redesignated as the 4th Infantry Division), and activated at Fort Benning, Georgia. Inactivated 23 February 1946 at Camp Butner, North Carolina. Activated 6 July 1948 at Fort Ord, California.

Reorganized and redesignated 1 April 1957 as Headquarters and Headquarters Company, 124th Signal Battalion (organic elements concurrently constituted and activated at Fort Lewis, Washington). Inactivated 15 December 1995 at Fort Carson, Colorado.

Activated 16 January 1996 at Fort Hood, Texas.

CAMPAIGN PARTICIPATION CREDIT

World War II
- Normandy (with arrowhead)
- Northern France
- Rhineland
- Ardennes-Alsace
- Central Europe

Vietnam
- Counteroffensive, Phase II
- Counteroffensive, Phase III
- Tet Counteroffensive
- Counteroffensive, Phase IV
- Counteroffensive, Phase V
- Counteroffensive, Phase VI
- Tet 69/Counteroffensive
- Summer–Fall 1969
- Winter–Spring 1970
- Sanctuary Counteroffensive
- Counteroffensive, Phase VII

DECORATIONS

Meritorious Unit Commendation (Army), Streamer embroidered EUROPEAN THEATER (4th Signal Company cited; Order of the Day No. 30, 4th Infantry Division, 12 September 1944)

Meritorious Unit Commendation (Army), Streamer embroidered VIETNAM 1967–1968 (124th Signal Battalion, 4th Infantry Division, cited; DA GO 48, 1969)

Belgian Fourragere 1940 (4th Signal Company cited; DA GO 43, 1950)

Cited in the Order of the Day of the Belgian Army for action in Belgium (4th Signal Company cited; DA GO 43, 1950)

Cited in the Order of the Day of the Belgian Army for action in the Ardennes (4th Signal Company cited; DA GO 43, 1950)

Republic of Vietnam Cross of Gallantry with Palm, Streamer embroidered VIETNAM 1966–1969 (124th Signal Battalion cited; DA GO 3, 1970)

Republic of Vietnam Cross of Gallantry with Palm, Streamer embroidered VIETNAM 1969–1970 (124th Signal Battalion cited; DA GO 52, 1971)

Republic of Vietnam Civil Action Honor Medal, First Class, Streamer embroidered VIETNAM 1966–1969 (124th Signal Battalion cited; DA GO 53, 1970)

Company A additionally entitled to:

Army Superior Unit Award, Streamer embroidered 1996–1997 (Company A, 124th Signal Battalion, cited as element of Combat Team [Provisional], 1st Brigade, 4th Infantry Division; DA GO 25, 2001)

Company B additionally entitled to:

Valorous Unit Award, Streamer embroidered QUANG NGAI PROVINCE (Company B, 124th Signal Battalion, cited; DA GO 43, 1972)

124th SIGNAL BATTALION BIBLIOGRAPHY

Alley, Lisa. "Division Structure Altering in Force XXI." *Army Communicator* 22 (June 1997): 8–9.

Babcock, Robert O., comp. *War Stories: Utah Beach to Pleiku, 4th Infantry Division*. Baton Rouge: Saint John's Press, 2001.

Bergen, John D. *Military Communications: A Test for Technology*. United States Army in Vietnam. Washington, D.C.: Center of Military History, United States Army, 1986.

Blumenson, Martin. *Breakout and Pursuit*. United States Army in World War II. Washington, D.C.: Office of the Chief of Military History, Department of the Army, 1961. 4th Infantry Division cited.

Chase, Welton, Jr. "Team Signal Excels in Army's First Digital Logistic-Focus National Training Center Rotation." *Army Communicator* 24 (Winter II 1999): 19–21.

Cole, Hugh M. *The Ardennes: Battle of the Bulge*. United States Army in World War II. Washington, D.C.: Office of the Chief of Military History, Department of the Army, 1964. 4th Infantry Division cited.

Daniels, Jeff. "Spiral Development and the Training Dilemma." *Army Communicator* 24 (Spring 1999): 5–7.

Fitz-Enz, David G. *Why A Soldier?: A Signal Corpsman's Tour from Vietnam to the Moscow Hot Line*. New York: Ballantine Books, 2000. Fitz-Enz served with the 124th Signal Battalion in Vietnam.

Fourth Infantry Division. Baton Rouge: Army and Navy Publishing Company, 1962.

4th Infantry Division, Fort Lewis, Washington. Baton Rouge: Army and Navy Publishing Company, 1965.

4th Infantry Division, Occupation of Germany, 1952. Atlanta: Albert Love Enterprises, 1952.

Harrison, Gordon A. *Cross-Channel Attack*. United States Army in World War II. Washington, D.C.: Office of the Chief of Military History, United States Army, 1951. 4th Infantry Division cited.

Hay, John H., Jr. *Tactical and Materiel Innovations*. Vietnam Studies. Washington, D.C.: Department of the Army, 1974.

Hymoff, Edward. *The Fourth Infantry Division, Vietnam*. New York: M. W. Lads Publishing Company, 1968.

MacDonald, Charles B. *The Last Offensive*. United States Army in World War II. Washington, D.C.: Office of the Chief of Military History, United States Army, 1973. 4th Infantry Division cited.

―――. *The Siegfried Line Campaign*. United States Army in World War II. Washington, D.C.: Office of the Chief of Military History, Department of the Army, 1963. 4th Infantry Division cited.

Martin, Patrick, Rosielynn Banzon, and John Cox. "Hood Signaleers Test Teamwork in Road Runner '00 Exercise." *Army Communicator* 25 (Spring 2000): 39–41.

Meadows, William C. *The Comanche Code Talkers of World War II*. Austin: University of Texas Press, 2002. Seventeen Comanche Indians were recruited for service with the 4th Signal Company.

Menetrey, Louis C., and A. R. McCahan. "Communications in the 4th Infantry Division (Mechanized)." *Army Communicator* 5 (Summer 1980): 52–55.

Raines, Rebecca Robbins. *Getting the Message Through: A Branch History of the U.S. Army Signal Corps*. Army Historical Series. Washington, D.C.: Center of Military History, United States Army, 1996.

Rienzi, Thomas M. *Communications-Electronics, 1962–1970*. Vietnam Studies. Washington, D.C.: Department of the Army, 1972.

Salazar, Hector, and Edward Seufert. "Infantry Division Tests ATM Switching in Experiment." *Army Communicator* 22 (Summer 1997): 25–27.

Shambo, Peter. "Company Perspective: Signal Support of Task Force Teaches Lessons on Digitization." *Army Communicator* 22 (Summer 1997): 17–18. Discusses Company A's support to the digitized brigade of the 4th Infantry Division at the National Training Center.

Stallings, Caroline. "3d Signal Brigade Provides 'Voice of Phantom Warriors' in 5-Month Exercise Series." *Army Communicator* 26 (Fall 2001): 16–18.

Thompson, George Raynor, and Dixie R. Harris. *The Signal Corps: The Outcome (Mid-1943 through 1945)*. United States Army in World War II. Washington, D.C.: Office of the Chief of Military History, United States Army, 1966.

Wood-Creighton, Tamasine. "124th Signal Battalion Tests Concepts, Equipment at National Training Center." *Army Communicator* 22 (Summer 1997): 14–17.

125th SIGNAL BATTALION

HERALDIC ITEMS

COAT OF ARMS

Shield: Per fess enhanced tenné and argent, in chief a diamond headed spear issuing from sinister fesswise of the second, and in base on and over a pale azure (bluebird) a fire beacon proper.

Crest: On a wreath of the colors argent and tenné a sea lion sejant of the first armed and langued azure, the tail encircling a Korean taeguk proper, and the paws grasping an annulet of bamboo or enclosing two lightning flashes palewise gules.

Motto: LEOKANI OKAUWILA (Voice of Lightning).

Symbolism: Orange and white are the colors traditionally associated with the Signal Corps. The blue is that of the Korean Service Ribbon. The spear with its diamond head represents the defense of Oahu on 7 December 1941 and the role of the 25th Infantry Division in spearheading the war in the Pacific. The fire signal against the three divisions of the bottom of the shield symbolizes the achievement of the unit in maintaining signal communications against three North Korean divisions in the Masan-Chinju operation in 1950.

The sea lion alludes to the Philippine Islands where the unit participated in the Philippine liberation and was awarded the Philippine Presidential Unit Citation. The taeguk refers to Korea where the organization participated in ten campaigns and was decorated with two Meritorious Unit Commendations and two Republic of Korea Presidential Unit Citations. The bamboo and the colors red and gold refer to Vietnam where the unit participated in twelve campaigns and was awarded two Meritorious Unit Commendations, indicated by the two lightning flashes.

DISTINCTIVE UNIT INSIGNIA

The distinctive unit insignia is the shield and motto of the coat of arms.

LINEAGE AND HONORS

RA
(25th Infantry Division) (active)

LINEAGE

Constituted 26 August 1941 in the Army of the United States as the 25th Signal Company and assigned to the 25th Infantry Division. Activated 1 October 1941 in Hawaii. Allotted 27 June 1949 to the Regular Army.

Reorganized and redesignated 1 February 1957 as Headquarters and Headquarters Company, 125th Signal Battalion (organic elements concurrently constituted and activated).

CAMPAIGN PARTICIPATION CREDIT

World War II
- Central Pacific
- Guadalcanal
- Northern Solomons
- Luzon

Korean War
- UN Defensive
- UN Offensive
- CCF Intervention
- First UN Counteroffensive
- CCF Spring Offensive
- UN Summer–Fall Offensive
- Second Korean Winter
- Korea, Summer–Fall 1952
- Third Korean Winter
- Korea, Summer 1953

Vietnam
- Counteroffensive
- Counteroffensive, Phase II
- Counteroffensive, Phase III
- Tet Counteroffensive
- Counteroffensive, Phase IV
- Counteroffensive, Phase V
- Counteroffensive, Phase VI
- Tet 69/Counteroffensive
- Summer–Fall 1969
- Winter–Spring 1970
- Sanctuary Counteroffensive
- Counteroffensive, Phase VII

DECORATIONS

Meritorious Unit Commendation (Army), Streamer embroidered KOREA 1950–1951 (25th Signal Company, 25th Infantry Division, cited; DA GO 84, 1951)

Meritorious Unit Commendation (Army), Streamer embroidered KOREA 1952–1953 (25th Signal Company, 25th Infantry Division, cited; DA GO 22, 1954)

Meritorious Unit Commendation (Army), Streamer embroidered VIETNAM 1966–1967 (125th Signal Battalion cited; DA GO 17, 1968)

Meritorious Unit Commendation (Army), Streamer embroidered VIETNAM 1967–1968 (125th Signal Battalion cited; DA GO 36, 1970)

Philippine Presidential Unit Citation, Streamer embroidered 17 OCTOBER 1944 TO 4 JULY 1945 (25th Infantry Division cited; DA GO 47, 1950)

Republic of Korea Presidential Unit Citation, Streamer embroidered MASAN-CHINJU (25th Signal Company cited; DA GO 35, 1951)

Republic of Korea Presidential Unit Citation, Streamer embroidered MUNSAN-NI (25th Signal Company cited; DA GO 19, 1955)

Republic of Vietnam Cross of Gallantry with Palm, Streamer embroidered VIETNAM 1966–1968 (125th Signal Battalion cited; DA GO 48, 1971)

Republic of Vietnam Cross of Gallantry with Palm, Streamer embroidered VIETNAM 1968–1970 (125th Signal Battalion cited; DA GO 5, 1973)

Republic of Vietnam Civil Action Honor Medal, First Class, Streamer embroidered VIETNAM 1966–1970 (125th Signal Battalion cited; DA GO 51, 1971)

Company B additionally entitled to:

Valorous Unit Award, Streamer embroidered QUANG NGAI PROVINCE (Company B, 125th Signal Battalion, cited; DA GO 43, 1972)

125th SIGNAL BATTALION BIBLIOGRAPHY

Appleman, Roy E. *South to the Naktong, North to the Yalu: June–November 1950.* United States Army in the Korean War. Washington, D.C.: Office of the Chief of Military History, Department of the Army, 1961. 25th Infantry Division cited.

Barnes, Sam. "Record Traffic from the Past." *Army Communicator* 4 (Fall 1979): 30–31. Vignette about battalion's service in Vietnam on Black Virgin Mountain.

Bergen, John D. *Military Communications: A Test for Technology.* United States Army in Vietnam. Washington, D.C.: Center of Military History, United States Army, 1986.

Burns, John C., ed. *1969, Vietnam: The U.S. 25th Infantry Division.* Tropic Lightning Association, 1970.

Clark, Michael H. *Tropic Lightning, Vietnam: 1 October 1967 to 1 October 1968.* Doraville, Ga.: Albert Love Enterprises, 1968.

Collins, Joseph Lawton, comp. *Operations of the 25th Infantry Division on Guadalcanal, 17 December 1942–4 February 1943.* N.p., c. 1943.

David, Allen A., ed. *Battleground Korea, The Story of the 25th Infantry Division.* Tokyo: Kyoya Company, 1951.

Eckhardt, George. *Command and Control.* Vietnam Studies. Washington, D.C.: Department of the Army, 1974. 25th Infantry Division cited.

Fulton, William B. *Riverine Operations.* Vietnam Studies. Washington, D.C.: Department of the Army, 1973. 25th Infantry Division cited.

Hay, John H., Jr. *Tactical and Materiel Innovations.* Vietnam Studies. Washington, D.C.: Department of the Army, 1974. 25th Infantry Division cited.

Heiser, Joseph M., Jr. *Logistics Support.* Vietnam Studies. Washington, D.C.: Department of the Army, 1974. 25th Infantry Division cited.

Hermes, Walter G. *Truce Tent and Fighting Front.* United States Army in the Korean War. Washington, D.C.: Office of the Chief of Military History, Department of the Army, 1966. 25th Infantry Division cited.

Karolevitz, Robert F., ed. *The 25th Division and World War II.* Baton Rouge: Army and Navy Publishing Company, 1946.

McPherson, Bill. "Signalers Restore Kauai's Voice." *Army* 43 (March 1993): 44–46.

Miller, John, Jr. *Cartwheel: The Reduction of Rabaul.* United States Army in World War II. Washington, D.C.: Office of the Chief of Military History, Department of the Army, 1959. 25th Infantry Division cited.

———. *Guadalcanal: The First Offensive.* United States Army in World War II. Washington, D.C.: Historical Division, Department of the Army, 1949. 25th Infantry Division cited.

Myer, Charles R. *Division-Level Communications, 1962–1973.* Vietnam Studies. Washington, D.C.: Department of the Army, 1982.

125th Signal Battalion, Cu Chi–Yah Ninh, Republic of Vietnam. N.p., n.d.

Operations of the 25th Infantry, Luzon, P.I., 17 January 1945 to 30 June 1945. n.p., 1945.

Operations of the 25th Infantry Division in the Central Solomons, New Georgia–Arundel–Vella Lavella, 16 August 1943–12 October 1943. N.p., c. 1943.

Pearson, Willard. *The War in the Northern Provinces, 1966–1968.* Vietnam Studies. Washington, D.C.: Department of the Army, 1975. 25th Infantry Division cited.

Petersen, Gregg. "125th Signal Support of Operation Iniki Response." *Army Communicator* 18 (Fall–Winter 1993): 20–24, 59–61.

Puchalski, R. Vincent, ed. *The 25th's 25th...in Combat. Tropic Lightning 1 October 1941–1 October 1966.* Doraville, Ga.: Albert Love Enterprises, 1966.

Pullen, Richard T., Robert E. Christensen, and James C. Totten, eds. *25th Infantry Division, Tropic Lightning in Korea.* Atlanta: Albert Love Enterprises, 1954.

Raines, Rebecca Robbins. *Getting the Message Through: A Branch History of the U.S. Army Signal Corps.* Army Historical Series. Washington, D.C.: Center of Military History, United States Army, 1996.

Rienzi, Thomas M. *Communications-Electronics, 1962–1970.* Vietnam Studies. Washington, D.C.: Department of the Army, 1972.

Rogers, Bernard W. *Cedar Falls–Junction City: A Turning Point.* Vietnam Studies. Washington, D.C.: Department of the Army, 1972. 25th Infantry Division cited.

Rottman, Larry, ed. *The 25th Infantry Division "Tropic Lightning," 1 October 1966–1 October 1967.* Doraville, Ga.: Albert Love Enterprises, 1967.

Rutherford, Williams de Jarnette. *165 Days: A Story of the 25th Division on Luzon.* Manila, 1945.

Smith, Robert Ross. *Triumph in the Philippines.* United States Army in World War II. Washington, D.C.: Office of the Chief of Military History, Department of the Army, 1963. 25th Infantry Division cited.

Thompson, George Raynor, Dixie R. Harris, Pauline M. Oakes, and Dulany Terrett. *The Signal Corps: The Test (December 1941 to July 1943).* United States Army in World War II. Washington, D.C.: Office of the Chief of Military History, Department of the Army, 1957.

25th Infantry Division History of the Occupation of Japan, May 1948. N.p., 1948.

127th SIGNAL BATTALION

HERALDIC ITEMS

COAT OF ARMS

Shield: Tenné, a patriachal cross argent charged with the insignia of the 7th Division proper (two black isosceles triangles placed palewise with vertices together on a red circle).

Crest: On a wreath of the colors argent and tenné a cross or composed of a torch palewise, flaming proper, and a thunderbolt fesswise emitting ten forks of lightning.

Motto: LA VICTOIRE PAR LA LIAISON (Victory by Communications).

Symbolism: Orange and white are the colors traditionally associated with the Signal Corps. The Cross of Lorraine represents service in the Lorraine campaign of World War I by the 10th Field Signal Battalion. Red and black are the colors of the 7th Infantry Division, the division the 127th Signal Battalion served. It is also the division to which the battalion's predecessor units, the 7th Signal Company and the 10th Field Signal Battalion, were assigned.

The crest includes the torch from the insignia of the Signal Corps and a thunderbolt emitting ten forks of lightning, the number corresponding to the numerical designation of the battalion. The thunderbolt is an ancient device, one of the emblems of Jupiter symbolizing power, used by the Romans on their standards and later employed by Napoleon. It is now symbolic of electricity and used to represent the Signal Corps organization. In addition, the thunderbolt appears in the arms of Metz. This battalion, as a part of the 7th Division, was engaged on the outer defenses of that city when the armistice was signed in 1918.

DISTINCTIVE UNIT INSIGNIA

The distinctive unit insignia is the shield and motto of the coat of arms.

LINEAGE AND HONORS

RA
(7th Infantry Division) (inactive)

LINEAGE

Constituted 3 June 1916 in the Regular Army as a Signal Corps battalion. Organized 10 July 1917 at Camp Alfred Vail, New Jersey, as the 10th Field Battalion, Signal Corps. Reorganized and redesignated 3 August 1917 as the 10th Field Signal Battalion. Assigned 10 November 1917 to the 7th Division (later redesignated as the 7th Infantry Division). Reorganized and redesignated 15 February 1921 as the

7th Signal Company. Inactivated 19 September 1921 at Camp Meade, Maryland. Activated 1 July 1940 at Camp Ord, California.

Reorganized and redesignated 1 July 1957 as Headquarters and Headquarters Company, 127th Signal Battalion (organic elements constituted 31 May 1957 and activated 1 July 1957 in Korea). Inactivated 2 April 1971 at Fort Lewis, Washington. Activated 21 July 1975 at Fort Ord, California. Inactivated 15 September 1993 at Fort Ord, California.

CAMPAIGN PARTICIPATION CREDIT

World War I
    Lorraine 1918

World War II
    Aleutian Islands (with arrowhead)
    Eastern Mandates
    Leyte
    Ryukyus

Korean War
    UN Defensive
    UN Offensive
    CCF Intervention
    First UN Counteroffensive
    CCF Spring Offensive
    UN Summer–Fall Offensive
    Second Korean Winter
    Korea, Summer–Fall 1952
    Third Korean Winter
    Korea, Summer 1953

Company B additionally entitled to:

Armed Forces Expeditions
    Panama

DECORATIONS

Meritorious Unit Citation (Army), Streamer embroidered PACIFIC THEATER (7th Signal Company cited; GO 57, 7th Infantry Division, 27 April 1945)

Meritorious Unit Commendation (Army), Streamer embroidered KOREA 1950–1951 (7th Signal Company, 7th Infantry Division, cited; DA GO 33, 1952)

Meritorious Unit Commendation (Army), Streamer embroidered KOREA 1951 (7th Signal Company, 7th Infantry Division, cited; DA GO 69, 1952)

Meritorious Unit Commendation (Army), Streamer embroidered KOREA 1951–1952 (7th Signal Company, 7th Infantry Division, cited; DA GO 19, 1953)

Meritorious Unit Commendation (Army), Streamer embroidered KOREA 1952–1953 (7th Signal Company, 7th Infantry Division, cited; DA GO 56, 1954)

Philippine Presidential Unit Citation, Streamer embroidered 17 OCTOBER 1944 TO 4 JULY 1945 (7th Signal Company cited; DA GO 47, 1950)

Republic of Korea Presidential Unit Citation, Streamer embroidered INCHON (7th Signal Company cited; DA GO 35, 1951)

Republic of Korea Presidential Unit Citation, Streamer embroidered KOREA 1950–1953 (7th Signal Company cited; DA GO 22, 1956)

Republic of Korea Presidential Unit Citation, Streamer embroidered KOREA 1945–1948; 1953–1971 (7th Infantry Division cited; DA GO 50, 1971)

127th SIGNAL BATTALION BIBLIOGRAPHY

American Battle Monuments Commission. *7th Division, Summary of Operations in the World War*. Washington, D.C.: Government Printing Office, 1944.

Appleman, Roy E. *South to the Naktong, North to the Yalu: June–November 1950*. United States Army in the Korean War. Washington, D.C.: Office of the Chief of Military History, Department of the Army, 1961. 7th Infantry Division cited.

Appleman, Roy E., James M. Burns, Russell A. Gugeler, and John Stevens. *Okinawa: The Last Battle*. United States Army in World War II. Washington, D.C.: Historical Division, Department of the Army, 1948. 7th Infantry Division cited.

Armeli, Thomas. "Lightfighter Communications in Operation JUST CAUSE." *Army Communicator* 15 (Winter–Spring 1990): 48–52.

Bayonet, A History of the 7th Infantry Division. 2d ed. Tokyo: Toppan Printing Company, 1952.

Bayonet, A History of the 7th Infantry Division. Tokyo: Toppan Printing Company, 1951.

The Bayonet, The History of the 7th Infantry Division in Korea. Tokyo: Dai Nippon Printing Company, 1953.

Cannon, M. Hamlin. *Leyte: The Return to the Philippines*. United States Army in World War II. Washington, D.C.: Office of the Chief of Military History, Department of the Army, 1954. 7th Infantry Division cited.

Crowl, Philip A., and Edmund G. Love. *Seizure of the Gilberts and Marshalls*. United States Army in World War II. Washington, D.C.: Office of the Chief of Military History, Department of the Army, 1955. 7th Signal Company cited.

Fell, Edgar T., comp. *History of the Seventh Division, United States Army, 1917–1919*. Philadelphia: George H. Buchanan Company, 1927.

Hermes, Walter G. *Truce Tent and Fighting Front*. United States Army in the Korean War. Washington, D.C.: Office of the Chief of Military History, United States Army, 1966. 7th Infantry Division cited.

Love, Edmund G. *The Hourglass: A History of the 7th Infantry Division in World War II*. Washington, D.C.: Infantry Journal Press, 1950.

Raines, Rebecca Robbins. *Getting the Message Through: A Branch History of the U.S. Army Signal Corps*. Army Historical Series. Washington, D.C.: Center of Military History, United States Army, 1996.

7th Infantry Division in Korea. Atlanta: Albert Love Enterprises, 1954.

The Seventh Division in Korea. Tokyo: FEC Printing Plant, 1948.

7th Infantry Division, 127th Signal Battalion, Camp Casey, Korea, 1963–1964. N.p., n.d. A pictorial history.

Waring, Paul C. *History of the 7th Infantry (Bayonet) Division*. Tokyo: Dai Nippon Printing Company, 1967.

129th SIGNAL BATTALION

HERALDIC ITEMS

COAT OF ARMS

Shield: Tenné, four lightning flashes saltirewise throughout celeste fimbriated argent, overall a torch of the last enflamed gules.

Crest: That for the regiments and separate battalions of the Maryland Army National Guard: On a wreath of the colors argent and tenné a cross bottony per cross quarterly gules and argent.

Motto: LIGHT THE FIRES.

Symbolism: Orange is a color traditionally associated with the Signal Corps. The motto LIGHT THE FIRES is alluded to by the torch, recalling the historic tradition of signal communications. The lightning flashes are a further reference to the Signal Corps and suggest the speed of modern global communications technology.

DISTINCTIVE UNIT INSIGNIA

The distinctive unit insignia is the shield and motto of the coat of arms.

LINEAGE AND HONORS

ARNG
(29th Infantry Division) (Maryland)

LINEAGE

Organized 1 July 1986 from new and existing units in the Maryland and Virginia Army National Guard as the 129th Signal Battalion, with Headquarters at Pikesville, Maryland, and assigned to the 29th Infantry Division. Location of Headquarters changed 1 July 1989 to Bel Air, Maryland. Reorganized 1 March 1990 in the Maryland Army National Guard.

Home Area: Central and Western Maryland

LINEAGES AND HERALDIC DATA

CAMPAIGN PARTICIPATION CREDIT

Company B (Reisterstown) entitled to:

World War I
    Silver Band without campaign inscription

World War II-EAME
    Normandy (with arrowhead)
    Northern France
    Rhineland
    Central Europe

DECORATIONS

Company B (Reisterstown) entitled to:

French Croix de Guerre with Palm, Streamer embroidered BEACHES OF NORMANDY (110th Field Artillery Battalion cited; DA GO 43, 1950)

129th SIGNAL BATTALION BIBLIOGRAPHY

Cooper John P. *The History of the 110th Field Artillery Battalion, with Sketches of Related Units*. Baltimore: War Records Division, Maryland Historical Society, 1953.

133d SIGNAL BATTALION

HERALDIC ITEMS

COAT OF ARMS

Shield: Tenné, a torteau fimbriated argent overall two spears saltirewise of the like; on a chief wavy silver three fleurs-de-lis azure.

Crest: That for the regiments and separate battalions of the Illinois Army National Guard: On a wreath of the colors argent and tenné upon a grassy field the blockhouse of old Fort Dearborn proper.

Motto: DISTANCE NO BAR.

Symbolism: Orange and white are the colors traditionally associated with the Signal Corps. The two areas of the shield joined by the wavy line stand for the two oversea areas in which the unit served during World War I and World War II. The three fleurs-de-lis refer to the battalion's participation in three World War I campaigns in France. The two spears stand for campaign participation on two South Sea islands during World War II. The roundel is scarlet in reference to the scarlet streamer awarded to the unit for the Meritorious Unit Commendation.

DISTINCTIVE UNIT INSIGNIA

The distinctive unit insignia is the shield and motto of the coat of arms.

LINEAGE AND HONORS

ARNG
(Illinois)

LINEAGE

Constituted 11 June 1897 in the Illinois National Guard as a company of Signal Corps troops and organized at Chicago. Mustered into Federal service 28 June 1916 as Company A, Signal Corps; mustered out of Federal service 1 January 1917. Mustered into Federal service 1 August 1917; drafted into Federal service 5 August 1917. Expanded, reorganized, and redesignated 24 September 1917 as the 108th Field Signal Battalion and assigned to the 33d Division. Demobilized 30 June 1919 at Camp Grant, Illinois.

Reorganized and federally recognized 8 June 1922 at Chicago as the 33d Signal Company, an element of the 33d Division (later redesignated as the 33d Infantry Division). Inducted into Federal service 5 March 1941 at Chicago. Inactivated 5 February 1946 in Japan.

Reorganized and federally recognized 5 June 1947 at Chicago. Reorganized and redesignated 1 March 1959 as Headquarters and Headquarters Company, 133d Signal Battalion (organic elements constituted 1 March 1959 and federally recognized 21 April 1959 at Chicago).

Battalion consolidated 1 February 1968 with the 109th Signal Company (organized and federally recognized 9 May 1949 at Chicago as the 179th Antiaircraft Artillery Operations Detachment), and consolidated unit reorganized and redesignated as the 433d Signal Company; concurrently relieved from assignment to the 33d Infantry Division.

Reorganized and redesignated 1 October 1980 as Headquarters and Headquarters Detachment, 133d Signal Battalion. Reorganized and redesignated 1 October 1985 as Headquarters and Headquarters Company, 133d Signal Battalion (organic elements concurrently organized from existing units).

Home Area: Statewide

CAMPAIGN PARTICIPATION CREDIT

World War I
  Somme Offensive
  Meuse-Argonne
  Lorraine 1918

World War II
  New Guinea
  Luzon

DECORATIONS

Meritorious Unit Commendation (Army), Streamer embroidered PACIFIC THEATER (33d Signal Company cited; GO 128, 33d Infantry Division, 14 June 1945)

Philippine Presidential Unit Citation, Streamer embroidered 17 OCTOBER 1944 TO 4 JULY 1945 (33d Infantry Division cited; DA GO 47, 1950)

133d SIGNAL BATTALION BIBLIOGRAPHY

American Battle Monuments Commission. *33d Division, Summary of Operations in the World War*. Washington, D.C.: Government Printing Office, 1944.

Harris, Barnett W., and Dudley J. Nelson. *33d Division Across No-Man's Land*. Kankakee, Ill.: Harris and Nickerson, 1919.

Huidekoper, Frederic L. *The History of the 33d Division, A.E.F.* 4 vols. Springfield: Illinois State Historical Library, 1921.

———. *33d Division, A.E.F., From Its Arrival in France Until the Armistice with Germany, November 11, 1918*. Luxembourg: Gustave Soupert, 1919.

Illinois in the World War: An Illustrated History of the Thirty-Third Division. 2 vols. Chicago: States Publications Society, 1920.

Judy, William L. *The Prairie Division*. N.p., 1919.

Roster of the Illinois National Guard and Illinois Naval Militia as Organized When Called by the President for World War Service. Springfield, Ill., 1929.

Roster of the Illinois National Guard on the Mexican Border, 1916–1917. Springfield, Ill., 1928.

Smith, Robert Ross. *Triumph in the Philippines*. United States Army in World War II. Washington, D.C.: Office of the Chief of Military History, Department of the Army, 1963. 33d Infantry Division cited.

33d Division Pictorial History, Army of the United States, Camp Forrest, 1941–1942. Atlanta: Army Press, 1942.

33d Infantry Division Historical Committee. *The Golden Cross: A History of the 33d Infantry Division in World War II*. Washington, D.C.: Infantry Journal Press, 1948.

Watters, Mary. *Illinois in the Second World War*. Springfield, Ill.: Illinois State Historical Library, 1951–52.

134th SIGNAL BATTALION

HERALDIC ITEMS

COAT OF ARMS

Shield: Argent, a chevron tenné between in dexter flank a mullet vert and in sinister a fleur-de-lis of the like. On a chief embattled of six of the second a bugle horn of the first.

Crest: That for the regiments and separate battalions of the Minnesota Army National Guard: On a wreath of the colors argent and tenné a sheaf of wheat proper.

Motto: VOCE RETONANTI (With Loud Resounding Voice).

Symbolism: Orange and white are the colors traditionally associated with the Signal Corps. The six embattlements of the chief refer to the six World War II campaigns in which the unit participated. The star and the fleur-de-lis represent the two decorations—the Meritorious Unit Commendation and the French Croix de Guerre—awarded to the unit and its current elements. The chevron denotes support, and the bugle horn denotes the martial spirit and mission of the unit.

DISTINCTIVE UNIT INSIGNIA

The distinctive unit insignia is the shield and motto of the coat of arms.

LINEAGE AND HONORS

ARNG
(34th Infantry Division) (Minnesota)

LINEAGE

Organized and federally recognized 18 November 1919 in the Minnesota National Guard at Minneapolis as the Service Battery, 1st Field Artillery. Redesignated 21 November 1921 as the Service Battery, 151st Field Artillery, an element of the 34th Division (later redesignated as the 34th Infantry Division). Consolidated (less Band Section) 1 July 1940 with Headquarters Battery, 151st Field Artillery, and consolidated unit designated as Headquarters Battery, 151st Field Artillery. Inducted into Federal service 10 February 1941 at Minneapolis.

Former Service Battery, 151st Field Artillery, reorganized and redesignated 1 April 1941 at Minneapolis as the Service Battery, 1st Battalion, 151st Field Artillery (former Headquarters Battery, 151st Field Artillery—hereafter separate lineage). Reorganized and redesignated 30 January 1942 as the Service Battery, 151st Field Artillery Battalion, an element of the 34th Infantry Division. Inactivated 3 November 1945 at Camp Patrick Henry, Virginia.

Reorganized and federally recognized 4 November 1946 at Minneapolis as the Service Battery, 151st Field Artillery Battalion, an element of the 47th Infantry Division. Ordered into active Federal service 16 January 1951 at Minneapolis (Service Battery, 151st Field Artillery Battalion [NGUS], organized and federally recognized 16 January 1953 at Minneapolis). Service Battery, 151st Field Artillery Battalion, released from active Federal service 2 December 1954 and reverted to state control. Federal recognition concurrently withdrawn from the Service Battery, 151st Field Artillery Battalion (NGUS).

Converted and redesignated 22 February 1959 as Headquarters and Headquarters Company, 147th Signal Battalion, an element of the 47th Infantry Division (organic elements concurrently organized from existing units). Location of Headquarters changed 1 July 1989 to Inver Grove Heights.

Redesignated 10 February 1991 as the 134th Signal Battalion; concurrently relieved from assignment to the 47th Infantry Division and assigned to the 34th Infantry Division. Location of Headquarters changed 2 June 1992 to Eagan; changed 1 April 1994 to St. Paul; changed 1 June 1998 to Inver Grove Heights.

Home Area: Statewide

CAMPAIGN PARTICIPATION CREDIT

World War II
  Tunisia
  Naples-Foggia (with arrowhead)
  Anzio
  Rome-Arno
  North Apennines
  Po Valley

DECORATIONS

French Croix de Guerre with Palm, World War II, Streamer embroidered BELVEDERE (151st Field Artillery Battalion cited; DA GO 43, 1950)

Company B (Hastings) additionally entitled to:

Meritorious Unit Commendation (Army), Streamer embroidered ITALY 1944 (Service Company, 135th Infantry, cited; GO 19, 34th Infantry Division, 21 January 1945)

134th SIGNAL BATTALION BIBLIOGRAPHY

Blumenson, Martin. *Salerno to Cassino*. United States Army in World War II. Washington, D.C.: Office of the Chief of Military History, United States Army, 1969. 135th Infantry and 151st Field Artillery Battalion cited.

Fisher, Ernest F., Jr. *Cassino to the Alps*. United States Army in World War II. Washington, D.C.: Office of the Chief of Military History, United States Army, 1977. 135th Infantry cited.

47th "Viking" Infantry Division, Pictorial Review, Camp Rucker, Alabama. Atlanta: Albert Love Enterprises, 1951.

Gammack, Gordon. *The 34th Division's Italian Campaign (to December 1943) and Other Selected Articles*. Des Moines, 1944.

Hedgepeth, Rob. "Five Nations Test Coalition Communications." *Army Communicator* 28 (Spring 2003): 27–28. United States, Great Britain, Canada, Australia, and New Zealand.

A History of the Minnesota National Guard. St. Paul, 1940.

Hougen, John H. *The Story of the 34th Infantry Division*. San Angelo, Tex.: Newsfoto Publishing Company, 1949. Reprint, Nashville: Battery Press, 1979

Howe, George F. *Northwest Africa: Seizing the Initiative in the West*. United States Army in World War II. Washington, D.C.: Office of the Chief of Military History, Department of the Army, 1957. 151st Field Artillery Battalion and 34th Infantry Division cited.

"Innovative Training." *National Guard* 35 (March 1981): 22–25.

Kreger, William G. *A Condensed History of the 135th Infantry from Gettysburg to the Po*. N.p., 1951.

Kunz, Virginia B. *Muskets to Missiles: A Military History of Minnesota*. St. Paul: Minnesota Statehood Centennial Commission, 1958.

Narrative History of the 151st Field Artillery Battalion for January 1, 1944 to January 31, 1944. Italy, 1944.

A Partial History: 135th Infantry Regiment, 34th "Red Bull" Division. N.p., 1945.

The Story of the 34th Infantry Division. Book I: Louisiana to Pisa. Book II: Pisa to Final Victory. Milan, Italy: Archetipografia de Milano, 1945.

Trask, David F. *History of the 135th Infantry Regiment*. Enterprise, Ala.: Enterprise Ledger, 1954.

Wilson, Richard. *The Gallant Fight of the 34th Division in the North African Campaign*. Des Moines Register and Tribune, 1943.

135th SIGNAL BATTALION

HERALDIC ITEMS

COAT OF ARMS

Shield: Sable, two lightning flashes saltirewise throughout tenné, overall a billet argent bearing an ermine spot of the first. On a chief argent a grizzly bear's head erased proper.

Crest: That for the regiments and separate battalions of the Missouri and Nebraska Army National Guard, in the order in which the states were admitted to the Union:

MISSOURI: On a wreath of the colors argent and sable a grizzly bear standing rampant proper.

NEBRASKA: On a wreath of the colors argent and sable an ear of corn in full ear partially husked proper.

Motto: FIRST FAST FLEXIBLE.

Symbolism: Orange and white are the colors traditionally associated with the Signal Corps. The white oblong, a heraldic billet, refers to correspondence and, together with the lightning flashes, denotes the swift communication facilities provided by the battalion. The grizzly bear represents the organization's original allotment to the Missouri Army National Guard. The ermine spot refers to the headquarters' location at St. Joseph, which was founded by a French fur trader.

DISTINCTIVE UNIT INSIGNIA

Description: A gold color metal and enamel device that consists of a gold grizzly bear's head on top of a white vertical oblong charged with a black ermine spot. Radiating from the sides of the oblong four diagonal orange lightning flashes, two on each side, all in front of a gold horizontal oval scored with rays and enclosed by a gold scroll folded at the sides and inscribed at the left FIRST, at the right FAST, and in base FLEXIBLE in black letters.

Symbolism: Orange and white are the colors traditionally associated with the Signal Corps. The white oblong, a heraldic billet, refers to correspondence and, together with the lightning flashes, denotes the swift communication facilities provided by the battalion. The grizzly bear represents the organization's original allotment to the Missouri Army National Guard. The ermine spot refers to the headquarters' location at St. Joseph, which was founded by a French fur trader. Additionally, the vertical oblong connotes "1" or FIRST, the flashes signify FAST, and the rays in every direction refer to FLEXIBLE, which together allude to the battalion's motto.

LINEAGE AND HONORS

ARNG

LINEAGE   (35th Infantry Division) (Missouri and Nebraska)

Constituted 26 March 1963 in the Missouri Army National Guard as Headquarters and Headquarters Detachment, 135th Signal Battalion, an element of the 35th Infantry Division. Organized and federally recognized 1 April 1963 at St. Joseph. Reorganized and redesignated 16 September 1985 as Headquarters and Headquarters Company, 135th Signal Battalion (organic elements concurrently organized from existing units in Missouri and Nebraska).

Home Area: Missouri and Nebraska

CAMPAIGN PARTICIPATION CREDIT

Headquarters Company (St. Joseph, Missouri) entitled to:

World War II-AP
Leyte
Ryukyus
Western Pacific

Company A (Omaha, Nebraska) entitled to:

World War II-AP
Aleutian Islands

World War II-EAME
Normandy
Northern France
Rhineland
Ardennes-Alsace
Central Europe

DECORATIONS

Headquarters Company (St. Joseph, Missouri) entitled to:

Philippine Presidential Unit Citation, Streamer embroidered 17 OCTOBER 1944 TO 4 JULY 1945 (242d Engineer Combat Battalion cited; DA GO 47, 1950)

Company A (Omaha, Nebraska) entitled to:

Presidential Unit Citation (Army), Streamer embroidered BASTOGNE (134th Infantry Regiment cited; DA GO 62, 1947)
French Croix de Guerre with Palm, World War II, Streamer embroidered ST. LO (134th Infantry Regiment cited; DA GO 43, 1950)

135th SIGNAL BATTALION BIBLIOGRAPHY

Blumenson, Martin. *Breakout and Pursuit.* United States Army in World War II. Washington, D.C.: Office of the Chief of Military History, Department of the Army, 1961. 134th Infantry cited.

Cole, Hugh M. *The Ardennes: Battle of the Bulge.* United States Army in World War II. Washington, D.C.: Office of the Chief of Military History, United States Army, 1965. 134th Infantry cited.

———. *The Lorraine Campaign.* United States Army in World War II. Washington, D.C.: Historical Division, United States Army, 1950. 134th Infantry cited.

Dod, Karl C. *The Corps of Engineers: The War Against Japan.* United States Army in World War II. Washington, D.C.: Office of the Chief of Military History, United States Army, 1966. 242d Engineer Combat Battalion cited.

MacDonald, Charles B. *The Last Offensive.* United States Army in World War II. Washington, D.C.: Office of the Chief of Military History, United States Army, 1973. 134th Infantry cited.

Miltonberger, Butler B., and James A. Huston. *134th Infantry Regiment Combat History of World War II.* N.p., 1946.

"Riot Reaction Force: The Guard in the April Disorders." *National Guardsman* 22 (May 1968): 2–16. 135th Signal Battalion cited.

136th SIGNAL BATTALION

HERALDIC ITEMS

COAT OF ARMS

Shield: Tenné, a mullet argent, overall five lightning flashes conjoined in fess point sable.

Crest: That for the regiments and separate battalions of the Texas Army National Guard: On a wreath of the colors argent and tenné a mullet argent encircled by a garland of live oak and olive proper conjoined at the stems with a ribbon or.

Motto: COMMAND ON THE MOVE.

Symbolism: Orange and white are the colors traditionally associated with the Signal Corps. The star is a symbol of Texas, the home of the unit, and denotes command and control. The five black lightning flashes radiating from the center of the star convey the ability to communicate with multidirectional capabilities day or night.

DISTINCTIVE UNIT INSIGNIA

Description: A silver color metal and enamel device that consists of the shield and crest of the coat of arms. Attached around the base of the shield a semicircular black scroll with silver spokes inscribed COMMAND ON THE MOVE in silver letters.

Symbolism: Orange and white (silver) are the colors traditionally associated with the Signal Corps. The star is a symbol of Texas, the home of the unit, and denotes command and control. The five black lightning flashes radiating from the center of the star convey the ability to communicate with multidirectional capabilities day or night. The crest is that of the state of Texas. The star alludes to the Texas flag; the oak and laurel wreath surrounding it highlight the virtues of strength and peace. The black scroll in the form of a stylized wheel emphasizes the mobile power of the unit.

LINEAGE AND HONORS

ARNG
(Texas)

LINEAGE

Organized 1 October 1989 from new and existing units in the Texas Army National Guard as the 136th Signal Battalion with Headquarters at Temple.

Home Area: Southern Texas

CAMPAIGN PARTICIPATION CREDIT

None.

DECORATIONS

None.

136th SIGNAL BATTALION BIBLIOGRAPHY

Campbell, Jerry L. "Leveler Training on the Mark." *Army Communicator* 15 (Summer–Fall 1990): 38–39. Discusses fielding of Mobile Subscriber Equipment (MSE) at Fort Hood.

Johnson, Danny M. *Military Communications Supporting Peacekeeping Operations in the Balkans: The Signal Corps at Its Best*. Mannheim, Germany: Headquarters, 5th Signal Command, 2000.

138th SIGNAL BATTALION

HERALDIC ITEMS

COAT OF ARMS

Shield: Per pale tenné and sable, a pile between a mullet of eight points and three kampilans bendwise in pale argent.

Crest: That for the regiments and separate battalions of the Indiana Army National Guard: On a wreath of the colors argent and tenné a demi-lion rampant argent holding in dexter paw a laurel branch vert.

Motto: SUCCESS OF COMMAND.

Symbolism: Orange and white are the colors traditionally associated with the Signal Corps. The three kampilans represent the unit's campaign service in the Philippines, and the star is for the Philippine Presidential Unit Citation. The searchlight in the center suggests one of the functions of the unit.

DISTINCTIVE UNIT INSIGNIA

The distinctive unit insignia is the shield and motto of the coat of arms.

LINEAGE AND HONORS

ARNG
(38th Infantry Division) (Indiana)

LINEAGE

Organized and federally recognized 7 October 1921 in the Indiana National Guard at Tipton as Headquarters, 2d Battalion, 152d Infantry, an element of the 38th Division (later redesignated as the 38th Infantry Division). Inducted into Federal service 17 January 1941 at Tipton. Inactivated 9 November 1945 at Camp Anza, California.

Reorganized and federally recognized 24 June 1947 at Anderson as Headquarters, 1st Battalion, 151st Infantry. Converted and redesignated 1 February 1959 as Headquarters, 138th Signal Battalion, an element of the 38th Infantry Division (organic elements converted and redesignated from existing units).

Home Area: Central Indiana

CAMPAIGN PARTICIPATION CREDIT

World War II
  New Guinea
  Leyte
  Luzon

DECORATIONS

Philippine Presidential Unit Citation, Streamer embroidered 17 OCTOBER 1944 TO 4 JULY 1945 (152d Infantry Regiment cited; DA GO 47, 1950)

138th SIGNAL BATTALION BIBLIOGRAPHY

Historical Annual, National Guard of the State of Indiana, 1938. Baton Rouge: Army and Navy Publishing Company, 1938.

Hodges, Peyton, et al., eds. *38th Infantry Division, "Avengers of Bataan."* Atlanta: Albert Love Enterprises, 1947.

Indiana Army National Guard 38th Infantry Division, 1967. N.p.: Newsfoto Publishing Company, c. 1967.

Moorhead, Robert G. "38th Infantry Division Is a Three-State Enterprise." *Army* 23 (October 1973): 99–102.

Pictorial History, Thirty-Eighth Division, Army of the United States, 1941. Atlanta: Army and Navy Publishing Company, 1941.

Smith, Robert Ross. *Triumph in the Philippines*. United States Army in World War II. Washington, D.C.: Office of the Chief of Military History, Department of the Army, 1963. 152d Infantry cited.

War History Commission. *Indiana in World War II*. Bloomington, 1948.

Watt, William J., and James R. H. Spears, eds. *Indiana's Citizen Soldiers: The Militia and National Guard in Indiana History*. Indianapolis: Indiana State Armory Board, 1980.

Webster, Leonard E. *A Military History of the Indiana National Guard, 1816–1966*. Indianapolis: Military Department of Indiana, 1966.

141st SIGNAL BATTALION
(The Communicators)

HERALDIC ITEMS

COAT OF ARMS

Shield: Per fess abased dancette sable and tenné, in chief between two flames a fire arrow fesswise argent.

Crest: On a wreath of the colors argent and sable a circlet of steel flamant superimposed by two demispears palewise proper.

Motto: ENSE ET VOCE (With Sword and Voice).

Symbolism: Orange and white are the colors traditionally associated with the Signal Corps. The black area represents Africa, the Dark Continent. The fire arrow, an early signaling device, represents the mission and battle experience of the unit. The mountainous terrain of Italy, where the unit served during World War II, is represented by the jagged division of the lower part of the shield.

The flaming circlet of steel commemorates the unit's service in Southwest Asia. The steel underscores the strength and resolve of the U.S. Army troops and materiel in Saudi Arabia and Kuwait. The flames allude to a signal fire or beacon and denote zeal and action. The spears represent combat readiness and participation in two wars, World War II and Southwest Asia.

DISTINCTIVE UNIT INSIGNIA

The distinctive unit insignia is the shield and motto of the coat of arms.

LINEAGE AND HONORS

RA
(1st Armored Division) (active)

LINEAGE

Constituted 1 June 1940 in the Regular Army as the 7th Signal Troop and activated at Fort Knox, Kentucky. Reorganized and redesignated 15 July 1940 as the 47th Signal Company and assigned to the 1st Armored Division. Redesignated 7 August 1941 as the 141st Signal Armored Company. Redesignated 1 January 1942 as the 141st Armored Signal Company. Inactivated 26 April 1946 at Camp Kilmer, New Jersey.

Activated 7 March 1951 at Fort Hood, Texas. Reorganized and redesignated 15 February 1957 as Headquarters and Headquarters Company, 141st Signal Battalion (organic elements constituted 11 February 1957 and activated 15 February 1957 at Fort Polk, Louisiana). Inactivated 23 December 1957 at Fort Polk, Louisiana (Company A activated 24 September 1960 at Fort Hood, Texas). Activated (less Company A) 3 February 1962 at Fort Hood, Texas.

CAMPAIGN PARTICIPATION CREDIT

World War II
    Algeria–French Morocco (with arrowhead)
    Tunisia
    Naples-Foggia
    Anzio
    Rome-Arno
    North Apennines
    Po Valley

Southwest Asia
    Defense of Saudi Arabia
    Liberation and Defense of Kuwait
    Cease-Fire

DECORATIONS

Meritorious Unit Commendation (Army), Streamer embroidered SOUTHWEST ASIA 1990–1991 (141st Signal Battalion [less Company B] cited; DA GO 1, 1996)

Army Superior Unit Award, Streamer embroidered 1995–1996 (141st Signal Battalion cited; DA GO 25, 2001)

Company B additionally entitled to:

Valorous Unit Award, Streamer embroidered IRAQ-KUWAIT (Company B, 141st Signal Battalion, cited; DA GO 27, 1994)

141st SIGNAL BATTALION BIBLIOGRAPHY

Blumenson, Martin. *Salerno to Cassino*. United States Army in World War II. Washington, D.C.: Office of the Chief of Military History, Department of the Army, 1969. 1st Armored Division cited.

1st Armored Division. Dallas, Tex.: Taylor Publishing Company, 1952.

1st Armored Division, Fort Hood, Texas. Baton Rouge: Army and Navy Publishing Company, 1963.

Fisher, Ernest F., Jr. *Cassino to the Alps*. United States Army in World War II. Washington, D.C.: Center of Military History, United States Army, 1977. 1st Armored Division cited.

Gerstein, Daniel. "Report from the Field: Recovering from Peace Operations." *Army Communicator* 23 (Spring 1998): 37–40.

———. "A Report from the Field: The Signal Mission in Bosnia-Herzegovina." *Army Communicator* 23 (Summer 1998): 48–51.

Historical and Pictorial Review, First Armored Division of the United States Army, Fort Knox, Kentucky, 1941. 6 vols. Baton Rouge: Army and Navy Publishing Company, 1941.

Howe, George F. *The Battle History of the 1st Armored Division, "Old Ironsides."* Washington, D.C.: Combat Forces Press, 1954. Reprint. Nashville, Tenn.: Battery Press, 1979.

———. *Northwest Africa: Seizing the Initiative in the West*. United States Army in World War II. Washington, D.C.: Office of the Chief of Military History, Department of the Army, 1957. 1st Armored Division cited.

Humphreys, David. "Team Cobra: 141st Signal Battalion's 'Tip of the Sword' in Iraq." *Army Communicator* 28 (Winter 2003): 37–39.

Johnson, Danny M. *Military Communications Supporting Peacekeeping Operations in the Balkans: The Signal Corps at Its Best*. Mannheim, Germany: Headquarters, 5th Signal Command, 2000.

Llanos, Andrew, and David Are. "The Tactical High-Speed Data Super Radio-Access Unit: A Success in Kosovo." *Army Communicator* 26 (Fall 2001): 24–29.

Savage, Jay R. "An Area Signal System." *Army Communicator* 4 (Spring 1979): 48–49.

———. "How to Hide a TAC." *Army Communicator* 3 (Fall 1978): 11–12.

Thompson, George Raynor, and Dixie R. Harris. *The Signal Corps: The Outcome (Mid-1943 through 1945)*. United States Army in World War II. Washington, D.C.: Office of the Chief of Military History, United States Army, 1966.

Thompson, George Raynor, Dixie R. Harris, Pauline M. Oakes, and Dulany Terrett. *The Signal Corps: The Test (December 1941 to July 1943)*. United States Army in World War II. Washington, D.C.: Office of the Chief of Military History, Department of the Army, 1957.

25th Anniversary, 1st Armored Division, Fort Hood, Texas. Baton Rouge: Army and Navy Publishing Company, 1965.

White, Wayne M. "Communicating on the Move." *Army Communicator* 16 (Summer 1991): 34–37. Discusses the battalion's activities during Operation DESERT STORM.

142d SIGNAL BATTALION

HERALDIC ITEMS

COAT OF ARMS

Shield: Per fess wavy enhanced tenné and argent, a point reversed counterchanged in chief a fleur-de-lis and issuing from base a cubic arm in armor grasping four lightning flashes, all of the last, between in dexter fess a palm tree proper and in sinister fess a bear rampant sable.
Crest: None approved.
Motto: FLEXIBILITY.
Symbolism: Orange and white are the colors traditionally associated with the Signal Corps. The arm grasping two lightning flashes symbolizes the communications support mission of the battalion to the armored division. The palm tree stands for the unit's World War II action in the Mediterranean area. The fleur-de-lis represents campaigns in France. The black bear, emblem of the city of Berlin, represents service in the Rhineland, Central Europe, and the occupation of the city of Berlin in 1945. The wavy line, representing the Meuse River, and the chevron, representing a highway in perspective, refer to the battalion's participation in the liberation of Belgium.

DISTINCTIVE UNIT INSIGNIA

The distinctive unit insignia is the shield and motto of the coat of arms.

LINEAGE AND HONORS

RA
(2d Armored Division) (inactive)

LINEAGE

Constituted 15 July 1940 in the Regular Army as the 48th Signal Company, assigned to the 2d Armored Division, and activated at Fort Benning, Georgia. Redesignated 7 August 1941 as the 142d Signal Armored Company. Redesignated 1 January 1942 as the 142d Armored Signal Company.

Reorganized and redesignated 1 July 1957 as Headquarters and Headquarters Company, 142d Signal Battalion (organic elements constituted 21 June 1957 and activated 1 July 1957 in Germany). Inactivated 15 September 1991 at Fort Hood, Texas. Activated 16 December 1992 at Fort Hood, Texas. Inactivated 15 January 1996 at Fort Hood, Texas.

CAMPAIGN PARTICIPATION CREDIT

World War II
  Algeria–French Morocco (with arrowhead)
  Sicily (with arrowhead)
  Normandy
  Northern France
  Rhineland
  Ardennes-Alsace
  Central Europe

Southwest Asia
  Defense of Saudi Arabia
  Liberation and Defense of Kuwait

DECORATIONS

Belgian Fourragere 1940 (142d Armored Signal Company cited; DA GO 43, 1950)

Cited in the Order of the Day of the Belgian Army for action in Belgium (142d Armored Signal Company cited; DA GO 43, 1950)

Cited in the Order of the Day of the Belgian Army for action in the Ardennes (142d Armored Signal Company cited; DA GO 43, 1950)

142d SIGNAL BATTALION BIBLIOGRAPHY

Blumenson, Martin. *Breakout and Pursuit*. United States Army in World War II. Washington, D.C.: Office of the Chief of Military History, Department of the Army, 1961. 2d Armored Division cited.

Cole, Hugh M. *The Ardennes: Battle of the Bulge*. United States Army in World War II. Washington, D.C.: Office of the Chief of Military History, Department of the Army, 1965. 2d Armored Division cited.

Dutchak, Eugene, ed. *2d Armored Division, Fort Hood, Texas, 1961–1962*. Topeka, Kans.: Josten Military Publications, 1962.

Edson, Ron. "Multiple Unit Training Assembly-5." *Army Communicator* 6 (Spring 1981): 49–51. Training exercise with Reserve component training partner, the 249th Signal Battalion.

Garland, Albert N., and Howard McGaw Smyth. *Sicily and the Surrender of Italy*. United States Army in World War II. Washington, D.C.: Office of the Chief of Military History, Department of the Army, 1965. 2d Armored Division cited.

Gilmore, John. "The One Army Concept." *Army Communicator* 11 (Summer 1986): 38–39.

Goins, Lorenzo A. "Task Force 142 Signal." *Army Communicator* 15 (Spring–Summer 1990): 13–15. On testing of mobile subscriber radio equipment during Centurion Shield '90 field exercise in Europe.

Harrison, Gordon A. *Cross-Channel Attack*. United States Army in World War II. Washington, D.C.: Office of the Chief of Military History, United States Army, 1951. 2d Armored Division cited.

Houston, Donald E. *Hell on Wheels, the Second Armored Division.* San Rafael, Calif.: Presidio Press, 1977.

Howe, George F. *Northwest Africa: Seizing the Initiative in the West.* United States Army in World War II. Washington, D.C.: Department of the Army, 1957. 2d Armored Division cited.

Lee, Gilbert R., III. "Converting a LEN Into a Tandem Switching Node." *Army Communicator* 16 (Winter 1991): 13–14. LEN is a large extension node, part of the battalion's mobile subscriber radio equipment.

MacDonald, Charles B. *The Last Offensive.* United States Army in World War II. Washington, D.C.: Office of the Chief of Military History, United States Army, 1973. 2d Armored Division cited.

———. *The Siegfried Line Campaign.* United States Army in World War II. Washington, D.C.: Office of the Chief of Military History, Department of the Army, 1963. 2d Armored Division cited.

2d Armored Division, Germany. Atlanta: Albert Love Enterprises, 1952.

2d Armored Division "Hell on Wheels," Fort Hood, Texas, 1965. Baton Rouge: Army and Navy Publishing Company, 1965.

Stokes, Carol E., ed. *The U.S. Army Signal Corps in Operation Desert Shield/Desert Storm.* Fort Gordon, Ga.: Office of the Command Historian, U.S. Army Signal Center and Fort Gordon, 1994.

Stokes, Carol E., and Kathy R. Coker. "Getting the Message Through in the Persian Gulf War." *Army Communicator* 17 (Summer–Winter 1992): 17–25.

Thompson, George Raynor, and Dixie R. Harris. *The Signal Corps: The Outcome (Mid-1943 through 1945).* United States Army in World War II. Washington, D.C.: Office of the Chief of Military History, United States Army, 1966.

Trahan, E.A., ed. *A History of the Second United States Armored Division, 1940–1946.* Atlanta: Albert Love Enterprises, 1946.

143d SIGNAL BATTALION

HERALDIC ITEMS

COAT OF ARMS

Shield: Chequy argent and tenné, on a pale sable a lion rampant or, and on a chief of the second five signal horns of the first—three and two—all fesswise.
Crest: None approved.
Motto: VOX FERRORUM (The Voice of Iron).
Symbolism: Orange and white are the colors traditionally associated with the Signal Corps. The chessboard pattern is based on the signal grid system and alludes to the battalion's tactical flexibility and strategy, as used in the game of chess. The organization's active participation in the invasion of Belgium, and the decorations given to the unit for service in Belgium during World War II, are symbolized by the colors black and gold and the lion rampant, both taken from the coat of arms of Belgium. The four divisions of the field allude to the four decorations given the organization. The horns, five in number for the five campaign honors earned by the battalion in the European Theater during World War II, are a variation of those used in the old German post system and allude to the organization's service in Germany, as well as its mission of communication.

DISTINCTIVE UNIT INSIGNIA

The distinctive unit insignia is the shield and motto of the coat of arms.

LINEAGE AND HONORS

RA
LINEAGE (3d Armored Division) (inactive)

Constituted 13 January 1941 in the Regular Army as the 46th Signal Company and assigned to the 3d Armored Division. Activated 15 April 1941 at Camp Beauregard, Louisiana. Redesignated 7 August 1941 as the 143d Signal Armored Company. Redesignated 1 January 1942 as the 143d Armored Signal Company. Inactivated 10 November 1945 in Germany.

Activated 30 July 1948 at Fort Knox, Kentucky. Reorganized and redesignated 1 October 1957 as Headquarters and Headquarters Company, 143d Signal Battalion (organic elements constituted 30 August 1957 and activated 1 October 1957 in Germany). Inactivated 15 April 1992 in Germany.

CAMPAIGN PARTICIPATION CREDIT

World War II
  Normandy
  Northern France
  Rhineland
  Ardennes-Alsace
  Central Europe

Southwest Asia
  Defense of Saudi Arabia
  Liberation and Defense of Kuwait
  Cease-Fire

DECORATIONS

Meritorious Unit Commendation (Army), Streamer embroidered EUROPEAN THEATER (143d Armored Signal Company cited; GO 89, 3d Armored Division, 12 July 1945)

Belgian Fourragere 1940 (143d Armored Signal Company cited; DA GO 43, 1950)

Cited in the Order of the Day of the Belgian Army for action in Belgium (143d Armored Signal Company cited; DA GO 43, 1950)

Cited in the Order of the Day of the Belgian Army for action in the Ardennes (143d Armored Signal Company cited; DA GO 43, 1950)

143d SIGNAL BATTALION BIBLIOGRAPHY

Blumenson, Martin. *Breakout and Pursuit.* United States Army in World War II. Washington, D.C.: Office of the Chief of Military History, United States Army, 1961. 3d Armored Division cited.

Cole, Hugh M. *The Ardennes: Battle of the Bulge.* United States Army in World War II. Washington, D.C.: Office of the Chief of Military History, Department of the Army, 1965. 3d Armored Division cited.

Editors of *Army Times. A History of the U.S. Army Signal Corps.* New York: G. P. Putnam's Sons, 1961.

Goda, Bryan S., and Robert M. Prudhomme. "Communications on a Mobile Battlefield in the 100 Hours War." *Army Communicator* 16 (Spring 1991): 42–47.

Historical and Pictorial Review, Third Armored Division of the United States Army, Camp Polk, Louisiana, 1942. 3 vols. Baton Rouge: Army and Navy Publishing Company, 1942.

MacDonald, Charles B. *The Last Offensive.* United States Army in World War II. Washington, D.C: Office of the Chief of Military History, United States Army, 1973. 3d Armored Division cited.

———. *The Siegfried Line Campaign.* United States Army in World War II. Washington, D.C.: Office of the Chief of Military History, United States Army, 1963. 3d Armored Division cited.

Spearhead in the West, 1941–1945, Third Armored Division. Frankfurt am Main, Germany: Kunst and Wervedruck, 1945. Reprint. Nashville, Tenn.: Battery Press, 1980.

Thompson, George Raynor, and Dixie R. Harris. *The Signal Corps: The Outcome (Mid-1943 through 1945).* United States Army in World War II. Washington, D.C.: Office of the Chief of Military History, United States Army, 1966.

144th SIGNAL BATTALION

HERALDIC ITEMS

COAT OF ARMS

Shield: Tenné, four bendlets enhanced and in dexter base a fleur-de-lis argent. On a chief of the last a lion passant guardant vert.

Crest: On a wreath of the colors argent and tenné a spray of oak leaves proper surmounted by a lineman's splice knot argent.

Motto: VOX VINCENTIS (Voice of the Victorious).

Symbolism: Orange and white are the colors traditionally associated with the Signal Corps. The four white diagonal bends suggest lines of communication and represent the unit's four World War II decorations. The fleur-de-lis, from the historic French coat of arms, indicates that the battalion has been decorated by the French government. The lion, a device from the arms of Normandy, is placed in the position of honor on the upper portion of the shield in commemoration of the unit's action against the enemy during the battle of Normandy. Green, the historic color for Armor, alludes to the organization's former designation, 144th Signal Armored Company.

The lineman's splice knot, symbolic of an effective communication system, and the oak leaves, identified with the Ardennes forest, are placed on a crest as a further position of honor in recognition of the unit's outstanding action during the battle of the Ardennes.

DISTINCTIVE UNIT INSIGNIA

The distinctive unit insignia is the shield and motto of the coat of arms.

LINEAGE AND HONORS

RA
(4th Armored Division) (inactive)

LINEAGE

Constituted 13 January 1941 in the Regular Army as the 49th Signal Company and assigned to the 4th Armored Division. Activated 15 April 1941 at Pine Camp, New York. Redesignated 7 August 1941 as the 144th Signal Armored Company. Redesignated 5 January 1942 as the 144th Armored Signal Company. Inactivated 24 April 1946 at Camp Kilmer, New Jersey.

Activated 15 June 1954 at Fort Hood, Texas. Reorganized and redesignated 1 April 1957 as Headquarters and Headquarters Company, 144th Signal Battalion (organic elements constituted 12 March 1957 and activated 1 April 1957 at Fort Hood, Texas). Inactivated 10 May 1971 in Germany.

CAMPAIGN PARTICIPATION CREDIT

World War II
    Normandy
    Northern France
    Rhineland
    Ardennes-Alsace
    Central Europe

DECORATIONS

Presidential Unit Citation (Army), Streamer embroidered ARDENNES (4th Armored Division cited; WD GO 54, 1945)

French Croix de Guerre with Palm, World War II, Streamer embroidered NORMANDY (144th Armored Signal Company cited; DA GO 43, 1950)

French Croix de Guerre with Palm, World War II, Streamer embroidered MOSELLE RIVER (144th Armored Signal Company cited; DA GO 43, 1950)

French Croix de Guerre, World War II, Fourragere (144th Armored Signal Company cited; DA GO 43, 1950)

144th SIGNAL BATTALION BIBLIOGRAPHY

Blumenson, Martin. *Breakout and Pursuit*. United States Army in World War II. Washington, D.C.: Office of the Chief of Military History, United States Army, 1961. 4th Armored Division cited.

Cole, Hugh M. *The Ardennes: Battle of the Bulge*. United States Army in World War II. Washington, D.C.: Office of the Chief of Military History, United States Army, 1965. 4th Armored Division cited.

Historical and Pictorial Review, Fourth Armored Division, United States Army, Camp Pine, New York. 6 vols. Baton Rouge: Army and Navy Publishing Company, 1942.

Jacobs, Bruce. *Breakthrough! The Story of the 4th Armored Division*. Kearny, N.J.: 4th Armored Division Association, 1956.

Koyen, Kenneth A. *The Fourth Armored Division From the Beach to Bavaria: The Story of the Fourth Armored Division in Combat*. Munich, Germany: Herder Druck, 1945.

MacDonald, Charles B. *The Last Offensive*. United States Army in World War II. Washington, D.C.: Office of the Chief of Military History, United States Army, 1973. 4th Armored Division cited.

146th SIGNAL BATTALION

HERALDIC ITEMS

COAT OF ARMS

Shield: Gules (crimson), between two flanks or a pheon point to chief in chief and a clarion in base of the like.

Crest: That for the regiments and separate battalions of the Florida Army National Guard: On a wreath of the colors or and gules an alligator statant proper.

Motto: SAINTS OF SERVICE.

Symbolism: The colors crimson and yellow (gold) are the colors of the unit's immediate predecessor, the 748th Armored Ordnance Battalion. The pheon and clarion allude to two battle honors (New Guinea with arrowhead and Southern Philippines) displayed by elements of the current battalion for service in World War II. The clarion is also a type of trumpet with clear, piercing tones and, being a form of signaling, refers to the unit's transition to a Signal Corps organization.

DISTINCTIVE UNIT INSIGNIA

The distinctive unit insignia is the shield and motto of the coat of arms.

LINEAGE AND HONORS

ARNG
(Florida)

LINEAGE

Constituted 1 November 1952 in the Florida Army National Guard as the 748th Ordnance Battalion and assigned to the 48th Infantry Division; concurrently organized from existing units at Jacksonville. Reorganized and redesignated 1 November 1955 as the 748th Armored Ordnance Battalion (48th Infantry Division concurrently reorganized and redesignated as the 48th Armored Division). Reorganized and redesignated 15 April 1959 as the 748th Ordnance Battalion.

Converted and redesignated 15 February 1963 as the 146th Signal Battalion and relieved from assignment to the 48th Armored Division.

Home Area: Jacksonville and Pensacola

CAMPAIGN PARTICIPATION CREDIT

Headquarters Company (Jacksonville) entitled to:

World War II-AP
New Guinea (with arrowhead)
Southern Philippines

Company B (Pensacola) entitled to:

World War II (Asiatic-Pacific Theater)
Silver Band without campaign inscription

Company C (Jacksonville) entitled to:

World War II-AP
New Guinea (with arrowhead)
Western Pacific
Southern Philippines

DECORATIONS

Headquarters Company (Jacksonville) entitled to:

Philippine Presidential Unit Citation, Streamer embroidered 17 OCTOBER 1944 TO 4 JULY 1945 (124th Infantry cited; DA GO 47, 1950)

Company C (Jacksonville) entitled to:

Presidential Unit Citation (Army), Streamer embroidered MINDANAO (2d Battalion, 124th Infantry cited; WD GO 38, 1946)
Philippine Presidential Unit Citation, Streamer embroidered 17 OCTOBER 1944 TO 4 JULY 1945 (124th Infantry cited; DA GO 47, 1950)

146th SIGNAL BATTALION BIBLIOGRAPHY

Morris, Al, Bill Hawkesworth, and Phyllis Prucino. "The 53d on REFORGER." *Army Communicator* 11 (Spring 1986): 26–29.

124th Infantry Gators at Fort Benning, Nineteen Hundred Forty-Three. N.p., 1943.

"Operation Fuerzas Unidas '84: Building a Road in Panama." *National Guard* 38 (July 1984): 20–24.

"Riot Reaction Force: The Guard in the April Disorders." *National Guardsman* 22 (May 1968): 2–16.

Smith, Robert Ross. *The Approach to the Philippines.* United States Army in World War II. Washington, D.C.: Office of the Chief of Military History, Department of the Army, 1953. 124th Infantry cited.

———. *Triumph in the Philippines.* United States Army in World War II. Washington, D.C.: Office of the Chief of Military History, Department of the Army, 1963. 124th Infantry cited.

151st SIGNAL BATTALION

HERALDIC ITEMS

COAT OF ARMS

Shield: Per bend azure and tenné, in bend a double-ended lightning flash throughout argent, its lower portion charged with a lightning flash sable, and in chief a branch of palmetto of the third.

Crest: That for the regiments and separate battalions of the South Carolina Army National Guard: On a wreath of the colors argent and tenné upon a mount vert a palmetto tree proper charged with a crescent argent.

Motto: UBIQUE AD FINEM (Everywhere to the End).

Symbolism: Orange and white are the colors traditionally associated with the Signal Corps. The lightning flash through the center denotes the unit's service both to South Carolina, represented by the blue, and Florida, represented by the orange. The palmetto branch indicates that the unit is assigned to the South Carolina Army National Guard, whose crest features the palmetto tree.

DISTINCTIVE UNIT INSIGNIA

The distinctive unit insignia is the shield and motto of the coat of arms.

LINEAGE AND HONORS

ARNG
(South Carolina)

LINEAGE

Constituted 23 March 1959 in the South Carolina Army National Guard as the 151st Signal Battalion and assigned to the 51st Infantry Division. Organized 1 April 1959 in central South Carolina from existing units with Headquarters at Columbia. Relieved 1 April 1963 from assignment to the 51st Infantry Division. Location of Headquarters changed 1 January 1968 to Newberry; changed 1 July 1980 to Greenville.

Home Area: Northwestern South Carolina

CAMPAIGN PARTICIPATION CREDIT

Headquarters and Headquarters Company (Greenville) entitled to:

World War I
  Somme Offensive
  Ypres-Lys
  Flanders 1918

World War II-EAME
  Northern France
  Rhineland

Company A (Laurens) entitled to:

World War II-EAME
　Naples-Foggia
　North Apennines
　Po Valley

DECORATIONS

Company A (Laurens) entitled to:

French Croix de Guerre with Silver-gilt Star, World War II, Streamer embroidered CASSINO (178th Field Artillery Battalion cited; DA GO 43, 1950)

151st SIGNAL BATTALION BIBLIOGRAPHY

American Battle Monuments Commission. *30th Division, Summary of Operations in the World War*. Washington, D.C.: Government Printing Office, 1944. 118th Infantry cited. HHC perpetuates Company G, 118th Infantry.

Brawders, Jean Marie. "CAPSTONE Effects Training Changes." *National Guard* 40 (November 1986): 30–34.

Crocker, Robert W. "Go Between Circuits IV." *Army Communicator* 6 (Summer 1981): 50–53.

Davis, Nora Marshall. *History of the 118th Infantry (Palmetto Regiment)*. Columbia, S.C., 1935.

Fisher, Ernest F., Jr. *Cassino to the Alps*. United States Army in World War II. Washington, D.C.: Center of Military History, United States Army, 1977. 178th Field Artillery Battalion cited. Company A perpetuates the Medical Detachment, 178th Field Artillery Battalion.

Historical and Pictorial Review, 30th Infantry Division, Army of the United States, Fort Jackson, South Carolina, 1941. Baton Rouge: Army and Navy Publishing Company, 1941.

Historical Annual, National Guard of the State of South Carolina, 1938. Baton Rouge: Army and Navy Publishing Company, 1938.

Murphy, Elmer A. *The Thirtieth Division in the World War*. Lepanto, Ark.: Old Hickory Publishing Company, 1936.

178th Field Artillery Battalion. Bassanodel Grappa, Italy, c. 1945.

Royall, Sam J. *History of the 118th Infantry, American Expeditionary Force, France*. Columbia, S.C.: State Company, 1919.

Theodore, Peter C. "Viewpoint: 67th Signal Battalion." *Army Communicator* 2 (Spring 1977): 57–58. In 1975 the 151st was affiliated with the 67th, a Regular Army unit, for training purposes.

154th SIGNAL BATTALION

HERALDIC ITEMS

COAT OF ARMS

Shield: Argent, two flanches azure overall a Maltese cross tenné charged with a lightning flash point to base of the first.
Crest: None approved.
Motto: LOS MEDIOS (The Means).
Symbolism: Orange and white (silver) are the colors traditionally associated with the Signal Corps. Panama is represented by the silver field between blue flanches, alluding to the oceans enclosing the isthmus. The Maltese cross refers to Christopher Columbus, explorer of the region, and to its Spanish heritage. The lightning flash alludes to the battalion's mission.

DISTINCTIVE UNIT INSIGNIA

Description: A silver color metal and enamel device that consists of a white shield with blue flanches. Centered overall an orange Maltese cross bearing a silver lightning flash issuant from the top of the cross, and attached below an orange scroll inscribed with the motto LOS MEDIOS in silver letters.
Symbolism: Orange and white (silver) are the colors traditionally associated with the Signal Corps. Panama and the isthmus are represented by the white field enclosed on each side by blue flanches, symbols of the Pacific Ocean and the Caribbean Sea. The shield, of a shape typical to sixteenth century Spain, represents that country's association with the region. The Maltese cross, insignia of Christopher Columbus, recalls his arrival in 1502 to found Nombre de Dios colony. The lightning flash alludes to the battalion's mission.

LINEAGE AND HONORS

RA
(inactive)

LINEAGE

Constituted 1 September 1985 in the Regular Army as the 154th Signal Battalion and activated in Panama. Inactivated 15 October 1997 in Panama.

CAMPAIGN PARTICIPATION CREDIT

Armed Forces Expeditions
  Panama

DECORATIONS

Army Superior Unit Award, Streamer embroidered 1994–1995 (154th Signal Battalion cited; DA GO 14, 1997)

154th SIGNAL BATTALION BIBLIOGRAPHY

Blocher, Bob. "Joint U.S.-Guatemalan Exercise." *Army Communicator* 16 (Winter 1991): 11–12.

———. "154th Proves Its Mettle During Just Cause." *Army Communicator* 15 (Winter–Spring 1990): 36–37.

———. "Training Becomes Reality." *Soldiers* 45 (April 1990): 10–11.

154th Signal Battalion 1986 Yearbook, Fort Clayton, Panama. N.p.

156th SIGNAL BATTALION

HERALDIC ITEMS

COAT OF ARMS

Shield: Tenné, issuant from a chevron of eight bars wavy argent and sable an oriental dragon rampant of the like grasping in dexter talon a stylized torch of the second and last flamant proper, all narrowly fimbriated of the second.

Crest: That for the regiments and separate battalions of the Michigan Army National Guard: On a wreath of the colors argent and tenné a griffin segreant or.

Motto: AUDIATUR VERBUM (Let the Word Be Heard).

Symbolism: Orange and white are the colors traditionally associated with the Signal Corps. The oriental dragon refers to action in the Asiatic-Pacific Theater during World War II. The wavy chevron alludes to the Rhine River and represents the European Theater. The division of eight bars alludes to battle honors earned during World Wars I and II. The torch represents the functions of the Signal Corps.

DISTINCTIVE UNIT INSIGNIA

The distinctive unit insignia is the shield and motto of the coat of arms.

LINEAGE AND HONORS

ARNG
(Michigan)

LINEAGE

Constituted 13 February 1959 in the Michigan Army National Guard as the 156th Signal Battalion. Organized from existing units in southern Michigan with Headquarters federally recognized 15 March 1959 at Detroit. Ordered into active Federal service 1 October 1961 at Detroit; released 9 August 1962 from active Federal service and reverted to state control. Ordered into active Federal service 24 July 1967 at home stations; released 2 August 1967 from active Federal service and reverted to state control. Location of Headquarters changed 1 February 1968 to Ypsilanti.

Home Area: Southern Michigan

CAMPAIGN PARTICIPATION CREDIT

Headquarters Company (Ypsilanti) entitled to:

Civil War
  Bull Run
  Manassas
  Antietam
  Fredericksburg
  Peninsula
  Chancellorsville
  Gettysburg
  Wilderness
  Spotsylvania
  Cold Harbor
  Petersburg
  Appomattox

World War I
  Aisne-Marne
  Oise-Aisne
  Meuse-Argonne
  Alsace 1918

World War II-AP
  Papua
  New Guinea
  Leyte

Company A (Kalamazoo) and Company B (Adrian) each entitled to:

Civil War
  Bull Run
  Peninsula
  Fredericksburg
  Vicksburg
  Wilderness
  Cold Harbor
  Petersburg
  Appomattox
  Mississippi 1863
  Tennessee 1863

World War I
  Aisne-Marne
  Oise-Aisne
  Meuse-Argonne
  Alsace 1918

World War II-AP
  Papua
  New Guinea (with arrowhead)
  Leyte
  Luzon

Company C (Ypsilanti) entitled to:

World War I
  Aisne-Marne
  Oise-Aisne
  Meuse-Argonne
  Alsace 1918

DECORATIONS

Headquarters Company (Ypsilanti) entitled to:

Presidential Unit Citation (Army), Streamer embroidered PAPUA (Papuan Forces, United States Army, Southwest Pacific Area, cited; WD GO 21, 1943)
Philippine Presidential Unit Citation, Streamer embroidered 17 OCTOBER 1944 TO 4 JULY 1945 (32d Signal Company cited; DA GO 47, 1950)

Company A (Kalamazoo) and Company B (Adrian) each entitled to:

Presidential Unit Citation (Army), Streamer embroidered PAPUA (Papuan Forces, United States Army, Southwest Pacific Area, cited; WD GO 21, 1943)
French Croix de Guerre with Palm, World War I, Streamer embroidered OISE-AISNE (126th Infantry cited; WD GO 11, 1924)
Philippine Presidential Unit Citation, Streamer embroidered 17 OCTOBER 1944 TO 4 JULY 1945 (126th Infantry cited; DA GO 47, 1950)

Company C (Ypsilanti) entitled to:

French Croix de Guerre with Palm, World War I, Streamer embroidered OISE-AISNE (126th Infantry cited; WD GO 11, 1924)

156th SIGNAL BATTALION BIBLIOGRAPHY

American Battle Monuments Commission. *32d Division, Summary of Operations in the World War*. Washington, D.C.: Government Printing Office, 1943. The battalion's companies perpetuate elements of the 32d Division.

Blakely, Harold W. *The 32d Infantry Division in World War II*. Madison, Wisc., 1957.

Cannon, M. Hamlin. *Leyte: The Return to the Philippines*. United States Army in World War II. Washington, D.C.: Office of the Chief of Military History, Department of the Army, 1954. 126th Infantry cited.

Carroll, Bill. "Gagetown '87." *Army Communicator* 13 (Winter 1988): 48–49. Field exercise held in New Brunswick, Canada.

Gansser, Emil B. *History of the 126th Infantry in the War with Germany*. Grand Rapids, Mich.: 126th Infantry Association, A.E.F., 1920.

Garlock, Glenn W. *Tales of the Thirty-Second*. West Salem, Wisc.: Badger Publishing Company, 1927.

Hanton, Carl. *The 32d Division in the World War 1917–1919*. Milwaukee: Wisconsin Printing Company, 1920.

Historical and Pictorial Review: National Guard of the State of Michigan. Baton Rouge: Army and Navy Publishing Company, 1940.

Hopper, George C. *First Michigan Infantry, Three Months and Three Years, Proceedings of 1891 Reunion at Detroit. Brief History of the Regiment by Major George C. Hopper. Roster of Living Members*. Coldwater, Mich.: Courier Print, 1891. Company A at Ypsilanti perpetuates Company H, 1st Michigan Infantry.

Lawrence, Warren J. "A History of Company C, 156th Signal Battalion (Combat Area), Michigan Army National Guard, in the Berlin Crisis, 1961–1962." Master's thesis, Western Michigan University, 1971.

Michigan. Adjutant General. *Record of First Michigan Infantry Civil War, 1861–1865*. Kalamazoo: Ihling Brothers and Everard, 1905.

Miller, John., *Cartwheel: The Reduction of Rabaul*. United States Army in World War II. Washington, D.C.: Office of the Chief of Military History, Department of the Army, 1959. 126th Infantry cited.

Milner, Samuel. *Victory in Papua*. United States Army in World War II. Washington, D.C.: Office of the Chief of Military History, Department of the Army, 1957. 126th Infantry cited.

"On Guard." *The National Guardsman* 16 (February 1962): 19.

Owen, Charles W. *The First Michigan Infantry, Three Months and Three Years, Brief History of the Regiment From Its Organization in May, 1861, Until Its Muster Out in July, 1865, Together with Personal Experiences of the Writer*. Quincy, Mich.: Quincy Herald Print, 1903.

Petzold, Herman. *Memoirs of the Second Michigan Infantry*. N.p., 1897. Company B at Adrian perpetuates Company D, 2d Michigan Infantry.

Record of Service of Michigan Volunteers in the Civil War, 1861–1865. 46 vols. Kalamazoo: Ihling Brothers and Everard, 1905.

Robertson, John. *Michigan in the War*. Lansing, Mich.: W. S. George, 1880.

Smith, Robert Ross. *The Approach to the Philippines*. United States Army in World War II. Washington, D.C.: Office of the Chief of Military History, Department of the Army, 1953. 126th Infantry cited.

―――. *Triumph in the Philippines*. United States Army in World War II. Washington, D.C.: Office of the Chief of Military History, Department of the Army, 1963. 126th Infantry cited.

163d SIGNAL BATTALION

HERALDIC ITEMS

COAT OF ARMS

Shield: Per pale tenné and argent, a flame emitting two smoke signals counterchanged.

Crest: That for the regiments and separate battalions of the Army Reserve: On a wreath of the colors argent and tenné the Lexington Minuteman proper. The statue of the Minuteman Capt. John Parker (H. H. Kitson, sculptor) stands on the Common in Lexington, Massachusetts.

Motto: A COUP SUR (With Sure Stroke).

Symbolism: Orange and white are the colors traditionally associated with the Signal Corps. The flame and smoke signals represent the universal and ancient method of conveying a message. The smoke clouds also allude to the organization's two battle honors earned during World War II.

DISTINCTIVE UNIT INSIGNIA

The distinctive unit insignia is the shield and motto of the coat of arms.

LINEAGE AND HONORS

AR
(63d Infantry Division) (inactive)

LINEAGE

Constituted 18 January 1943 in the Army of the United States as the 563d Signal Company, an element of the 63d Infantry Division. Activated 15 June 1943 at Camp Blanding, Florida. Inactivated 29 September 1945 at Camp Myles Standish, Massachusetts. Allotted 22 February 1952 to the Organized Reserve Corps. Activated 1 March 1952 at Los Angeles, California. (Organized Reserve Corps redesignated 9 July 1952 as the Army Reserve.)

Reorganized and redesignated 1 May 1959 as Headquarters and Headquarters Company, 163d Signal Battalion, an element of the 63d Infantry Division; location concurrently changed to Gardenia, California. (Companies A and B constituted 31 March 1959 and activated 1 May 1959 at Los Angeles, California.) (Company C constituted 27 March 1963 and activated 1 April 1963 at Gardenia, California.)

Reorganized and redesignated 1 October 1963 as Headquarters and Headquarters Detachment, 163d Signal Battalion. Location changed 1 January 1964 to Torrance, California. Battalion (less Company C) inactivated 31 December 1965 at Torrance, California (Company C concurrently inactivated at Gardenia, California).

CAMPAIGN PARTICIPATION CREDIT

World War II
  Rhineland
  Central Europe

DECORATIONS

None.

163d SIGNAL BATTALION BIBLIOGRAPHY

Blood and Fire, Victory in Europe, 63d Infantry Division. Esslingen, Germany: J. F. Schreiber, 1945.

Historical Background 63d Infantry Division. Maywood, Calif.: Headquarters, 63d Infantry Division, 1963.

MacDonald, Charles B. *The Last Offensive.* United States Army in World War II. Washington, D.C.: Office of the Chief of Military History, United States Army, 1973. 63d Infantry Division cited.

"The 63d Infantry Division." *Army Reserve* 11 (March 1965): 9–10.

The 63d Infantry Division, United States Army, June 1943–September 1945. N.p., n.d.

179th SIGNAL BATTALION

HERALDIC ITEMS

COAT OF ARMS

Shield: Per fess wavy enhanced argent semé-de-lis sable and tenné, radiant to base from honor point seven lightning flashes of the first.

Crest: That for the regiments and separate battalions of the Army Reserve: On a wreath of the colors argent and tenné the Lexington Minuteman proper. The statue of the Minuteman Capt. John Parker (H. H. Kitson, sculptor) stands on the Common in Lexington, Massachusetts.

Motto: VALOR ET SCIENTIA (Valor and Knowledge).

Symbolism: Orange and white are the colors traditionally associated with the Signal Corps. Fleurs-de-lis appear frequently in coats of arms of French provinces in the area of the battalion's war service. The wavy line represents the Rhine River, alluding to service in Germany. The seven lightning flashes symbolize the battalion's battle honors.

DISTINCTIVE UNIT INSIGNIA

The distinctive unit insignia is the shield and motto of the coat of arms.

LINEAGE AND HONORS

AR
(79th Infantry Division) (inactive)

LINEAGE

Constituted 1 July 1916 in the Enlisted Reserve Corps as a Signal Corps battalion. Organized March–October 1917 in Maryland as the 7th Reserve Field Signal Battalion. Ordered into active military service 5 October 1917 at Camp Meade, Maryland; concurrently redesignated as the 304th Field Signal Battalion and assigned to the 79th Division. Demobilized 27 May 1919 at Camp Dix, New Jersey.

Reconstituted 24 June 1921 in the Organized Reserves as the 79th Signal Company, an element of the 79th Division (later redesignated as the 79th Infantry Division). Organized in December 1921 at Philadelphia, Pennsylvania. Ordered into active military service 15 June 1942 at Camp Pickett, Virginia. Inactivated 15 December 1945 at Camp Kilmer, New Jersey. Activated 28 January 1947 at Philadelphia, Pennsylvania. (Organized Reserves redesignated 25 March 1948 as the Organized Reserve Corps; redesignated 9 July 1952 as the Army Reserve.)

Reorganized and redesignated 6 April 1959 as Headquarters and Headquarters Company, 179th Signal Battalion, an element of the 79th Infantry Division (Companies A and B constituted 17 March 1959 and activated 20 April 1959 at Reading, Pennsylvania, and Wilkes-Barre, Pennsylvania, respectively). Battalion inactivated (less Company A) 28 February 1963 at Philadelphia, Pennsylvania. (Company A inactivated 28 March 1963 at Reading, Pennsylvania.)

CAMPAIGN PARTICIPATION CREDIT

World War I
Meuse-Argonne
Lorraine 1918

World War II
Normandy
Northern France
Rhineland
Ardennes-Alsace
Central Europe

DECORATIONS

Meritorious Unit Commendation (Army), Streamer embroidered EUROPEAN THEATER (79th Signal Company cited; GO 64, 79th Infantry Division, 29 April 1945)

French Croix de Guerre with Palm, World War II, Streamer embroidered NORMANDY TO PARIS (79th Signal Company cited; DA GO 43, 1950)

French Croix de Guerre with Palm, World War II, Streamer embroidered PARROY FOREST (79th Signal Company cited; DA GO 43, 1950)

French Croix de Guerre, World War II, Fourragere (79th Signal Company cited; DA GO 43, 1950)

179th SIGNAL BATTALION BIBLIOGRAPHY

American Battle Monuments Commission. *79th Division, Summary of Operations in the World War*. Washington, D.C.: Government Printing Office, 1944.

Barber, J. Frank, comp. and ed. *History of the Seventy-Ninth Division, A.E.F., During the World War, 1917–1919*. Lancaster, Pa.: Steinman and Steinman, 1922.

Blumenson, Martin. *Breakout and Pursuit*. United States Army in World War II. Washington, D.C.: Office of the Chief of Military History, Department of the Army, 1961. 79th Infantry Division cited.

Cole, Hugh M. *The Lorraine Campaign*. United States Army in World War II. Washington, D.C.: Historical Division, Department of the Army, 1950. 79th Infantry Division cited.

The Cross of Lorraine, A Combat History of the 79th Infantry Division, June 1942–December 1945. Baton Rouge: Army and Navy Publishing Company, 1946.

Harrison, Gordon A. *Cross-Channel Attack*. United States Army in World War II. Washington, D.C.: Office of the Chief of Military History, United States Army, 1951. 79th Infantry Division cited.

The History of Company C, 304th Field Signal Battalion, U.S. Army, American Expeditionary Forces. A Brief History and Roster of the Outpost Company of the Signal Battalion of the 79th Division, from Organization to Demobilization, 1917–1919. Philadelphia: Shade Printing Company, 1920.

MacDonald, Charles B. *The Last Offensive*. United States Army in World War II. Washington, D.C.: Office of the Chief of Military History, United States Army, 1973. 79th Infantry Division cited.

181st SIGNAL BATTALION

HERALDIC ITEMS

COAT OF ARMS

Shield: Tenné, between four double-ended lightning flashes radiating from fess point argent a cross of the like charged in fess with a Philippine sun azure, bearing a torteaux fimbriated of the second. Overall issuant from base a demitorch sable detailed and flamed of the second.

Crest: That for the regiments and separate battalions of the Army Reserve: On a wreath of the colors argent and tenné the Lexington Minuteman proper. The statue of the Minuteman Capt. John Parker (H. H. Kitson, sculptor) stands on the Common in Lexington, Massachusetts.

Motto: RAPIDA COLLIQUA OMNIA (Rapid Communications Everywhere).

Symbolism: Orange and white are the colors traditionally associated with the Signal Corps. The torch and four lightning flashes, symbolic of signal fire and electrical communications, allude to the mission of the unit. The four lightning flashes also represent the four battle honors earned by the unit during World Wars I and II. The Philippine sun symbolizes the Pacific area in which the unit served during World War II. The cross (from the seal of the province of Leyte) identifies the part of the Philippine Islands where the unit fought, for which it received the Philippine Presidential Unit Citation. The colors red, white, and blue are symbolic of that award.

DISTINCTIVE UNIT INSIGNIA

The distinctive unit insignia is the shield and motto of the coat of arms.

LINEAGE AND HONORS

LINEAGE

AR (81st Infantry Division) (inactive)

Constituted 1 July 1916 in the Enlisted Reserve Corps as a Signal Corps battalion. Organized March–October 1917 in South Carolina as the 8th Reserve Field Signal Battalion. Ordered into active military service 5 October 1917 at Camp Jackson, South Carolina; concurrently redesignated as the 306th Field Signal Battalion and assigned to the 81st Division. Demobilized 22 June 1919 at Camp Jackson, South Carolina.

Reconstituted 24 June 1921 in the Organized Reserves as the 81st Signal Company, an element of the 81st Division (later redesignated as the 81st Infantry Division). Organized 1 December 1921 at Nashville, Tennessee. Ordered into active military service 15 June 1942 at Camp Rucker, Alabama. Inactivated 20 January 1946 in Japan. Activated 12 January 1948 at Atlanta, Georgia. (Organized Reserves redesignated 25 March 1948 as the Organized Reserve Corps; redesignated 9 July 1952 as the Army Reserve.)

Reorganized and redesignated 1 May 1959 as Headquarters and Headquarters Company, 181st Signal Battalion, an element of the 81st Infantry Division (organic elements constituted 10 April 1959 and activated 1 May 1959 at Clemson, South Carolina). Redesignated 1 October 1963 as Headquarters and Headquarters Detachment, 181st Signal Battalion. Inactivated 31 December 1965 at Atlanta, Georgia (organic elements concurrently inactivated).

CAMPAIGN PARTICIPATION CREDIT

World War I
Meuse-Argonne
Lorraine 1918

World War II
Western Pacific
Leyte

DECORATIONS

Philippine Presidential Unit Citation, Streamer embroidered 17 OCTOBER 1944 TO 4 JULY 1945 (81st Signal Company cited; DA GO 47, 1950)

181st SIGNAL BATTALION BIBLIOGRAPHY

American Battle Monuments Commission. *81st Division, Summary of Operations in the World War*. Washington, D.C.: Government Printing Office, 1944.

81st Wildcat Division Historical Committee. *The 81st Infantry Wildcat Division in World War II*. Washington, D.C.: Infantry Journal Press, 1948.

Irwin, Warren W., ed. *World War History of the 306th Field Signal Battalion, 81st Division*. Rochester, New York, 1938.

Operation Report 81st Infantry Division: Operation on Peleliu Island, 23 September–27 November 1944. N.p., 1944.

Operation Report 81st Infantry Division: Palau Islands to New Caledonia to Leyte, P.I. to Japan 5 Jan. 1945 to 10 Jan. 1946. N.p., 1946.

Smith, Robert Ross. *The Approach to the Philippines*. United States Army in World War II. Washington, D.C.: Office of the Chief of Military History, United States Army, 1953. 81st Infantry Division cited.

190th SIGNAL BATTALION

HERALDIC ITEMS

COAT OF ARMS

Shield: Per quarter tenné and argent between in first a mullet and in third a torch issuant both of the second, two lightning flashes bend sinisterwise azure.

Crest: That for the regiments and separate battalions of the Army Reserve: On a wreath of the colors argent and tenné the Lexington Minuteman proper. The statue of the Minuteman Capt. John Parker (H. H. Kitson, sculptor) stands on the Common in Lexington, Massachusetts.

Motto: THE VITAL LINK.

Symbolism: Orange and white are the colors traditionally associated with the Signal Corps. The lightning flashes are from the Signal Corps symbol on military maps. The blue alludes to the water of the Moselle and Saar (Sarre) Rivers and represents the unit's decoration for service in that region. The four quarters, plus the charges on them, denote the eight campaigns in which the unit participated during World Wars I and II. The mullet is for the Lone Star State of Texas, the unit's former location. The torch, an early signaling device, represents the basic function of the organization.

DISTINCTIVE UNIT INSIGNIA

The distinctive unit insignia is the shield and motto of the coat of arms.

LINEAGE AND HONORS

AR
(90th Infantry Division) (inactive)

LINEAGE

Constituted 1 July 1916 in the Enlisted Reserve Corps as a Signal Corps battalion. Organized March–October 1917 in Texas as the 16th Reserve Field Signal Battalion. Ordered into active military service 5 October 1917 at Fort Sam Houston, Texas; concurrently redesignated as the 315th Field Signal Battalion and assigned to the 90th Division. Demobilized 25 June 1919 at Camp Bowie, Texas.

Reconstituted 24 June 1921 in the Organized Reserves as the 90th Signal Company, an element of the 90th Division (later redesignated as the 90th Infantry Division). Organized in December 1921 at San Antonio, Texas. Ordered into active military service 25 March 1942 at Camp Barkeley, Texas. Inactivated 22 December 1945 at Camp Patrick Henry, Virginia. Activated 24 March 1947 at San Antonio, Texas. (Organized Reserves redesignated 25 March 1948 as the Organized Reserve Corps; redesignated 9 July 1952 as the Army Reserve.)

Reorganized and redesignated 1 April 1959 as Headquarters and Headquarters Company, 190th Signal Battalion, an element of the 90th Infantry Division (Companies A and B constituted 19 March 1959; activated 1 April 1959 at Lubbock and Austin, Texas, respectively). Battalion (less Company A) inactivated 31 December 1965 at San Antonio, Texas (Company A concurrently inactivated at Lubbock, Texas).

CAMPAIGN PARTICIPATION CREDIT

World War I
St. Mihiel
Meuse-Argonne
Lorraine 1918

World War II
Normandy
Northern France
Rhineland
Ardennes-Alsace
Central Europe

DECORATIONS

Meritorious Unit Commendation (Army), Streamer embroidered EUROPEAN THEATER JAN–FEB 1944 (90th Signal Company cited; GO 631, 90th Infantry Division, 23 August 1945)

Meritorious Unit Commendation (Army), Streamer embroidered EUROPEAN THEATER MAR–AUG 1944 (90th Signal Company cited; GO 631, 90th Infantry Division, 23 August 1945)

Meritorious Unit Commendation (Army), Streamer embroidered EUROPEAN THEATER SEP 1944–FEB 1945 (90th Signal Company cited; GO 631, 90th Infantry Division, 23 August 1945)

French Croix de Guerre with Palm, World War II, Streamer embroidered MOSELLE-SARRE RIVERS (90th Signal Company cited; DA GO 43, 1950)

190th SIGNAL BATTALION BIBLIOGRAPHY

Abrams, Joe I. *A History of the 90th Division in World War II, 6 June 1944 to 9 May 1945.* Baton Rouge: Army and Navy Publishing Company, 1946.

American Battle Monuments Commission. *90th Division, Summary of Operations in the World War.* Washington, D.C.: Government Printing Office, 1944.

Blumenson, Martin. *Breakout and Pursuit.* United States Army in World War II. Washington, D.C.: Office of the Chief of Military History, United States Army, 1961. 90th Infantry Division cited.

Cole, Hugh M. *The Lorraine Campaign.* United States Army in World War II. Washington, D.C.: Historical Division, Department of the Army, 1950. 90th Infantry Division cited.

From D Day Plus Two to V-E Day with the 90th Signal Company. Weiden, Germany: Ferdinand Nickl, 1945.

Harrison, Gordon A. *Cross-Channel Attack.* United States Army in World War II. Washington, D.C.: Office of the Chief of Military History, United States Army, 1951. 90th Infantry Division cited.

MacDonald, Charles B. *The Siegfried Line Campaign.* United States Army in World War II. Washington, D.C.: Office of the Chief of Military History, Department of the Army, 1963. 90th Infantry Division cited.

Operations 90th Division, American Expeditionary Forces, August 18, 1918–November 11, 1918. Fort Leavenworth, Kans.: General Service Schools, 1918.

Operations 90th Division, American Expeditionary Forces, November 11, 1918 to May 6, 1919. Fort Leavenworth, Kans.: General Service Schools, 1919.

Wythe, George. *A History of the 90th Division.* New York: De Vinne Press, 1920.

HEADQUARTERS AND HEADQUARTERS DETACHMENT
198th SIGNAL BATTALION
(First Delaware)

HERALDIC ITEMS

COAT OF ARMS

Shield: Argent, a fleur-de-lis gules and on a chief azure eleven mullets—five and six—or.

Crest: That for the regiments and separate battalions of the Delaware Army National Guard: On a wreath of the colors argent and gules a griffin's head erased azure, eared and beaked or, langued gules, and collared sable fimbriated argent and thereon three plates.

Motto: FIRST REGIMENT OF FIRST STATE.

Symbolism: The shield is white, the former color of Infantry. The eleven mullets represent the eleven campaigns in which the organization served during the Civil War. The red fleur-de-lis is for World War I service; red is the color of the Coast Artillery and alludes to the unit's earlier mission.

DISTINCTIVE UNIT INSIGNIA

The distinctive unit insignia is the shield and motto of the coat of arms.

LINEAGE AND HONORS

ARNG
(Delaware)

LINEAGE

Constituted 9 December 1775 in the Continental Army as the Delaware Regiment (also known as Haslet's Regiment). Organized during January–March 1776 for one year's service under the command of Colonel John Haslet. Mustered into Continental service 11–12 April 1776 at Dover and Lewistown. Reorganized 12 December 1776–1 March 1777 as Colonel David Hall's Regiment. Reorganized September 1780–August 1781 from new and existing companies. Mustered out of Continental service 3 November 1783 at Christiana Bridge.

Light Infantry, 1st Regiment, reorganized 10 October 1793 in the Delaware Militia at Wilmington, under the command of Captain David Bush. Mustered into Federal service 23 May 1813 at Wilmington; mustered out of Federal service 31 July 1813; mustered into Federal service 28 August 1814; mustered out of Federal service 3 January–13 March 1815.

Artillery Company, 2d Brigade, reorganized prior to 9 April 1793 at Dover, under the command of Captain Furbee. Mustered into Federal service 23 May 1813 at Dover; mustered out of Federal service 2 September 1814.

1st Company, Light Infantry, 8th Regiment, reorganized prior to 22 February 1799 at Georgetown, under the command of Captain Benton Harris. Mustered into Federal service 2 March 1813; mustered out of Federal service 4 May 1813 at Lewes. Mustered into Federal service 6 May 1813; mustered out of Federal service 31 July 1813. Mustered into Federal service 6 August 1814; mustered out of Federal service 11 January 1815. Reorganized 6 March 1825 as the 1st Company of Light Infantry, 1st Battalion.

Light Infantry, 1st Regiment; Artillery Company, 2d Brigade; and 1st Company of Light Infantry, 1st Battalion, reorganized with new units in 1831 as the Light Infantry Battalion, attached to the 8th Regiment. Reorganized from 1849–1861 as independent volunteer companies.

Reorganized 2–22 May 1861 as the 1st Delaware Volunteer Infantry Regiment and mustered into Federal service at Wilmington; mustered out of Federal service 2–26 August 1861. Reorganized 10 September–19 October 1861 and mustered into Federal service for three years at Wilmington; mustered out of Federal service 12 July 1865 near Munson's Hill, Virginia.

Reorganized 4 April 1869 in the Delaware Volunteers as the 1st Zouave Regiment. Reorganized in 1880 in the Organized Militia of Delaware as the 1st Regiment of Infantry. (Organized Militia of Delaware redesignated 17 April 1885 as the Delaware National Guard.) Mustered into Federal service 9–19 May 1898 at Middletown as the 1st Delaware Volunteer Infantry; mustered out of Federal service (less Companies A, B, G, and M) 16 November 1898 at Wilmington (Companies A, B, G, and M mustered out of Federal service 19 December 1898 at Wilmington).

Reorganized 1899–1900 in the Delaware National Guard as the 1st Infantry Regiment. Mustered into Federal service 8–9 July 1916 at New Castle; mustered out of Federal service 15–16 February 1917. Drafted into Federal service 5 August 1917. (Companies of the 1st and 2d Battalions transferred in October 1917 to the 3d Battalion, 114th Infantry, and other units of the 29th Division.) Personnel of the entire former 1st Infantry Regiment, Delaware National Guard, withdrawn 17 January 1918 from the 29th Division and regiment reorganized and redesignated as the 59th Pioneer Infantry. Demobilized (less Companies B, C, and D) 8 July 1919 at Camp Dix, New Jersey (Companies B, C, and D demobilized 7 August 1919 at Camp Upton, New York).

Former elements of the 1st Infantry Regiment, Delaware National Guard, reorganized and federally recognized 15 September 1921 as the 198th Artillery (Coast Artillery Corps) with Headquarters at Wilmington, and the Separate Battalion, Coast Artillery (see ANNEX). 198th Artillery (Coast Artillery Corps) redesignated 16 August 1924 as the 198th Coast Artillery. Inducted into Federal service 16 September 1940 at Wilmington. (3d Battalion organized 1 January 1943 while in Federal service.) Regiment broken up 1 March 1944 and its elements reorganized and redesignated as follows: Headquarters and Headquarters Battery as Headquarters Battery, 198th Antiaircraft Artillery Group; 1st Battalion as the 736th Antiaircraft Artillery Gun Battalion; and 2d Battalion as the 945th Antiaircraft Artillery Automatic Weapons Battalion; (3d Battalion as the 373d Antiaircraft Artillery Gun Battalion—hereafter separate lineage).

Headquarters and Headquarters Battery, 198th Antiaircraft Artillery Group, inactivated 24 December 1945 at Camp Anza, California. Reorganized and federally recognized 27 August 1946 at Wilmington.

736th Antiaircraft Artillery Gun Battalion inactivated 2 January 1946 at Camp Stoneman, California. Reorganized and federally recognized 16 October 1946 at Wilmington. Expanded 10 October 1949 to form the 736th Antiaircraft Artillery Gun Battalion and the 156th Antiaircraft Artillery Automatic Weapons Battalion. 736th Antiaircraft Artillery Gun Battalion ordered into active Federal service 19 August 1950 at Wilmington. Released from active Federal service 2 August 1952 and reverted to state control. Redesignated 1 October 1953 as the 736th Antiaircraft Artillery Battalion.

156th Antiaircraft Artillery Automatic Weapons Battalion redesignated 20 July 1951 as the 156th Antiaircraft Artillery Gun Battalion. Redesignated 1 October 1953 as the 156th Antiaircraft Artillery Battalion.

945th Antiaircraft Artillery Automatic Weapons Battalion inactivated 15 February 1946 in Japan. Reorganized and federally recognized 17 October 1946 with Headquarters at Dover. Reorganized and redesignated 24 October 1949 as the 193d Antiaircraft Artillery Gun Battalion. Redesignated 1 October 1953 as the 193d Antiaircraft Artillery Battalion.

Headquarters and Headquarters Battery, 198th Antiaircraft Artillery Group; 280th (see ANNEX), 736th, 156th, 193d, and 945th (organized in 1953 as the 286th Antiaircraft Artillery Operations Detachment [NGUS]) Antiaircraft Artillery Battalions consolidated 1 April 1959 to form the 198th Artillery, a parent regiment under the Combat Arms Regimental System, to consist of the 1st, 2d, 4th, and 5th Gun Battalions, the 3d Automatic Weapons Battalion, and the 6th Detachment. Reorganized 1 April 1962 to consist of the 1st, 2d, 3d, 4th, and 5th Automatic Weapons Battalions and the 6th Detachment. Reorganized 1 May 1963 to consist of the 1st, 2d, 3d, and 4th Automatic Weapons Battalions and the 6th Detachment. Reorganized 31 January 1968 to consist of the 1st, 2d, and 3d Battalions.

1st and 2d Battalions, 198th Artillery, consolidated 1 January 1970 to form the 198th Signal Battalion with Headquarters at New Castle (3d Battalion concurrently broken up and reorganized as various elements in the Delaware Army National Guard—hereafter separate lineages). 198th Signal Battalion reorganized 15 April 1989 in the Delaware and South Carolina Army National Guard.

Headquarters and Headquarters Company reorganized and redesignated 1 September 1990 in the Delaware Army National Guard at Wilmington as Headquarters and Headquarters Detachment, 198th Signal Battalion (organic elements concurrently reorganized as various elements of the Delaware and South Carolina Army National Guard—hereafter separate lineages).

ANNEX

Separate Battalion, Coast Artillery redesignated 24 March 1924 as the 1st Separate Battalion, Coast Artillery. Redesignated 10 July 1925 as the 261st Coast Artillery Battalion. Reorganized and redesignated 15 April 1940 as the 1st Battalion, 261st Coast Artillery. Consolidated 27 January 1941 with Headquarters, 261st Coast Artillery, and consolidated unit designated as the 261st Coast Artillery Battalion; concurrently inducted into Federal service at Georgetown. Battalion disbanded 1 October 1944 (organic elements hereafter separate lineages). 261st Coast Artillery Battalion (less former Headquarters, 261st Coast Artillery) reconstituted 24 October 1949 as the 945th Antiaircraft Artillery Automatic Weapons Battalion with Headquarters at Georgetown. Redesignated 1 October 1953 as the 945th Antiaircraft Artillery Battalion. Reorganized and redesignated 20 November 1956 as the 280th Antiaircraft Artillery Battalion.

Home Station: Wilmington

CAMPAIGN PARTICIPATION CREDIT

Revolutionary War
- Long Island
- Trenton
- Princeton
- Brandywine
- Germantown
- Cowpens
- Guilford Court House
- Yorktown
- Monmouth
- New York 1776
- New York 1777
- South Carolina 1780
- South Carolina 1781
- North Carolina 1781
- South Carolina 1782

War of 1812
- Delaware 1813
- Delaware 1814
- Delaware 1815

Civil War
- Peninsula
- Antietam
- Fredericksburg
- Chancellorsville
- Gettysburg
- Wilderness
- Spotsylvania
- Cold Harbor
- Petersburg
- Appomattox
- Virginia 1863

World War I
- Meuse-Argonne

World War II
- Northern Solomons (with arrowhead)

DECORATIONS

None.

198th SIGNAL BATTALION BIBLIOGRAPHY

Anderson, Enoch. *Personal Recollections of Captain Enoch Anderson, an Officer of the Delaware Regiments in the Revolutionary War.* Edited by Henry Hobart Bellas. Wilmington: Historical Society of Delaware, 1896.

Anderson, Thomas. "Journal of Lieutenant Thomas Anderson of the Delaware Regiment 1780–1782." *Historical Magazine*, 2d ser., 1 (1867): 207–11.

Bellas, Henry Hobart. *A History of the Delaware State Society of the Cincinnati From Its Organization to the Present Time. To Which is Appended a Brief Account of the Delaware Regiments in the War of the Revolution.* Wilmington: Historical Society of Delaware, 1895.

Bennett, C[aleb] P[rew]. "The Delaware Regiment in the Revolution." *Pennsylvania Magazine of History and Biography* 9 (1885): 451–62.

———. "Orderly Book of Caleb Prew Bennett at the Battle of Yorktown, 1781." Edited by Charles W. Dickens. *Delaware History* 4 (1950): 105–48.

Blanton, Nancy C. "Go Between Circuits III." *Army Communicator* 5 (Summer 1980): 19–23.

Conner, William H., and Leon de Valinger, Jr. *Delaware's Role in World War II, 1940–1946*. Dover: State of Delaware, Public Archives Commission, 1955.

Dyer, Frederick H. *A Compendium of the War of the Rebellion*. Des Moines: Dyer Publishing Company, 1908.

Gordon, Martin K. "Operation BOB CAT: The National Guard on Bora Bora." *Push Pin Post* 8 (May 1979). 198th Coast Artillery cited.

Hancock, Harold B., ed. "Revolutionary War Period Material in the Hall of Records, 1775–1787: Four Little Known Sources." *Delaware History* 17 (1976): 54–85.

Historical and Pictorial Review, National Guard of the State of Delaware. Baton Rouge: Army and Navy Publishing Company, 1940.

History of the 59th Pioneer Infantry, 1918–1919, American Expeditionary Forces. Toul, France: Imprimerie Lemaire, 1919.

Kirkwood, Robert. *The Journal and Order Book of Captain Robert Kirkwood of the Delaware Regiment of the Continental Line*. Edited by Joseph Brown Turner. Wilmington: Historical Society of Delaware, 1910.

Kushner, Ervan F. *Bogged Down in Bora Bora*. Paterson, N.J.: Ervan F. Kushner Books, 1984.

McBarron, H. Charles and James P. Simpson. "Colonel John Haslet's Delaware Regiment 1776 (Delaware Blues)." *Military Collector and Historian* 17 (Summer 1965): 49–50.

———. "Colonel David Hall's Regiment, Delaware Line, 1777–1783." *Military Collector and Historian* 18 (Summer 1966): 48–50.

McCulloch, Robert P. *A Brief Sketch of the Military Operations on the Delaware During the Late War: Together with a copy of the muster-rolls of the several volunteer-corps which composed the Advance Light Brigade, as they stood at the close of the campaign of one thousand eight hundred and fourteen*. Philadelphia: Robert P. M'Culloh, 1820.

Marine, William M. *The Bombardment of Lewes by the British, April 6 and 7, 1813*. Wilmington: Historical Society of Delaware, 1901.

Miller, John, Jr. *Cartwheel: The Reduction of Rabaul*. United States Army in World War II. Washington: Office of the Chief of Military History, United States Army, 1959.

Murphy, Thomas G. *Four Years in the War: The History of the First Regiment of Delaware Veteran Volunteers (Infantry)*. Philadelphia: James S. Claxton, 1866.

Rodney, Caesar. *Letters To and From Caesar Rodney 1756–1784*. Edited by George Herbert Ryden. Philadelphia: University of Pennsylvania Press of the Historical Society of Delaware, 1933.

Seville, William P. *History of the First Regiment Delaware Volunteers*. Wilmington: Historical Society of Delaware, 1884.

Seymour, William. *A Journal of the Southern Expedition, 1780–1783*. Wilmington: Historical Society of Delaware, 1896.

"Training Can Be 'Different!'" *The National Guardsman* 26 (December 1972): 8–14.
Ward, Christopher. *The Delaware Continentals, 1776–1783*. Wilmington: Historical Society of Delaware, 1941.
Wilson, W. Emerson, ed. *Delaware in the Civil War*. Dover, 1962.
Wright, Robert K., Jr. *The Continental Army*. Army Lineage Series. Washington, D.C.: Center of Military History, United States Army, 1983.

202d SIGNAL BATTALION

HERALDIC ITEMS

COAT OF ARMS

Shield: Tenné, in pile two lightning flashes issuant from chief argent. In fess on a plate charged with an annulet sable a trivet brazier inflamed, ascending therefrom three columns of smoke proper.

Crest: That for the regiments and separate battalions of the Army Reserve: On a wreath of the colors argent and tenné the Lexington Minuteman proper. The statue of the Minuteman Capt. John Parker (H. H. Kitson, sculptor) stands on the Common in Lexington, Massachusetts.

Motto: GOOD NEWS TRAVELS FAST.

Symbolism: Orange and white are the colors traditionally associated with the Signal Corps. The fourteenth century European gunner's brazier refers to the unit's service in Central Europe. The three columns of smoke ascending from the brazier is an American Indian signal meaning "good news." The two lightning flashes conjoined at base to form a victory symbol represent the battalion's battle honors.

DISTINCTIVE UNIT INSIGNIA

The distinctive unit insignia is the shield of the coat of arms.

LINEAGE AND HONORS

AR
(102d Infantry Division) (inactive)

LINEAGE

Constituted 24 June 1921 in the Organized Reserves as the 102d Signal Company, an element of the 102d Division (later redesignated as the 102d Infantry Division). Organized in November 1921 at St. Louis, Missouri. Ordered into active military service 15 September 1942 at Camp Maxey, Texas. Inactivated 21 March 1946 at Camp Kilmer, New Jersey. Activated 6 August 1947 at Bloomington, Illinois. (Organized Reserves redesignated 25 March 1948 as the Organized Reserve Corps; redesignated 9 July 1952 as the Army Reserve.) Location changed 3 July 1948 to St. Louis, Missouri.

Reorganized and redesignated 1 June 1959 as Headquarters and Headquarters Company, 202d Signal Battalion, an element of the 102d Infantry Division (organic elements concurrently constituted and activated at St. Louis, Missouri). Reorganized and redesignated 1 October 1963 as Headquarters and Headquarters Detachment, 202d Signal Battalion. Inactivated 31 December 1965 at St. Louis, Missouri (organic elements concurrently inactivated).

CAMPAIGN PARTICIPATION CREDIT

World War II
   Rhineland
   Central Europe

DECORATIONS

Meritorious Unit Commendation (Army), Streamer embroidered EUROPEAN THEATER (102d Signal Company cited; GO 82, 102d Infantry Division, 5 June 1945)

202d SIGNAL BATTALION BIBLIOGRAPHY

History 102d Infantry Division USAR. N.p., 1958.

MacDonald, Charles B. *The Last Offensive.* United States Army in World War II. Washington, D.C.: Office of the Chief of Military History, United States Army, 1973. 102d Infantry Division cited.

———. *The Siegfried Line Campaign.* United States Army in World War II. Washington, D.C.: Office of the Chief of Military History, United States Army, 1963. 102d Infantry Division cited.

Mick, Allan H., ed. *With the 102d Infantry Division through Germany.* Vimperk, Czechoslovakia: J. Steinbrener, 1945. Reprint. Nashville, Tenn.: Battery Press, 1980.

———. *With the 102d Infantry Division through Germany.* Washington, D.C.: Infantry Journal Press, 1947.

Pictorial History, 102d Infantry Division. Atlanta: Albert Love Enterprises, 1944.

212th SIGNAL BATTALION

HERALDIC ITEMS

COAT OF ARMS

Shield: Tenné, within a mascle argent a plate charged with a mullet azure voided of the second.

Crest: That for the regiments and separate battalions of the Arkansas Army National Guard: On a wreath of the colors argent and tenné, above two sprays of apple blossoms proper, a diamond argent charged with four mullets azure, one in upper point and three in lower, within a bordure of the last bearing twenty-five mullets of the second.

Motto: COMMUNICATIONS ALWAYS.

Symbolism: Orange and white are the colors traditionally associated with the Signal Corps. The white diamond was suggested by the Arkansas state flag, the four sides alluding to northern, southern, eastern, and western Arkansas. The star refers to Little Rock, the capital of the state and the former headquarters of the battalion. The diamond also simulates a radio antenna and the disc, which represents the diaphragm in telephonic equipment, symbolizes a sounding board for all types of signal apparatus.

DISTINCTIVE UNIT INSIGNIA

The distinctive unit insignia is the shield and motto of the coat of arms.

LINEAGE AND HONORS

ARNG
(Arkansas)

LINEAGE

Constituted 1 January 1954 in the Arkansas Army National Guard as the 212th Signal Battalion. Organized and federally recognized 3 May 1954 in central Arkansas with Headquarters at Little Rock. Ordered into active Federal service 24 September 1957 at home stations; released 23 October 1957 from active Federal service and reverted to state control. Ordered into active Federal service 25 January 1991 at home stations; released 26 March 1991 from active Federal service and reverted to state control.

Home Area: Central Arkansas

CAMPAIGN PARTICIPATION CREDIT

Company A (Hot Springs) entitled to:

World War II-AP
    Aleutian Islands

World War II-EAME
    Rhineland
    Central Europe

Company C (Pine Bluff) entitled to:

World War II-AP
    Aleutian Islands

DECORATIONS

None.

212th SIGNAL BATTALION BIBLIOGRAPHY

Brinkerhoff, John R., Ted Silva, and John A. Seitz. *The Signal Support Dilemma: The 335th Signal Command*. United States Army Reserve in Operation Desert Storm. N.p.: ANDRULIS Research Corp., 1992.

Campbell, Jerry L. "Leveler Training on the Mark." *Army Communicator* 15 (Summer–Fall 1990): 38–39. On fielding of mobile subscriber radio equipment (MSE) at Fort Hood.

Goldstein, Donald, and Katherine V. Dillon. *The Williwaw War: The Arkansas National Guard in the Aleutians in World War II*. Fayetteville: University of Arkansas Press, 1992. 206th Artillery cited; Company A perpetuates Company H of the regiment.

Holland, William F. *History, Arkansas Army and Air National Guard, 1820–1965*. Little Rock: Military Department, State of Arkansas, 1965.

"Riot Reaction Force: The Guard in the April Disorders." *National Guardsman* 22 (May 1968): 2–16. Company C cited.

Walthall, Melvin Curtis. *We Can't All Be Heroes: A History of the Separate Infantry Regiments in World War II*. Hicksville, N.Y.: Exposition Press, 1975. 153d Infantry cited; Company C perpetuates the Antitank Platoon, Headquarters Company, of the regiment.

230th SIGNAL BATTALION

HERALDIC ITEMS

COAT OF ARMS

Shield: Per bend azure and gules, a bendlet wavy argent between four fleurs-de-lis in base and, issuing from chief, a lightning bolt bendwise, all gold.

Crest: That for the regiments and separate battalions of the Tennessee Army National Guard: On a wreath of the colors argent and azure upon a mount vert a hickory tree proper charged with three mullets—one and two—argent.

Motto: WE SOUND THE CALL.

Symbolism: The color yellow refers to the unit's original assignment to the 30th Armored Division. The wavy bendlet denotes overseas duty, and the two divisions of the shield are used to signify World Wars I and II. The four fleurs-de-lis allude to service in Europe where four awards were earned by elements of the organization during those wars. The lightning bolt is symbolic of speed and direct action, signifying efficiency of signal communications.

DISTINCTIVE UNIT INSIGNIA

The distinctive unit insignia is the shield and motto of the coat of arms.

LINEAGE AND HONORS

ARNG
(Tennessee and New York)

LINEAGE

Constituted 24 February 1959 in the Tennessee Army National Guard as the 230th Signal Battalion and assigned to the 30th Armored Division. Organized 1 March 1959 from existing units in western Tennessee with Headquarters at Jackson. Headquarters and Headquarters Company reorganized and redesignated 1 November 1973 as Headquarters and Headquarters Detachment, 230th Signal Battalion, and relieved from assignment to the 30th Armored Division; location concurrently changed to Humboldt (remainder of 230th Signal Battalion—hereafter separate lineages).

Reorganized and redesignated 1 April 1980 in the North Carolina, Tennessee, and Virginia Army National Guard as the 230th Signal Battalion with Headquarters at Humboldt, Tennessee.

Reorganized 16 April 1993 in the North Carolina and Tennessee Army National Guard. Reorganized 1 October 1996 in the Tennessee and New York Army National Guard.

Home Area: Western Tennessee and southeastern New York

CAMPAIGN PARTICIPATION CREDIT

Company B (Yonkers, New York) and Company C (Orangeburg, New York) each entitled to:

Korean War
    First UN Counteroffensive
    CCF Spring Offensive
    UN Summer–Fall Offensive
    Second Korean Winter
    Korea, Summer–Fall 1952
    Third Korean Winter
    Korea, Summer 1953

DECORATIONS

Company B (Yonkers, New York) and Company C (Orangeburg, New York) each entitled to:

    Meritorious Unit Commendation (Army), Streamer embroidered KOREA 1951–1952 (101st Signal Battalion, Corps, cited; DA GO 28, 1953)
    Republic of Korea Presidential Unit Citation, Streamer embroidered KOREA 1952–1953 (101st Signal Battalion, Corps, cited; DA GO 89, 1953)

230th SIGNAL BATTALION BIBLIOGRAPHY

Crocker, Robert W. "Go Between Circuits IV." *Army Communicator* 6 (Summer 1981): 50–53.

Robbins, Rebecca. "Record Traffic From the Past." *Army Communicator* 5 (Summer 1980): 30–31. 101st Signal Battalion cited.

"Signal Company Gets New Name, Commo Duties." *Virginia Guardpost* (Summer 1980): 16. Company D, 230th Signal Battalion, cited.

30th Armored Division, Tennessee National Guard, 1959 Summer Encampment, 28 June–12 July 1959, Fort Stewart, Georgia. N.p., 1959.

Toland, Ray B. "Training to the Army Standard." *Army Communicator* 9 (Winter 1984): 13–14.

234th SIGNAL BATTALION

HERALDIC ITEMS

COAT OF ARMS

Shield: Tenné, a fess wavy azure (celestial) fimbriated argent between in chief a pheon within a crescent and in base a mullet of eight points, all of the last.

Crest: That for the regiments and separate battalions of the Iowa Army National Guard: On a wreath of the colors argent and tenné a hawk's head erased proper.

Motto: A SUPERIOR PERFORMANCE.

Symbolism: The coat of arms is based on the service of the battalion's subordinate elements at the time the battalion was organized in 1959. The crescent and arrowhead allude to the assault landing in Algeria-French Morocco during World War II. The eight-pointed star symbolizes World War II service in Italy, and the blue bend represents World War II service in Central Europe.

DISTINCTIVE UNIT INSIGNIA

The distinctive unit insignia consists of elements of the shield and the motto of the coat of arms.

LINEAGE AND HONORS

ARNG
(Iowa)

LINEAGE

Constituted 22 April 1959 in the Iowa Army National Guard as the 234th Signal Battalion and assigned to the 34th Infantry Division. Organized 1 May 1959 from existing units in central Iowa with Headquarters at Des Moines. Relieved 1 March 1963 from assignment to the 34th Infantry Division. Location of Headquarters changed 1 October 1979 to Cedar Rapids.

Home Area: Eastern Iowa

LINEAGES AND HERALDIC DATA

CAMPAIGN PARTICIPATION CREDIT

Headquarters Company (Cedar Rapids) entitled to:

World War I
    Silver Band without campaign inscription

World War II-EAME
    Tunisia
    Naples-Foggia
    Anzio
    Rome-Arno
    North Apennines
    Po Valley

Company B (Clinton) entitled to:

World War II-EAME
    Naples-Foggia
    Anzio
    Rome-Arno
    North Apennines
    Rhineland
    Ardennes-Alsace
    Central Europe

Company C (Marshalltown) entitled to:

World War II-EAME
    Algeria-French Morocco (with arrowhead)
    Tunisia
    Naples-Foggia
    Anzio
    Rome-Arno
    North Apennines
    Po Valley

DECORATIONS

Headquarters Company (Cedar Rapids) entitled to:

    Presidential Unit Citation (Army), Streamer embroidered NORTHERN ITALY (1st Battalion, 133d Infantry, cited; WD GO 113, 1946)
    French Croix de Guerre with Palm, World War II, Streamer embroidered BELVEDERE (133d Infantry cited; DA GO 43, 1950)

Company C (Marshalltown) entitled to:

    Presidential Unit Citation (Army), Streamer embroidered CERVARO, ITALY (2d Battalion, 168th Infantry, cited; WD GO 6, 1945)
    French Croix de Guerre with Palm, World War II, Streamer embroidered BELVEDERE (168th Infantry cited; DA GO 43, 1950)

234th SIGNAL BATTALION BIBLIOGRAPHY

Blumenson, Martin. *Salerno to Cassino*. United States Army in World War II. Washington, D.C.: Office of the Chief of Military History, Department of the Army, 1969. 133d and 168th Infantry cited.

Conard, Bruce. *History in Brief, Iowa National Guard*. N.p., c. 1975.

Fisher, Ernest F., Jr. *Cassino to the Alps*. United States Army in World War II. Washington, D.C.: Center of Military History, United States Army, 1977. 133d and 168th Infantry cited.

Hedgepeth, Rob. "Five Nations Test Coalition Communications." *Army Communicator* 28 (Spring 2003): 27–28. United States, Great Britain, Canada, Australia, and New Zealand.

History of the 168th Infantry Regiment from January 1, 1944, to January 31, 1944. Italy: Headquarters, 168th Infantry Regiment, 1944.

Hougen, John H. *The Story of the 34th Infantry Division*. San Angelo, Tex.: Newsfoto Publishing Company, 1949. Reprint. Nashville, Tenn.: Battery Press, 1979.

Howe, George F. *Northwest Africa: Seizing the Initiative in the West*. United States Army in World War II. Washington, D.C.: Office of the Chief of Military History, Department of the Army, 1957. 133d and 168th Infantry cited.

Scott, Peter T. *Shoot, Move, and Communicate, Old Artillery Adage. 194th Field Artillery Battalion, U.S. Army*. Munich: F. Bruckmann KG, 1945. Company B at Clinton perpetuates Company A of the 194th.

Starr, Chester G., ed. *From Salerno to the Alps: A History of the Fifth Army, 1943–1945*. Washington, D.C.: Infantry Journal Press, 1948. Reprint. Nashville, Tenn.: Battery Press, 1979. 133d and 168th Infantry cited.

The Story of the 34th Infantry Division. Book I: Louisiana to Pisa. Italy: Information-Education Section, MTOUSA, 1945. *Book II: Pisa to Final Victory*. Milan: Archetipografia de Milano, 1945. (133d and 168th Infantry cited).

240th SIGNAL BATTALION

HERALDIC ITEMS

COAT OF ARMS

Shield: Per chevron reversed gules and or, in chief between three mullets—two and one of the last—that in fess point barbed to chief, a Korean taeguk proper fimbriated and issuant of three lightning flashes to chief gold, and in base a lion passant guardant tenné.

Crest: That for the regiments and separate battalions of the California Army National Guard: On a wreath of the colors or and gules, the setting sun behind a grizzly bear passant on a grassy field, all proper.

Motto: KEYSTONE OF COMMAND.

Symbolism: Orange is a color traditionally associated with the Signal Corps. The lion in base is adapted from the arms of Normandy province in France where elements of the battalion served during World War II. The award of the Philippine Presidential Unit Citation to elements of the battalion is suggested by the scarlet triangular area with the stars denoting three World War II campaigns in the Asiatic-Pacific Theater, and the lower star is barbed to indicate participation in an assault landing on Luzon. Korean War service and three awards of the Korean Presidential Unit Citation are symbolized by the taeguk and three lightning flashes; the lightning flashes further symbolize the signal function of the battalion.

DISTINCTIVE UNIT INSIGNIA

The distinctive unit insignia is the shield and motto of the coat of arms.

LINEAGE AND HONORS

LINEAGE

ARNG
(40th Infantry Division) (California)

Constituted 28 December 1973 in the California Army National Guard as the 240th Signal Battalion and assigned to the 40th Infantry Division. Organized 13 January 1974 from existing units in the Los Angeles area with Headquarters at Long Beach. Location of Headquarters changed 24 September 1974 to Stanton; changed 1 March 1981 to Long Beach; changed 1 September 1997 to Compton.

Home Area: Los Angeles area

CAMPAIGN PARTICIPATION CREDIT

Headquarters Company (Compton) entitled to:

World War II-EAME
Normandy
Northern France
Rhineland
Ardennes-Alsace
Central Europe

Korean War
Second Korean Winter
Korea, Summer–Fall 1952
Third Korean Winter
Korea, Summer 1953

Company A (Long Beach) and Company C (Compton) each entitled to:

World War II-AP
Bismarck Archipelago
Luzon (with arrowhead)
Southern Philippines

Korean War
Second Korean Winter
Korea, Summer–Fall 1952
Third Korean Winter
Korea, Summer 1953

DECORATIONS

Headquarters Company (Compton) entitled to:

Cited in the Order of the Day of the Belgian Army for action along the Meuse River (981st Field Artillery Battalion cited; DA GO 43, 1950)
Republic of Korea Presidential Unit Citation, Streamer embroidered KOREA 1952–1954 (981st Field Artillery Battalion cited; DA GO 50, 1954)

Company A (Long Beach) and Company C (Compton) each entitled to:

Philippine Presidential Unit Citation, Streamer embroidered 17 OCTOBER 1944 TO 4 JULY 1945 (160th Infantry cited; DA GO 47, 1950)
Republic of Korea Presidential Unit Citation, Streamer embroidered KOREA 1952–1953 (160th United States Infantry Regiment cited; DA GO 24, 1954)
Republic of Korea Presidential Unit Citation, Streamer embroidered KOREA 1952–1954 (160th and 223d Infantry cited; DA GO 50, 1954)

240th SIGNAL BATTALION BIBLIOGRAPHY

40th Infantry Division: The Years of World War II, 7 December 1941–7 April 1946. Baton Rouge: Army and Navy Publishing Company, 1947.

Hermes, Walter G. *Truce Tent and Fighting Front.* United States Army in Korea. Washington, D.C.: Office of the Chief of Military History, United States Army, 1966. 160th Infantry cited.

Historical and Pictorial Review, 40th Infantry Division, Army of the United States, Camp San Luis Obispo, California, 1941. Baton Rouge: Army and Navy Publishing Company, 1941.

History of the 40th Infantry Division in the Philippines. 657th Engineer Topographic Battalion, 1945.

McCreedy, William W. *Sunburst Saga, A Story of the 160th Infantry Regiment.* Louisville, Ky.: Bishop's Press, 1947.

160th Infantry, Camp San Luis Obispo, 1941. Baton Rouge: Army and Navy Publishing Company, 1941.

Penney, Robert E. *The 223d Goes to Camp.* Pasadena, Calif.: 1949. Company C perpetuates elements of the 223d Infantry.

Smith, Robert Ross. *Triumph in the Philippines.* United States Army in World War II. Washington, D.C.: Office of the Chief of Military History, Department of the Army, 1963. 160th Infantry cited.

249th SIGNAL BATTALION

HERALDIC ITEMS

COAT OF ARMS

Shield: Argent, a pale tenné charged with a lightning flash of the field on a chief of the second four billets of the first.

Crest: That for the regiments and separate battalions of the Texas Army National Guard: On a wreath of the colors argent and tenné, a mullet argent encircled by a garland of live oak and olive proper conjoined at the stems with a ribbon or.

Motto: GET THE MESSAGE THROUGH.

Symbolism: Orange and white are the colors traditionally associated with the Signal Corps. The lightning flash also denotes the Signal Corps. The billets represent the unit's former home area of Dallas, San Antonio, Austin, and Fort Worth. The pale and chief simulate a capital "T" and allude to the state of Texas and the organization's allocation.

DISTINCTIVE UNIT INSIGNIA

The distinctive unit insignia is the shield and motto of the coat of arms.

LINEAGE AND HONORS

ARNG
(49th Armored Division) (Texas)

LINEAGE

Organized and federally recognized 1 November 1973 from existing units in the Texas Army National Guard as the 249th Signal Battalion, an element of the 49th Armored Division, with Headquarters at Dallas.

Home Area: Northeastern Texas

CAMPAIGN PARTICIPATION CREDIT

Company C (Mexia) entitled to:

World War II-EAME
Naples-Foggia (with arrowhead)
Anzio
Rome-Arno
Southern France (with arrowhead)
Rhineland
Ardennes-Alsace
Central Europe

DECORATIONS

Company C (Mexia) entitled to:

Presidential Unit Citation (Army), Streamer embroidered ALSACE (1st Battalion, 143d Infantry, cited; WD GO 1, 1947)

French Croix de Guerre with Palm, Streamer embroidered VOSGES (143d Infantry cited; WD GO 43, 1950)

249th SIGNAL BATTALION BIBLIOGRAPHY

Alley, Lisa. "249th Signal Battalion Deploys to Support 49th Armored Division." *Army Communicator* 25 (Spring 2000): 9–10.

Blumenson, Martin. *Salerno to Cassino*. United States Army in World War II. Washington, D.C.: Office of the Chief of Military History, Department of the Army, 1969. 143d Infantry cited.

Campbell, Jerry L. "Leveler Training on the Mark." *Army Communicator* 15 (Summer–Fall 1990): 38–39. On fielding of mobile subscriber radio equipment (MSE) at Fort Hood.

Edson, Ron. "Multiple Unit Training Assembly-5." *Army Communicator* 6 (Spring 1981): 49–51. Training exercise with Regular Army training partner 142d Signal Battalion.

Fisher, Ernest F., Jr. *Cassino to the Alps*. United States Army in World War II. Washington, D.C.: Center of Military History, United States Army, 1977. 143d Infantry cited.

Gilmore, John. "The One Army Concept." *Army Communicator* 11 (Summer 1986): 38–39.

Johnson, Danny M. *Military Communications Supporting Peacekeeping Operations in the Balkans: The Signal Corps at Its Best*. Mannheim, Germany: Headquarters, 5th Signal Command, 2000.

250th SIGNAL BATTALION

HERALDIC ITEMS

COAT OF ARMS

Shield: Tenné, a bend wavy between two fleurs-de-lis argent, on a chief sable a lion passant of the second charged with a pheon of the first.

Crest: That for the regiments and separate battalions of the New Jersey Army National Guard: On a wreath of the colors argent and tenné, a lion's head erased or collared four fusils gules.

Motto: SOUND OF MIGHT.

Symbolism: Orange and white are the colors traditionally associated with the Signal Corps. The two fleurs-de-lis allude to the battalion's service in France during World War I. The wavy bend refers to the Rhineland and Central Europe. The lion, taken from the coat of arms of Normandy and charged with an arrowhead, refers to the Normandy invasion, for which an element of the battalion received the French Croix de Guerre.

DISTINCTIVE UNIT INSIGNIA

The distinctive unit insignia is the shield, crest, and motto of the coat of arms.

LINEAGE AND HONORS

ARNG
LINEAGE (42d Infantry Division) (New Jersey)

Organized 21 February 1917 in the New Jersey National Guard at Newark as Headquarters Company, 1st Infantry. Drafted into Federal service 5 August 1917. Reorganized and redesignated 11 October 1917 as Headquarters Company, 113th Infantry, an element of the 29th Division. Demobilized 27 May 1919 at Camp Dix, New Jersey.

Reorganized and federally recognized 30 June 1919 in the New Jersey National Guard at Newark as Headquarters Company, 6th Infantry. Redesignated 17 June 1921 as Headquarters Company, 113th Infantry, a element of the 44th Division. Inducted into Federal service 16 September 1940 at Newark. (113th Infantry relieved 20 February 1942 from assignment to the 44th Division.) Inactivated 25 September 1945 at Camp Rucker, Alabama.

Converted and redesignated 1 August 1946 as the 50th Armored Signal Company and assigned to the 50th Armored Division. Reorganized and federally recognized 10 February 1947 at Newark. Location changed 31 January 1957 to Plainfield.

Reorganized and redesignated 1 March 1959 as Headquarters and Headquarters Company, 250th Signal Battalion, and remained assigned to the 50th Armored Division (organic elements concurrently organized from new and existing units).

Location of Headquarters changed 1 February 1968 to Orange; changed 1 November 1973 to Plainfield. Relieved 1 September 1993 from assignment to the 50th Armored Division and assigned to the 42d Infantry Division. Location of Headquarters changed 1 November 1994 to Westfield.

Home Area: Westfield and vicinity

CAMPAIGN PARTICIPATION CREDIT

World War I
   Meuse-Argonne
   Alsace 1918

Company C (Somerset) additionally entitled to:

World War II-EAME
   Normandy (with arrowhead)
   Northern France
   Rhineland
   Ardennes-Alsace
   Central Europe

DECORATIONS

Company C (Somerset) entitled to:

French Croix de Guerre with Palm, World War II, Streamer embroidered BEACHES OF NORMANDY (102d Cavalry Reconnaissance Squadron cited; DA GO 43, 1950)

250th SIGNAL BATTALION BIBLIOGRAPHY

American Battle Monuments Commission. *29th Division, Summary of Operations in the World War*. Washington, D.C.: Government Printing Office, 1944.

Combat History, 44th Infantry Division, 1944–1945. Atlanta: Albert Love Enterprises, 1946.

Cutchins, John A. and George Scott Stewart, Jr. *History of the Twenty-Ninth Division, "Blue and Gray," 1917–1919*. Philadelphia: McCalla and Company, 1921.

50th Armored Division, New Jersey National Guard, 1954. Red Bank, N.J.: Deerin Publications, 1954.

50th Armored Division, New Jersey National Guard, 1946–1956. New York: Publications Associates, 1956.

Harrison, Gordon A. *Cross-Channel Attack*. United States Army in World War II. Washington, D.C.: Office of the Chief of Military History, United States Army, 1951. 102d Cavalry Squadron cited.

Historical and Pictorial Review, National Guard of the State of New Jersey, 1940. Baton Rouge: Army and Navy Publishing Company, 1940.

Route of March 102 Cavalry Reconnaissance Squadron. Pilsen, Czechoslovakia, 1945.

Source Book, Operations of the 29th Division, East of the Meuse River, October 8th to 30th, 1918. Fort Monroe, Va.: Coast Artillery School, 1922.

Walthall, Melvin Curtis. *We Can't All Be Heroes: A History of the Separate Infantry Regiments in World War II.* Hicksville, N.Y.: Exposition Press, 1975. 113th Infantry cited.

With the European Phase of World War II Now History and the Deeds of the 102d Cavalry Reconnaissance Squadron Mechanized an Integral Part of That History ... Pilsen, Czechoslovakia, 1945.

279th SIGNAL BATTALION

HERALDIC ITEMS

COAT OF ARMS

Shield: Gules, a bend wavy between the chief semé of bird bolts and in base a seal couchant on a rock or.

Crest: That for the regiments and separate battalions of the Alabama Army National Guard: On a wreath of the colors or and gules a slip of cotton plant with full bursting boll proper.

Motto: STRIKE FAST AND SURE.

Symbolism: Scarlet and yellow are the colors traditionally associated with the Artillery. The bird bolts symbolize the former antiaircraft mission of the organization. The wavy diagonal band represents the Tennessee River, which courses through the area of Alabama where the battalion was reorganized. The seal denotes the origin of a portion of the battalion as a coast artillery unit that was activated in Alaska, as well as the battalion's World War II service in the Pacific area.

DISTINCTIVE UNIT INSIGNIA

The distinctive unit insignia is the shield and motto of the coat of arms.

LINEAGE AND HONORS

ARNG
(Alabama)

LINEAGE

Organized and federally recognized 22 August 1926 in the Alabama National Guard from new and existing units in northeastern Alabama as the 127th Engineer Battalion, with Headquarters at Huntsville. Reorganized and redesignated 1 June 1931 as the 127th Engineer Squadron. Redesignated 1 April 1936 as the 127th Squadron, Corps of Engineers. Redesignated 13 July 1936 as the 127th Engineer Squadron. Expanded, reorganized, and redesignated 1 November 1940 as the 151st Engineers. Inducted into Federal service 27 January 1941 at home stations. Redesignated 12 September 1942 as the 151st Engineer Combat Regiment.

Regiment broken up 11 July 1944 and its elements reorganized and redesignated as follows: 1st Battalion as the 151st Engineer Combat Battalion. (Headquarters, Headquarters and Service Company as Headquarters and Headquarters Company, 1169th Engineer Combat Group; 2d Battalion as the 1343d Engineer Combat Battalion—hereafter separate lineages.) 151st Engineer Combat Battalion inactivated 27 December 1945 at Camp Kilmer, New Jersey.

Reorganized and federally recognized 16 January 1947 with Headquarters at Huntsville. Ordered into active Federal service 14 August 1950 at home stations;

released 21 February 1955 from active Federal service and reverted to state control; concurrently consolidated with the 279th Antiaircraft Artillery Battalion (see ANNEX) and consolidated unit designated as the 279th Antiaircraft Artillery Battalion.

Converted and redesignated 2 May 1959 as the 279th Signal Battalion. Ordered into active Federal service 1 October 1961 at home stations; released 10 August 1962 from active Federal service and reverted to state control. Ordered into active Federal service 11 June 1963 at home stations; released 16 June 1963 from active Federal service and reverted to state control. Ordered into active Federal service 10 September 1963 at home stations; released 12 September 1963 from active Federal service and reverted to state control.

ANNEX

Constituted 25 May 1944 in the Army of the United States as the 279th Coast Artillery Battalion. Activated 31 July 1944 at Shemya, Alaska. Inactivated 28 November 1945 at Fort Lawton, Washington. Redesignated 22 January 1951 as the 279th Antiaircraft Artillery Gun Battalion and allotted to the Alabama Army National Guard. Organized and federally recognized 19 February 1951 in northeastern Alabama with Headquarters at Huntsville. Reorganized and redesignated 1 June 1951 as the 279th Antiaircraft Artillery Automatic Weapons Battalion. Redesignated 1 October 1953 as the 279th Antiaircraft Artillery Battalion.

Home Area: Northern Alabama

CAMPAIGN PARTICIPATION CREDIT

World War II
Aleutian Islands
European-African-Middle Eastern Theater, Streamer without inscription

Korean War
First UN Counteroffensive
CCF Spring Offensive
UN Summer–Fall Offensive
Second Korean Winter
Korea, Summer–Fall 1952
Third Korean Winter
Korea, Summer 1953

Company C (Albertville) additionally entitled to:

World War II-AP
New Guinea (with arrowhead)
Western Pacific (with arrowhead)
Southern Philippines

Company D (Jasper) additionally entitled to:

World War II-AP
  India-Burma
  China Defensive
  Central Burma

DECORATIONS

Republic of Korea Presidential Unit Citation, Streamer embroidered KOREA 1951–1952 (151st Engineer Combat Battalion cited; DA GO 33, 1953, as amended by DA GO 38, 1954)

Company C (Albertville) additionally entitled to:

Philippine Presidential Unit Citation, Streamer embroidered 17 OCTOBER 1944 TO 4 JULY 1945 (167th Infantry cited; DA GO 47, 1950)

279th SIGNAL BATTALION BIBLIOGRAPHY

Dod, Karl C. *The Corps of Engineers: The War Against Japan*. United States Army in World War II. Washington, D.C.: Office of the Chief of Military History, United States Army, 1966. 151st Engineer Combat Regiment cited.

Historical Annual, National Guard of the State of Alabama, 1938. Baton Rouge: Army and Navy Publishing Company, 1938.

167th Infantry, Camp Blanding, 1941. Baton Rouge: Army and Navy Publishing Company, 1941.

Smith, Robert Ross. *The Approach to the Philippines*. United States Army in World War II. Washington, D.C.: Office of the Chief of Military History, Department of the Army, 1953. 167th Infantry cited.

―――. *Triumph in the Philippines*. United States Army in World War II. Washington, D.C.: Office of the Chief of Military History, Department of the Army, 1963. 167th Infantry cited.

"Southern Guardsmen Aid After Tornadoes Strike." *National Guardsman* 22 (February 1968): 33–34.

280th SIGNAL BATTALION

HERALDIC ITEMS

COAT OF ARMS

Shield: Argent, three lightning flashes conjoined in base tenné, a chief of the last two laurel branches crossed in saltire of the first.

Crest: That for the regiments and separate battalions of the Delaware Army National Guard: On a wreath of the colors argent and tenné a griffin's head erased azure, eared and beaked or, langued gules, and collared sable fimbriated argent and thereon three plates.

Motto: HONOR DUTY CONSTANCY.

Symbolism: Orange and white are the colors traditionally associated with the Signal Corps. The lightning flashes symbolize speed and communications; joined together they form a strong base and, branching out from this central point, suggest versatility and scope. The laurel branches allude to excellence of achievement and the highest values and efforts of a military unit.

DISTINCTIVE UNIT INSIGNIA

Description: A silver color metal and enamel device that consists of three orange lightning flashes conjoined in base and surmounting a silver wreath of laurel enclosed in base by an orange tripartite scroll with the sections folded over on each other and inscribed HONOR DUTY CONSTANCY in silver letters.

Symbolism: Orange and white (silver) are the colors traditionally associated with the Signal Corps. The lightning flashes symbolize speed and communications; joined together they form a strong base and, branching out from this central point, suggest versatility and scope. The wreath alludes to excellence of achievement and the highest values and efforts of a military unit, principles that are echoed by the unit's motto.

LINEAGE AND HONORS

ARNG
(Delaware and Connecticut)

LINEAGE

Organized and federally recognized 8 July 1936 in the Delaware National Guard at Georgetown as Battery B, 261st Coast Artillery Battalion. Reorganized and redesignated 15 April 1940 as Battery B, 261st Coast Artillery. Inducted into Federal service 27 January 1941 at Georgetown. Reorganized and redesignated 1 October 1944 as Battery D, 21st Coast Artillery Battalion. Inactivated 1 April 1945 at Fort Miles, Delaware.

Redesignated 16 May 1946 as Battery B, 945th Antiaircraft Artillery Automatic Weapons Battalion. Organized and federally recognized 23 April 1947 at Georgetown. Disbanded 16 October 1949 at Georgetown.

Reconstituted and federally recognized 24 October 1949 at Georgetown as Headquarters Battery, 945th Antiaircraft Artillery Automatic Weapons Battalion. Redesignated 1 October 1953 as Headquarters Battery, 945th Antiaircraft Artillery Battalion. Reorganized and redesignated 20 November 1956 as Headquarters Battery, 280th Antiaircraft Artillery Battalion. Reorganized and redesignated 1 April 1959 as Headquarters Battery, 3d Automatic Weapons Battalion, 198th Artillery. Consolidated 1 May 1963 with Headquarters Battery, 5th Automatic Weapons Battalion, 198th Artillery (see ANNEX) and consolidated unit reorganized and redesignated as Headquarters Battery, 3d Automatic Weapons Battalion, 198th Artillery, at Laurel. Reorganized and redesignated 31 January 1968 as Headquarters Battery, 3d Battalion, 198th Artillery.

Converted and redesignated 1 January 1970 as Headquarters and Headquarters Detachment, 198th Transportation Battalion; location concurrently changed to Milford.

Converted and redesignated 1 November 1971 as Headquarters and Headquarters Detachment, 280th Signal Battalion. Location changed 1 June 1974 to Georgetown. Redesignated 1 April 1979 as Headquarters and Headquarters Company, 280th Signal Battalion; organic elements organized 1 April to 1 June 1979 in Delaware, Connecticut, and Rhode Island. Reorganized 1 September 1993 in the Delaware and Connecticut Army National Guard.

ANNEX

Organized and federally recognized 15 September 1953 in the Delaware Army National Guard at Laurel as the 286th Antiaircraft Artillery Operations Detachment (NGUS). Redesignated 1 October 1953 as the 286th Antiaircraft Artillery Detachment (NGUS). Reorganized and redesignated 18 March 1955 as the 286th Antiaircraft Artillery Detachment. Reorganized and redesignated 20 November 1956 as Headquarters Battery, 945th Antiaircraft Artillery Battalion. Reorganized and redesignated 1 April 1959 as Headquarters Battery, 5th Gun Battalion, 198th Artillery. Reorganized and redesignated 1 April 1962 as Headquarters Battery, 5th Automatic Weapons Battalion, 198th Artillery.

Home Area: Delaware and Connecticut

CAMPAIGN PARTICIPATION CREDIT

Company A (Seaford, Delaware) entitled to:

World War I
    Meuse-Argonne

DECORATIONS

None.

280th SIGNAL BATTALION BIBLIOGRAPHY

Carroll, Bill. "Testing Rapid Deployment." *Army Communicator* 8 (Summer 1983): 35–38.

Conner, William H., and Leon de Valinger, Jr. *Delaware's Role in World War II, 1940–1946.* Dover: State of Delaware, Public Archives Commission, 1955.

History of the 59th Pioneer Infantry, 1918–1919, American Expeditionary Forces. Toul, France: Imprimerie Lemaire, 1919. Company A perpetuates Company I, 59th Pioneer Infantry.

Johnson, John. "280th Signal Battalion Brings Commo to 10,000-Soldier Reserve Exercise." *Army Communicator* 24 (Winter II 1999): 35–37.

Orme, Nate. "280th Signal Battalion Provides Commo at Exercise." *Army Communicator* 27 (Fall 2002): 30–31. Companies A and B provide support to Petroleum, Oil, and Lubricants Exercise (POLEX) and Grecian Firebolt.

"REFORGER: Holding Freedom's Line." *National Guard* 38 (December 1984): 12–16.

"Training Can Be 'Different!'" *National Guardsman* 26 (December 1972): 8–14.

Vance, Derick. "Company C Signaleers Make the Connection." *Army Communicator* 27 (Fall 2002): 28–29. Support to POLEX and Grecian Firebolt.

Worrall, George. "Army Reserve, Air National Guard Pass Joint Signals." *Army Communicator* 27 (Winter 2002):66–67. Discusses the 280th's participation in Grecian Firebolt '02 exercise, but incorrectly refers to it as an Army Reserve unit.

HEADQUARTERS AND HEADQUARTERS DETACHMENT
302d SIGNAL BATTALION

HERALDIC ITEMS

COAT OF ARMS

Shield: Tenné, a chevron abased argent semé-de-lis azure overall a telephone pole radiant with four lightning flashes of the second.

Crest: On a wreath of the colors argent and tenné a disc of the last fimbriated and with a bend wavy of the first between two fleurs-de-lis in fess or charged with a bear's head couped and langued proper. Overall two lightning flashes chevronwise reversed from base or.

Motto: VIRTUTE ET LABORE (By Courage and Work).

Symbolism: Orange and white are the colors traditionally associated with the Signal Corps. The unit's World War II European campaign honors are symbolized by the fleurs-de-lis. The unit's historic affiliation with a telephone company and its former signal construction mission are depicted by the telephone pole, which also represents the organization's former headquarters in Maryland, a state noted as the home of the first telegraph line.

Orange and white are the colors traditionally associated with the Signal Corps. The bear's head and two fleurs-de-lis refer to World War II campaigns in Central Europe, Northern France, and Normandy. The wavy bend refers to the Rhineland and is taken from heraldic symbolism used in the region. The lightning flashes represent the signal mission and communication expertise. Gold denotes excellence; white signifies high ideals.

DISTINCTIVE UNIT INSIGNIA

The distinctive unit insignia is the shield and motto of the coat of arms.

LINEAGE AND HONORS

RA
(inactive)

LINEAGE

Constituted 29 July 1921 in the Organized Reserves as the 302d Signal Battalion. Organized in January 1922 at New York, New York. Redesignated 8 December

1942 as the 302d Signal Operation Battalion. Ordered into active military service 23 February 1943 at Camp Swift, Texas. Inactivated 1 June 1946 in Germany.

Redesignated 8 January 1947 as the 302d Signal Heavy Construction Battalion. Activated 17 January 1947 at Louisville, Kentucky. (Organized Reserves redesignated 25 March 1948 as the Organized Reserve Corps; redesignated 9 July 1952 as the Army Reserve.) Location changed 31 December 1948 to Philadelphia, Pennsylvania. Inactivated 5 September 1950 at Philadelphia, Pennsylvania.

Redesignated 16 April 1951 as the 302d Signal Aviation Construction Battalion. Activated 18 April 1951 at Frederick, Maryland. Reorganized and redesignated 10 April 1952 as the 302d Signal Construction Battalion. Reorganized and redesignated 28 October 1953 as the 302d Signal Battalion.

Battalion broken up 25 May 1959 and its elements reorganized, redesignated, or disbanded as follows: Headquarters and Headquarters Detachment reorganized; Companies A and B reorganized and redesignated as the 558th and 559th Signal Companies, respectively—hereafter separate lineages; Companies C and D disbanded.

Headquarters and Headquarters Detachment, 302d Signal Battalion, inactivated 20 February 1963 at Frederick, Maryland. Withdrawn 15 June 1969 from the Army Reserve and allotted to the Regular Army. Activated 14 July 1969 in Thailand. Inactivated 30 June 1971 in Thailand.

Activated 23 August 1991 in Germany. Inactivated 15 September 1994 in Germany.

CAMPAIGN PARTICIPATION CREDIT

World War II
Normandy
Northern France
Rhineland
Central Europe

DECORATIONS

None.

302d SIGNAL BATTALION BIBLIOGRAPHY

A History of the 302d Signal Operation Battalion. Heidelberg, Germany, 1945.

304th SIGNAL BATTALION

HERALDIC ITEMS

COAT OF ARMS

Shield: Per fess engrailed arched and enhanced gray and sable, a foot engrailed azure fimbriated argent, overall issuing from dexter chief a lightning flash tenné fimbriated of the fourth.

Crest: On a wreath of the colors argent and sable a sea lion sejant sable armed and langued azure grasping a trumpet of the first, pendant therefrom and tied of the last a banderole emblazoned parti per bend wavy of two gules and azure bearing in pale two mullets silver within a border of the last.

Motto: PRET TOUJOURS PRET (Ready Always Ready).

Symbolism: The lightning flash in the colors of the Signal Corps symbolizes the rapid communication provided by the battalion. The blue foot with white fimbriation represents ocean waves, exemplifying the many amphibious operations made by the Eighth Army during World War II and supported by this organization. The engrailed line across the shield represents the typical shoreline of the islands assaulted. The gray upper portion of the shield is symbolic of the early morning sky during an amphibious attack.

The design commemorates the actions for which the battalion received unit decorations during World War II and the Korean War. The sea lion is from the flag of the president of the Philippines and refers to the unit's service in the Leyte campaign. The trumpet or bugle symbolizes Army communication, which is the battalion's function. The two stars on the red and blue tabard represent the actions in Korea for which the battalion received two Meritorious Unit Commendations.

DISTINCTIVE UNIT INSIGNIA

The distinctive unit insignia is the shield and motto of the coat of arms.

LINEAGE AND HONORS

RA
(active)

LINEAGE

Constituted 29 July 1921 in the Organized Reserves as the 304th Signal Battalion. Organized in March 1922 at Atlanta, Georgia. Redesignated 8 December 1942 as the 304th Signal Operation Battalion. Ordered into active military service 1 June 1943 at Camp Swift, Texas. (Organized Reserves redesignated 25 March 1948 as the Organized Reserve Corps; redesignated 9 July 1952 as the Army Reserve.) Reorganized and redesignated 25 January 1953 as the 304th Signal Battalion. Withdrawn 15 June 1953 from the Army Reserve and allotted to the Regular Army.

CAMPAIGN PARTICIPATION CREDIT

World War II
   New Guinea
   Leyte

Korean War
   UN Defensive
   UN Offensive
   CCF Intervention
   First UN Counteroffensive
   CCF Spring Offensive
   UN Summer–Fall Offensive
   Second Korean Winter
   Korea, Summer–Fall 1952
   Third Korean Winter
   Korea, Summer 1953

DECORATIONS

Meritorious Unit Commendation (Army), Streamer embroidered ASIATIC-PACIFIC THEATER (304th Signal Operations Battalion cited; GO 38, Eighth Army, 19 April 1946)

Meritorious Unit Commendation (Army), Streamer embroidered KOREA 1950–1951 (304th Signal Operation Battalion; DA GO 72, 1951)

Meritorious Unit Commendation (Army), Streamer embroidered KOREA 1952–1953 (304th Signal Battalion [Operation] cited; DA GO 68, 1953)

Philippine Presidential Unit Citation, Streamer embroidered 17 OCTOBER 1944 TO 4 JULY 1945 (304th Signal Operations Battalion cited; DA GO 47, 1950)

304th SIGNAL BATTALION BIBLIOGRAPHY

Austin, Robert L., Jr. "Signal Keeps It Secret." *KORUS* 20 (October 1992): 16.

Fuller, Tom. "Communications on Keumdansan." *Army Communicator* 10 (Summer 1985): 30–31. Troposphere Platoon, Company C, cited.

Raines, Rebecca Robbins. *Getting the Message Through: A Branch History of the U.S. Army Signal Corps*. Army Historical Series. Washington, D.C.: Center of Military History, United States Army, 1996.

Rolak, Bruno J. *History of the U.S. Army Communications Command (1964–1976)*. Fort Huachuca, Ariz.: United States Army Communications Command, 1976.

Westover, John G. *Combat Support in Korea*. Washington, D.C.: Combat Forces Press, 1955.

306TH SIGNAL BATTALION

HERALDIC ITEMS

COAT OF ARMS

Shield: Gules, a dragonfly volant in chief bendwise sable fimbriated or, overall a spider web throughout of the last.
Crest: That for the regiments and separate battalions of the Army Reserve: On a wreath of the colors or and gules the Lexington Minuteman proper. The statue of the Minuteman Capt. John Parker (H. H. Kitson, sculptor) stands on the Common in Lexington, Massachusetts.
Motto: DOMINUS RETAE (Master of the Snare).
Symbolism: The spider web is distinctive of a barrage balloon battalion. The scarlet of the shield is for the Coast Artillery Corps. The dragonfly represents the enemy aircraft. The spider web indicates the web of cable that not only blocks out but also enmeshes and destroys enemy aircraft.

DISTINCTIVE UNIT INSIGNIA

The distinctive unit insignia is the shield and motto of the coat of arms.

LINEAGE AND HONORS

AR
(inactive)

LINEAGE

Constituted 26 August 1942 in the Army of the United States as the 316th Coast Artillery Barrage Balloon Battalion. Activated 5 December 1942 at Camp Tyson, Tennessee. Reorganized and redesignated 15 July 1943 as the 316th Antiaircraft Balloon Battalion, Very Low Altitude. Converted and redesignated 7 April 1944 as the 49th Signal Light Construction Battalion. Reorganized and redesignated 1 September 1944 as the 49th Signal Heavy Construction Battalion. Inactivated 15 January 1946 on Guam.

Redesignated 12 February 1947 as the 306th Signal Heavy Construction Battalion and allotted to the Organized Reserves. Activated 26 February 1947 with Headquarters at Springfield, Illinois. (Organized Reserves redesignated 25 March 1948 as the Organized Reserve Corps; redesignated 9 July 1952 as the Army Reserve.) Inactivated 15 November 1950 at Springfield, Illinois. Redesignated 18 August 1959 as the 306th Signal Battalion. Activated 1 October 1959 with Headquarters at Oak Park, Illinois. Inactivated 4 March 1963 at Oak Park, Illinois.

CAMPAIGN PARTICIPATION CREDIT

World War II
    Air Offensive, Japan

Company A additionally entitled to:

World War II-AP
    Western Pacific

DECORATIONS

Company A entitled to:

Meritorious Unit Commendation (Army), Streamer embroidered GUAM (Company A, 49th Signal Heavy Construction Battalion, cited; GO 144, Western Pacific Base Command, 23 November 1945)

306th SIGNAL BATTALION BIBLIOGRAPHY

No published histories.

307th SIGNAL BATTALION

HERALDIC ITEMS

COAT OF ARMS

Shield: Per fess enhanced rayonné argent and tenné, in chief a grape leaf vert between two lightning flashes gules and in base an oriental dragon of the first.

Crest: On a wreath of the colors argent and tenné a castle wall of the first bearing an escutcheon gules charged with a lightning bolt argent and issuing three demispears with bamboo shafts pilewise proper ferrules azure garnished of the third.

Motto: OPTIME MERENTI (To the Best Deserving).

Symbolism: Orange and white are the colors traditionally associated with the Signal Corps. The grape leaf refers to service in the Rhineland during World War II, and the oriental dragon refers to service in Vietnam. The rayonné line simulates an active electrical field; with lightning flashes it symbolizes the speed of communications. The flashes are pictured in red to represent the unit's Meritorious Unit Commendation.

The castle wall symbolizes strength and defense; its two towers represent the unit's World War II service in the American Theater and the Rhineland. The red escutcheon commemorates a Meritorious Unit Commendation. The lightning bolt highlights speed and electronic warfare. The bamboo spear shafts allude to Vietnam and the unit's three campaigns there. The spearheads are red, white, and blue, reflecting our national colors.

DISTINCTIVE UNIT INSIGNIA

The distinctive unit insignia is the shield and motto of the coat of arms.

LINEAGE AND HONORS

RA
(active)

LINEAGE

Constituted 27 May 1942 in the Army of the United States as the 313th Coast Artillery Barrage Balloon Battalion. Activated 15 June 1942 in the Canal Zone. Reorganized and redesignated 27 January 1944 as the 313th Antiaircraft Balloon Battalion, Low Altitude. Converted and redesignated 10 April 1944 as the 48th Signal Light Construction Battalion. Reorganized and redesignated 26 June 1944 as the 48th Signal Heavy Construction Battalion. Inactivated 29 November 1945 at Fort Monmouth, New Jersey.

Redesignated 26 February 1947 as the 307th Signal Heavy Construction Battalion and allotted to the Organized Reserves. Activated 11 March 1947 with Headquarters at Cincinnati, Ohio (organic elements activated 24 April 1947). (Organized Reserves redesignated 25 March 1948 as the Organized Reserve Corps; redesignated 9 July 1952 as the Army Reserve.) Reorganized and redesignated 1 March 1950 as the 307th Signal Construction Battalion. Location of Headquarters changed 5 February 1951 to Fort Thomas, Kentucky. Reorganized and redesignated 28 October 1953 as the 307th Signal Battalion. Location of Headquarters changed 1 July 1957 to Cincinnati, Ohio. (Companies A-D disbanded 24 April 1959 at Cincinnati, Ohio; Hamilton, Ohio; Marion, Ohio; and Springfield, Ohio, respectively.) Headquarters and Headquarters Detachment, 307th Signal Battalion, inactivated 15 January 1963 at Cincinnati, Ohio.

Withdrawn 1 March 1970 from the Army Reserve, allotted to the Regular Army, and activated in Vietnam. Inactivated 30 April 1971 in Vietnam. Reorganized and redesignated 31 July 1971 as Headquarters and Headquarters Company, 307th Signal Battalion, and activated in Korea (organic elements concurrently reconstituted in the Regular Army and activated in Korea). Battalion inactivated 1 October 1977 in Korea. (Company A activated 16 May 1987 in Korea.) Activated (less Company A) 16 March 1988 in Korea.

CAMPAIGN PARTICIPATION CREDIT

World War II
  American Theater, Streamer without inscription
  Rhineland

Vietnam
  Winter–Spring 1970
  Sanctuary Counteroffensive
  Counteroffensive, Phase VII

DECORATIONS

Meritorious Unit Commendation (Army), Streamer embroidered EUROPEAN THEATER (48th Signal Heavy Construction Battalion cited; GO 142, Communications Zone, U.S. Forces, European Theater, 22 July 1945)

307th SIGNAL BATTALION BIBLIOGRAPHY

No published histories.

318th SIGNAL BATTALION

HERALDIC ITEMS

COAT OF ARMS

Shield: Or, on a bend tenné a lightning flash of the first and in chief a bell azure.

Crest: That for the regiments and separate battalions of the Army Reserve: On a wreath of the colors or and tenné the Lexington Minuteman proper. The statue of the Minuteman Capt. John Parker (H. H. Kitson, sculptor) stands on the Common in Lexington, Massachusetts.

Motto: WE ARE THERE.

Symbolism: The design is arbitrary in nature and symbolic of the functions of a Signal Corps organization.

DISTINCTIVE UNIT INSIGNIA

The distinctive unit insignia is the shield of the coat of arms.

LINEAGE AND HONORS

AR
(inactive)

LINEAGE

Constituted 3 November 1941 in the Army of the United States as the 94th Signal Battalion. Activated 15 May 1942 at Camp Crowder, Missouri. Inactivated 4 December 1945 at Camp Myles Standish, Massachusetts.

Redesignated 3 November 1948 as the 318th Signal Battalion and allotted to the Organized Reserve Corps. Activated 22 November 1948 with Headquarters at Fairfield, Connecticut. Location of Headquarters changed 26 April 1950 to Bridgeport, Connecticut. Reorganized and redesignated 6 July 1950 as the 318th Signal Battalion, Corps. (Organized Reserve Corps redesignated 9 July 1952 as the Army Reserve.) Reorganized and redesignated 29 December 1953 as the 318th Signal Battalion. Location of Headquarters changed 11 March 1957 to Fairfield, Connecticut. Inactivated 31 January 1968 at Fairfield, Connecticut.

CAMPAIGN PARTICIPATION CREDIT

World War II
    Rhineland
    Ardennes-Alsace
    Central Europe

DECORATIONS

Presidential Unit Citation (Army), Streamer embroidered RHINE RIVER (94th Signal Battalion cited; WD GO 76, 1945)

318th SIGNAL BATTALION BIBLIOGRAPHY

No published histories.

319th SIGNAL BATTALION

HERALDIC ITEMS

COAT OF ARMS

Shield: Tenné, in pale two smoke puffs argent charged with an eagle displayed and a horse rampant sable above a bonfire issuant from base of the second.

Crest: That for the regiments and separate battalions of the Army Reserve: On a wreath of the colors argent and tenné the Lexington Minuteman proper. The statue of the Minuteman Capt. John Parker (H. H. Kitson, sculptor) stands on the Common in Lexington, Massachusetts.

Motto: TOGETHER WE WILL.

Symbolism: Orange and white are the colors traditionally associated with the Signal Corps. The smoke puffs above the flames symbolize the American Indian method of signal communication. The horse from the arms of the province of Naples and the eagle from that of Rome indicate the two battle honors awarded for service in those areas.

DISTINCTIVE UNIT INSIGNIA

The distinctive unit insignia is the shield and motto of the coat of arms.

LINEAGE AND HONORS

AR
(active)

LINEAGE

Constituted 25 June 1943 in the Army of the United States as the 984th Signal Service Company and activated at Fort Dix, New Jersey. Inactivated 29 May 1946 in Italy. Allotted 30 June 1947 to the Organized Reserves. Activated 11 July 1947 at Tulsa, Oklahoma. (Organized Reserves redesignated 25 March 1948 as the Organized Reserve Corps; redesignated 9 July 1952 as the Army Reserve.) Reorganized and redesignated 17 December 1948 as Company A, 319th Signal Battalion (remainder of battalion not organized). Inactivated 16 November 1950 at Tulsa, Oklahoma.

Redesignated 17 July 1956 as Headquarters and Headquarters Company, 319th Signal Battalion. Activated 1 August 1956 at Tulsa, Oklahoma. Inactivated 1 April 1959 at Tulsa, Oklahoma. Activated 17 September 1988 at Stockton, California (organic elements concurrently constituted and activated). Location of Headquarters changed 15 September 1994 to Sacramento, California; changed 10 March 1998 to Rancho Cordova, California; changed 15 January 2000 to Sacramento, California.

CAMPAIGN PARTICIPATION CREDIT

World War II
   Naples-Foggia
   Rome-Arno

DECORATIONS

None.

319th SIGNAL BATTALION BIBLIOGRAPHY

Conder, Terry L. "Total Army Force Works Together." *Army Communicator* 14 (Winter 1989): 50–51. Companies A and B participated in Natural Team IV, an exercise hosted by the Nevada Army National Guard.

Frailey, Fred. "Reserve Battalion Holds Joint Training Operations with Navy Detachment." *Army Communicator* 23 (Summer 1998): 55.

Ward, Jim. "319th Signal Battalion: A Force Multiplier." *Army Communicator* 22 (Fall 1997): 20–21

———."319th Signal Battalion Leads Way in Communications During Wild Boar '97." *Army Communicator* 22 (Fall 1997): 18–19.

HEADQUARTERS AND HEADQUARTERS COMPANY 324th SIGNAL BATTALION

HERALDIC ITEMS

COAT OF ARMS

Shield: Argent, two lightning bolts saltirewise tenné between four radiating pheons sable, overall a hurt gridlined of the first. On a chief wavy of the second a fleur-de-lis argent.

Crest: That for the regiments and separate battalions of the Army Reserve: On a wreath of the colors argent and tenné the Lexington Minuteman proper. The statue of the Minuteman Capt. John Parker (H. H. Kitson, sculptor) stands on the Common in Lexington, Massachusetts.

Motto: READY ANYWHERE ANYTIME.

Symbolism: Orange and white are the colors traditionally associated with the Signal Corps. The lightning bolts emitting from the globe represent the battalion's quickness to respond anytime and the worldwide scope of its mission. Blue stands for honor and loyalty. The fleur-de-lis and wavy division refer to the location of the unit's World War II campaigns in Normandy, Northern France, Rhineland, and Central Europe. The spearheads, pointing to the four major geographical directions, symbolize readiness for military action anywhere and also reflect the total number of the battalion's campaign participation credits.

DISTINCTIVE UNIT INSIGNIA

The distinctive unit insignia is the shield and motto of the coat of arms.

LINEAGE AND HONORS

AR
(active)

LINEAGE

Constituted 27 December 1943 in the Army of the United States as the 3111th Signal Service Battalion. Activated 20 January 1944 at Fort Monmouth, New Jersey. Inactivated 28 December 1945 at Camp Shanks, New York.

Redesignated 6 June 1950 as Headquarters, 324th Signal Service Battalion, and allotted to the Organized Reserve Corps. Activated 1 September 1950 at Newark, New Jersey. (Organized Reserve Corps redesignated 9 July 1952 as the Army Reserve.) Reorganized and redesignated 9 February 1953 as Headquarters, 324th Signal Battalion. Reorganized and redesignated 31 March 1955 as Headquarters and

Headquarters Detachment, 324th Signal Battalion. Location changed 9 November 1955 to Kearny, New Jersey; changed 28 October 1957 to Jersey City, New Jersey. Inactivated 1 June 1959 at Jersey City, New Jersey.

Redesignated 16 October 1984 as Headquarters and Headquarters Company, 324th Signal Battalion, and activated at Fort Gordon, Georgia. (328th [see ANNEX 1] and 543d [see ANNEX 2] Signal Companies reorganized and redesignated 16 September 1987 as Companies A and B, 324th Signal Battalion, respectively: Company C, 324th Signal Battalion, constituted 29 July 1987 in the Army Reserve and activated 16 April 1988 at Athens, Georgia.)

ANNEX 1

Constituted 1 March 1944 in the Army of the United States as the 3128th Signal Port Service Company. Activated 15 March 1944 at Camp Crowder, Missouri. Reorganized and redesignated 3 July 1944 as the 3128th Signal Service Company. Inactivated 20 December 1945 in Germany. Redesignated 1 February 1956 as the 328th Signal Company and allotted to the Army Reserve. Activated 13 February 1956 at Greenwood, South Carolina. Inactivated 31 December 1957 at Greenwood, South Carolina. Activated 15 March 1972 at Clemson, South Carolina.

ANNEX 2

Constituted 24 May 1944 in the Army of the United States as the 543d Signal Base Depot Company. Activated 15 June 1944 at Fort Monmouth, New Jersey. Inactivated 20 June 1948 in Germany. Redesignated 27 May 1959 as the 543d Signal Company and allotted to the Army Reserve. Activated 15 June 1959 at Huntsville, Alabama.

CAMPAIGN PARTICIPATION CREDIT

World War II
  Normandy
  Northern France
  Rhineland
  Central Europe

DECORATIONS

None.

324th SIGNAL BATTALION BIBLIOGRAPHY

Thompson, George Raynor, and Dixie R. Harris. *The Signal Corps: The Outcome (Mid-1943 through 1945)*. United States Army in World War II. Washington, D.C.: Office of the Chief of Military History, United States Army, 1966.

HEADQUARTERS AND HEADQUARTERS DETACHMENT
325th SIGNAL BATTALION

HERALDIC ITEMS

COAT OF ARMS

None approved.

DISTINCTIVE UNIT INSIGNIA

Description: A silver color metal and enamel device that consists of a diamond of four diamonds with the top and bottom ones white and the lateral ones orange surmounted by a cross formed of two lightning flashes. The horizontal white and the vertical orange, all on a silver cable, form a loop with a square knot splice of three wrappings with the diamond overlapping the lower part of the splice at the top and extending beyond the edges of the cable at the sides and resting on the inner rim above the inscription ONE STEP AHEAD on the encircling loop in black.

Symbolism: Orange and white (silver) are the colors traditionally associated with the Signal Corps. The splice represents continuity and symbolizes the direction and coordination of the battalion. The two lightning flashes refer to the command control of two to seven signal companies. The diamonds, arranged to support one another, emulate the action of logistical, personnel, and area installation aspects of the unit's mission. The rounded portion of the cable simulates a wheel and denotes the organization's high percentage of mobility.

LINEAGE AND HONORS

RA
(inactive)

LINEAGE

Constituted 7 July 1944 in the Army of the United States as Headquarters and Headquarters Detachment, 3216th Signal Service Battalion. Activated 23 August 1944 in Algeria. Inactivated 26 September 1945 in Italy.

Redesignated 29 June 1950 as Headquarters, 325th Signal Service Battalion, and allotted to the Organized Reserve Corps. Activated 25 July 1950 at Providence, Rhode Island. (Organized Reserve Corps redesignated 9 July 1952 as the Army Reserve.) Reorganized and redesignated 1 January 1953 as Headquarters, 325th Signal Battalion. Reorganized and redesignated 1 April 1955 as Headquarters and Headquarters Detachment, 325th Signal Battalion. Location changed 1

April 1960 to Warwick, Rhode Island. Inactivated 1 February 1963 at Warwick, Rhode Island.

Withdrawn 30 March 1967 from the Army Reserve and allotted to the Regular Army. Activated 2 June 1967 at Fort George G. Meade, Maryland. Inactivated 31 July 1968 at Fort George G. Meade, Maryland. Activated 14 July 1969 in Thailand. Inactivated 31 December 1970 in Thailand.

CAMPAIGN PARTICIPATION CREDIT

World War II
  European-African-Middle Eastern Theater, Streamer without inscription

DECORATIONS

None.

325th SIGNAL BATTALION BIBLIOGRAPHY

No published histories.

327th SIGNAL BATTALION

HERALDIC ITEMS

COAT OF ARMS

Shield: Sable, in base an annulet argent, overall a pile of the like bearing a hawk in stoop of the first between two lightning flashes pilewise tenné.

Crest: On a wreath of the colors argent and sable a sun in splendor surmounted by two swords saltirewise and a scimitar palewise points down proper tied by a cord gules.

Motto: SPEED AND ACCURACY.

Symbolism: Orange and white are the colors traditionally associated with the Signal Corps. Black refers to the unit's mascot and logo, the "Nighthawk." The lightning flashes symbolize tactical communication and speed. The flashes and annulet simulate an arrow hitting a bull's-eye, underscoring the unit's motto SPEED AND ACCURACY. The hawk represents the spirit, pride, and strength of the warrior. This bird of prey dives and strikes at incredible speeds.

The three blades represent war service in World War II, Vietnam, and Southwest Asia. The scimitar highlights the unit's service in Southwest Asia, and the sun alludes to the desert heat of Saudi Arabia as well as the tropical nature of Vietnam. The red cord suggests the battalion's commendations and denotes valor and sacrifice while underscoring unity and cooperation.

DISTINCTIVE UNIT INSIGNIA

Description: A silver color metal and enamel device that consists of the shield and motto of the coat of arms. Attached around the base of the shield a black tripartite scroll inscribed SPEED AND ACCURACY in silver letters.

Symbolism: The arched top of the device alludes to a military parachute and recalls the unit's airborne capability.

LINEAGE AND HONORS

RA
(active)

LINEAGE

Constituted 26 May 1952 in the Organized Reserve Corps as Headquarters and Headquarters Company, 327th Signal Support Battalion. Activated 30 June 1952 at Tampa, Florida. (Organized Reserve Corps redesignated 9 July 1952 as the

Army Reserve.) Reorganized and redesignated 15 September 1953 as Headquarters and Headquarters Detachment, 327th Signal Battalion. Inactivated 7 July 1959 at Tampa, Florida.

Withdrawn 18 April 1967 from the Army Reserve and allotted to the Regular Army. Activated 1 August 1967 at Fort Bragg, North Carolina. Reorganized and redesignated 16 September 1980 as Headquarters and Headquarters Company, 327th Signal Battalion; concurrently, the 416th Signal Company (see ANNEX 1) and the 221st Signal Company (see ANNEX 2) reorganized and redesignated, as Company A and Company B, 327th Signal Battalion, respectively.

ANNEX 1

Constituted 29 August 1940 in the Regular Army as the 316th Signal Aviation Company. Activated 20 September 1940 at Mitchel Field, New York. Redesignated 5 March 1941 as the 316th Signal Company, Air Wing. Redesignated 24 October 1941 as the 416th Signal Company, Aviation. Inactivated 16 October 1945 in Italy. Redesignated 15 December 1954 as the 416th Signal Aviation Company. Activated 7 February 1955 at Fort Huachuca, Arizona.

Reorganized and redesignated 26 May 1961 as the 416th Signal Company. Inactivated 2 February 1963 at Fort Huachuca, Arizona. Activated 18 August 1965 at Fort Lee, Virginia.

ANNEX 2

Constituted 3 November 1941 in the Regular Army as the 221st Signal Depot Company. Activated 14 August 1943 at Fort Monmouth, New Jersey. Inactivated 20 June 1948 in Germany. Redesignated 8 January 1952 as the 221st Signal Base Depot Company. Activated 22 January 1952 at Atlanta, Georgia. Reorganized and redesignated 4 October 1954 as the 221st Signal Company.

Inactivated 1 September 1965 at Sacramento, California. Activated 1 June 1966 at Fort Monmouth, New Jersey. Inactivated 1 July 1974 at Schofield Barracks, Hawaii. Activated 16 September 1979 at Fort Bragg, North Carolina.

CAMPAIGN PARTICIPATION CREDIT

Southwest Asia
  Defense of Saudi Arabia
  Liberation and Defense of Kuwait

Company A additionally entitled to:

World War II-EAME
  Antisubmarine
  Tunisia
  Naples-Foggia
  Rome-Arno

LINEAGES AND HERALDIC DATA

Company B additionally entitled to:

World War II-EAME
  Normandy
  Northern France
  Rhineland

Vietnam
  Counteroffensive, Phase III
  Tet Counteroffensive
  Counteroffensive, Phase IV
  Counteroffensive, Phase V
  Counteroffensive, Phase VI
  Tet 69/Counteroffensive
  Summer–Fall 1969
  Winter–Spring 1970
  Sanctuary Counteroffensive
  Counteroffensive, Phase VII
  Consolidation I
  Consolidation II

DECORATIONS

Meritorious Unit Commendation (Army), Streamer embroidered SOUTHWEST ASIA 1990–1991 (327th Signal Battalion cited; Memorandum, TAPC-PDA, subject: Meritorious Unit Commendation, 20 April 1995)

Company A additionally entitled to:

Meritorious Unit Commendation (Army), Streamer embroidered EUROPEAN THEATER (416th Signal Company, Aviation, cited; GO 631, Fifteenth Air Force, 12 February 1945)

Company B additionally entitled to:

Meritorious Unit Commendation (Army), Streamer embroidered VIETNAM 1969–1970 (221st Signal Company cited; DA GO 48, 1971)

327th SIGNAL BATTALION BIBLIOGRAPHY

"Airborne Signal Battalion Reorganizes for Contingencies." *Army Communicator* 21 (Winter 1996): 42.

"Calling All Units." *Army Communicator* 10 (Summer 1985): 43.

Guidotti, John A. "The 35th Signal's New Go-to-War Concept." *Army Communicator* 16 (Fall–Winter 1991): 20–23.

Kennedy, Randy. "35th Signal Brigade." *Army Communicator* 12 (Fall 1987): 30–33.

Raines, Rebecca Robbins. *Getting the Message Through: A Branch History of the U.S. Army Signal Corps*. Army Historical Series. Washington, D.C.: Center of Military History, United States Army, 1996. 221st Signal Company cited.

Rienzi, Thomas M. *Communications-Electronics, 1962–1970*. Vietnam Studies. Washington, D.C.: Department of the Army, 1972. 221st Signal Company cited.

Stokes, Carol E., ed. *The U.S. Army Signal Corps in Operation Desert Shield/Desert Storm*. Fort Gordon, Ga.: Office of the Command Historian, U.S. Army Signal Center and Fort Gordon, 1994.

Stokes, Carol E. and Kathy R. Coker. "Getting the Message Through in the Persian Gulf War." *Army Communicator* 17 (Summer–Winter 1992): 17–25.

Thompson, George Raynor, and Dixie R. Harris. *The Signal Corps: The Outcome (Mid-1943 through 1945)*. United States Army in World War II. Washington, D.C.: Office of the Chief of Military History, United States Army, 1966. 221st Signal Depot Company cited.

Thompson, L. Carrington. "The Cable Dogs of the 327th." *Army Communicator* 9 (Fall 1984): 26–29. Company B cited.

HEADQUARTERS AND HEADQUARTERS DETACHMENT
352d SIGNAL BATTALION

HERALDIC ITEMS

None approved.

LINEAGE AND HONORS

LINEAGE

AR
(inactive)

Constituted 10 October 1944 in the Army of the United States as Headquarters and Headquarters Detachment, 3352d Signal Service Battalion. Activated 2 November 1944 in France. Inactivated 31 March 1947 in Germany.

Redesignated 16 September 1955 as Headquarters and Headquarters Detachment, 352d Signal Battalion, and allotted to the Army Reserve. Activated 1 November 1955 at New York, New York. Inactivated 1 March 1963 at New York, New York.

CAMPAIGN PARTICIPATION CREDIT

World War II
  European-African-Middle Eastern Theater, Streamer without inscription

DECORATIONS

None.

352d SIGNAL BATTALION BIBLIOGRAPHY

No published histories.

360th SIGNAL BATTALION

HERALDIC ITEMS

COAT OF ARMS

Shield: Argent, a lightning flash, its point a fleur-de-lis tenné, and a coconut palm tree of the like fructed or in saltire surmounted at the junction by a compass rose white fimbriated of the second debruised by a base rayonné of the last.

Crest: None approved.

Motto: ALL ENCOMPASSING.

Symbolism: Orange and white are the colors traditionally associated with the Signal Corps. The coconut palm tree alludes to campaign participation by the battalion during World War II in the Asiatic-Pacific Theater. The postwar organization of the unit in France is depicted by the lightning flash and fleur-de-lis. The compass rose and motto refer to the battalion's capability to perform its mission in many directions. The three lobes of the fleur-de-lis, six flames of the signal fire, and basic circular shape allude to the numerical designation of the unit.

DISTINCTIVE UNIT INSIGNIA

Description: A gold color metal and enamel device that consists of a gold disc bearing at center a white compass rose of eight rays and surmounting an orange fire of six flames issuing from base between saltirewise throughout an orange palm tree with gold coconuts and an orange lightning flash terminating in a fleur-de-lis with the tops extending over a circular twofold gold scroll around the disc and inscribed ALL at the top and ENCOMPASSING at the bottom in black.

Symbolism: Orange and white are the colors traditionally associated with the Signal Corps. The coconut palm tree alludes to campaign participation by the battalion during World War II in the Asiatic-Pacific Theater. The postwar organization of the unit in France is depicted by the lightning flash and fleur-de-lis. The compass rose and motto refer to the battalion's capability to perform its mission in many directions. The three lobes of the fleur-de-lis, six flames of the signal fire, and basic circular shape allude to the numerical designation of the unit.

LINEAGE AND HONORS

TRADOC
(inactive)

LINEAGE

Constituted 18 December 1944 in the Army of the United States as Headquarters and Headquarters Detachment, 3360th Signal Service Battalion. Activated 3 January 1945 at Philadelphia, Pennsylvania. Inactivated 10 April 1946 in the Philippine Islands.

Redesignated 7 May 1964 as Headquarters and Headquarters Company, 360th Signal Battalion, and allotted to the Regular Army. Activated 24 September 1964 in France. Inactivated 13 November 1967 in Germany.

Headquarters transferred 23 September 1986 to the United States Army Training and Doctrine Command and activated at Fort Gordon, Georgia. Inactivated 24 July 1993 at Fort Gordon, Georgia.

CAMPAIGN PARTICIPATION CREDIT

World War II
　　Asiatic-Pacific Theater, Streamer without inscription

DECORATIONS

None.

360th SIGNAL BATTALION BIBLIOGRAPHY

Sheldon, John J., and Bozidar W. Brown. "Reorganizing Training at the Signal School." *Army Communicator* 15 (Winter–Spring 1990): 26–28.

361st SIGNAL BATTALION

HERALDIC ITEMS

COAT OF ARMS

None approved.

DISTINCTIVE UNIT INSIGNIA

Description: A gold color metal and enamel device that consists of two diagonal orange lightning flashes above three red chevronels that contain within their angle two concentric rings with seven spokes, all in black. Issuant vertically from its center point overall an orange lightning flash terminating at the apex of the chevronels and surmounted by a red demi-fleur-de-lis between the points of the diagonal lightning flashes. The above contained in base by a curving black scroll inscribed with the words THE ELITE in gold letters.

Symbolism: The three red chevronels on the gold background are symbolic of the flag of South Vietnam. Further, the red chevronels, along with the demi-fleur-de-lis at the apex (simulating a cartographer's symbol for north), allude to Long Lines Battalion North, the unit that preceded the 361st in Vietnam. The lightning flashes refer to the unit's signal function. The circular symbol in base, representing a scatter antenna, refers to the battalion's former role as long-haul communicators.

LINEAGE AND HONORS

TRADOC
(inactive)

LINEAGE

Constituted 10 October 1944 in the Army of the United States as Headquarters and Headquarters Detachment, 3361st Signal Service Battalion. Activated 27 October 1944 in India. Inactivated 8 November 1945 in India.

Redesignated 15 June 1969 as Headquarters and Headquarters Company, 361st Signal Battalion, allotted to the Regular Army, and activated in Vietnam. Inactivated 30 May 1971 in Vietnam.

Headquarters transferred 23 September 1986 to the United States Army Training and Doctrine Command and activated at Fort Gordon, Georgia. Inactivated 15 March 1991 at Fort Gordon, Georgia.

CAMPAIGN PARTICIPATION CREDIT

World War II
   Asiatic-Pacific Theater, Streamer without inscription

Vietnam
   Summer–Fall 1969
   Winter–Spring 1970
   Sanctuary Counteroffensive
   Counteroffensive, Phase VII

DECORATIONS

Meritorious Unit Commendation (Army), Streamer embroidered ASIATIC-PACIFIC THEATER (3361st Signal Service Battalion cited; GO 5, Army Service Forces, Office of the Chief Signal Officer, 6 July 1945)

Meritorious Unit Commendation (Army), Streamer embroidered VIETNAM 1969 (361st Signal Battalion cited; DA GO 43, 1972 as amended by DA GO 13, 1978)

361st SIGNAL BATTALION BIBLIOGRAPHY

Bergen, John D. *Military Communications: A Test for Technology.* United States Army in Vietnam. Washington, D.C.: Center of Military History, United States Army, 1986.

Clarke, Jeffrey J. *Advice and Support: The Final Years, 1965–1973.* United States Army in Vietnam. Washington, D.C.: Center of Military History, United States Army, 1988.

Raines, Rebecca Robbins. *Getting the Message Through: A Branch History of the U.S. Army Signal Corps.* Army Historical Series. Washington, D.C.: Center of Military History, United States Army, 1996.

Rienzi, Thomas M. *Communications-Electronics, 1962–1970.* Vietnam Studies. Washington, D.C.: Department of the Army, 1972.

Sheldon, John J., and Bozidar W. Brown. "Reorganizing Training at the Signal School." *Army Communicator* 15 (Winter–Spring 1990): 26–28.

366th SIGNAL BATTALION

HERALDIC ITEMS

COAT OF ARMS

None approved.

DISTINCTIVE UNIT INSIGNIA

Description: A silver color metal and enamel device that consists of a vertical orange quill pen with arrowhead for point in base between two orange lightning flashes radiant from the top and terminating above a black scroll looped from the base on each side and arched across the center of the device inscribed COMBAT SIGNAL SUPPORT in silver letters.

Symbolism: Orange and white (silver) are the colors traditionally associated with the Signal Corps. The quill pen terminating in an arrowhead denotes the battalion's effective capabilities for providing communications during combat operations. The lightning flashes radiant from a single point refer to the coordination and control of a widespread communications system and speed in performance of the unit's mission. The triangular configuration of the device is symbolic of the support mission of the organization.

LINEAGE AND HONORS

TRADOC
(inactive)

LINEAGE

Constituted 10 October 1944 in the Army of the United States as Headquarters and Headquarters Detachment, 3366th Signal Service Battalion. Activated 15 November 1944 on New Caledonia. Inactivated 6 May 1946 on Okinawa.

Redesignated 16 February 1953 as Headquarters, 366th Signal Battalion, and allotted to the Regular Army. Activated 25 March 1953 at Camp Gordon, Georgia. Reorganized and redesignated 4 April 1955 as Headquarters and Headquarters Detachment, 366th Signal Battalion. Inactivated 20 December 1957 at Fort Gordon, Georgia. Activated 22 March 1968 at Fort Hood, Texas. Inactivated 21 September 1972 at Fort Hood, Texas.

Headquarters transferred 23 September 1986 to the United States Army Training and Doctrine Command and activated at Fort Gordon, Georgia. Inactivated 30 September 1994 at Fort Gordon, Georgia.

CAMPAIGN PARTICIPATION CREDIT

World War II
Asiatic-Pacific Theater, Streamer without inscription

DECORATIONS

None.

366th SIGNAL BATTALION BIBLIOGRAPHY

Sheldon, John J., and Bozidar W. Brown. "Reorganizing Training at the Signal School." *Army Communicator* 15 (Winter–Spring 1990): 26–28.

369th SIGNAL BATTALION

HERALDIC ITEMS

COAT OF ARMS

Shield: Per bend sinister tenné and azure, issuant from dexter base a satellite dish argent detailed of the second issuing a lightning flash bendwise sinister or between four mullets of six as the constellation Southern Cross white. On a chief of the second a demibezant surmounted by four short rays reversed between five longer of the like, all radiant from fess point yellow.

Crest: On a wreath of the colors or and tenné a demi–polar bear to dexter and a demidragon combatant argent, each gorged with a collar gules supporting between them a plate charged with five bars wavy azure.

Motto: QUALITY ALL WAYS.

Symbolism: Orange and white are the colors traditionally associated with the Signal Corps. The microwave antenna issuing a lightning flash represents the battalion's former mission of operating and maintaining signal facilities and communication service. The four stars simulate the constellation Southern Cross, visible from Vietnam where the unit participated in four campaigns. The rays on a gold demidisc suggest the Northern Lights, Aurora Borealis, and reflect the unit's World War II campaign credits while serving in Alaska.

The polar bear, symbolic of service in Alaska, is gorged with a red collar to commemorate the Meritorious Unit Commendation awarded the battalion for its World War II service. The dragon, also gorged with a red collar, honors the unit's receipt of the Meritorious Unit Commendation for service in Vietnam from 1968 to 1970. The dragon and the polar bear grasp a plate bearing five wavy bars, which suggest waves or water and allude to the unit's service in the Pacific.

DISTINCTIVE UNIT INSIGNIA

Description: A gold color metal and enamel device that consists of an equilateral triangle with arched, convex sides, one point down evenly divided diagonally from upper right to lower left orange and blue. The left side is surmounted by a representation of a microwave dish-type antenna, white with gold ribs emitting on the diagonal partition line between four white six-pointed stars—two and two—a gold lightning flash. Issuing from the top of the triangle nine gold concentric rays, five long alternating with four shorter rays, all above a gold scroll inscribed QUALITY ALL WAYS in black letters. The base of the triangle extends slightly on to the scroll.

LINEAGES AND HERALDIC DATA 353

Symbolism: Orange and white are the colors traditionally associated with the Signal Corps. The microwave antenna represents equipment for sending and receiving communications, and the lightning flash stands for a radio signal. Together they refer to the battalion's former mission of operating and maintaining signal facilities and service. The gold rays represent the Northern Lights, the Aurora Borealis, and commemorate the battalion's service in Alaska during World War II, for which it received the Meritorious Unit Commendation. The arrangement of four white stars simulates the Southern Cross, a constellation of southern skies visible from Vietnam, and refers to the battalion's war service in that country. The gold color represents the precious metal gold, symbol of quality and value. The three sides of the triangle, six points of the stars, and nine rays of the lights also allude to the battalion's numerical designation.

LINEAGE AND HONORS

TRADOC
(active)

LINEAGE

Constituted 10 October 1944 in the Army of the United States as Headquarters and Headquarters Detachment, 3369th Signal Service Battalion. Activated 9 November 1944 in Alaska. Inactivated 11 March 1947 in Alaska.

Redesignated 15 June 1969 as Headquarters and Headquarters Company, 369th Signal Battalion, allotted to the Regular Army, and activated in Vietnam. Inactivated 30 June 1971 in Vietnam.

Headquarters transferred 23 September 1986 to the United States Army Training and Doctrine Command and activated at Fort Gordon, Georgia.

CAMPAIGN PARTICIPATION CREDIT

World War II
  Asiatic-Pacific Theater, Streamer without inscription

Vietnam
  Summer–Fall 1969
  Winter–Spring 1970
  Sanctuary Counteroffensive
  Counteroffensive, Phase VII

DECORATIONS

Meritorious Unit Commendation (Army), Streamer embroidered PACIFIC THEATER (3369th Signal Service Battalion cited; GO 33, Alaskan Department, 20 February 1946)

Meritorious Unit Commendation (Army), Streamer embroidered VIETNAM 1968–1970 (369th Signal Battalion cited; DA GO 2, 1971)

Company A additionally entitled to:

Army Superior Unit Award, Streamer embroidered 1999–2000 (Company A, 369th Signal Battalion, cited; DA GO 29, 2001)

369th SIGNAL BATTALION BIBLIOGRAPHY

Bergen, John D. *Military Communications: A Test for Technology*. United States Army in Vietnam. Washington, D.C.: Center of Military History, United States Army, 1986.

Clarke, Jeffrey J. *Advice and Support: The Final Years, 1965–1973*. United States Army in Vietnam. Washington, D.C.: Center of Military History, United States Army, 1988.

Rienzi, Thomas M. *Communications-Electronics, 1962–1970*. Vietnam Studies. Washington, D.C.: Government Printing Office, 1972.

Sheldon, John J., and Bozidar W. Brown. "Reorganizing Training at the Signal School." *Army Communicator* 15 (Winter–Spring 1990): 26–28.

379th SIGNAL BATTALION

HERALDIC ITEMS

COAT OF ARMS

Shield: Tenné, a pair of torches pilewise in base silver gray, the flames respectant or and of the field supporting a mullet argent.

Crest: From a wreath of the colors or and tenné a hurt charged with a Torii Gate or, the lower crossbeam gules fimbriated yellow.

Motto: ACCURACY, SPEED, CONTINUITY.

Symbolism: Orange and white are the colors traditionally associated with the Signal Corps. The star symbolizes the atmosphere and the source of electrical impulses, and the torches lighting their flames from the star allude to the battalion's mission in transmitting information and intelligence. The motto ACCURACY, SPEED, CONTINUITY was submitted by the organization.

The hurt represents the Pacific theater in which the unit served in World War II. The Torii Gate is symbolic of the Ryukyu Islands and represents the battalion's service there. The red bar on the gate denotes the Meritorious Unit Commendation awarded to the unit for service in the Pacific area during the Vietnam era.

DISTINCTIVE UNIT INSIGNIA

Description: A silver color metal and enamel device that consists of two silver torches at right angles and joined at base and issuant therefrom two orange flames, swirling to a point and meeting in the center of a silver star. In base and surmounting the torches a black scroll bears the inscription ACCURACY, SPEED, CONTINUITY in silver letters.

Symbolism: Orange and white (silver) are the colors traditionally associated with the Signal Corps. The star symbolizes the atmosphere and the source of electrical impulses, and the torches lighting their flames from the star allude to the signal battalion's mission in transmitting information and intelligence. The motto ACCURACY, SPEED, CONTINUITY was submitted by the organization.

LINEAGE AND HONORS

TRADOC
(inactive)

LINEAGE

Constituted 17 February 1945 in the Army of the United States as Headquarters and Headquarters Detachment, 3796th Signal Service Battalion. Activated 27 February 1945 in Hawaii. Inactivated 25 March 1947 in Korea.

Redesignated 12 September 1952 as Headquarters and Headquarters Company, 379th Signal Support Battalion, and allotted to the Regular Army. Activated 1 November 1952 at Camp Gordon, Georgia. Reorganized and redesignated 8 October 1953 as Headquarters and Headquarters Detachment, 379th Signal Battalion. Inactivated 1 October 1961 in Germany. Activated 25 August 1963 in Thailand. Inactivated 30 June 1971 in Thailand.

Headquarters transferred 23 September 1986 to the United States Army Training and Doctrine Command and activated at Fort Gordon, Georgia. Inactivated 1 October 1987 at Fort Gordon, Georgia.

CAMPAIGN PARTICIPATION CREDIT

World War II
  Ryukyus

DECORATIONS

Meritorious Unit Commendation (Army), Streamer embroidered PACIFIC AREA (379th Signal Battalion cited; DA GO 20, 1967)

379TH SIGNAL BATTALION BIBLIOGRAPHY

Bergen, John D. *Military Communications: A Test for Technology*. United States Army in Vietnam. Washington, D.C.: Center of Military History, United States Army, 1986.

Rienzi, Thomas M. *Communications-Electronics, 1962–1970*. Vietnam Studies. Washington, D.C.: Government Printing Office, 1972.

HEADQUARTERS AND HEADQUARTERS DETACHMENT 392d SIGNAL BATTALION

HERALDIC ITEMS

COAT OF ARMS

Shield: Or, a lion rampant sable grasping a lightning bolt tenné; on a fess azure three fleurs-de-lis of the first.

Crest: That for the regiments and separate battalions of the Army Reserve: On a wreath of the colors or and sable the Lexington Minuteman proper. The statue of the Minuteman Capt. John Parker (H. H. Kitson, sculptor) stands on the Common in Lexington, Massachusetts.

Motto: WE SERVE TO HONOR.

Symbolism: Orange is a color traditionally associated with the Signal Corps. Gold is emblematic of honor and high achievement, and blue is for loyalty. Black and gold allude to the night and day, around the clock mission of the Signal Corps. The three fleurs-de-lis commemorate the unit's World War II campaigns in Normandy, Northern France, and Ardennes-Alsace, and the lion represents the Central Europe campaign. The lion embodies courage and strength, and the lightning bolt it grasps symbolizes electronic technology and quick response.

DISTINCTIVE UNIT INSIGNIA

The distinctive unit insignia is the shield and motto of the coat of arms.

LINEAGE AND HONORS

AR
(active)

LINEAGE

Constituted 23 July 1942 in the Army of the United States as the 392d Signal Company, Aviation. Activated 1 August 1942 at MacDill Field, Florida. Redesignated 16 January 1944 as the 392d Signal Company, Air Force. Reorganized and redesignated 26 August 1944 as the 1709th Signal Service Battalion. Inactivated 12 November 1945 at Camp Shanks, New York.

Redesignated 16 March 1954 as Headquarters, 392d Signal Battalion, and allotted to the Army Reserve. Activated 1 May 1954 at New York, New York. Inactivated 1 February 1956 at New York, New York. Redesignated 8 August 1956 as Headquarters and Headquarters Detachment, 392d Signal Battalion. Activated 1 October 1956 at Concord, New Hampshire. Inactivated 1 February 1963 at Concord, New Hampshire. Activated 16 October 1995 at West Hazleton, Pennsylvania.

CAMPAIGN PARTICIPATION CREDIT

World War II
    Normandy
    Northern France
    Ardennes-Alsace
    Central Europe

DECORATIONS

None.

392d SIGNAL BATTALION BIBLIOGRAPHY

No published histories.

HEADQUARTERS AND HEADQUARTERS DETACHMENT 417th SIGNAL BATTALION

HERALDIC ITEMS

COAT OF ARMS

Shield: Per chevron enhanced tenné and argent, between two lightning flashes chevronwise of the first a triangle gules charged with a mullet of seven white above two barrulets couped wavy azure, and on a chief per chevron of the second four palm fronds chevronwise vert.

Crest: That for the regiments and separate battalions of the Florida Army National Guard: On a wreath of the colors argent and tenné an alligator statant proper.

Motto: GUARDS THE PEACE.

Symbolism: Orange and white are the colors traditionally associated with the Signal Corps. The red and white were suggested by the colors of the flag of the state of Florida, the unit's home base. The blue, white, and red refer to the tricolor of France where the organization served during World War I, and also denote the Philippine Presidential Unit Citation awarded the unit for the Southern Philippines campaign during World War II. The lightning flashes simulate an arrowhead, the palms typify tropical growth, the gold area and the wavy blue bars together represent an island, and the seven-pointed white star is from the flag of Australia. All are used to symbolize Australia, where the unit was activated during World War II, and the island of New Guinea, where the unit made an assault landing; the wavy blue bars simulate the Presidential Unit Citation streamer awarded to the unit for that action.

DISTINCTIVE UNIT INSIGNIA

Description: A gold color metal and enamel device that consists of two orange lightning flashes chevronwise issuing from apex four green palm fronds faced left and right and bearing in the lower area between the flashes a seven pointed white star above two wavy bars all above a red scroll arced to base, lined gold and inscribed GUARDS THE PEACE in gold letters; the interior areas between the flashes, star, wavy bars, and scroll all of gold.

LINEAGE AND HONORS

ARNG
(Florida)

LINEAGE

Organized 4 March 1897 in the Florida State Troops at Tallahassee as Company C (Governor's Guards), 4th Battalion of Infantry. (4th Battalion of Infantry consolidated 14 May 1898 with the 1st, 2d, and 3d Battalions of Infantry, reorganized, and mustered into Federal service 20–25 May 1898 at Tampa as the 1st Florida Volunteer Infantry; mustered out of Federal service 3 December 1898 at Tampa and 27 January 1899 at Huntsville, Alabama.) Reorganized in 1899 at Tallahassee as Company G, 1st Regiment of Infantry. Redesignated between 1900 and 1902 as Company D, 1st Regiment of Infantry. Disbanded 15 July 1904 at Tallahassee.

Reconstituted 7 June 1907 in the Florida State Troops at Tallahassee as Company C, 1st Regiment of Infantry. (Florida State Troops redesignated in 1909 as the Florida National Guard.) Redesignated 19 March 1915 as Company I, 1st Regiment of Infantry. Disbanded 14 June 1916 at Tallahassee.

Reconstituted 29 May 1917 in the Florida National Guard and reorganized at Tallahassee as Company B, 1st Regiment of Infantry. Drafted into Federal service 5 August 1917 at Jacksonville as an element of the 31st Division. Converted and redesignated 1 October 1917 as the 2d Company, 56th Depot Brigade. (56th Depot Brigade demobilized 31 October 1917 at Camp Wheeler, Georgia, and its personnel transferred to other organizations in the 31st Division.)

Reconstituted 26 June 1924 in the Florida National Guard at Tallahassee as Company M, 124th Infantry, an element of the 31st Division. Inducted into Federal service 25 November 1940 at Tallahassee. (124th Infantry relieved 15 December 1941 from assignment to the 31st Division.) Inactivated 2 March 1944 at Fort Jackson, South Carolina. Activated 5 April 1944 in Australia as an element of the 31st Infantry Division. Inactivated 16 December 1945 at Camp Stoneman, California. (124th Infantry relieved 13 June 1946 from assignment to the 31st Infantry Division; assigned 5 July 1946 to the 48th Infantry Division.)

Reorganized and federally recognized 4 February 1947 at Tallahassee as Company A, 124th Infantry. Reorganized and redesignated 1 November 1955 as Headquarters and Service Company, 124th Armored Infantry Battalion, an element of the 48th Armored Division. Consolidated 15 April 1959 with the Medical Detachment, 124th Armored Infantry Battalion (organized and federally recognized 1 November 1955 at Tallahassee), and consolidated unit designated as Headquarters Company, 1st Armored Rifle Battalion, 124th Infantry. Converted and redesignated 15 February 1963 as Headquarters and Headquarters Company, 260th Engineer Group, and relieved from assignment to the 48th Armored Division.

Consolidated 20 January 1968 with the 489th Medical Detachment (organized and federally recognized 1 March 1964 at Tallahassee), and consolidated unit converted and redesignated as Headquarters and Headquarters Detachment, 53d Signal Group. Reorganized and redesignated 1 October 1985 as Headquarters and Headquarters Company, 53d Signal Brigade.

Reorganized and redesignated 1 October 1997 as Headquarters and Headquarters Detachment, 417th Signal Battalion.

LINEAGES AND HERALDIC DATA 361

Home Station: Tallahassee

CAMPAIGN PARTICIPATION CREDIT

World War I
  Streamer without inscription

World War II
  New Guinea (with arrowhead)
  Southern Philippines

DECORATIONS

Presidential Unit Citation (Army), Streamer embroidered NEW GUINEA (3d Battalion, 124th Infantry, cited; WD GO 122, 1946)
Philippine Presidential Unit Citation, Streamer embroidered 17 OCTOBER 1944 TO 4 JULY 1945 (124th Infantry cited; DA GO 47, 1950)

417th SIGNAL BATTALION BIBLIOGRAPHY

Beall, Jean Marie. "REFORGER's Ma Bell: 53d Signal Brigade Makes the Connection." *National Guard* 44 (May 1990): 28–30, 32.
Hasenauer, Heike. "Grecian Firebolt." *Soldiers* 39 (September 1994): 37–40. 53d Signal Brigade cited.
Historical and Pictorial Review of the 31st Division, Army of the United States, Camp Blanding, Florida, 1941. Baton Rouge: Army and Navy Publishing Company, 1941.
History of the 31st Infantry Division in Training and Combat, 1940–1945. Baton Rouge: Army and Navy Publishing Company, 1945.
"Level Heads." *National Guard* 37 (November 1983): 35. 53d Signal Brigade cited.
Morris, Al, et al. "The 53d on REFORGER." *Army Communicator* 11 (Spring 1986): 26–29.
124th Infantry Gators at Fort Benning, Nineteen Hundred Forty-Three. N.p., 1943.
"Riot Reaction Force: The Guard in the April Disorders." *National Guardsman* 22 (May 1968): 2–16. 53d Signal Group cited.
Smith, Robert Ross. *The Approach to the Philippines.* United States Army in World War II. Washington, D.C.: Office of the Chief of Military History, Department of the Army, 1953. 124th Infantry cited.

HEADQUARTERS AND HEADQUARTERS DETACHMENT 421st SIGNAL BATTALION

HERALDIC ITEMS

None approved.

LINEAGE AND HONORS

AR
(inactive)

LINEAGE

Constituted 7 July 1944 in the Army of the United States as Headquarters and Headquarters Detachment, 3214th Signal Service Battalion. Activated 8 August 1944 in Italy. Inactivated 30 September 1945 in Italy.

Redesignated 25 March 1954 as Headquarters, 421st Signal Battalion, and allotted to the Army Reserve. Activated 19 April 1954 at Reading, Pennsylvania. Reorganized and redesignated 27 June 1955 as Headquarters and Headquarters Detachment, 421st Signal Battalion. Inactivated 28 February 1963 at Reading, Pennsylvania.

CAMPAIGN PARTICIPATION CREDIT

World War II
  Rome-Arno

DECORATIONS

None.

421st SIGNAL BATTALION BIBLIOGRAPHY

No published histories.

HEADQUARTERS AND HEADQUARTERS DETACHMENT
422d SIGNAL BATTALION

HERALDIC ITEMS

COAT OF ARMS

Shield: Celeste, a lozenge argent voided tenné charged with a mullet of the second, all between two lightning flashes in chief chevronwise or, and in base two laurel branches chevronwise reversed of the second.

Crest: That for the regiments and separate battalions of the Nevada Army National Guard: On a wreath of the colors argent and celeste within a garland of sagebrush a sledge and miner's drill crossed in saltire behind a pickax in pale proper.

Motto: BATTLE BORN.

Symbolism: Orange and white (silver) are the colors traditionally associated with the Signal Corps. The square on square refers to the Signal Corps flag and the battalion's mission. The lightning flashes symbolize speed and communications. The silver star and laurel branches, adapted from the shoulder sleeve insignia of the Nevada Army National Guard, refer to the unit's location and denote excellence and achievement. The light blue alludes to the Virginia Blues, the first organized state militia in Nevada.

DISTINCTIVE UNIT INSIGNIA

The distinctive unit insignia consists of elements of the shield and the motto of the coat of arms.

LINEAGE AND HONORS

ARNG
(Nevada)

LINEAGE

Organized and federally recognized 21 June 1928 in the Nevada National Guard at Reno as the 40th Military Police Company, an element of the 40th Division. Converted and redesignated 1 January 1941 as Headquarters Battery, 121st Separate Coast Artillery Battalion, and relieved from assignment to the 40th Division. Inducted into Federal service 23 June 1941 at Reno.

Reorganized and redesignated 10 September 1943 as Headquarters Battery, 121st Antiaircraft Artillery Gun Battalion. Reorganized and redesignated 4 January 1945 as Headquarters Battery, 1st Rocket Battalion. Reorganized and redesignated 13 April 1945 as Headquarters Battery, 421st Rocket Field Artillery Battalion. Inactivated 15 January 1946 at Fort Lawton, Washington.

Consolidated with Battery A, 421st Rocket Field Artillery Battalion (see ANNEX 1), and consolidated unit reorganized and federally recognized 19 January 1949 at Reno as Headquarters Battery, 421st Antiaircraft Artillery Gun Battalion. Reorganized and redesignated 1 December 1952 as Headquarters Battery, 421st Antiaircraft Artillery Automatic Weapons Battalion. Redesignated 1 October 1953 as Headquarters Battery, 421st Antiaircraft Artillery Battalion.

Consolidated 1 April 1959 with the Medical Detachment, 421st Antiaircraft Artillery Battalion (see ANNEX 2), and consolidated unit reorganized and redesignated as Headquarters Battery, 1st Gun Battalion, 221st Artillery. Reorganized and redesignated 1 June 1962 as Headquarters Battery, 1st Automatic Weapons Battalion, 221st Artillery.

Converted and redesignated 15 December 1967 as Headquarters Troop, 3d Squadron, 116th Armored Cavalry. Converted and redesignated 1 March 1972 as Headquarters Detachment, 150th Composite Battalion. Redesignated 1 March 1973 as Headquarters and Headquarters Detachment, 150th Service Battalion. Location changed 1 October 1975 to Stead.

Personnel transferred 1 October 1978 to the Command and Control Headquarters, Nevada Army National Guard; transferred 1 March 1981 to Headquarters and Headquarters Detachment, 422d Signal Battalion, at Reno.

ANNEX 1

Organized and federally recognized 28 June 1929 in the Nevada National Guard at Reno as Company D, 115th Engineers. Converted and redesignated 1 January 1941 as Battery A, 121st Separate Coast Artillery Battalion. Inducted into Federal service 23 June 1941 at Reno. Reorganized and redesignated 10 September 1943 as Battery A, 121st Antiaircraft Artillery Gun Battalion. Reorganized and redesignated 4 January 1945 as Battery A, 1st Rocket Battalion. Reorganized and redesignated 13 April 1945 as Battery A, 421st Rocket Field Artillery Battalion. Inactivated 15 January 1946 at Fort Lawton, Washington.

ANNEX 2

Organized and federally recognized 8 April 1936 in the Nevada National Guard at Reno as the Medical Detachment, 2d Battalion, 115th Engineers. Reorganized and redesignated 1 January 1941 as the Medical Detachment, 121st Separate Coast Artillery Battalion. Inducted into Federal service 23 June 1941 at Reno. Reorganized and redesignated 10 September 1943 as the Medical Detachment, 121st Antiaircraft Artillery Gun Battalion. Reorganized and redesignated 4 January 1945 as the Medical Detachment, 1st Rocket Battalion. Reorganized and redesignated 13 April 1945 as the Medical Detachment, 421st Rocket Field Artillery Battalion. Inactivated 15 January 1946 at Fort Lawton, Washington. Reorganized and federally recognized 12 July 1949 as the Medical Detachment, 421st Antiaircraft Artillery Gun Battalion. Reorganized and redesignated 1 December 1952 as the Medical Detachment, 421st Antiaircraft Artillery Automatic Weapons Battalion. Redesignated 1 October 1953 as the Medical Detachment, 421st Antiaircraft Artillery Battalion.

Home Station: Reno

CAMPAIGN PARTICIPATION CREDIT

World War II
  Ryukyus

DECORATIONS

None.

422d SIGNAL BATTALION BIBLIOGRAPHY

Appleman, Roy E., James M. Burns, Russell A. Gugeler, and John Stevens. *Okinawa: The Last Battle*. Washington, D.C.: Historical Division, Department of the Army, 1948. 421st Rocket Field Artillery Battalion participated in the Ryukyus campaign.

Conder, Terry L. "Active, Reserve Soldiers Improvise, Use New Technology to Overcome Problem in Grecian Firebolt '98." *Army Communicator* 23 (Fall 1998): 33–34.

———. "Total Army Force Works Together." *Army Communicator* 14 (Winter 1989): 50–51.

Hernandez, Chris E. *A History of the Desert Wolf, Present Designation 421st Rocket FA Battalion, Former Designations, 121st Separate Battalion CA (AA), 121st AAA Gun Battalion, 1st Rocket Battalion, 1940–1950*. Glendale, Calif.: Griffin Patterson Company, 1946.

Ranson, Steven R. "422d Signal Avoids Washout From Joint Thunder Hail, Rain, Sleet." *Army Communicator* 28 (Fall 2003): 40–42.

426th SIGNAL BATTALION

HERALDIC ITEMS

COAT OF ARMS

Shield: Argent, between a chevron per chevron embattled vert and gules four roundels engrailed of eight—three in chief one and two and one in base tenné—each charged with an annulet or.
Crest: None approved.
Motto: THE COMMANDING VOICE.
Symbolism: Orange and white are the colors traditionally associated with the Signal Corps. The four roundels stand for the four area signal centers that were installed, operated, and maintained by the battalion. The radiant edges indicate the emission and transmission of signal information, and the gold annulets refer to circuit control. The chevron alludes to the mountains of Italy and stands for the battalion's two campaigns in that country during World War II. Green, white, and red are the Italian national colors. The embattled division line refers to combat service and also indicates that the unit was organized as a signal combat battalion.

DISTINCTIVE UNIT INSIGNIA

The distinctive unit insignia is the shield and motto of the coat of arms.

LINEAGE AND HONORS

RA
(inactive)

LINEAGE

Constituted 28 June 1942 in the Army of the United States as the 426th Signal Battalion. Activated 1 August 1942 at Fresno, California. Reorganized and redesignated 19 January 1943 as the 426th Signal Construction Battalion, Aviation. Reorganized and redesignated 1 July 1944 as the 426th Signal Heavy Construction Battalion. Inactivated 8 November 1945 in Italy.

Redesignated 2 March 1967 as the 426th Signal Battalion and allotted to the Regular Army. Activated 25 April 1967 at Fort Bragg, North Carolina. Inactivated 15 April 1993 at Fort Bragg, North Carolina.

CAMPAIGN PARTICIPATION CREDIT

World War II
  Rome-Arno
  North Apennines

Southwest Asia
  Defense of Saudi Arabia
  Liberation and Defense of Kuwait

DECORATIONS

Meritorious Unit Commendation (Army), Streamer embroidered SOUTHWEST ASIA 1990–1991 (426th Signal Battalion cited; DA GO 12, 1994)

426th SIGNAL BATTALION BIBLIOGRAPHY

Crocker, Robert W. "Go Between Circuits IV." *Army Communicator* 6 (Summer 1981): 50–53.

Kennedy, Randy. "35th Signal Brigade." *Army Communicator* 12 (Fall 1987): 30–33.

Stokes, Carol E., ed. *The U.S. Army Signal Corps in Operation Desert Shield/Desert Storm*. Fort Gordon, Ga.: Office of the Command Historian, U.S. Army Signal Center and Fort Gordon, 1994.

Stokes, Carol E., and Kathy R. Coker. "Getting the Message Through in the Persian Gulf War." *Army Communicator* 17 (Summer–Winter 1992): 17–25.

440th SIGNAL BATTALION

HERALDIC ITEMS

COAT OF ARMS

Shield: Tenné, issuant from base a telegraph pole arraswise with two cross beams, each arm holding four insulators with a like number of circuit wires bendsinisterwise, and issuant from the ends of the cross beams three lightning flashes, all argent.

Crest: On a wreath of the colors argent and tenné a pair of carabao horns argent, bound gules in front of a Korean temple azure.

Motto: MAINTAINING CONTACT.

Symbolism: The telegraph pole symbolizes the functions of the battalion. The four circuits represent the four former components—two construction companies, headquarters company, and medical detachment—of the organization.

The crest commemorates the organization's distinguished service in the Philippines during World War II and in Korea. The unit's six decorations—two for the Philippines and four for Korea—are represented by the two horns of the carabao and the four apertures of the temple. The colors blue and red refer to the awards of the Presidential Unit Citation and the Meritorious Unit Commendation.

DISTINCTIVE UNIT INSIGNIA

The distinctive unit insignia is the shield and motto of the coat of arms.

LINEAGE AND HONORS

RA
(active)

LINEAGE

Constituted 18 March 1942 in the Army of the United States as the 440th Signal Battalion. Activated 25 March 1942 at Geiger Field, Washington. Reorganized and redesignated 14 December 1942 as the 440th Signal Construction Battalion. Reorganized and redesignated 23 July 1944 as the 440th Signal Heavy Construction Battalion. Reorganized and redesignated 12 April 1949 as the 440th Signal Aviation Heavy Construction Battalion. Reorganized and redesignated 25 May 1951 as the 440th Signal Aviation Construction Battalion. Inactivated 16 May 1956 in Korea.

Redesignated 29 September 1961 as the 440th Signal Battalion and allotted to the Regular Army. Activated 1 October 1961 in Germany.

CAMPAIGN PARTICIPATION CREDIT

World War II
　Papua
　New Guinea
　Leyte
　Luzon

Korean War
　CCF Intervention
　First UN Counteroffensive
　CCF Spring Offensive
　Korea, Summer 1953

Company A additionally entitled to:

Korean War
　UN Defensive
　UN Offensive

DECORATIONS

Presidential Unit Citation (Army), Streamer embroidered KOREA (440th Signal Aviation Construction Battalion cited; GO 457, Far East Air Forces, 28 September 1951)

Meritorious Unit Commendation (Army), Streamer embroidered PACIFIC THEATER (440th Signal Heavy Construction Battalion, Aviation, cited; GO 1813, Far East Air Forces, 15 August 1945)

Army Superior Unit Award, Streamer embroidered 1995–1996 (440th Signal Battalion cited; DA GO 25, 2001)

Air Force Outstanding Unit Award, Streamer embroidered KOREA (440th Signal Aviation Construction Battalion cited; DA GO 46, 1957)

Philippine Presidential Unit Citation, Streamer embroidered 17 OCTOBER 1944 TO 4 JULY 1945 (440th Signal [Heavy] Construction Battalion [Aviation] cited; DA GO 47, 1950)

Republic of Korea Presidential Unit Citation, Streamer embroidered KOREA 1950 (440th Signal Aviation Construction Battalion cited; GO 84, Far East Air Forces, 17 February 1953)

Republic of Korea Presidential Unit Citation, Streamer embroidered KOREA 1950–1953 (440th Signal Aviation Construction Battalion cited; GO 35, Far East Air Forces, 4 March 1954)

Company A additionally entitled to:

Presidential Unit Citation (Army), Streamer embroidered PAPUA (Papuan Forces United States Army, Southwest Pacific Area, cited; WD GO 21, 1943)

440th SIGNAL BATTALION BIBLIOGRAPHY

Johnson, Danny M. *Military Communications Supporting Peacekeeping Operations in the Balkans: The Signal Corps at Its Best*. Mannheim, Germany: Headquarters, 5th Signal Command, 2000.

Thompson, George Raynor, and Dixie R. Harris. *The Signal Corps: The Outcome (Mid-1943 through 1945)*. United States Army in World War II. Washington, D.C.: Office of the Chief of Military History, United States Army, 1966.

442d SIGNAL BATTALION

HERALDIC ITEMS

COAT OF ARMS

Shield: Per cross tenné and sable, overall three multibarbed South Pacific spears—two saltirewise surmounted by one in pale argent—within a cable entwined with a lineman's loop that terminates in two lightning flashes fesswise throughout or.

Crest: On a wreath of the colors argent and tenné a conch shell fesswise or, supporting upon its upper rim a sea lion naiant, grasping in dexter paw a sword of the first.

Motto: READY RAPID RELIABLE.

Symbolism: Orange and white (silver) are the colors traditionally associated with the Signal Corps. The three multibarbed spears commemorate the unit's historic campaign service in the Asiatic-Pacific Theater during World War II. The battalion's former assignment in the United States Army Strategic Communications Command is indicated by the four divisions of the shield, alluding to the four corners of the world. Together with the lightning flashes they signify readiness for worldwide deployment to fulfill communication requirements. The looped cable refers to the battalion's capabilities in installing, operating, and maintaining signal centers.

The conch shell, a South Pacific war trumpet, and the sea lion from the coat of arms of the president of the Philippine Commonwealth allude to the World War II battle honor, the Philippine Presidential Unit Citation.

DISTINCTIVE UNIT INSIGNIA

The distinctive unit insignia is the shield and motto of the coat of arms.

LINEAGE AND HONORS

TRADOC
(active)

LINEAGE

Constituted 19 July 1942 in the Army of the United States as the 442d Signal Construction Battalion, Aviation. Activated 1 August 1942 in Puerto Rico. Reorganized and redesignated 1 August 1944 as the 442d Signal Heavy Construction Battalion. Inactivated 30 June 1946 in Japan.

Redesignated 6 November 1967 as the 442d Signal Battalion, allotted to the Regular Army, and activated in Thailand. (Companies A, B, and C inactivated 14

July 1969 in Thailand.) Headquarters and Headquarters Detachment, 442d Signal Battalion, inactivated 30 June 1971 in Thailand.

Headquarters transferred 23 September 1986 to the United States Army Training and Doctrine Command and activated at Fort Gordon, Georgia.

CAMPAIGN PARTICIPATION CREDIT

World War II
  New Guinea
  Leyte
  Luzon

DECORATIONS

Meritorious Unit Commendation (Army), Streamer embroidered PACIFIC AREA (442d Signal Battalion cited; DA GO 37, 1972)

Army Superior Unit Award, Streamer embroidered 1999–2000 (Headquarters and Company A, Company C, 442d Signal Battalion, cited; DA GO 29, 2001)

Philippine Presidential Unit Citation, Streamer embroidered 17 OCTOBER 1944 TO 4 JULY 1945 (442d Signal [Heavy] Construction Battalion cited; DA GO 57, 1950)

442d SIGNAL BATTALION BIBLIOGRAPHY

Lane, Charles. "Integrated MSE Training Helps Produce Total Signaleer." *Army Communicator* 15 (Winter–Spring 1990): 20–22. Discusses mobile subscriber radio equipment (MSE) training provided by Company D at Fort Gordon.

Rienzi, Thomas M. *Communications-Electronics 1962–1970*. Vietnam Studies. Washington, D.C.: Government Printing Office, 1972.

Thompson, George Raynor, and Dixie R. Harris. *The Signal Corps: The Outcome (Mid-1943 through 1945)*. United States Army in World War II. Washington, D.C.: Office of the Chief of Military History, United States Army, 1966.

447th SIGNAL BATTALION

HERALDIC ITEMS

COAT OF ARMS

Shield: Tenné, four beacons argent, the flames proper fimbriated of the last.

Crest: On a wreath of the colors argent and tenné a lightning bolt fesswise of the first supporting a lion passant or charged on the shoulder with a fleur-de-lis azure.

Motto: SIGNA VICTORIAE (Signals for Victory).

Symbolism: Orange and white are the colors traditionally associated with the Signal Corps. The beacons are an ancient symbol of signal service, and the four symbolize the organization's campaigns in Europe during World War II.

The lion, symbolic of strength and courage, is combined with a fleur-de-lis to commemorate service during World War II in France and Central Europe. Gold is emblematic of honor and high achievement. The lightning bolt represents quick response and electronic capabilities.

DISTINCTIVE UNIT INSIGNIA

The distinctive unit insignia is the shield and motto of the coat of arms.

LINEAGE AND HONORS

TRADOC
(active)

LINEAGE

Constituted 10 August 1942 in the Army of the United States as the 447th Signal Construction Battalion, Aviation. Activated 29 August 1942 at Dale Mabry Field, Florida. Reorganized and redesignated 5 October 1944 as the 447th Signal Heavy Construction Battalion. Inactivated 25 October 1945 at Camp Shanks, New York.

Redesignated 3 December 1954 as the 447th Signal Battalion and allotted to the Regular Army. Activated 28 January 1955 in Germany. Inactivated 19 August 1963 in Germany. Activated 14 February 1964 in Germany. Inactivated 13 November 1967 in Germany.

Headquarters transferred 23 September 1986 to the United States Army Training and Doctrine Command and activated at Fort Gordon, Georgia.

CAMPAIGN PARTICIPATION CREDIT

World War II
    Normandy
    Northern France
    Rhineland
    Central Europe

DECORATIONS

Company A entitled to:

Army Superior Unit Award, Streamer embroidered 1999–2000 (Company A, 447th Signal Battalion, cited; DA GO 29, 2001)

447th SIGNAL BATTALION BIBLIOGRAPHY

Sheldon, John J., and Bozidar W. Brown. "Reorganizing Training at the Signal School." *Army Communicator* 15 (Winter–Spring 1990): 26–28.

Tingle, Earl. "The 447th Signal Battalion: Yesterday and Today." *Army Communicator* 14 (Summer 1989): 42–44.

459th SIGNAL BATTALION

HERALDIC ITEMS

COAT OF ARMS

Shield: Per pale argent and tenné, on a bend wavy azure between two fleurs-de-lis counterchanged a lion passant guardant of the first.
Crest: None approved.
Motto: A TERRA AD ASTRA (From the Earth to the Stars).
Symbolism: Orange and white are the colors traditionally associated with the Signal Corps. Blue alludes to the unit's service during World War II with the Army Air Forces. The three campaign honors awarded the organization for service in Europe during World War II are represented by the lion "passant guardant" from the coat of arms of Normandy and the two fleurs-de-lis. The wavy stripe alludes to the unit's landing at Omaha Beach in Normandy in July 1944.

DISTINCTIVE UNIT INSIGNIA

The distinctive unit insignia is the shield and motto of the coat of arms.

LINEAGE AND HONORS

RA
(inactive)

LINEAGE

Constituted 10 August 1942 in the Army of the United States as the 459th Signal Construction Battalion, Aviation. Activated 29 August 1942 at Morris Field, North Carolina. Reorganized and redesignated 5 October 1944 as the 459th Signal Heavy Construction Battalion, Aviation. Inactivated 24 December 1945 at Camp Pinedale, California.

Redesignated 3 April 1962 as the 459th Signal Battalion and allotted to the Regular Army. Activated 25 May 1962 at Fort Huachuca, Arizona. Inactivated 30 November 1971 in Vietnam. Activated 16 September 1993 in Germany. Inactivated 15 September 1994 in Germany.

CAMPAIGN PARTICIPATION CREDIT

World War II
  Normandy
  Northern France
  Central Europe

Vietnam
  Counteroffensive, Phase II
  Counteroffensive, Phase III
  Tet Counteroffensive
  Counteroffensive, Phase IV
  Counteroffensive, Phase V
  Counteroffensive, Phase VI
  Tet 69/Counteroffensive
  Summer–Fall 1969
  Winter–Spring 1970
  Sanctuary Counteroffensive
  Counteroffensive, Phase VII
  Consolidation I

DECORATIONS

Meritorious Unit Commendation (Army), Streamer embroidered VIETNAM 1966–1968 (459th Signal Battalion [Combat Area] cited; DA GO 48, 1969)

Company D additionally entitled to:

Meritorious Unit Commendation (Army), Streamer embroidered VIETNAM 1967–1968 (Company D, 459th Signal Battalion, cited; DA GO 42, 1969)

459th SIGNAL BATTALION BIBLIOGRAPHY

Bergen, John D. *Military Communications: A Test for Technology.* United States Army in Vietnam. Washington, D.C.: Center of Military History, United States Army, 1986.

Pearson, Willard. *The War in the Northern Provinces, 1966–1968.* Vietnam Studies. Washington: Department of the Army, 1975.

Rienzi, Thomas M. *Communications-Electronics, 1962–1970.* Vietnam Studies. Washington, D.C.: Department of the Army, 1972.

460th SIGNAL BATTALION

HERALDIC ITEMS

COAT OF ARMS

Shield: Argent, in pale a rice stalk of two leaves tenné surmounted in middle base by a hurt bearing a mullet and fimbriated of the field accosted by two flames of the second.

Crest: That for the regiments and separate battalions of the Army Reserve: On a wreath of the colors argent and tenné the Lexington Minuteman proper. The statue of the Minuteman Capt. John Parker (H. H. Kitson, sculptor) stands on the Common in Lexington, Massachusetts.

Motto: AFFIRMATIVE.

Symbolism: Orange and white are the colors traditionally associated with the Signal Corps. The rice stalk with its two leaves refers to the Pacific areas where the unit served during World War II. The blue circle and white star, alluding to the identification marking on Army Air Forces aircraft, refer to the unit's wartime function as an aviation signal battalion. The fire, a basic method of signaling, is a symbol of the unit's mission.

DISTINCTIVE UNIT INSIGNIA

The distinctive unit insignia is the shield and motto of the coat of arms.

LINEAGE AND HONORS

LINEAGE
AR (inactive)

Constituted 10 August 1942 in the Army of the United States as the 460th Signal Construction Battalion, Aviation. Activated 17 August 1942 at Langley Field, Virginia. Reorganized and redesignated 20 December 1944 as the 460th Signal Heavy Construction Battalion, Aviation. Inactivated 24 February 1946 in the Ryukyus Islands.

Redesignated 8 April 1959 as the 460th Signal Battalion and allotted to the Army Reserve. Activated 15 May 1959 with Headquarters at Miami, Florida. Inactivated 15 January 1963 at Miami, Florida.

CAMPAIGN PARTICIPATION CREDIT

World War II
    Western Pacific
    Ryukyus

DECORATIONS

None.

460th SIGNAL BATTALION BIBLIOGRAPHY

No published histories.

501st SIGNAL BATTALION

HERALDIC ITEMS

COAT OF ARMS

Shield: Per chevron argent and tenné, in base a pelican feather of the first charged with a lightning flash of the second.

Crest: On a wreath of the colors argent and tenné an American bald eagle rising, wings addorsed proper armed and langued gules bearing in dexter talons two arrows saltirewise points up vert, armed Azure, and flighted of the fourth.

Motto: VOX AQUILAE (Voice of the Eagle).

Symbolism: Orange and white are the colors traditionally associated with the Signal Corps. The lightning flash on the pelican feather was the badge of the 101st Airborne Signal Company from which the battalion is descended. The lightning flash illustrates the function of the company, and the pelican's feather represents the state of Louisiana, where the company was organized in 1942. The "per chevron" background alludes to the unit's assault landing in Normandy.

The two arrowheads, which refer to the assault landings in Normandy and in the Rhineland, are blue in color in reference to the two Presidential Unit Citations awarded the unit for the Normandy assault and the action at Bastogne during World War II. The green shafts and red feathers allude to the award of the French Croix de Guerre and the Belgian Fourragere. Arrows also appear in the coat of arms of the Netherlands and refer to the award of the Orange Lanyard. Red also denotes the Meritorious Unit Commendation awarded the unit for service in Vietnam.

DISTINCTIVE UNIT INSIGNIA

The distinctive unit insignia is the shield and motto of the coat of arms.

LINEAGE AND HONORS

RA
LINEAGE (101st Airborne Division) (active)

Constituted 23 July 1918 in the National Army as the 626th Field Signal Battalion and assigned to the 101st Division. (101st Division only partially organized October–November 1918; demobilized 11 December 1918.) Reconstituted 24 June 1921 in the Organized Reserves as the 101st Signal Company and assigned to the 101st Division. Organized in October 1921 in Wisconsin. Withdrawn 15 August 1942 from the Organized Reserves and allotted to the Army of the United States; concurrently reorganized at Camp Claiborne, Louisiana, as the 101st Airborne Signal Company, an element of the 101st Airborne Division. Inactivated 30 November 1945 in France.

Allotted 25 June 1948 to the Regular Army. Activated 6 July 1948 at Camp Breckinridge, Kentucky. Inactivated 1 April 1949 at Camp Breckinridge, Kentucky. Activated 25 August 1950 at Camp Breckinridge, Kentucky. Inactivated 1 December 1953 at Camp Breckinridge, Kentucky. Activated 15 May 1954 at Fort Jackson, South Carolina.

Reorganized and redesignated 1 July 1956 as Headquarters, Headquarters and Service Detachment, 501st Airborne Signal Battalion, an element of the 101st Airborne Division (516th Signal Company [see ANNEX 1] and 299th Signal Company [see ANNEX 2] concurrently redesignated as the Operations Company and the Installation Company, 501st Airborne Signal Battalion, respectively, and activated at Fort Campbell, Kentucky).

Reorganized and redesignated 25 April 1957 as the 501st Signal Battalion (Operations and Installation Companies concurrently reorganized and redesignated as Companies A and B, respectively).

ANNEX 1

Constituted 11 May 1942 in the Army of the United States as the 246th Signal Operation Company. Activated 15 April 1943 at Camp Crowder, Missouri. Inactivated 30 November 1945 at Fort Monmouth, New Jersey. Redesignated 15 March 1949 as the 516th Signal Company. Activated 1 April 1949 in Austria. Allotted 20 February 1951 to the Regular Army. Inactivated 31 July 1955 in Austria.

ANNEX 2

Constituted 8 December 1942 in the Army of the United States as the 299th Signal Installation Company. Activated 24 September 1943 at Camp Crowder, Missouri. Redesignated 26 May 1945 as the 299th Signal Service Company. Inactivated 21 March 1946 in France. Redesignated 16 February 1953 as the 299th Signal Company and allotted to the Regular Army. Activated 25 March 1953 at Camp Gordon, Georgia. Inactivated 27 June 1955 at Camp Gordon, Georgia.

CAMPAIGN PARTICIPATION CREDIT

World War II
  Normandy (with arrowhead)
  Rhineland (with arrowhead)
  Ardennes-Alsace
  Central Europe

Vietnam
  Counteroffensive, Phase III
  Tet Counteroffensive
  Counteroffensive, Phase IV
  Counteroffensive, Phase V
  Counteroffensive, Phase VI
  Tet 69/Counteroffensive
  Summer–Fall 1969
  Winter–Spring 1970
  Sanctuary Counteroffensive
  Counteroffensive, Phase VII
  Consolidation I
  Consolidation II

Southwest Asia
    Defense of Saudi Arabia
    Liberation and Defense of Kuwait

DECORATIONS

Presidential Unit Citation (Army), Streamer embroidered NORMANDY (101st Airborne Signal Company cited; WD GO 89, 1944)

Presidential Unit Citation (Army), Streamer embroidered BASTOGNE (101st Airborne Division cited; WD GO 17, 1945)

Meritorious Unit Commendation (Army), Streamer embroidered VIETNAM 1968 (501st Signal Battalion cited; DA GO 39, 1970)

French Croix de Guerre with Palm, World War II, Streamer embroidered NORMANDY (101st Signal Company cited; DA GO 43, 1950)

Belgian Croix de Guerre 1940 with Palm, Streamer embroidered BASTOGNE; cited in the Order of the Day of the Belgian Army for action at Bastogne (101st Signal Company cited; DA GO 27, 1959)

Belgian Fourragere 1940 (101st Signal Company cited; DA GO 43, 1950)

Cited in the Order of the Day of the Belgian Army for action in France and Belgium (101st Signal Company cited: DA GO 43, 1950)

Netherlands Orange Lanyard (101st Signal Company cited; DA GO 43, 1950)

Republic of Vietnam Cross of Gallantry with Palm, Streamer embroidered VIETNAM 1968–1969 (501st Signal Battalion cited; DA GO 43, 1970)

Republic of Vietnam Cross of Gallantry with Palm, Streamer embroidered VIETNAM 1971 (501st Signal Battalion cited; DA GO 6, 1974)

Republic of Vietnam Civil Action Honor Medal, First Class, Streamer embroidered VIETNAM 1968–1970 (501st Signal Battalion cited; DA GO 48, 1971)

Company B additionally entitled to:

Republic of Vietnam Cross of Gallantry with Palm, Streamer embroidered VIETNAM 1968 (Company B, 501st Signal Battalion, cited; DA GO 21, 1969)

501st SIGNAL BATTALION BIBLIOGRAPHY

Ackerman, Robert K. "An Air Assault Division Leaps Forward." *Signal* 59 (September 2004): 23–26.

Benton, Lewis E., ed. *History of the 101st Airborne Division, 1942–1968*. Vietnam, 1968.

Bergen, John D. *Military Communications: A Test for Technology*. United States Army in Vietnam. Washington, D.C.: Center of Military History, United States Army, 1986.

Cole, Hugh M. *The Ardennes: Battle of the Bulge*. United States Army in World War II. Washington, D.C.: Office of the Chief of Military History, Department of the Army, 1965. 101st Airborne Division cited.

Harrison, Gordon A. *Cross-Channel Attack*. United States Army in World War II. Washington, D.C.: Office of the Chief of Military History, United States Army, 1951. 101st Airborne Division cited.

Jaeger, John F., et al. *History of the 101st Airborne Division, 1942–1964*. Fort Campbell, Ky.: 101st Airborne Division, 1964.

MacDonald, Charles B. *The Last Offensive*. United States Army in World War II. Washington, D.C.: Office of the Chief of Military History, United States Army, 1973. 101st Airborne Division cited.

──────. *The Siegfried Line Campaign*. United States Army in World War II. Washington, D.C.: Office of the Chief of Military History, Department of the Army, 1963. 101st Airborne Division cited.

Myer, Charles R. *Division-Level Communications, 1963–1973*. Vietnam Studies. Washington, D.C.: Department of the Army, 1982.

Pfefferman, Mark W. "Experimenting With an MSE End User Concept." *Army Communicator* 15 (Summer–Fall 1990): 34–36.

Raines, Rebecca Robbins. *Getting the Message Through: A Branch History of the U.S. Army Signal Corps*. Army Historical Series. Washington, D.C.: Center of Military History, United States Army, 1996. 101st Airborne Signal Company cited.

Rapport, Leonard, and Arthur Northwood, Jr. *Rendezvous with Destiny, A History of the 101st Airborne Division*. Washington, D.C.: Infantry Journal Press, 1948. Rev. ed. Greeneville, Tenn.: 101st Airborne Division Association, 1965.

Roberts, Arch E., et al. *"Screaming Eagles" 101st Airborne*. Nashville: Benson Printing Company, 1957.

Salerno, Dennis P., and Thomas F. Washer. "Air Assault Communications: Desert Storm." *Army Communicator* 16 (Fall–Winter 1991): 52–60.

Shapiro, Milton J. *The Screaming Eagles, The 101st Airborne Division in World War II*. New York: Messner, 1976.

Thompson, George Raynor, and Dixie R. Harris. *The Signal Corps: The Outcome (Mid-1943 through 1945)*. United States Army in World War II. Washington, D.C.: Office of the Chief of Military History, United States Army, 1966.

Tolson, John J. *Airmobility 1961–1971*. Vietnam Studies. Washington, D.C.: Department of the Army, 1973. 101st Airborne Division cited.

Washer, Thomas F., II, and Richard S. Gatewood. "Expanding the Division Communications Network on the Air-Assault Battlefield." *Army Communicator* 20 (Spring 1995): 15–18.

Washer, Tom. "High-Speed Multiplexing on the Air-Assault Battlefield." *Army Communicator* 24 (Spring 1999): 18.

HEADQUARTERS AND HEADQUARTERS DETACHMENT
503d SIGNAL BATTALION

HERALDIC ITEMS

None approved.

LINEAGE AND HONORS

LINEAGE

AR (inactive)

Constituted 7 July 1944 in the Army of the United States as Headquarters and Headquarters Detachment, 3212th Signal Service Battalion. Activated 8 August 1944 in Italy. Inactivated 30 September 1945 in Italy.

Redesignated 8 January 1947 as Headquarters and Headquarters Detachment, 503d Signal Service Battalion. Activated 31 December 1946 in Japan. Inactivated 15 March 1948 in Japan. Redesignated 28 July 1953 as Headquarters, 503d Signal Battalion, and allotted to the Army Reserve. Activated 31 August 1953 at Mobile, Alabama. Reorganized and redesignated 31 March 1955 as Headquarters and Headquarters Detachment, 503d Signal Battalion. Inactivated 15 January 1963 at Mobile, Alabama.

CAMPAIGN PARTICIPATION CREDIT

World War II
    Rome-Arno

DECORATIONS

None.

503d SIGNAL BATTALION BIBLIOGRAPHY

No published histories.

HEADQUARTERS AND HEADQUARTERS DETACHMENT
504th SIGNAL BATTALION

HERALDIC ITEMS

COAT OF ARMS

Shield: Per pale tenné and argent, a hand couped grasping a lightning flash fesswise emitting two flames arched to chief, all counterchanged, and in base four barrulets wavy of the like.

Crest: On a wreath of the colors argent and tenné a mural crown sable mortared of the first issuing flames or and gules, and a dexter hand proper grasping a lightning flash palewise azure.

Motto: THINK, GO, DO.

Symbolism: Orange and white are the colors traditionally associated with the Signal Corps. The shield is divided into two parts to represent the dual functions of the unit: supply and maintenance. The hand grasping the lightning flash symbolizes the mission of the unit. The flames denote the zeal and readiness of the organization to carry out its mission. The four wavy barrulets refer to Italy, Germany, Japan, and the United States, the four places of the unit's activation. The wavy barrulets also allude to the Arno River, the area in which the unit earned a battle honor for services during World War II.

The lightning flash, a symbol of the Signal Corps mission, represents the unit's World War II campaign in Italy. The mural crown further recalls European service during that war. The flames symbolize signal fires used in the past and refer to the worldwide conflict during which the unit saw distinguished service. The lightning flash denotes speedy response and is blue, alluding to modern electronics and telecommunications. Red stands for courage, yellow (gold) for excellence, and black for stability and strength.

DISTINCTIVE UNIT INSIGNIA

The distinctive unit insignia is the shield and motto of the coat of arms.

LINEAGE AND HONORS

LINEAGE

RA
(active)

Constituted 7 July 1944 in the Army of the United States as Headquarters and Headquarters Detachment, 3213th Signal Service Battalion. Activated 8 August 1944 in Italy. Inactivated 30 September 1945 in Italy.

Redesignated 31 December 1946 as Headquarters and Headquarters Detachment, 504th Signal Service Battalion, and activated in Japan. Inactivated 15 September 1948 in Japan. Redesignated 8 January 1952 as Headquarters, 504th Signal Service Battalion, and allotted to the Regular Army. Activated 15 February 1952 at Camp San Luis Obispo, California. Reorganized and redesignated 12 March 1953 as Headquarters, 504th Signal Battalion. Reorganized and redesignated 4 April 1955 as Headquarters and Headquarters Detachment, 504th Signal Battalion. Inactivated 15 December 1958 at Fort Huachuca, Arizona. Activated 10 March 1961 at Tobyhanna Signal Depot, Pennsylvania. Inactivated 14 September 1965 in Germany. Activated 16 April 1993 at Fort Huachuca, Arizona.

CAMPAIGN PARTICIPATION CREDIT

World War II
  Rome-Arno

DECORATIONS

Army Superior Unit Award, Streamer embroidered 1993–1994 (Headquarters and Headquarters Detachment, 504th Signal Battalion, cited; DA GO 1, 1996)

504th SIGNAL BATTALION BIBLIOGRAPHY

Ackerman, Robert K. "Tactical Signalers Learn to Pack Light, Travel Right." *Signal* 54 (April 2000): 37–39.

Ward, Jim. "Commo Support Worldwide." *Soldiers* 51 (November 1996): 46–47.

———. "Major Changes Arrive for Army Signal Command." *Army Communicator* 22 (Spring 1997): 16–17.

HEADQUARTERS AND HEADQUARTERS DETACHMENT 509th SIGNAL BATTALION

HERALDIC ITEMS

COAT OF ARMS

Shield: Argent, a lightning bolt barbed between two lightning bolts flory radiating from point tenné, and a chief arched sable.

Crest: On a wreath of the colors argent and tenné two demispears with bamboo shafts proper, all in front of an oriental dragon passant or, armed and langued gules, and garnished vert.

Motto: FACIEMUS FORTIUS (We Shall Act Bravely).

Symbolism: Orange and white are the colors traditionally associated with the Signal Corps. The fleurs-de-lis commemorate the two campaign honors awarded the battalion for service in Europe during World War II. The conjoined lightning bolts refer to the unit's coordination and swift communication capabilities, and the lightning bolt with arrowhead alludes to the organization's readiness and aggressive action. The arch alludes to the globe and represents the scope of the organization's worldwide mission. The colors black and white symbolize the night and day vigilance of the Signal Corps.

The two spears commemorate the two campaign honors the unit was awarded for service in Vietnam. The dragon symbolizes strength and vigilance.

DISTINCTIVE UNIT INSIGNIA

Description: A silver color metal and enamel device that consists of a demi-disc superimposed by three orange lightning bolts conjoined in base, the center bolt terminating in an arrowhead and either side bolt terminating in a demi-fleur-de-lis, all superimposed at the bottom by a black bipartite scroll inscribed FACIEMUS FORTIUS in silver letters.

Symbolism: Orange and white (silver) are the colors traditionally associated with the Signal Corps. The fleurs-de-lis commemorate the two campaign honors awarded the battalion for service in Europe during World War II. The conjoined lightning bolts refer to the unit's coordination and swift communication facilities, and the lightning bolt with arrowhead alludes to the organization's readiness and aggressive action. The hemisphere represents the battalion's widespread service.

LINEAGE AND HONORS

RA
(active)

LINEAGE

Constituted 11 December 1944 in the Army of the United States as Headquarters and Headquarters Detachment, 3906th Signal Service Battalion. Activated 17 January 1945 in France. Inactivated 31 August 1946 in the Ryukyus Islands.

Redesignated 27 June 1947 as Headquarters and Headquarters Detachment, 509th Signal Service Battalion. Activated 20 July 1947 in Korea. Inactivated 25 January 1949 in Korea. Redesignated 8 January 1952 as Headquarters, 509th Signal Service Battalion, and allotted to the Regular Army. Activated 15 February 1952 at Camp San Luis Obispo, California. Reorganized and redesignated 12 March 1953 as Headquarters, 509th Signal Battalion. Inactivated 3 December 1954 at Fort Sheridan, Illinois.

Redesignated 1 March 1963 as Headquarters and Headquarters Detachment, 509th Signal Battalion. Activated 25 March 1963 at Fort Chaffee, Arkansas. Inactivated 10 January 1968 in Vietnam. Activated 1 December 1976 in Italy.

CAMPAIGN PARTICIPATION CREDIT

World War II
  Rhineland
  Central Europe

Vietnam
  Counteroffensive, Phase II
  Counteroffensive, Phase III

DECORATIONS

None.

509th SIGNAL BATTALION BIBLIOGRAPHY

Bergen, John D. *Military Communications: A Test for Technology.* United States Army in Vietnam. Washington, D.C.: Center of Military History, United States Army, 1986.

Clements, Judith A. *The 509th Signal Battalion, A Unit History.* Camp Darby, Italy, 1978.

Fitzgerald, Peter. "509th Operations in Northern Iraq." *Army Communicator* 28 (Fall 2003): 3–4.

Page, Joseph T., Jr. "Communications-Italian Style." *Army Communicator* 3 (Spring 1978): 40–41.

511th SIGNAL BATTALION

HERALDIC ITEMS

None approved.

LINEAGE AND HONORS

RA
(11th Airborne Division) (inactive)

LINEAGE

Constituted 12 November 1942 in the Army of the United States as the 511th Airborne Signal Company and assigned to the 11th Airborne Division. Activated 25 February 1943 at Camp Mackall, North Carolina. Allotted 15 November 1948 to the Regular Army.

Reorganized and redesignated 1 March 1957 as Headquarters and Headquarters Detachment, 511th Signal Battalion (organic elements constituted 20 February 1957 and activated 1 March 1957 in Germany). Inactivated 1 July 1958 in Germany. Headquarters and Headquarters Detachment, 511th Signal Battalion, redesignated 1 February 1963 as Headquarters and Headquarters Company, 511th Signal Battalion. (Company A, 511th Signal Battalion, activated 7 February 1963 at Fort Bragg, North Carolina.) Headquarters and Headquarters Company, 511th Signal Battalion, activated 1 May 1964 at Fort Benning, Georgia. Battalion inactivated 30 June 1965 at Fort Benning, Georgia.

CAMPAIGN PARTICIPATION CREDIT

World War II
    New Guinea
    Leyte
    Luzon (with arrowhead)

DECORATIONS

Presidential Unit Citation (Army), Streamer embroidered LUZON (511th Airborne Signal Company cited; WD GO 71, 1945)

Philippine Presidential Unit Citation, Streamer embroidered 17 OCTOBER 1944 TO 4 JULY 1945 (511th Airborne Signal Company cited; DA GO 47, 1950)

511th SIGNAL BATTALION BIBLIOGRAPHY

"The Angels," A History of the 11th Airborne Division. N.p., c. 1963.

"The Angels in Action," 11th Airborne Infantry Division, Fort Campbell, Kentucky. Baton Rouge: Army and Navy Publishing Company, 1955.

Cannon, M. Hamlin. *Leyte: The Return to the Philippines*. United States Army in World War II. Washington, D.C.: Office of the Chief of Military History, Department of the Army, 1954. 11th Airborne Division cited.

11th Airborne Division. Atlanta: Albert Love Enterprises, 1944.

11th Airborne Division. Baton Rouge: Army and Navy Publishing Company, 1950.

11th Airborne Division, Fort Campbell, Kentucky. Dallas: Taylor Publishing Company, 1952.

Flanagan, Edward M., Jr. *The Angels. A History of the 11th Airborne Division*. Novato, Calif.: Presidio Press, 1989.

———. *The Angels: A History of the 11th Airborne Division, 1943–1946*. Washington, D.C.: Infantry Journal Press, 1948.

Pictorial Review of the 11th Airborne Division from Fort Campbell to Germany. Baton Rouge: Army and Navy Publishing Company, 1956.

Smith, Robert Ross. *Triumph in the Philippines*. United States Army in World War II. Washington, D.C.: Office of the Chief of Military History, Department of the Army, 1963.

523d SIGNAL BATTALION

HERALDIC ITEMS

COAT OF ARMS

Shield: Per fess rayonné tenné and azure, a pile argent bearing a fleur-de-lis of the second between in chief two ermine spots and in base as many fleurs-de-lis, all of the third.
Crest: None approved.
Motto: WHO DARES WINS.
Symbolism: Orange and white are the colors traditionally associated with the Signal Corps. Blue and white are the colors for Infantry. The rayonne per fess refers to the principle of a coordinated integral operation between the unit and the Infantry. The pile simulates a beam of light and symbolizes a continually open channel of information. The three fleurs-de-lis represent France and the honors awarded the organization for the Ardennes-Alsace, Northern France, and Normandy campaigns. The ermine spots relate to Europe and are used to represent the Central Europe and Rhineland campaigns during World War II.

DISTINCTIVE UNIT INSIGNIA

The distinctive unit insignia is the shield and motto of the coat of arms.

LINEAGE AND HONORS

RA
(23d Infantry Division) (inactive)

LINEAGE

Constituted 29 February 1944 in the Army of the United States as the 3132d Signal Service Company. Activated 1 March 1944 at Pine Camp, New York. Inactivated 25 September 1945 at Pine Camp, New York.

Redesignated 31 July 1951 as the 503d Signal Radio Operation Company and allotted to the Regular Army. Activated 15 September 1951 at Camp Cooke, California. Reorganized and redesignated 15 January 1953 as the 503d Signal Company. Inactivated 20 October 1953 in Germany.

Redesignated 1 December 1954 as the 123d Signal Company. Assigned 2 December 1954 to the 23d Infantry Division and activated at Fort Clayton, Canal Zone. Inactivated 10 April 1956 at Fort Clayton, Canal Zone. Relieved 8 April 1960 from assignment to the 23d Infantry Division. Activated 25 April 1960 in Korea. Inactivated 1 January 1966 in Korea.

Redesignated 10 January 1968 as Headquarters and Headquarters Detachment, 523d Signal Battalion; concurrently assigned to the 23d Infantry Division and activated in Vietnam (organic elements concurrently constituted and activated in Vietnam). Inactivated 30 November 1971 at Fort Lewis, Washington. Activated 16 September 1993 in Germany. Inactivated 15 September 1994 in Germany.

CAMPAIGN PARTICIPATION CREDIT

World War II
  Normandy
  Northern France
  Rhineland
  Ardennes-Alsace
  Central Europe

Vietnam
  Counteroffensive, Phase III
  Tet Counteroffensive
  Counteroffensive, Phase IV
  Counteroffensive, Phase V
  Counteroffensive, Phase VI
  Tet 69/Counteroffensive
  Summer–Fall 1969
  Winter–Spring 1970
  Sanctuary Counteroffensive
  Counteroffensive, Phase VII
  Consolidation I

DECORATIONS

Republic of Vietnam Cross of Gallantry with Palm, Streamer embroidered VIETNAM 1969, 1970 (523d Signal Battalion cited; DA GO 42, 1972)

Headquarters and Headquarters Detachment additionally entitled to:

Republic of Vietnam Cross of Gallantry with Palm, Streamer embroidered VIETNAM 1971 (Headquarters and Headquarters Detachment, 523d Signal Battalion, cited; DA GO 6, 1974)

523d SIGNAL BATTALION BIBLIOGRAPHY

Rienzi, Thomas M. *Communications-Electronics, 1962–1970.* Vietnam Studies. Washington, D.C.: Department of the Army, 1972.
Walker, Joseph H., ed. *The Americal Division.* Vietnam, 1970.

551st SIGNAL BATTALION

HERALDIC ITEMS

COAT OF ARMS

Shield: Argent, on a pile tenné a bell of the first; two flaunches of the second, fretty of the field.

Crest: On a wreath of the colors argent and tenné a sea lion or gorged with a collar barry of three—azure, argent, and gules—and grasping in dexter claw a lightning bolt barbed palewise celeste.

Motto: VIDEO ET MONEO (I Watch and Warn).

Symbolism: Orange and white are the colors traditionally associated with the Signal Corps. The wedge-shaped pile is symbolic of the driving force of the organization, and the bell represents contact. The V-shaped pile is also symbolic of victory; the interlacing or grill on each side represents the former plotting functions of the organization.

The sea lion, adapted from the Philippine presidential flag, commemorates the unit's campaign participation in the Philippines during World War II, and the collar reflects the colors of the Philippine Presidential Unit Citation as well as our national colors. Electronic capabilities are represented by the lightning bolt, whose barbs allude to combat readiness. The light blue color refers to the South Seas and the geographical area of the Philippines.

DISTINCTIVE UNIT INSIGNIA

The distinctive unit insignia is the shield and motto of the coat of arms.

LINEAGE AND HONORS

TRADOC
(active)

LINEAGE

Constituted 10 December 1941 in the Army of the United States as the 551st Signal Aircraft Warning Battalion, Separate. Activated 15 December 1941 at Fort Dix, New Jersey. Redesignated 12 December 1942 as the 551st Signal Aircraft Warning Battalion. Inactivated 1 February 1946 in the Philippine Islands.

Redesignated 23 September 1986 as the 551st Signal Battalion and allotted to the Regular Army. Headquarters concurrently transferred to the United States Army Training and Doctrine Command and activated at Fort Gordon, Georgia.

LINEAGES AND HERALDIC DATA

CAMPAIGN PARTICIPATION CREDIT

World War II
    Northern Solomons
    Leyte
    Southern Philippines

DECORATIONS

Philippine Presidential Unit Citation, Streamer embroidered 17 OCTOBER 1944 TO 4 JULY 1945 (551st Signal Air Warning Battalion cited; DA GO 47, 1950)

Company A additionally entitled to:

Army Superior Unit Award, Streamer embroidered 1999–2000 (Company A, 551st Signal Battalion, cited; DA GO 29, 2001)

551st SIGNAL BATTALION BIBLIOGRAPHY

No published histories.

560th SIGNAL BATTALION

HERALDIC ITEMS

COAT OF ARMS

Shield: Per fess enhanced dancetté of two argent and tenné, in chief a cross throughout vert (bottle green), and in base issuant from a nucleus five broad lightning flashes form an inverted pentagon of the first.

Crest: None approved.

Motto: COPIAS CONJUNGE (Link the Forces).

Symbolism: Orange and white are the colors traditionally associated with the Signal Corps. The five lightning flashes allude to the mission of the unit, the sending and receiving of messages, and also represent the five battle honors awarded the unit for service in the European Theater during World War II. The dancetté of two refers to the Alps and the Apennines, areas of operations during World War II. The cross represents an airstrip and alludes to the aviation element in the former mission of the battalion. The color green, from the flag of the Italian Republic, is symbolic of the unity of purpose of the battalion and Italian forces in the common goal of preserving and defending liberty and freedom.

DISTINCTIVE UNIT INSIGNIA

The distinctive unit insignia is the shield and motto of the coat of arms.

LINEAGE AND HONORS

TRADOC
(inactive)

LINEAGE

Constituted 28 February 1942 in the Army of the United States as the 560th Signal Aircraft Warning Battalion, Separate. Activated 14 June 1942 at Drew Field, Florida. Reorganized and redesignated 14 March 1943 as the 560th Signal Aircraft Warning Battalion. Disbanded 31 January 1945 in Italy.

Reconstituted 4 August 1945 in the Army of the United States as the 560th Signal Aircraft Warning Battalion. Redesignated 25 October 1961 as the 560th Signal Battalion and allotted to the Regular Army. Activated 15 November 1961 in Italy. Inactivated 18 March 1971 in Italy.

Headquarters transferred 30 June 1987 to the United States Army Training and Doctrine Command and activated at Lowry Air Force Base, Colorado. Inactivated 30 September 1992 at Lowry Air Force Base, Colorado.

CAMPAIGN PARTICIPATION CREDIT

World War II
    Tunisia
    Naples-Foggia
    Rome-Arno
    Southern France
    North Apennines

DECORATIONS

Air Force Outstanding Unit Award, Streamer embroidered 1989 (560th Signal Battalion cited; DA GO 8, 1991)

560th SIGNAL BATTALION BIBLIOGRAPHY

Thompson, George Raynor, Dixie R. Harris, Pauline M. Oakes, and Dulany Terrett. *The Signal Corps: The Test (December 1941 to July 1943)*. United States Army in World War II. Washington, D.C.: Office of the Chief of Military History, Department of the Army, 1957.

711th SIGNAL BATTALION

HERALDIC ITEMS

COAT OF ARMS

Shield: Tenné, on a saltire argent a lightning flash and arrow, point up, crossed saltirewise gules.

Crest: That for the regiments and separate battalions of the Alabama Army National Guard: On a wreath of the colors argent and tenné a slip of cotton plant with full bursting boll proper.

Motto: SMASH TO THE STARS.

Symbolism: Orange and white are the colors traditionally associated with the Signal Corps. The saltire taken from the state flag of Alabama alludes to the Confederate flag and symbolizes the organization's Civil War service. The arrow refers to the unit's service in the Indian Wars against the Creeks, and the lightning flash is a symbol of celerity and force.

DISTINCTIVE UNIT INSIGNIA

The distinctive unit insignia is the shield and motto of the coat of arms.

LINEAGE AND HONORS

ARNG
(Alabama)

LINEAGE

Organized in 1836 at Mobile as the Mobile Artillery Company (also known as the Alabama Artillery and the Alabama State Artillery). Mustered into Federal service in 1836 at Mobile as an element of Colonel Smith's Regiment of Alabama Mounted Volunteers; mustered out of Federal service 27 July 1836 at Mobile and continued as an independent volunteer company. Mustered into Federal service 23 May 1846 at Mobile as an element of Colonel J.M. Withers' 1st Alabama Volunteers; mustered out of Federal service 16 June 1846 at Mobile and continued as an independent volunteer company.

Mustered into Confederate service 4 May 1861 at Mobile as Ketchum's Battery, Alabama State Artillery. (While in Confederate service Alabama State Artillery expanded to battalion size.) Surrendered 4 May 1865 with the Army of the Department of Alabama, Mississippi, and East Louisiana.

Reorganized in July 1872 in the Alabama Volunteer Militia at Mobile as the State Artillery Company. (Alabama Volunteer Militia redesignated 9 February 1877 as Alabama State Troops.) Redesignated in 1887 as Battery A, Field Artillery. Redesignated about 1894 as Battery A, 1st Artillery Battalion. (Alabama State Troops redesignated 18 February 1897 as the Alabama National Guard.) Reorganized and redesignated 14 January 1908 as Company A, Coast Artillery Battalion. Mustered out of state service 28 February 1910.

LINEAGES AND HERALDIC DATA

Reconstituted 9 January 1947 in the Alabama National Guard as the 711th Antiaircraft Artillery Gun Battalion; concurrently organized and federally recognized with Headquarters at Mobile. Ordered into active Federal service 4 September 1950 at home stations; released 3 September 1952 from active Federal service and reverted to state control. Redesignated 1 October 1953 as the 711th Antiaircraft Artillery Battalion.

Converted and redesignated 2 May 1959 as the 711th Signal Battalion. Ordered into active Federal service 15 October 1961 at home stations; released 5 August 1962 from active Federal service and reverted to state control. Ordered into active Federal service 11 June 1963 at home stations; released 16 June 1963 from active Federal service and reverted to state control. Ordered into active Federal service 10 September 1963 at home stations; released 12 September 1963 from active Federal service and reverted to state control. Redesignated 1 February 1972 as the 711th Command Signal Operations Battalion. Redesignated 1 March 1974 as the 711th Signal Battalion.

Home Area: Southwestern Alabama

CAMPAIGN PARTICIPATION CREDIT

Indian Wars
  Creeks

Civil War (Confederate service)
  Shiloh
  Murfreesborough
  Chickamauga
  Chattanooga
  Atlanta
  Franklin
  Nashville
  Kentucky 1862
  Mississippi 1862
  Alabama 1865

Headquarters Company (Mobile) additionally entitled to:

World War II-AP
  New Guinea (with arrowhead)

Company B (Grove Hill) additionally entitled to:

World War II-EAME
  Anzio
  Naples-Foggia
  Rome-Arno
  Southern France (with arrowhead)
  Rhineland
  Ardennes-Alsace
  Central Europe

Company C (Foley) additionally entitled to:

World War II-AP
New Guinea
Southern Philippines

DECORATIONS

Company C (Foley) entitled to:

Meritorious Unit Commendation (Army), Streamer embroidered PACIFIC THEATER (31st Quartermaster Company cited; GO 26, 31st Infantry Division, 2 February 1945)

Philippine Presidential Unit Citation, Streamer embroidered 17 OCTOBER 1944 TO 4 JULY 1945 (31st Quartermaster Company cited; DA GO 47, 1950)

711th SIGNAL BATTALION BIBLIOGRAPHY

Alabama in the Civil War. Montgomery: State Department of Archives and History, 1963.

Bergeron, Arthur W., Jr. *Confederate Mobile*. Jackson: University Press of Mississippi, 1991.

Brewer, Willis. *Alabama, Her History, Resources, War Record, and Public Record from 1540–1872*. Montgomery: Barrett and Brown, Printers, 1872.

Downey, Fairfax. *Indian Wars of the U.S. Army (1776–1865)*. Garden City, New York: Doubleday and Company, Inc., 1963.

History of the 31st Infantry Division in Training and Combat, 1940–1945. Baton Rouge: Army and Navy Publishing Company, 1946.

Pumpey, Sherman L. *Muster Lists of Alabama Confederate Troops*. 3 vols. Independence, Calif.: Historical and Genealogical Publishing Company, 1965.

"Riot Reaction Force: The Guard in the April Disorders." *National Guardsman* 22 (May 1968): 2–16.

711th AAA Gun Battalion, Camp Stewart, Georgia, 1951. Baton Rouge: Army and Navy Publishing Company, 1951.

Toland, Ray B. "Training to the Army Standard." *Army Communicator* 9 (Winter 1984): 13–14.

Utley, Robert M., and Wilcomb E. Washburn. *The American Heritage History of the Indian Wars*. New York: American Heritage Publishing Company, 1977.

HEADQUARTERS AND HEADQUARTERS DETACHMENT
835th SIGNAL BATTALION

HERALDIC ITEMS

None approved.

LINEAGE AND HONORS

LINEAGE

AR (inactive)

Constituted 13 February 1942 in the Army of the United States as the 835th Signal Service Company. Activated 17 February 1942 at Fort DuPont, Delaware. Redesignated 18 February 1943 as the 835th Signal Service Battalion. Inactivated 28 April 1946 in India.

Redesignated 18 October 1950 as Headquarters, 835th Signal Service Battalion, and allotted to the Organized Reserve Corps. Activated 9 November 1950 at Fort Myer, Virginia. (Organized Reserve Corps redesignated 9 July 1952 as the Army Reserve.) Reorganized and redesignated 11 June 1953 as Headquarters, 835th Signal Battalion. Reorganized and redesignated 27 June 1955 as Headquarters and Headquarters Detachment, 835th Signal Battalion. Location changed 1 December 1960 to Riverdale, Maryland. Inactivated 28 February 1963 at Riverdale, Maryland.

CAMPAIGN PARTICIPATION CREDIT

World War II
Asiatic-Pacific Theater, Streamer without inscription

DECORATIONS

None.

835th SIGNAL BATTALION BIBLIOGRAPHY

Hawkins, John, and Ward Hawkins. *History of the 835th Signal Service Battalion, 1942–1946.* N.p., n.d.

Hunter, Charles N. *GALAHAD.* San Antonio: Naylor Company, 1963.

Romanus, Charles F., and Riley Sunderland. *Stilwell's Mission to China.* United States Army in World War II. Washington, D.C.: Office of the Chief of Military History, Department of the Army, 1953.

Thompson, George Raynor, and Dixie R. Harris. *The Signal Corps: The Outcome (Mid-1943 through 1945).* United States Army in World War II. Washington, D.C.: Office of the Chief of Military History, United States Army, 1966.

Thompson, George Raynor, Dixie R. Harris, Pauline M. Oakes, and Dulany Terrett. *The Signal Corps: The Test (December 1941 to July 1943).* United States Army in World War II. Washington, D.C.: Office of the Chief of Military History, Department of the Army, 1957.

HEADQUARTERS AND HEADQUARTERS DETACHMENT 845th SIGNAL BATTALION

HERALDIC ITEMS

COAT OF ARMS

Shield: Per saltire argent and sable, two lightning bolts in saltire tenné between in chief a stylized magnolia blossom leaved of three proper and in base a crescent vert.

Crest: That for the regiments and separate battalions of the Army Reserve: On a wreath of the colors argent and tenné the Lexington Minuteman proper. The statue of the Minuteman Capt. John Parker (H. H. Kitson, sculptor) stands on the Common in Lexington, Massachusetts.

Motto: None approved.

Symbolism: Orange is a color traditionally associated with the Signal Corps. The crossed lightning bolts symbolize the unit's ability to readily provide support with signal communications facilities. The three magnolia leaves and blossom, the state flower of Mississippi, represent the 845th Signal Battalion's home area of Pascagoula, Mississippi, and its assignment at one time to the Third Army. The crescent, a symbol of North Africa, refers to the unit's campaign service in North Africa during World War II. The colors black and white allude to day and night alertness.

DISTINCTIVE UNIT INSIGNIA

The distinctive unit insignia is an adaptation of the shield of the coat of arms.

LINEAGE AND HONORS

AR
(active)

LINEAGE

Constituted 7 October 1942 in the Army of the United States as the 845th Signal Service Battalion. Activated 1 November 1942 at Camp Crowder, Missouri. Inactivated 7 March 1944 in North Africa.

Headquarters and Headquarters Company, 845th Signal Service Battalion, redesignated 2 May 1952 as Headquarters and Headquarters Company, 845th Signal Support Battalion, and allotted to the Organized Reserve Corps. Activated 15 May 1952 at Hopkinsville, Kentucky. (Organized Reserve Corps redesignated 9 July 1952 as the Army Reserve.) Reorganized and redesignated 28 October 1953 as Headquarters and Headquarters Detachment, 845th Signal Battalion. Inactivated

5 February 1954 at Hopkinsville, Kentucky. Activated 9 September 1955 at Pascagoula, Mississippi.

CAMPAIGN PARTICIPATION CREDIT

World War II
European-African-Middle Eastern Theater, Streamer without inscription

DECORATIONS

None.

845th SIGNAL BATTALION BIBLIOGRAPHY

No published histories.

HEADQUARTERS AND HEADQUARTERS DETACHMENT
850th SIGNAL BATTALION

HERALDIC ITEMS

COAT OF ARMS

Shield: Argent, a conventionalized sphinx sejant tenné charged on the body with a lightning flash or.
Crest: None approved.
Motto: SPEED, SOLIDARITY, SUPERIORITY.
Symbolism: Orange and white are the colors traditionally associated with the Signal Corps. The lightning flash represents the signal functions of the organization, and the sphinx symbolizes omniscience and secrecy.

DISTINCTIVE UNIT INSIGNIA

The distinctive unit insignia is a modification of the shield of the coat of arms.

LINEAGE AND HONORS

LINEAGE

AR
(inactive)

Constituted 26 May 1942 in the Army of the United States as the 850th Signal Service Battalion. Activated 25 August 1942 at Camp Crowder, Missouri. Inactivated 30 September 1945 in Italy.

Headquarters and Headquarters Company, 850th Signal Service Battalion, redesignated 4 December 1952 as Headquarters, 850th Signal Service Battalion, and allotted to the Army Reserve. Activated 1 January 1953 at Spartanburg, South Carolina. Reorganized and redesignated 31 March 1953 as Headquarters, 850th Signal Battalion. Reorganized and redesignated 31 March 1955 as Headquarters and Headquarters Detachment, 850th Signal Battalion. Location changed 31 October 1957 to Clemson, South Carolina. Inactivated 15 January 1963 at Clemson, South Carolina.

CAMPAIGN PARTICIPATION CREDIT

World War II
    Rome-Arno

DECORATIONS

Meritorious Unit Commendation (Army), Streamer embroidered EUROPEAN THEATER (Headquarters and Headquarters Company, 850th Signal Service Battalion, cited; GO 139, Mediterranean Theater of Operations, 29 November 1944)

850th SIGNAL BATTALION BIBLIOGRAPHY

No published histories.

HEADQUARTERS AND HEADQUARTERS DETACHMENT 980th SIGNAL BATTALION

HERALDIC ITEMS

None approved.

LINEAGE AND HONORS

AR
(inactive)

LINEAGE

Constituted 6 December 1943 in the Army of the United States as the 980th Signal Service Company. Activated 15 December 1943 at Fort Monmouth, New Jersey. Inactivated 20 January 1946 at Camp Anza, California.

Redesignated 16 July 1947 as the 980th Signal Long Lines Company and allotted to the Organized Reserves. Activated 1 August 1947 at Nashville, Tennessee. (Organized Reserves redesignated 25 March 1948 as the Organized Reserve Corps; redesignated 9 July 1952 as the Army Reserve.) Reorganized and redesignated 1 December 1950 as the 980th Signal Operations Company. Reorganized and redesignated 1 May 1952 as the 980th Signal Support Company.

Reorganized and redesignated 30 September 1953 as Headquarters, 980th Signal Battalion. Reorganized and redesignated 31 March 1955 as Headquarters and Headquarters Detachment, 980th Signal Battalion. Inactivated 15 January 1963 at Nashville, Tennessee.

CAMPAIGN PARTICIPATION CREDIT

World War II
    Normandy
    Northern France
    Rhineland
    Ardennes-Alsace
    Central Europe

DECORATIONS

Meritorious Unit Commendation (Army), Streamer embroidered EUROPEAN THEATER 1944 (980th Signal Service Company cited; GO 52, Communications Zone, European Theater of Operations, 12 April 1945)

Meritorious Unit Commendation (Army), Streamer embroidered EUROPEAN THEATER 1944–1945 (980th Signal Service Company cited; GO 143, Communications Zone, U.S. Forces, European Theater, 23 July 1945)

980th SIGNAL BATTALION BIBLIOGRAPHY

Thompson, George Raynor, and Dixie R. Harris. *The Signal Corps: The Outcome (Mid-1943 through 1945)*. United States Army in World War II. Washington, D.C.: Office of the Chief of Military History, United States Army, 1966.

Glossary of Lineage Terms

ACTIVATE. To transfer a constituted Regular Army or Army Reserve unit from the inactive to the active rolls of the United States Army. The unit is usually stationed at a specific location and assigned personnel and equipment at this time; however, a unit may be active at zero strength—that is, without personnel or equipment. This term was not used before 1921. It is never used when referring to National Guard units, and only since World War II has it been used in connection with Army Reserve units (*See also* ORGANIZE.)

ALLOT. To allocate a unit to one of the components of the United States Army. The present components are the Regular Army (RA), the Army National Guard (ARNG), and the Army Reserve (AR), formerly known as the Organized Reserves and the Organized Reserve Corps. During World War I, units were also allotted to the National Army, and during World War II to the Army of the United States. An Army National Guard unit is usually further allotted to a particular state or group of states. A unit may be withdrawn from any component except the Army National Guard and allotted to another. The new allotment, however, does not change the history, lineage, and honors of the unit.

ASSIGN. To make a unit part of a larger organization and place it under that organization's command and control until it is relieved from the assignment. As a rule, only assignments to divisions and separate combined arms brigades are shown in unit lineages.

CONSOLIDATE. To merge two or more units into a single unit. The unit may retain the designation of one of the former units or have a new designation, but it inherits the history, lineage, and honors of all of the units affected by the merger. Active as well as inactive units may be consolidated.

CONSTITUTE. To place the designation of a new unit on the official rolls of the United States Army.

CONVERT. To transfer a unit from one branch of the Army to another—for example, from signal to military intelligence. Such a change always requires a redesignation; however, there is no break in the historical continuity of the unit. Active as well as inactive units may be converted; but if the unit is active, it must also be reorganized under a new table of organization and equipment (TOE).

DEMOBILIZE. To remove the designation of a unit from the rolls of the Army. If the unit is active, it must also be inactivated. This term is used in unit lineages only when referring to the period during and immediately after World War I. (For other periods see Disband)

DESIGNATION. The official name of a unit, consisting usually of a number, a branch or function, and a command echelon; for example, 5th Signal Command. Additional descriptive terms may appear in parentheses, but such parenthetical identifiers are not part of the unit's official designation.

DISBAND. To remove the designation of a Regular Army or Army Reserve unit from the official rolls of the United States Army. If the unit is active, it must also be inactivated. Disbandment is intended to be permanent and irreversible, except in extraordinary circumstances.

ELEMENT. A unit that is assigned to or is part of a larger organization. (*See also ORGANIC ELEMENT.*)

FEDERALLY RECOGNIZE. To accept an Army National Guard unit into the force structure of the United States Army after the unit has been inspected by a Federal representative and found to be properly stationed, organized, and equipped in accordance with Army requirements.

FEDERAL SERVICE. Active duty of an Army National Guard unit while under the control of the United States government, rather than the control of its home state. Units enter federal service by order of the president of the United States, as authorized by Congress. For most wars prior to World War I, units were *mustered into federal service*, and during World War I they were *drafted into federal service*. The phrase *inducted into federal service* was used during World War II. Since World War II, the phrase *ordered into active federal service* has been used. A unit remains in federal service until released by the federal government, at which time it reverts to the control of its home state.

INACTIVATE. To place a Regular Army or Army Reserve unit not currently needed in the force structure in an inoperative status without assigned personnel or equipment for a limited period of time. The unit is transferred to the inactive rolls of the United States Army, but can be activated again whenever needed. Upon reactivation, the unit retains its former history, lineage, and honors. The term *inactivate* has been used only since 1921. Before that time, units remained active, were consolidated with other units, or were removed from the rolls of the Army.

NATIONAL GUARD OF THE UNITED STATES (NGUS). As used in this volume, an NGUS unit was a temporary organization within a state that took the place of a unit in Federal service during the Korean War. It usually had the same designation and was organized in the same general area as the replaced unit.

ORDER INTO ACTIVE FEDERAL SERVICE. To place an Army National Guard unit on full-time active duty under the control of the United States government. The unit remains in federal service until released by the federal government, at which time it reverts to the control of its home state or states.

ORDER INTO ACTIVE MILITARY SERVICE. To place an Army Reserve unit on full-time active duty, usually during a war or a crisis. After completing its active duty, the unit may be inactivated or it may be released from active military service, reverting to reserve status. This term does not apply to Army Reserve units on annual active duty for training.

ORGANIC ELEMENT. A unit that is an integral part of a larger organization; for example, a lettered company of a battalion.

ORGANIZE. To assign personnel and equipment to a unit and make it operative—that is, capable of performing its mission. For Army National Guard units, this term is used instead of ACTIVATE (*see above*).

RECONSTITUTE. To restore to the official rolls of the United States Army a unit that has been disbanded, demobilized, or had its Federal recognition withdrawn. The reconstituted unit may have a new designation, but retains its former history, lineage, and honors.

REDESIGNATE. To change a unit's official name. Active as well as inactive units may be redesignated, but personnel and equipment of an active unit are not changed

GLOSSARY OF LINEAGE TERMS

unless the unit is reorganized at the same time. Redesignation is a change of name only; the unit's history, lineage, and honors remain the same. (*See also* CONVERT)

REORGANIZE. To change the structure of a unit in accordance with a new table of organization and equipment (TOE) within the same branch of the Army. When referring to the Army National Guard, this term also means to organize an inactive unit again. (*See also* CONVERT *for reorganizations involving a new branch.*)

SPECIAL DESIGNATION. An official unit nickname. There are two types of special designations—a traditional designation (one that a unit has used continuously for the last thirty years or more) and a distinctive designation (one that a unit has used for less than thirty years or one with which a unit wishes to be associated). The special designation, if any, appears in parentheses after the unit's official designation. It should not be confused with a unit's motto, which is part of its heraldic items.

WITHDRAW FEDERAL RECOGNITION. To remove the designation of an Army National Guard unit from the official rolls of the United States Army. Federal recognition is withdrawn when the unit no longer meets Army requirements or is no longer needed in the force structure.

Signal Corps Unit Index

Airborne Signal Battalions
    112th: 223
    501st: 379
Airborne Signal Companies
    82d. *See* Signal Battalion, 82d, 195.
    101st. *See* Signal Battalion, 501st, 379.
    511th. *See* Signal Battalion, 511th, 388.
    512th. *See* Signal Battalion, 112th, 223.
Aircraft Warning Battalions (World War II)
    551st. *See* Signal Battalion, 551st, 392.
    560th. *See* Signal Battalion, 560th, 394.
Antiaircraft Artillery Battalions
    104th (Alabama National Guard, 1947–1954). *See* Signal Battalion, 115th, 227.
    121st (Nevada National Guard, 1943–1945). *See* Signal Battalion, 422d, 363.
    156th (Delaware National Guard, 1949–1959). *See* Signal Battalion, 198th, 296.
    193d (Delaware National Guard, 1949–1959). *See* Signal Battalion, 198th, 296.
    278th (Alabama National Guard, 1953–1959). *See* Signal Battalion, 115th, 227.
    279th (South Carolina National Guard, 1951–1959). *See* Signal Battalion, 279th, 319.
    280th (Delaware National Guard, 1956–1959). *See* Signal Battalions, 198th and 280th, 296, 322.
    421st (Nevada National Guard, 1949–1959). *See* Signal Battalion, 422d, 363.
    711th (Alabama National Guard, 1947–1959). *See* Signal Battalion, 711th, 396.
    736th (Delaware National Guard, 1944–1959). *See* Signal Battalion, 198th, 296.
    945th (Delaware National Guard, 1944–1949; 1956–1959). *See* Signal Battalion,198th, 296.
        Battery B (1946–1949). *See* Signal Battalion, 280th, 322.
        Headquarters Battery (1949–1956) *See* Signal Battalion, 280th, 322
Antiaircraft Artillery Brigades
    68th (Delaware National Guard, 1943–1946). *See* Signal Brigade, 261st, 58.
    261st (Delaware National Guard, 1946–1970). *See* Signal Brigade, 261st, 58.
Antiaircraft Artillery Detachments
    179th (Illinois National Guard). *See* Signal Battalion, 133d, 254.
    286th (Delaware National Guard, 1953–1956). *See* Signal Battalions, 198th and 280th, 296, 322.
Antiaircraft Artillery Group
    198th, Headquarters and Headquarters Battery (1944–1959). *See* Signal Battalion, 198th, 296.
Antiaircraft Balloon Battalions
    313th (1944). *See* Signal Battalion, 307th, 331.
    316th (1943–1944) *See* Signal Battalion, 306th, 329.

Armored Cavalry Regiment
    116th, Headquarters Troop, 3d Squadron (Nevada National Guard,
        1967–1972). *See* Signal Battalion, 422d, 363.
Armored Ordnance Battalion
    748th (Florida National Guard, 1952–1959). *See* Signal Battalion, 146th, 277.
Armored Signal Companies
    50th (New Jersey National Guard, 1946-1959). *See* Signal Battalion, 250th, 316.
    141st (1941-1957). *See* Signal Battalion, 141st, 267.
    142d (1941-1957). *See* Signal Battalion, 142d, 270.
    143d (1941-1957). *See* Signal Battalion, 143d, 273.
    144th (1941-1957). *See* Signal Battalion, 144th, 275.
Army National Guard Units
    28th Signal Battalion (Pennsylvania): 112
    105th Signal Battalion (South Carolina): 217
    115th Signal Battalion (Alabama): 227
    129th Signal Battalion (Maryland): 252
    133d Signal Battalion (Illinois): 254
    134th Signal Battalion (Minnesota): 257
    135th Signal Battalion (Missouri and Nebraska): 260
    142d Signal Brigade (Alabama): 51
    136th Signal Battalion (Texas): 263
    138th Signal Battalion (Indiana): 265
    146th Signal Battalion (Florida): 277
    151st Signal Battalion (South Carolina): 279
    156th Signal Battalion (Michigan): 283
    198th Signal Battalion (Delaware): 296
    212th Signal Battalion (Arkansas): 304
    228th Signal Brigade (South Carolina): 55
    230th Signal Battalion (Tennessee and New York): 306
    234th Signal Battalion (Iowa): 308
    240th Signal Battalion (California): 311
    249th Signal Battalion (Texas): 314
    250th Signal Battalion (New Jersey): 316
    261st Signal Brigade (Delaware): 58
    279th Signal Battalion (Alabama): 319
    280th Signal Battalion (Delaware and Connecticut): 322
    417th Signal Battalion (Florida): 359
    422d Signal Battalion (Nevada): 363
    711th Signal Battalion (Alabama): 396
Artillery Regiments
    Alabama Artillery (from 1836). *See* Signal Battalion, 711th, 396.
    1st Field, Service Battery (Minnesota National Guard, 1919–1921). *See* Signal
        Battalion, 134th, 257.
    151st Field, Service Battery (Minnesota National Guard, 1921–1940). *See*
        Signal Battalion, 134th, 257.
    198th (Delaware National Guard, 1921–1924; 1959–1970). *See* Signal Battalion,
        198th, 296. *See also* Coast Artillery Units, 198th; Signal Battalion, 280th, 322.

UNIT INDEX

Artillery Regiments—Continued
    206th, Company H (World War II). *See* Signal Battalion, 212th, Company A, 304.
    221st (Nevada National Guard, 1959–1967). *See* Signal Battalion, 422d, 363.
    278th, 1st Automatic Weapons Battalion (Alabama National Guard, 1959). *See* Signal Battalion, 115th, 227.

Cavalry Reconnaissance Squadron
    102d. *See* Signal Battalion, 250th, Company C, 316.

Coast Artillery Units
    21st Coast Artillery Battalion, Battery D (World War II). *See* Signal Battalion, 280th, 322.
    121st Separate Coast Artillery Battalion, Headquarters Battery (Nevada National Guard, 1941–1943). *See* Signal Battalion, 422d, 363.
    198th Coast Artillery regiment (Delaware National Guard, 1924–1944). *See* Signal Battalion, 198th, 296.
    261st Coast Artillery Battalion/261st Coast Artillery regiment ((Delaware National Guard, 1925–1944). *See* Signal Battalions, 198th and 280th, 296, 322.
    279th Coast Artillery Battalion (1944–1945). *See* Signal Battalion, 279th, 319.
    313th Barrage Balloon Battalion (1942–1944). *See* Signal Battalion, 307th, 331.
    316th Barrage Balloon Battalion (1942–1943). *See* Signal Battalion, 306th, 329.
    318th Balloon Battalion (1942–1944). *See* Signal Battalion, 78th, 193.
    261st Coast Artillery Battalion, Battery B (Delaware National Guard, 1936–1940). *See* Signal Battalion, 280th, 322.
    261st Coast Artillery, Battery B (Delaware National Guard, 1940–1944). *See* Signal Battalion, 280th, 322.
    316th Coast Artillery Barrage Balloon Battalion (1942–1943). *See* Signal Battalion, 306th, 329.

Constabulary Unit
    97th Constabulary Signal Squadron (1946–1950). *See* Signal Battalion, 97th, 206.

Delaware Regiment (Continental Army). *See* Signal Battalion, 198th, 296.

Divisions (signal units assigned to)
    1st Armored. *See* Signal Battalion, 141st, 267.
    1st Cavalry. *See* Signal Battalion, 13th, 96.
    1st Expeditionary (1917). *See* Signal Battalion, 121st, 229.
    1st Infantry. *See* Signal Battalion, 121st, 229.
    2d Armored. *See* Signal Battalion, 142d, 270.
    2d Infantry. *See* Signal Battalion, 122d, 234.
    3d Armored *See* Signal Battalion, 143d, 273.
    3d Infantry. *See* Signal Battalion, 123d, 238.
    4th Armored. *See* Signal Battalion, 144th, 275.
    4th Infantry
        1917–1939. *See* Signal Battalion, 4th. 79.
        since 1940. *See* Signal Battalion, 124th, 241.
    5th Infantry. *See* Signal Battalion, 5th, 81.
    6th Infantry. *See* Signal Battalion, 6th, 83.
    7th Infantry. *See* Signal Battalion, 127th, 249.

Divisions (signal units assigned to)—Continued
    8th Infantry. *See* Signal Battalion, 8th, 87.
    9th Infantry. *See* Signal Battalion, 9th, 89.
    10th Mountain. *See* Signal Battalion, 10th, 92.
    11th Airborne. *See* Signal Battalion, 511th, 388.
    15th Cavalry. See Signal Battalion, 11th, 94.
    23d Infantry. *See* Signal Battalion, 523d, 390.
    24th Infantry. *See* Signal Battalion, 24th, 105.
    25th Infantry. *See* Signal Battalion, 125th, 245.
    28th Infantry. *See* Signal Battalion, 28th, 112.
    29th Infantry. *See* Signal Battalion, 129th, 252.
    30th Armored (1959–1973). *See* Signal Battalion, 230th, 306.
    33d Infantry (1917–1949). *See* Signal Battalion, 133d, 254.
    34th Infantry
        (since 1991). *See* Signal Battalion, 134th. 257.
        (1959–1963). *See* Signal Battalion, 234th, 308.
    35th Infantry (since 1963). *See* Signal Battalion, 135th, 260.
    38th Infantry. *See* Signal Battalion, 138th, 265.
    40th Infantry. *See* Signal Battalion, 240th, 311.
    42d Infantry. *See* Signal Battalion, 250th, 316.
    47th Infantry (147th Signal Battalion, 1959–1991). *See* Signal Battalion, 134th, 257.
    49th Armored. *See* Signal Battalion, 249th, 314.
    50th Armored (1946–1993). See Signal Battalion, 250th, 316.
    51st Infantry (1959–1963) *See* Signal Battalion, 151st, 279.
    63d Infantry. *See* Signal Battalion, 163d, 287.
    77th Infantry. *See* Signal Battalion, 77th, 191.
    79th Infantry. *See* Signal Battalion, 179th, 289.
    81st Infantry. *See* Signal Battalion, 181st, 291.
    82d Airborne. *See* Signal Battalion, 82d, 195.
    83d Infantry. *See* Signal Battalion, 83d, 198.
    90th Infantry. *See* Signal Battalion, 190th, 293.
    94th Infantry (1921–1963). *See* Signal Battalion, 94th, 203.
    96th Infantry (1918–1963). *See* Signal Battalion, 96th, 204.
    101st Airborne. *See* Signal Battalion, 501st, 379.
    102d Infantry. *See* Signal Battalion, 202d, 302.
    103d Infantry (1921–1963). *See* Signal Battalion, 103d, 215.
    Hawaiian. *See* Signal Battalion, 24th, 105.
Engineer Battalions
    127th (Alabama National Guard, 1926–1931). *See* Signal Battalion, 279th, 319.
    151st Combat (World War II). *See* Signal Battalion, 279th, 319.
    242d (World War II). *See* Signal Battalion, 135th, Headquarters Company, 261.
    1343d (1944–1946). *See* Signal Battalion, 115th, 227.
Engineer Regiments
    115th (Nevada National Guard). *See* Signal Battalion, 422d, 363.
    151st (Alabama National Guard)

UNIT INDEX

Engineer Regiments—Continued
    1st Battalion. *See* Signal Battalion, 279th, 319.
    2d Battalion (1940–1942). *See* Signal Battalion, 115th, 227.

Field Artillery Battalions (or elements of)
    110th (World War II). *See* Signal Battalion, 129th, Company B, 253.
    151st (Minnesota National Guard). See Signal Battalion, 134th, 257.
    178th (World War II). *See* Signal Battalion, 151st, Company A, 280.
    194th (World War II). *See* Signal Battalion, 234th, Company B, 309.
    421st (1945–1946). *See* Signal Battalion, 422d, 363.
    981st (World War II and Korea). *See* Signal Battalion, 240th, 311.

Field Artillery Group
    178th, Headquarters Battery (World War II). *See* Signal Battalion, 111th, Company A, 222.

Hampton Guards. *See* Signal Brigade, 228th, 55.

Haslet's Regiment (Continental Army). *See* Signal Battalion, 198th, 296.

Infantry Regiment (War with Spain)
    1st Florida. *See* Signal Battalion, 417th, 359.

Infantry Regiments (Civil War)
    1st Delaware Volunteer. *See* Signal Battalion, 198th, 296.
    1st Michigan. *See* Signal Battalion, 156th, Company A, 284.
    2d Michigan. *See* Signal Battalion, 156th, Company B, 284.

Infantry Regiments (elements of)
    59th Pioneer (World War I). *See* Signal Battalion, 280th, 322.
    113th, Headquarters Company (World Wars I and II). *See* Signal Battalion, 250th, 316.
    118th
        Company F (World Wars I and II). *See* Signal Brigade, 228th, 55.
        Company G. *See* Signal Battalion, 151st, Headquarters and Headquarters Company, 279.
    124th (World War II). *See* Signal Battalions, 146th and 417th, 277, 359.
    126th (World War II). *See* Signal Battalion, 156th, 283.
    133d (World War II). *See* Signal Battalion, 234th, Headquarters Company, 309.
    134th (World War II). *See* Signal Battalion, 135th, Company A, 261.
    135th (World War II). *See* Signal Battalion, 134th, Company B, 258.
    143d (World War II). *See* Signal Battalion, 249th, 314.
    151st, Headquarters, 1st Battalion (Indiana National Guard, 1947–1959). *See* Signal Battalion, 138th, 265.
    152d, Headquarters, 2d Battalion (Indiana National Guard, 1921–1947). *See* Signal Battalion, 138th, 265.
    153d, Antitank Platoon, Headquarters Company. *See* Signal Battalion, 212th, Company C, 305.
    160th (World War II and Korean War). *See* Signal Battalion, 240th, 311.
    167th (World War II) *See* Signal Battalion, 279th, 319.
    168th (World War II). *See* Signal Battalion, 234th, 308.
    218th (1947–1959). *See* Signal Brigade, 228th, 55.
    223d (Korean War). *See* Signal Battalion, 240th, 311.

Maintenance Battalion
    62d (1966–1998). *See* Signal Battalion, 62d, 173.
Military Police Company
    40th (1928–1941). *See* Signal Battalion, 422d, 363.
Mobile Artillery Company. *See* Signal Battalion, 711th, 396.
Nicknames. *See* Special Designations.
Ordnance Battalion
    748th (Florida National Guard, 1952–1963). *See* Signal Battalion, 146th, 277.
Quartermaster Battalion
    51st (South Carolina National Guard, 1963–1968). *See* Signal Brigade, 228th, 55.
Quartermaster Company
    31st (World War II). *See* Signal Battalion, 711th, Company C, 398.
Rocket Battalion
    1st (1945). *See* Signal Battalion, 422d, 363.
Signal Battalions
    1st Field (1916–1921). *See* Signal Battalion, 122d, 234.
    1st Reserve Field (1917). *See* Signal Battalion, 77th, 191.
    1st Telegraph (1916–1917). *See* Signal Battalion, 50th, 150.
    1st: 77
    2d Field (1916–1921). *See* Signal Battalion, 121st, 229.
    3d Field, Company B (1916–1921). *See* Signal Battalion, 24th, 105.
    3d Telegraph, Company E (1916–1917). *See* Signal Battalion, 24th, 105.
    4th: 79
    5th: 81
    5th Construction (1931–1941). *See* Signal Battalion, 26th, 110.
    5th Field (1917–1921). *See* Signal Battalion, 123d, 238.
    5th Telegraph (1916–1917). *See* Signal Battalion, 51st, 153.
    6th: 83
    7th: 86
    7th Field (1917–1921). *See* Signal Battalion, 11th, 94.
    7th Reserve Field (1917). *See* Signal Battalion, 179th, 289.
    8th: 87
    8th Field (1917–1921). *See* Signal Battalion, 6th, 83.
    8th Reserve (1917). *See* Signal Battalion, 181st, 291.
    9th: 89
    9th Field (1917–1921). *See* Signal Battalion, 5th, 81.
    10th Field (1917–1921). *See* Signal Battalion, 127th, 249.
    10th Reserve Field (1917). *See* Signal Battalion, 8th, 87.
    10th: 92
    11th: 94
    13th Reserve Field (1917). *See* Signal Battalion, 82d, 195.
    13th: 96
    15th. *See* Signal Brigade, 15th, 37.
    16th: 101
    16th Reserve Field (1917) *See* Signal Battalion, 190th, 293.
    17th: 103
    20th Reserve Field (1917). *See* Signal Battalion, 82d, 195.

UNIT INDEX

Signal Battalions—Continued
    24th: 105
    25th: 108
    26th: 110
    28th: 112
    29th: 115
    30th: 117
    31st: 119
    32d: 121
    33d: 123
    34th: 125
    35th: 127
    36th: 129
    37th: 131
    38th: 133
    39th: 135
    40th: 138
    41st: 141
    43d: 144
    44th: 147
    48th Signal Construction (1944–1945). *See* Signal Battalion, 307th, 331.
    49th Signal Construction (1944–1946). *See* Signal Battalion, 306th, 329.
    50th: 150
    51st: 153
    51st Telegraph (1917–1921). *See* Signal Battalion, 50th, 150.
    52d: 156
    52d Telegraph (1916–1921). *See* Signal Battalion, 50th, 150.
    53d: 158
    53d Telegraph, Company E (1917–1921). *See* Signal Battalion, 24th, 105.
    54th: 160
    55th Telegraph (1917–1921). *See* Signal Battalion, 51st, 153.
    56th: 163
    57th: 165
    58th: 167
    59th (1927–1941). *See* Signal Battalion, 1st, 77.
    59th: 169
    60th: 171
    62d: 173
    63d: 175
    65th: 178
    67th: 179
    68th: 181
    69th: 183
    72d: 186
    73d: 188
    75th: 190
    77th: 191

Signal Battalions—Continued
    78th: 193
    82d: 195
    83d: 198
    86th: 200
    93d. *See* Signal Brigade, 93d, 46.
    94th: 203
    94th (1941–1948). *See* Signal Battalion, 318th. 333.
    96th: 204
    97th: 206
    98th: 208
    99th: 210
    101st (former elements of). *See* Signal Battalion, 230th, 306.
    102d: 213
    103d: 215
    105th: 217
    108th: 219
    108th Field Signal (1917–1919). *See* Signal Battalion, 133d, 254.
    111th: 221
    112th: 223
    114th: 226
    115th: 227
    121st: 229
    122d: 234
    123d: 238
    124th: 241
    125th: 245
    127th: 249
    129th: 252
    133d: 254
    134th: 257
    135th: 260
    136th: 263
    138th: 265
    141st: 267
    142d: 270
    143d: 273
    144th: 275
    146th: 277
    147th (1959–1991). *See* Signal Battalion, 134th, 257.
    151st: 279
    154th: 281
    156th: 283
    163d: 287
    179th: 289
    181st: 291
    190th: 293

UNIT INDEX

Signal Battalions—Continued
- 198th: 296
- 202d: 302
- 209th Field ((1918–1919). *See* Signal Battalion, 9th, 89.
- 212th: 304
- 230th: 306
- 234th: 308
- 240th: 311
- 249th: 314
- 250th: 316
- 279th: 319
- 280th: 322
- 302d: 325
- 302d Field (1917–1919). *See* Signal Battalion, 77th, 191.
- 304th: 327
- 304th Field (1917–1919). *See* Signal Battalion, 179th, 289.
- 306th: 329
- 306th Field (1917–1919). *See* Signal Battalion, 181st, 291.
- 307th: 331
- 307th Field (1917–1921). *See* Signal Battalion, 82d, 195.
- 308th Field (1917–1921). *See* Signal Battalion, 83d, 198.
- 315th Field (1917–1919). *See* Signal Battalion, 190th, 293.
- 318th: 333
- 319th: 335
- 320th Field (1917–1919). *See* Signal Battalion, 8th, 87.
- 324th: 337
- 325th: 339
- 327th: 341
- 352d: 345
- 360th: 346
- 361st: 348
- 366th: 350
- 369th: 352
- 379th: 355
- 392d: 357
- 417th: 359
- 421st: 362
- 422d: 363
- 426th: 366
- 440th: 368
- 442d: 371
- 447th: 373
- 459th: 375
- 460th: 377
- 501st: 379
- 503d: 383
- 504th: 384

Signal Battalions—Continued
    509th: 386
    511th: 388
    516th. *See* Signal Brigade, 516th, 63.
    523d: 390
    551st: 392
    560th: 394
    621st Field (1918–1919). *See* Signal Battalion, 96th, 204.
    626th Field (1918). *See* Signal Battalion, 501st, 379.
    711th: 396
    835th: 399
    845th: 401
    850th: 403
    928th (1942–1966). *See* Signal Brigade, 29th, 41.
    931st (1943–1967). *See* Signal Brigade, 35th, 43.
    932d (1943–1963). *See* Signal Brigade, 106th, 49.
    935th (1945–1963). *See* Signal Group, 12th, 70.
    972d (1944–1997). *See* Signal Command, 9th, 12.
    980th: 405
    1709th Signal Service (1944–1954). *See* Signal Battalion, 392d, 357.
    3101st Signal Service (1943–1948). *See* Signal Battalion, 7th, 86.
    3103d Signal Service (1943–1964). *See* Signal Brigade, 11th, 33.
    3111th Signal Service (1943–1950). *See* Signal Battalion, 324th, 337.
    3112th Signal Service (1944–1952). *See* Signal Command, 311th, 14.
    3114th Signal Service (1944–1947). *See* Signal Battalion, 75th, 190.
    3160th Signal Service (1945–1954). *See* Signal Brigade, 160th, 53.
    3181st Signal Service (1944–1946). *See* Signal Battalion, 11th, 94.
    3186th Signal Service (1944–1947). *See* Signal Battalion, 72d, 186.
    3212th Signal Service (1944–1947). *See* Signal Battalion, 503d, 383.
    3213th Signal Service (1944–1946). *See* Signal Battalion, 504th, 384.
    3214th Signal Service (1944–1954). *See* Signal Battalion, 421st, 362.
    3216th Signal Service (1944–1950). *See* Signal Battalion, 325th, 339.
    3352d Signal Service (1944–1955). *See* Signal Battalion, 352d, 345.
    3359th Signal Service (1944–1955). *See* Signal Brigade, 359th, 61.
    3360th Signal Service (1944–1964). See Signal Battalion, 360th, 346.
    3361st Signal Service (1944–1969). *See* Signal Battalion, 361st, 348.
    3364th Signal Service (1944–1959). *See* Signal Battalion, 114th, 226.
    3366th Signal Service (1944–1953). *See* Signal Battalion, 366th, 350.
    3367th Signal Service (1944–1947). *See* Signal Brigade, 516th, 63.
    3369th Signal Service (1944–1969). *See* Signal Battalion, 369th, 352.
    3796th Signal Service (1945–1952). *See* Signal Battalion, 379th, 355.
    3906th Signal Service (1944–1947). *See* Signal Battalion, 509th, 386.
    3907th Signal Service (1944–1951). *See* Signal Battalion, 39th, 135.
    4026th Signal Photographic (1945–1954). *See* Signal Battalion, 73d, 188.
Signal Brigades
    1st: 23
    2d: 26

UNIT INDEX

Signal Brigades—Continued
    3d: 29
    7th: 31
    11th: 33
    15th: 37
    22d: 39
    29th: 41
    35th: 43
    53d (1985–1997). *See* Signal Battalion, 417th, 359.
    93d: 46
    106th: 49
    142d: 51
    160th: 53
    228th: 55
    261st: 58
    335th: *See* Signal Command, 335th, 16.
    359th: 61
    516th: 63
Signal Center
    1st: 18
Signal Commands
    1st: 5
    5th: 6
    6th: 8
    7th: 10
    9th: 12
    261st. *See* Signal Brigade, 261st, 58.
    311th: 14
    335th: 16
Signal Companies
    1st (1921–1957). *See* Signal Battalion, 121st, 229.
    1st Provisional (1916). *See* Signal Battalion, 50th, 150.
    2d (1921–1957). *See* Signal Battalion, 122d, 234.
    3d (1921–1957). *See* Signal Battalion, 123d, 238.
    4th
        1917–1939. *See* Signal Battalion, 6th, 83.
        1940–1957. *See* Signal Battalion, 124th, 241.
   5th. *See* Signal Battalion, 5th, 81.
   6th. *See* Signal Battalion, 6th, 83.
   7th (1921–1957). *See* Signal Battalion, 127th, 249.
   8th. *See* Signal Battalion, 8th, 87.
   9th (1923–1948). *See* Signal Battalion, 9th, 89.
   9th Service (1918–1922). *See* Signal Command, 9th, 12.
   9th Signal Service (1925–1943). *See* Signal Command, 9th, 12.
   11th (1921–1941). *See* Signal Battalion, 24th, 105.
   13th. *See* Signal Battalion, 13th, 96.
   24th. *See* Signal Battalion, 24th, 105.

Signal Companies—Continued
    25th (1941–1957). *See* Signal Battalion, 125th, 245.
    28th (Pennsylvania National Guard). *See* Signal Battalion, 28th, 112.
    32d (World War II). *See* Signal Battalion, 156th, Headquarters Company, 283.
    33d (1922–1947). *See* Signal Battalion, 133d, 254.
    46th (1941). *See* Signal Battalion, 143d, 273.
    47th (1940–1941). *See* Signal Battalion, 141st, 267.
    48th (1940–1941). *See* Signal Battalion, 142d, 270.
    49th (1941). *See* Signal Battalion, 144th, 275.
    50th Armored (1946–1959). *See* Signal Battalion, 250th, 316.
    77th (1921–1959). *See* Signal Battalion, 77th, 191.
    79th (1921–1959). *See* Signal Battalion, 179th, 289.
    81st (1921–1959). *See* Signal Battalion, 181st, 291.
    82d Airborne. *See* Signal Battalion, 82d, 195.
    83d. *See* Signal Battalion, 83d, 198.
    90th (1921–1959). *See* Signal Battalion, 190th, 293.
    94th. *See* Signal Battalion, 94th, 203.
    96th. *See* Signal Battalion, 96th, 204.
    101st Airborne. *See* Signal Battalion, 501st, 379.
    102d (1921–1959). *See* Signal Battalion, 202d, 302.
    103d. *See* Signal Battalion, 103d, 215.
    109th (Illinois National Guard). *See* Signal Battalion, 133d, 254.
    110th Mountain. *See* Signal Battalion, 10th, 92.
    123d (1954–1968). *See* Signal Battalion, 523d, 390.
    141st Armored. *See* Signal Battalion, 141st, 267.
    142d Armored. *See* Signal Battalion, 142d, 270.
    143d Armored. *See* Signal Battalion, 143d, 273.
    144th Armored. *See* Signal Battalion, 144th, 275.
    216th Signal Depot. *See* Signal Depot, 216th, Headquarters and Headquarters Company, 19.
    221st (1941–1980). *See* Signal Battalion, 327th, Company B, 341.
    246th Signal Operation (1942–1949). *See* Signal Battalion, 501st, Company A, 379.
    299th (1942–1956). *See* Signal Battalion, 501st, Company B, 379.
    316th Signal Aviation (1940–1941). *See* Signal Battalion, 327th, Company A, 341.
    328th (1956–1987). *See* Signal Battalion, 324th, Company A, 337.
    392d (1942–1944). *See* Signal Battalion, 392d, 357.
    416th (1941–1980). *See* Signal Battalion, 327th, Company A, 341.
    433d (Illinois National Guard, 1968–1980). *See* Signal Battalion, 133d, 254.
    503d (1951–1954). *See* Signal Battalion, 523d, 390.
    511th Airborne. *See* Signal Battalion, 511th, 388.
    512th Airborne. *See* Signal Battalion, 112th, 223.
    516th (1949–1956). *See* Signal Battalion, 501st, Company A, 379.
    543d (1944–1987). *See* Signal Battalion, 324th, Company B, 337.
    563d (1943–1959). *See* Signal Battalion, 163d, 287.
    583d Signal Depot (1943–1947). *See* Signal Depot, 801st, 20.
    801st (1947–1953). *See* Signal Depot, 801st, 20.

UNIT INDEX 423

Signal Companies—Continued
    835th Signal Service (1942–1943). *See* Signal Battalion, 835th, 399.
    972d Signal Service (1943–1944). *See* Signal Command, 9th, 12.
    980th (1943-1953). *See* Signal Battalion, 980th, 405.
    984th Signal Service (1943–1948). *See* Signal Battalion, 319th, 335.
    3128th Signal Service (1944-1956). *See* Signal Battalion, 324th, Company A, 337.
    3132d Signal Service (1944–1951). *See* Signal Battalion, 523d, 390.
    3181st Signal Service (1946–1947). *See* Signal Battalion, 11th, 94.
    A, Signal Corps (1898–1916). *See* Signal Battalion, 121st, 229.
    A (Illinois National Guard, 1916–1917). *See* Signal Battalion, 133d, 254.
    A (Pennsylvania National Guard, 1908–1916). *See* Signal Battalion, 28th, 112.
    B, 1st Field Battalion (Pennsylvania National Guard, 1917). *See* Signal Battalion, 28th, 112.
    B, 3d Field Battalion, Signal Corps (1916–1921). *See* Signal Battalion, 24th, 105.
    B, 103d Field Signal Battalion (Pennsylvania National Guard, World War I). *See* Signal Battalion, 28th, 112.
    D, Signal Corps (1898–1916). *See* Signal Battalion, 121st, 229.
    E, Signal Corps (1899–1916). *See* Signal Battalion, 122d, 234.
    E, 3d Telegraph Battalion (1916–1917). *See* Signal Battalion, 24th, 105.
    E, 53d Telegraph Battalion (1917–1921). *See* Signal Battalion, 24th, 105.
    H, Signal Corps (1899–1916). *See* Signal Battalion, 50th, 150.
    I, Signal Corps (1904–1916). *See* Signal Battalion, 122d, 234.
    L, Signal Corps (1905–1916). *See* Signal Battalion, 24th, 105.
    M, Signal Corps (1909–1916). *See* Signal Battalion, 24th, 105.
    Service Company Number 9 (1922–1925). *See* Signal Command, 9th, 12.
    Wire Company, Field Battalion, Signal Troops (Pennsylvania National Guard, 1916–1917). *See* Signal Battalion, 28th, 112.
Signal Depots
    216th: 19
    801st: 20
    803d: 22
    3911th (1944–1948). *See* Signal Depot, 803d, 22
Signal Groups
    1st: 65
    2d Signal Service. *See* Signal Brigade, 2d, 26.
    4th: 67
    7th: 69
    11th. *See* Signal Brigade, 11th, 33.
    12th: 70
    21st: 72
    22d Signal Service. *See* Signal Brigade, 22d, 39.
    29th. *See* Signal Brigade, 29th, 41.
    35th. *See* Signal Brigade, 35th, 43.
    53d (Florida National Guard, 1968–1985). *See* Signal Battalion, 417th, 359.
    106th. *See* Signal Brigade, 106th, 49.

Signal Groups—Continued
    142d. *See* Signal Brigade, 142d, 51.
    160th. *See* Signal Brigade, 160th, 53.
    199th: 74
    228th. *See* Signal Brigade, 228th, 55.
    311th. *See* Signal Command, 311th, 14.
    332d: 75
    335th. *See* Signal Command, 335th, 16.
    359th. *See* Signal Brigade, 359th, 61.
    505th: 76
    516th. *See* Signal Brigade, 516th, 63.
    3146th Signal Service. *See* Signal Group, 505th, 76.
    3348th Signal Service. *See* Signal Brigade, 2d, 26.
    4025th Signal Service. *See* Signal Group, 4th, 67.
Signal Platoon
    110th (1943–1944). See Signal Battalion, 10th, 92.
Signal Regiments
    15th Signal Service. *See* Signal Brigade, 15th, 37.
    15th Signal Training. *See* Signal Brigade, 15th, 37.
Signal Squadron
    97th Constabulary. *See* Signal Battalion, 97th, 206.
Signal Troops
    1st. *See* Signal Battalion, 13th, 96.
    7th. *See* Signal Battalion, 141st, 267.
    13th. *See* Signal Battalion, 13th, 96.
Special Designations
    Always Professional. *See* Signal Battalion, 43d, 144.
    Desert Thunderbirds. *See* Signal Brigade, 11th, 33.
    Dragon Warriors. *See* Signal Command, 5th, 6.
    First to Communicate. *See* Signal Brigade, 1st, 23.
    First Delaware. *See* Signal Battalion, 198th, 296.
    First Voice Heard. *See* Signal Battalion, 86th, 200.
    The Communicators. *See* Signal Battalion, 141st, 267.
Special Operations. *See* Signal Battalion, 112th, 223.
Strategic Communications Command, U.S. Army
    261st (Delaware National Guard, 1971–1974). *See* Signal Brigade, 261st, 58.
Training and Doctrine Command (TRADOC), U.S. Army (signal units assigned to)
    15th Signal Brigade: 37
    29th Signal Brigade: 41
    360th Signal Battalion: 346
    361st Signal Battalion: 348
    366th Signal Battalion: 350
    369th Signal Battalion: 352
    442d Signal Battalion: 371
    447th Signal Battalion: 373
    551st Signal Battalion: 392
    560th Signal Battalion: 394

UNIT INDEX 425

Transportation Units
    113th Transportation Detachment (South Carolina National Guard, 1995–1996).
        See Signal Battalion, 105th, 217.
    118th Transportation Detachment (South Carolina National Guard, 1992–1995).
        See Signal Battalion, 105th, 217.
    151st Transportation Battalion (South Carolina National Guard, 1959–1953).
        See Signal Brigade, 228th, 55.
    198th Transportation Battalion (Delaware National Guard, 1970–1971).
        See Signal Battalion, 280th, 322.
West Point, New York (signal battalions assigned to U.S. Military Academy)
    1958–1966. *See* Signal Battalion, 6th, 83.
    since 1966. *See* Signal Battalion, 4th, 79.

Made in the USA
Coppell, TX
01 March 2023